Glider Flying Handbook

2013

U.S. Department of Transportation
FEDERAL AVIATION ADMINISTRATION
Flight Standards Service

FAA-H-8083-13A
Glider Flying Handbook
Updated May 11, 2015

Errata as of May 11, 2015

1. In the first bullet under "Other Airspeed Limitations" in the left column of page 4-6, the first sentence should be changed to: "Maneuvering speed (V_a) – a structural design airspeed used in determining the strength requirements for the glider and its control surfaces. The structural design requirements do not cover multiple inputs in one axis or control inputs in more than one axis at a time at any speed, even below V_a."

2. On page G-4 of the glossary, the following definition should be added: "Maneuvering speed (V_a) – a structural design airspeed used in determining the strength requirements for the glider and its control surfaces. The structural design requirements do not cover multiple inputs in one axis or control inputs in more than one axis at a time at any speed, even below V_a."

Errata as of October 21, 2013

1. In Figure 7-2 on page 7-3, the upper center and upper right labels regarding towing are reversed. The upper center label should read, "Towplane please turn left" and the upper right label should read, "Towplane please turn right."

2. In Figure 7-34 on page 7-35, the label pointing to the rudder should read, "Rudder deflected left."

Errata as of September 17, 2013

1. On page 1-3, the caption under Figure 1-5 should read, "A DG Flugzeugbau GmbH DG-800B glider."

Errata as of September 11, 2013

1. In the Acknowledgements (page v), the web address for the Soaring Society of America, Inc. should read, "www.ssa.org."

Preface

The Glider Flying Handbook is designed as a technical manual for applicants who are preparing for glider category rating and for currently certificated glider pilots who wish to improve their knowledge. Certificated flight instructors will find this handbook a valuable training aid, since detailed coverage of aeronautical decision-making, components and systems, aerodynamics, flight instruments, performance limitations, ground operations, flight maneuvers, traffic patterns, emergencies, soaring weather, soaring techniques, and cross-country flight is included. Topics such as radio navigation and communication, use of flight information publications, and regulations are available in other Federal Aviation Administration (FAA) publications.

The discussion and explanations reflect the most commonly used practices and principles. Occasionally, the word "must" or similar language is used where the desired action is deemed critical. The use of such language is not intended to add to, interpret, or relieve a duty imposed by Title 14 of the Code of Federal Regulations (14 CFR). Persons working towards a glider rating are advised to review the references from the applicable practical test standards (FAA-G-8082-4, Sport Pilot and Flight Instructor with a Sport Pilot Rating Knowledge Test Guide, FAA-G-8082-5, Commercial Pilot Knowledge Test Guide, and FAA-G-8082-17, Recreational Pilot and Private Pilot Knowledge Test Guide). Resources for study include FAA-H-8083-25, Pilot's Handbook of Aeronautical Knowledge, FAA-H-8083-2, Risk Management Handbook, and Advisory Circular (AC) 00-6, Aviation Weather For Pilots and Flight Operations Personnel, AC 00-45, Aviation Weather Services, as these documents contain basic material not duplicated herein. All beginning applicants should refer to FAA-H-8083-25, Pilot's Handbook of Aeronautical Knowledge, for study and basic library reference.

It is essential for persons using this handbook to become familiar with and apply the pertinent parts of 14 CFR and the Aeronautical Information Manual (AIM). The AIM is available online at www.faa.gov. The current Flight Standards Service airman training and testing material and learning statements for all airman certificates and ratings can be obtained from www.faa.gov.

This handbook supersedes FAA-H-8083-13, Glider Flying Handbook, dated 2003. Always select the latest edition of any publication and check the website for errata pages and listing of changes to FAA educational publications developed by the FAA's Airman Testing Standards Branch, AFS-630.

This handbook is published by the United States Department of Transportation, Federal Aviation Administration, Airman Testing Standards Branch, AFS-630, P.O. Box 25082, Oklahoma City, OK 73125.

Comments regarding this publication should be sent, in email form, to the following address:

AFS630comments@faa.gov

John M. Allen
Director, Flight Standards Service

Acknowledgments

The Glider Flying Handbook was produced by the Federal Aviation Administration (FAA) with the assistance of Safety Research Corporation of America (SRCA). The FAA wishes to acknowledge the following contributors:

Sue Telford of Telford Fishing & Hunting Services for images used in Chapter 1

JerryZieba (www.dianasailplanes.com) for images used in Chapter 2

Tim Mara (www.wingsandwheels.com) for images used in Chapters 2 and 12

Uli Kremer of Alexander Schleicher GmbH & Co for images used in Chapter 2

Richard Lancaster (www.carrotworks.com) for images and content used in Chapter 3

Dave Nadler of Nadler & Associates for images used in Chapter 6

Dave McConeghey for images used in Chapter 6

John Brandon (www.raa.asn.au) for images and content used in Chapter 7

Patrick Panzera (www.contactmagazine.com) for images used in Chapter 8

Jeff Haby (www.theweatherprediction) for images used in Chapter 8

National Soaring Museum (www.soaringmuseum.org) for content used in Chapter 9

Bill Elliot (www.soaringcafe.com) for images used in Chapter 12.

Tiffany Fidler for images used in Chapter 12.

Additional appreciation is extended to the Soaring Society of America, Inc. (www.ssa.com), the Soaring Safety Foundation, and Mr. Brad Temeyer and Mr. Bill Martin from the National Oceanic and Atmospheric Administration (NOAA) for their technical support and input.

Table of Contents

Preface iii

Acknowledgments v

Table of Contents vii

Chapter 1
Gliders and Sailplanes 1-1
Introduction 1-1
Gliders—The Early Years 1-2
Glider or Sailplane? 1-3
Glider Pilot Schools 1-4
    14 CFR Part 141 Pilot Schools 1-5
    14 CFR Part 61 Instruction 1-5
Glider Certificate Eligibility Requirements 1-5
Common Glider Concepts 1-6
    Terminology 1-6
    Converting Metric Distance to Feet 1-6

Chapter 2
Components and Systems 2-1
Introduction 2-1
Glider Design 2-2
The Fuselage 2-4
    Wings and Components 2-4
Lift/Drag Devices 2-5
Empennage 2-6
    Towhook Devices 2-7
Powerplant 2-7
    Self-Launching Gliders 2-7
    Sustainer Engines 2-8
Landing Gear 2-8
    Wheel Brakes 2-8

Chapter 3
Aerodynamics of Flight 3-1
Introduction 3-1
Forces of Flight 3-2
    Newton's Third Law of Motion 3-2
    Lift 3-2

The Effects of Drag on a Glider 3-3
    Parasite Drag 3-3
        Form Drag 3-3
        Skin Friction Drag 3-3
        Interference Drag 3-5
    Total Drag 3-6
    Wing Planform 3-6
        Elliptical Wing 3-6
        Rectangular Wing 3-7
        Tapered Wing 3-7
        Swept-Forward Wing 3-7
        Washout 3-7
    Glide Ratio 3-8
        Aspect Ratio 3-9
    Weight 3-9
    Thrust 3-9
Three Axes of Rotation 3-9
Stability 3-10
    Flutter 3-11
    Lateral Stability 3-12
Turning Flight 3-13
Load Factors 3-13
    Radius of Turn 3-14
    Turn Coordination 3-15
    Slips 3-15
        Forward Slip 3-16
        Sideslip 3-17
    Spins 3-17
Ground Effect 3-19

Chapter 4
Flight Instruments 4-1
Introduction 4-1
Pitot-Static Instruments 4-2
    Impact and Static Pressure Lines 4-2
    Airspeed Indicator 4-2
        The Effects of Altitude on the Airspeed
        Indicator 4-3
        Types of Airspeed 4-3

Airspeed Indicator Markings	4-5
Other Airspeed Limitations	4-6
Altimeter	4-6
Principles of Operation	4-6
Effect of Nonstandard Pressure and Temperature	4-7
Setting the Altimeter (Kollsman Window)	4-9
Types of Altitude	4-10
Variometer	4-11
Total Energy System	4-14
Netto	4-14
Electronic Flight Computers	4-15
Magnetic Compass	4-16
Yaw String	4-16
Inclinometer	4-16
Gyroscopic Instruments	4-17
G-Meter	4-17
FLARM Collision Avoidance System	4-18

Chapter 5
Glider Performance 5-1

Introduction	5-1
Factors Affecting Performance	5-2
High and Low Density Altitude Conditions	5-2
Atmospheric Pressure	5-2
Altitude	5-3
Temperature	5-3
Wind	5-3
Weight	5-5
Rate of Climb	5-7
Flight Manuals and Placards	5-8
Placards	5-8
Performance Information	5-8
Glider Polars	5-8
Weight and Balance Information	5-10
Limitations	5-10
Weight and Balance	5-12
Center of Gravity	5-12
Problems Associated With CG Forward of Forward Limit	5-12
Problems Associated With CG Aft of Aft Limit	5-13
Sample Weight and Balance Problems	5-13
Ballast	5-14

Chapter 6
Preflight and Ground Operations 6-1

Introduction	6-1
Assembly and Storage Techniques	6-2
Trailering	6-3
Tiedown and Securing	6-4
Water Ballast	6-4
Ground Handling	6-4
Launch Equipment Inspection	6-5
Glider Preflight Inspection	6-6
Prelaunch Checklist	6-7
Glider Care	6-7
Preventive Maintenance	6-8

Chapter 7
Launch and Recovery Procedures and Flight Maneuvers 7-1

Introduction	7-1
Aerotow Takeoff Procedures	7-2
Signals	7-2
Prelaunch Signals	7-2
Inflight Signals	7-3
Takeoff Procedures and Techniques	7-3
Normal Assisted Takeoff	7-4
Unassisted Takeoff	7-5
Crosswind Takeoff	7-5
Assisted	7-5
Unassisted	7-6
Aerotow Climb-Out	7-6
Aerotow Release	7-8
Slack Line	7-9
Boxing the Wake	7-10
Ground Launch Takeoff Procedures	7-11
CG Hooks	7-11
Signals	7-11
Prelaunch Signals (Winch/Automobile)	7-11
Inflight Signals	7-12
Tow Speeds	7-12
Automobile Launch	7-14
Crosswind Takeoff and Climb	7-14
Normal Into-the-Wind Launch	7-15
Climb-Out and Release Procedures	7-16
Self-Launch Takeoff Procedures	7-17
Preparation and Engine Start	7-17
Taxiing	7-18
Pretakeoff Check	7-18
Normal Takeoff	7-19
Crosswind Takeoff	7-19
Climb-Out and Shutdown Procedures	7-19
Landing	7-21
Gliderport/Airport Traffic Patterns and Operations	7-22
Normal Approach and Landing	7-22
Crosswind Landing	7-25
Slips	7-25
Downwind Landing	7-27
After Landing and Securing	7-27

Performance Maneuvers 7-27	Procedures..8-14
Straight Glides..7-27	Abnormal Procedures...8-14
Turns..7-28	Emergency Procedures...8-14
Roll-In...7-29	Self-Launch Takeoff Emergency Procedures 8-15
Roll-Out..7-30	Emergency Procedures...8-15
Steep Turns 7-31	Spiral Dives..8-15
Maneuvering at Minimum Controllable Airspeed ...7-31	Spins...8-15
Stall Recognition and Recovery 7-32	Entry Phase...8-17
Secondary Stalls..7-34	Incipient Phase 8-17
Accelerated Stalls 7-34	Developed Phase 8-17
Crossed-Control Stalls 7-35	Recovery Phase 8-17
Operating Airspeeds..7-36	Off-Field Landing Procedures 8-18
Minimum Sink Airspeed 7-36	Afterlanding Off Field 8-20
Best Glide Airspeed...7-37	Off-Field Landing Without Injury 8-20
Speed to Fly...7-37	Off-Field Landing With Injury 8-20
	System and Equipment Malfunctions 8-20
Chapter 8	Flight Instrument Malfunctions.............................8-20
Abnormal and Emergency Procedures 8-1	Airspeed Indicator Malfunctions 8-21
Introduction..8-1	Altimeter Malfunctions......................................8-21
Porpoising 8-2	Variometer Malfunctions...................................8-21
Pilot-Induced Oscillations (PIOs) 8-2	Compass Malfunctions 8-21
PIOs During Launch..8-2	Glider Canopy Malfunctions.................................8-21
Factors Influencing PIOs 8-2	Broken Glider Canopy 8-22
Improper Elevator Trim Setting...........................8-3	Frosted Glider Canopy.......................................8-22
Improper Wing Flaps Setting..............................8-3	Water Ballast Malfunctions...................................8-22
Pilot-Induced Roll Oscillations During Launch.........8-3	Retractable Landing Gear Malfunctions 8-22
Pilot-Induced Yaw Oscillations During Launch 8-4	Primary Flight Control Systems 8-22
Gust-Induced Oscillations...8-5	Elevator Malfunctions 8-22
Vertical Gusts During High-Speed Cruise 8-5	Aileron Malfunctions...8-23
Pilot-Induced Pitch Oscillations During Landing 8-6	Rudder Malfunctions 8-24
Glider-Induced Oscillations 8-6	Secondary Flight Controls Systems 8-24
Pitch Influence of the Glider Towhook Position........8-6	Elevator Trim Malfunctions 8-24
Self-Launching Glider Oscillations During	Spoiler/Dive Brake Malfunctions......................8-24
Powered Flight 8-7	Miscellaneous Flight System Malfunctions................8-25
Nosewheel Glider Oscillations During Launches	Towhook Malfunctions 8-25
and Landings 8-7	Oxygen System Malfunctions 8-25
Tailwheel/Tailskid Equipped Glider Oscillations	Drogue Chute Malfunctions 8-25
During Launches and Landings...............................8-8	Self-Launching Gliders...8-26
Aerotow Abnormal and Emergency Procedures...........8-8	Self-Launching/Sustainer Glider Engine Failure
Abnormal Procedures..8-8	During Takeoff or Climb.......................................8-26
Towing Failures...8-10	Inability to Restart a Self-Launching/Sustainer
Tow Failure With Runway To Land and Stop......8-11	Glider Engine While Airborne 8-27
Tow Failure Without Runway To Land Below	Self-Launching Glider Propeller Malfunctions.......8-27
Returning Altitude 8-11	Self-Launching Glider Electrical System
Tow Failure Above Return to Runway Altitude...8-11	Malfunctions...8-27
Tow Failure Above 800' AGL 8-12	In-flight Fire 8-28
Tow Failure Above Traffic Pattern Altitude.........8-13	Emergency Equipment and Survival Gear...................8-28
Slack Line..8-13	Survival Gear Checklists.......................................8-28
Ground Launch Abnormal and Emergency	Food and Water 8-28

Clothing	8-28
Communication	8-29
Navigation Equipment	8-29
Medical Equipment	8-29
Stowage	8-30
Parachute	8-30
Oxygen System Malfunctions	8-30
Accident Prevention	8-30

Chapter 9
Soaring Weather 9-1

Introduction	9-1
The Atmosphere	9-2
Composition	9-2
Properties	9-2
Temperature	9-2
Density	9-2
Pressure	9-2
Standard Atmosphere	9-3
Layers of the Atmosphere	9-4
Scale of Weather Events	9-4
Thermal Soaring Weather	9-6
Thermal Shape and Structure	9-6
Atmospheric Stability	9-7
Air Masses Conducive to Thermal Soaring	9-9
Cloud Streets	9-9
Thermal Waves	9-9
Thunderstorms	9-10
Lifted Index	9-12
K-Index	9-12
Weather for Slope Soaring	9-14
Mechanism for Wave Formation	9-16
Lift Due to Convergence	9-19
Obtaining Weather Information	9-21
Preflight Weather Briefing	9-21
Weather-Related Information	9-21
Interpreting Weather Charts, Reports, and Forecasts	9-23
Graphic Weather Charts	9-23
Winds and Temperatures Aloft Forecast	9-23
Composite Moisture Stability Chart	9-24

Chapter 10
Soaring Techniques 10-1

Introduction	10-1
Thermal Soaring	10-2
Locating Thermals	10-2
Cumulus Clouds	10-2
Other Indicators of Thermals	10-3
Wind	10-4
The Big Picture	10-5

Entering a Thermal	10-5
Inside a Thermal	10-6
Bank Angle	10-6
Speed	10-6
Centering	10-7
Collision Avoidance	10-9
Exiting a Thermal	10-9
Atypical Thermals	10-10
Ridge/Slope Soaring	10-10
Traps	10-10
Procedures for Safe Flying	10-12
Bowls and Spurs	10-13
Slope Lift	10-13
Obstructions	10-14
Tips and Techniques	10-15
Wave Soaring	10-16
Preflight Preparation	10-17
Getting Into the Wave	10-18
Flying in the Wave	10-20
Soaring Convergence Zones	10-23
Combined Sources of Updrafts	10-24

Chapter 11
Cross-Country Soaring 11-1

Introduction	11-1
Flight Preparation and Planning	11-2
Personal and Special Equipment	11-3
Navigation	11-5
Using the Plotter	11-5
A Sample Cross-Country Flight	11-5
Navigation Using GPS	11-8
Cross-Country Techniques	11-9
Soaring Faster and Farther	11-11
Height Bands	11-11
Tips and Techniques	11-12
Special Situations	11-14
Course Deviations	11-14
Lost Procedures	11-14
Cross-Country Flight in a Self-Launching Glider	11-15
High-Performance Glider Operations and Considerations	11-16
Glider Complexity	11-16
Water Ballast	11-17
Cross-Country Flight Using Other Lift Sources	11-17

Chapter 12
Towing 12-1

Introduction	12-1
Equipment Inspections and Operational Checks	12-2
Tow Hook	12-2
Schweizer Tow Hook	12-2

Tost Tow Hook	12-2
Tow Ring Inspection	12-4
Tow Rope Inspection	12-4
Tow Rope Strength Requirements	12-4
Take Off Planning	12-5
On the Airport	12-6
Ground Signals	12-6
Takeoff and Climb	12-7
Tow Positions, Turns, and Release	12-8
Glider Tow Positions	12-8
Turns on Tow	12-8
Approaching a Thermal	12-9
Release	12-9
Descent, Approach and Landing	12-10
Descent	12-10
Approach and Landing	12-10
Cross-Country Aerotow	12-10
Emergencies	12-11
Takeoff Emergencies	12-11
Tow Plane Power Failure on the Runway During Takeoff Roll	12-11
Glider Releases During Takeoff With Tow Plane Operation Normal	12-11
Tow Plane Power Failure or Tow Rope Break After Takeoff but Below 200 Feet Above Ground Level	12-11
Tow Plane Power Failure or Tow Rope Break After Takeoff Above 200 Feet	12-11
Glider Climbs Excessively High During Takeoff	12-11
Airborne Emergencies	12-12
Glider Release Failure	12-12
Glider Problem	12-12
Immediate Release	12-12

Chapter 13
Human Factors 13-1

Introduction	13-1
Learning from Past Mistakes	13-2
Recognizing Hazardous Attitudes	13-2
Complacency	13-2
Indiscipline	13-3
Overconfidence	13-3
Human Error	13-3
Types of Errors	13-3
Unintentional	13-3
Intentional	13-4
Human and Physiological Factors that Affect Flight	13-4
Fatigue	13-4
Hyperventilation	13-5
Inner Ear Discomfort	13-5
Spatial Disorientation	13-6
Dehydration	13-6
Heatstroke	13-6
Cold Weather	13-6
Cockpit Management	13-7
Personal Equipment	13-7
Oxygen System	13-7
Transponder Code	13-9
Definitions	13-9
Risk Management	13-9
Safety Management System (SMS)	13-9
Aeronautical Decision-Making (ADM)	13-10

Appendix A
Soaring Safety Foundation (SSF):
Safety Advisory 00-1, Glider Critical
Assembly Procedures A-1

Introduction	A-1
History	A-1
Ensuring Airworthiness	A-2
Critical Items	A-2

Glossary G-1

Index I-1

Chapter 1
Gliders and Sailplanes

Introduction

Welcome to the world of soaring. Whether it has been a lifelong dream or a new interest, the pleasure of flying is truly addictive and exhilarating. The intellectual challenge combined with the quiet and beauty of flying high above the earth are two of the many reasons that people both young and old get hooked on flying gliders. If contemplating learning more about the sport, an introductory flight absolutely helps make the decision. Soaring gracefully through the air, along with the meditative silence that surrounds you, is refreshing and exciting. Organizations such as the Soaring Society of America (SSA) have developed excellent programs not only to track a pilot's learning progression, but also issue badges for flight and knowledge accomplishments. Glider clubs are located all over the country and offer great flight training schools and pilot camaraderie.

The Glider Flying Handbook is designed to aid pilots in achieving their goals in aviation and to provide the knowledge and practical information needed to attain private, commercial, and flight instructor category ratings for gliders. This handbook, in conjunction with the Pilot's Handbook of Aeronautical Knowledge, FAA-H-8083-25 (as revised), is a source of basic knowledge for certification as a glider pilot and instructor. There are numerous other commercial sources available to the pilot for reference that should be obtained for additional information.

Gliders—The Early Years

The fantasy of flight led people to dream up intricate designs in an attempt to imitate the flight of birds. Leonardo da Vinci sketched a vision of flying machines in his 15th century manuscripts. His work consisted of a number of wing designs including a human-powered ornithopter, the name derived from the Greek word for bird. Centuries later, when others began to experiment with his designs, it became apparent that the human body could not sustain flight by flapping wings like birds. *[Figure 1-1]* The dream of human flight continued to capture the imagination of many, but it was not until 1799 when Sir George Cayley, a Baronet in Yorkshire, England, conceived a craft with stationary wings to provide lift, flappers to provide thrust, and a movable tail to provide control.

Otto Lilienthal was a German pioneer of human flight who became known as the Glider King. *[Figure 1-2]* He was the first person to make well-documented, repeated, successful gliding flights beginning in 1891. *[Figure 1-3]* He followed an experimental approach established earlier by Sir George

Figure 1-2. *Otto Lilienthal (May 23, 1848–August 10, 1896) was a German pioneer of human aviation.*

Cayley. Newspapers and magazines published photographs of Lilienthal gliding, favorably influencing public and scientific opinion about the possibility of flying machines becoming practical.

By the early 1900s, the famed Wright Brothers were experimenting with gliders and gliding flight in the hills

Figure 1-1. *A human-powered ornithopter is virtually incapable of flight due to its poor strength-to-weight ratio.*

Figure 1-3. *Otto Lilienthal in flight.*

of Kitty Hawk, North Carolina. *[Figure 1-4]* The Wrights developed a series of gliders while experimenting with aerodynamics, which was crucial to developing a workable control system. Many historians, and most importantly the Wrights themselves, pointed out that their game plan was to learn flight control and become pilots specifically by soaring, whereas all the other experimenters rushed to add power without refining flight control. By 1903, Orville and Wilbur Wright had achieved powered flight of just over a minute by putting an engine on their best glider design.

Figure 1-4. *Orville Wright (left) and Dan Tate (right) launching the Wright 1902 glider off the east slope of the Big Hill, Kill Devil Hills, North Carolina on October 17, 1902. Wilbur Wright is flying the glider.*

By 1906, the sport of gliding was progressing rapidly. An American glider meet was sponsored by the Aero Club of America on Long Island, New York. By 1911, Orville Wright had set a world duration record of flying his motorless craft for 9 minutes and 45 seconds.

By 1920, the sport of soaring was coming into its own. Glider design was spurred on by developments in Germany where the World War I Treaty of Versailles banned flying power aircraft. New forms of lift were discovered that made it possible to gain altitude and travel distances using these previously unknown atmospheric resources. In 1921, Dr. Wolfgang Klemperer broke the Wright Brothers 1911 soaring duration record with a flight of 13 minutes using ridge lift. In 1928, Austrian Robert Kronfeld proved that thermal lift could be used by a sailplane to gain altitude by making a short out and return flight. In 1929, the National Glider Association was founded in Detroit, Michigan; by 1930, the first USA National Glider Contest was held in Elmira, New York. In 1937, the first World Championships were held at the Wasserkuppe in Germany.

By the 1950s, soaring was developing rapidly with the first American, Dr. Paul MacCready, Jr., taking part in a World Soaring Championships held in Sweden. Subsequently, Dr. MacCready went on to become the first American to win a World Soaring Championship in 1956 in France.

The period of the 1960s and 1980s found soaring growing rapidly. During this period, there was also a revival of hang gliders and ultralight aircraft as new materials and a better understanding of low-speed aerodynamics made new designs possible.

By the late 1990s, aviation had become commonplace with jet travel becoming critical to the world economy. Soaring had grown into a diverse and interesting sport. Modern high performance gliders are made from composite materials and take advantage of highly refined aerodynamics and control systems. Today, soaring pilots use sophisticated instrumentation, including global positioning system (GPS) and altitude information (variometer) integrated into electronic glide computers to go farther, faster, and higher than ever before.

Glider or Sailplane?

The Federal Aviation Administration (FAA) defines a glider as a heavier-than-air aircraft that is supported in flight by the dynamic reaction of the air against its lifting surfaces, and whose free flight does not depend principally on an engine. *[Figure 1-5]* The term "glider" is used to designate the rating

Figure 1-5. *A Schleicher ASK 21 glider.*

that can be placed on a pilot certificate once a person successfully completes required glider knowledge and practical tests.

Another widely accepted term used in the industry is sailplane. A sailplane is a glider (heavier-than-air fixed-wing aircraft) designed to fly efficiently and gain altitude solely from natural forces, such as thermals and ridge waves. *[Figure 1-6]* Older gliders and those used by the military were not generally designed to gain altitude in lifting conditions, whereas modern day sailplanes are designed to gain altitude in various conditions of lift. Some sailplanes are equipped with sustaining engines to enable level flight even in light sink, or areas of descending air flow. More sophisticated sailplanes may have engines powerful enough to allow takeoffs and climbs to soaring altitudes. In both cases, the powerplants and propellers are designed to be stopped in flight and retracted into the body of the sailplane to retain the high efficiency necessary for nonpowered flight.

Figure 1-6. *A sailplane is a glider designed to fly efficienctly and gain altitude solely from natural forces, such as thermals and ridge waves.*

Gliding, that is flying a glider or sailplane, is relatively easy to learn, but soaring, which is gaining altitude and traveling without power, is much more difficult and immensely satisfying when accomplished. Soaring refers to the sport of flying sailplanes, which usually includes traveling long distances and remaining aloft for extended periods of time. Gliders were designed and built to provide short flights off a hill down to a landing area. Since their wings provided relatively low lift and high drag, these simple gliders were generally unsuitable for sustained flight using atmospheric lifting forces. Both terms are acceptable and are synonymous. Early gliders were easy and inexpensive to build, and they played an important role in flight training. The most well-known example today of a glider is the space shuttle, which literally glides back to earth. The space shuttle, like gliders that remain closer to the earth, cannot sustain flight for long periods of time.

Self-launching gliders are equipped with engines; with the engine shut down, they display the same flight characteristics as nonpowered gliders. *[Figure 1-7]* The engine allows them to be launched under their own power. Once aloft, pilots of self-launching gliders can shut down the engine and fly with the power off. The additional training and procedures required to earn a self-launch endorsement are covered later in this handbook.

Figure 1-7. *An ASH 26 E self-launching sailplane with the propeller extended.*

Glider Pilot Schools

Most airports or glider bases have some type of pilot training available, either through FAA-approved pilot schools or individual FAA-certificated flight instructors. FAA-approved glider schools usually provide a wide variety of training aids, special facilities, and greater flexibility in scheduling. A number of colleges and universities also provide glider pilot training as a part of their overall pilot training curricula. However, most glider training is conducted by individual flight instructors through a membership in a glider club. Also, there are several commercial glider companies located around the United States offering flight training, sightseeing glider rides, and glider towing services.

Choosing the right facility or instructor for your glider training should be both exciting and educational. Many factors need to be considered when choosing the right school, such as location, type of certification, part- or full-time training, and cost. The quality of training received should be the most important factor. Before interviewing schools, potential student pilots should be educated on the types of training curriculums that are available. Pilot training is conducted in accordance with one of two regulatory categories: Title 14 of the Code of Federal Regulations (14 CFR) part 141 or 14 CFR part 61. Students can receive exceptional flight training under either part 141 or 61 training programs, as both have the same teaching and testing requirements. What differs is the way you are taught in order to meet those same requirements.

14 CFR Part 141 Pilot Schools

Pilot schools that are certificated under 14 CFR part 141 provide a more structured training program with a standardized FAA-approved training syllabus. This ensures that all necessary skills are taught in a specific order through approved lesson plans. Under part 141, students are also required to complete a specific number of hours of formal ground instruction either in a classroom or one on one with an FAA-certificated flight instructor. Students are also required to pass the FAA knowledge and practical tests. In order to obtain approval and maintain their part 141 certification, pilot schools must adhere to several FAA regulations.

Because part 141 pilot schools must adhere to the approved training regiment, their students are allowed to complete the pilot certificate or rating in fewer flight training hours than required by part 61. However, most students generally exceed the reduced part 141 flight training hour requirements in order to meet the proficiency standards to pass the practical test.

14 CFR Part 61 Instruction

Pilot training conducted under 14 CFR part 61 offers a somewhat more flexible and less structured training program than that conducted under part 141. A part 61 training syllabus is not subject to FAA approval; therefore, flight instructors have the flexibility to rearrange lesson plans to suit the individual needs of their students. However, it is important to understand that flight instructors must adhere to the requirements of part 61 and train their students to the standards of part 61.

Training under part 61 does not require the student to complete a formal ground school. Instead, students have the following three options: (1) attend a ground school course, (2) complete a home-study program, or (3) hire a certificated flight or ground instructor to teach and review any materials that they choose. Regardless of which option a student chooses to take, all students are required to pass the FAA knowledge and practical tests for the pilot certificate or rating for which they are applying. The requirements for pilot training under part 61 are less structured than those under part 141, and part 61 may require more flight training hours to obtain a pilot certificate or rating than part 141.

Most glider training programs can be found on the SSA website at www.ssa.org. Once you choose a general location, make a checklist of things to look for in a training organization. By talking to pilots, visiting the facility, and reading articles in pilot magazines, a checklist can be made and used to evaluate your options. Your choice might depend on whether you are planning to obtain a sport or private pilot certificate or pursuing a higher pilot certificate or a flight instructor certificate toward becoming a professional glider pilot. The quality of training is very important and should be the first priority when choosing a course of training. Prior to making a final decision, visit the facility being considered and talk with management, instructors, and both current and former students. Evaluate all training requirements using a checklist, and then take some time to think things over before making a decision.

After deciding where to learn to fly and making the necessary arrangements, training can begin. An important fact: ground and flight training should be obtained as regularly and frequently as possible. This assures maximum retention of instruction and the achievement of proficiency for which every pilot should strive.

Glider Certificate Eligibility Requirements

To be eligible to fly a glider solo, an individual must be at least 14 years of age and demonstrate satisfactory aeronautical knowledge on a test developed by an instructor. A student must also have received and logged ground and flight training for the maneuvers and procedures in 14 CFR part 61 that are appropriate to the make and model of aircraft to be flown. A student pilot must demonstrate satisfactory proficiency and safety. Only after all of these requirements are met can an instructor endorse a student's certificate and logbook for solo flight.

To be eligible for a private pilot certificate with a glider rating, an individual must be at least 16 years of age, complete the specific training and flight time requirements described in 14 CFR part 61, pass a knowledge test, and successfully complete a practical test.

To be eligible for a commercial or flight instructor glider certificate, an individual must be 18 years of age, complete the specific training requirements described in 14 CFR part 61, pass the required knowledge tests, and pass another practical test. If currently a pilot for a powered aircraft is adding a glider category rating on that certificate, the pilot is exempt from the knowledge test but must satisfactorily complete the practical test. Certificated glider pilots are not required to hold an airman medical certificate to operate a glider. However, they must not have any medical deficiencies.

The FAA Practical Test Standards (PTS) establish the standards for the knowledge and skills necessary for the issuance of a pilot certificate. It is important to reference the PTS, FAA Advisory Circular (AC) 60-22, Aeronautical Decision Making, Pilots Handbook of Aeronautical Knowledge (FAA-H-8083-25), and the Risk Management Handbook (FAA-H-8083-2) to understand the knowledge, skills, and experience required to obtain a pilot certificate to fly a glider. For more information on the certification of the gliders themselves, refer to 14 CFR part 21, the European Aviation Safety Agency (EASA) Certification Specifications (CS) 22.221, and the Weight and Balance Handbook (FAA-H-8083-1).

Common Glider Concepts

Terminology

There are a number of terms used in gliding that all glider pilots should be familiar with. The list is not comprehensive, but includes the following:

- Knot—one nautical mile per hour (NMPH). A nautical mile is 6,076.115 feet as opposed to 5,280 feet in a statute mile. Rounded that is 6,000 feet, which divided by 60 minutes equals 100 feet per minute (fpm). Hence, this gives 1 on a variometer, which means one knot per hour or approximately 100 fpm. A 4-knot thermal lifts the glider at 400 fpm.
- Lift—measured in knots, rising air lifting the glider higher.
- Sink—falling air that forces the glider to lose height and is measured in knots.
- Attitude—the orientation of an aircraft in the air with respect to the horizon. If the aircraft is diving, then it is said to have a "nose-down attitude about its lateral axes." Attitude can also be a roll or bank as referenced to the longitudinal axis and pitch up or down as referenced to lateral axis.
- Pitch—the up and down movement around the lateral axis for pitch. Increasing the pitch lifts the nose and drops the tail. Decreasing the pitch drops the nose and lifts the tail.
- Roll—movement around a line between the nose and tail longitudinal axes. Rolling right drops the right wing while lifting the left wing.
- Yaw—a turning motion in which the nose of the aircraft moves to the right or left about its vertical axis.
- Cable—steel wire used to connect the glider to the winch. It is approximately 5mm wide and should be avoided at all times until after the correct training for safe handling. There are some winch operations using composite fiber cable that is stronger and lighter than steel.
- Strop—a special part of the winch cable that is designed to be handled. The strop has the tost rings that are attached to the glider.
- Weak link—a safety device in the winch cable or tow line. They come in various strengths (indicated by their color) and the correct one must be used with a given glider.
- Elevator—a moveable section in the tailplane (the small wing at the back of the glider) that effectively controls whether the glider climbs or dives in flight.
- Thermal—a bubble or column of warm rising air. Pilots try to find these columns of rising air and stay within them to gain altitude.

Converting Metric Distance to Feet

A glider pilot must also be able to convert distance in meters to distance in feet, using the following conversion:

$$1 \text{ meter} = 3.2808 \text{ feet}$$

Multiply the number of meters by 3.2808

To convert kilometers to nautical miles and nautical miles to kilometers or statute miles, use the following:

$$1 \text{ nautical mile (NM)} = 1.852 \text{ kilometers (km)}$$
$$1 \text{ nautical mile (NM)} = 1.151 \text{ statute miles (SM)}$$
$$1 \text{ km} = 0.53996 \text{ NM}$$

Chapter 2
Components and Systems

Introduction

Although gliders come in an array of shapes and sizes, the basic design features of most gliders are fundamentally the same. All gliders conform to the aerodynamic principles that make flight possible. When air flows over the wings of a glider, the wings produce a force called lift that allows the aircraft to stay aloft. Glider wings are designed to produce maximum lift with minimum drag.

Glider Design

The earlier gliders were made mainly of wood with metal fastenings, stays, and control cables. Subsequent designs led to a fuselage made of fabric-covered steel tubing glued to wood and fabric wings for lightness and strength. New materials, such as carbon fiber, fiberglass, glass reinforced plastic (GRP), and Kevlar® are now being used to developed stronger and lighter gliders. Modern gliders are usually designed by computer-aided software to increase performance. The first glider to use fiberglass extensively was the Akaflieg Stuttgart FS-24 Phönix, which first flew in 1957. *[Figure 2-1]* Fiberglass is still used because of its high strength to weight ratio and its ability to give a smooth exterior finish to reduce drag. Drag has also been minimized by more aerodynamic shapes and retractable undercarriages. Flaps were installed when technology improved and are fitted to the trailing edges of the wings on some gliders to minimize the drag and to allow lower landing speeds.

Figure 2-1. *The Akaflieg Stuttgart FS-24 Phönix, made in Germany, was first flown on November 27, 1957.*

Most high-performance gliders are built of composites, instead of metal or wood, with a gel-coat finish. The gel coat is susceptible to damage from exposure to ultraviolet (UV) radiation from the sun, as well as prolonged exposure to moisture. At some soaring sites, pilots can keep the glider assembled in a hangar, but the composite glider is more frequently rigged before flying and derigged after flying. The transition to high-performance gliders necessitates development of checklists and discipline during glider assembly and disassembly. Other considerations for gel-coat care include extreme cold soaking. There is evidence that flying a composite glider with a gel-coat finish to very high and cold altitudes followed by a quick descent to warmer levels can seriously reduce the life of the gel coat. Composite gliders appear to be more susceptible to flutter than metal gliders. Flutter is a function of true airspeed. The GFM/POH of composite gliders sometimes presents a table of the indicated V_{NE} for different heights. For instance, a popular two-seat composite glider shows 135 knots as the sea level V_{NE}, 128 knots at 10,000 feet MSL, 121 knots at 13,000 feet MSL, etc. Read the GFM/POH carefully and obey the limitations set forth in the manual.

With each generation of new materials and development and improvements in aerodynamics, the performance of gliders has increased. One measure of performance is glide ratio. A glide ratio of 30:1 means that in smooth air a glider can travel forward 30 feet while only losing 1 foot of altitude. Glide ratio is discussed further in Chapter 5, Glider Performance.

Due to the critical role that aerodynamic efficiency plays in the performance of a glider, gliders often have aerodynamic features seldom found in other aircraft. The wings of a modern racing glider have a specially designed low-drag laminar flow airfoil. After the wing surfaces have been shaped by a mold with great accuracy, they are highly polished and painted with a gel coat (light fiberglass spray/sealer). Some high performance gliders have winglets installed at the ends of the wings. These winglets are computer designed to decrease drag and improve handling performance. *[Figure 2-2]* To continually ensure the best in aerodynamics, manufacturers use specially designed seals in the vicinity of the flight controls (i.e., ailerons, rudder, and elevator) to prevent the flow of air in the opposite direction through the control surface gaps, which causes turbulence over the area.

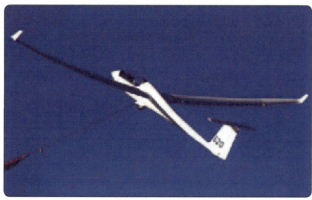

Figure 2-2. *Schempp-Hirth Ventus-2 glider with factory winglets installed.*

Additional high-technology designs include such items as bug wipers. These are very similar to a car windshield wiper. They may be installed to wipe the wings while in flight and remove insects that are disturbing the smooth flow of air over the wing by sliding back and forth along the leading edge of the wing. *[Figure 2-3]* Bug wipers can be operated by small electrical motors or by aerodynamics.

Modern competition gliders carry water ballast that can be jettisoned. This water acts as ballast in the wings and sometimes in the vertical stabilizer. The extra weight provided by the water ballast is advantageous if the lift is likely to be strong, and may also be used to adjust the glider's center of gravity (CG) during flight. Moving the CG toward the rear by carrying water in the vertical tail section reduces some

Figure 2-3. *Mechanical bug wipers can be installed to slide back and forth along the leading edge of the wing.*

of the required down force from the horizontal stabilizer aerodynamics and the resultant drag from that down force. Although heavier gliders have a slight disadvantage when climbing in rising air, they achieve a higher speed at any given glide angle. This is an advantage in strong conditions when the gliders spend only little time climbing in thermals. The pilot can jettison the water ballast before it becomes a disadvantage in weaker thermal conditions. Another use of water ballast is to dampen air turbulence that may be encountered during ridge soaring. To avoid undue stress on the airframe, gliders may jettison any water ballast before landing. *[Figure 2-4]* This is discussed further in Chapter 5, Glider Performance.

Figure 2-4. *Sailplane dropping water ballast before landing.*

Most gliders are built in Europe and are designed to meet the requirements of the European Aviation Safety Agency (EASA), similar to the United States Federal Aviation Administration (FAA). The EASA Certification Specification CS-22 (previously Joint Aviation Requirements (JAR)-22), defines minimum standards for safety in a wide range of characteristics such as controllability and strength. For example, it must have design features to minimize the possibility of incorrect assembly (gliders are often stowed in disassembled configuration with at least the wings being detached). Automatic connection of the controls during rigging is the common method of achieving this.

Throughout the years, flying gliders has not only been a recreational past time but are built and used for sport as well. Many glider pilots take part in gliding competitions that usually involve racing. Modern gliding competitions now comprise closed tasks; everyone races on an aerial route around specified turnpoints, plus start and finish points that bring everybody back to base. The weather forecast and the performance of the gliders, as well as the experience level of the pilots, dictate the length of the task. Today, most of the points are speed points, and the rule is to set the task so all pilots have a fair chance of completing it.

With the advent of global positioning systems (GPS), new types of tasks were introduced, such as speed or distance tasks within assigned areas and speed or distance tasks with pilot-selected turn points. Despite the use of pilot-selected turn points made possible by GPS, tasks over a fixed course are still used frequently. The Fédération Aéronautique Internationale (FAI), the world's air sports federation, is a nongovernmental and nonprofit international organization with the basic aim of furthering aeronautical and astronautical activities worldwide. The FAI Gliding Commission is the sporting body overseeing air sports at the international level so that essentially the same classes and class definitions are followed in all countries.

The following is an overview of the seven classes of gliders that are currently recognized by the FAI and are eligible for European and World Championships:

1. Standard class—no flaps, 15 meter (49.2 feet) wingspan, water ballast allowed.

2. 15 meter class—flaps allowed, 15 meter (49.2 feet) wingspan, water ballast allowed.

3. 18 meter class—flaps allowed, 18 meter (59 feet) wingspan, water ballast allowed.

4. Open class—no restrictions on wingspan, except a limit of 850 kg (1,874 pounds for the maximum all-up weight). Open classes may have wingspans in excess of 85 feet or more. *[Figure 2-5]*

5. Two-seat class—maximum wingspan of 20 meters (65.6 feet), also known by the German name of Doppelsitzer. *[Figure 2-6]*

6. Club class—this class allows a wide range of older, small gliders with different performance. The scores must be adjusted by handicapping. Water ballast is not allowed.

Figure 2-5. *The Schempp-Hirth Nimbus-4 is a family of high performance Fédération Aéronautique Internationale (FAI) open class gliders.*

7. World class—the FAI Gliding Commission, which is part of the FAI and an associated body called Organization Scientifique et Technique du Vol à Voile (OSTIV), announced a competition in 1989 for a low-cost glider that had moderate performance, was easy to assemble and handle, and was safe for low-hours pilots to fly. The winning design was announced in 1993 as the Warsaw Polytechnic PW-5. This allows competitions to be run with only one type of glider.

Glider airframes are designed with a fuselage, wings, and empennage or tail section. Self-launching gliders are equipped with an engine that enables them to launch without assistance and return to an airport under engine power if soaring conditions deteriorate.

The Fuselage

The fuselage is the portion of the airframe to which the wings and empennage are attached. The fuselage houses the cockpit and contains the controls for the glider, as well as a seat for each occupant. Glider fuselages can be formed from wood, fabric over steel tubing, aluminum, fiberglass, Kevlar® or other composites, or a combination of these materials. *[Figure 2-7]*

Wings and Components

Glider wings incorporate several components that help the pilot maintain the attitude of the glider and control lift and drag. These include ailerons and lift and drag devices, such as spoilers, dive brakes, and flaps. Glider wings vary in size and span from 12.2 meters (40 feet) to 30 meter (101.38 feet).

Figure 2-6. *The DG Flugzeugbau DG-1000 of the two-seater class.*

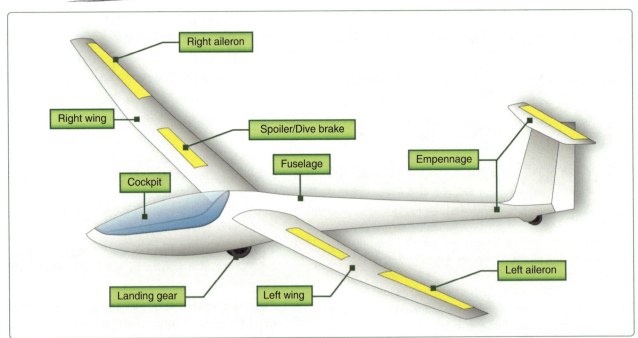

Figure 2-7. *Components of a glider.*

A wing may consist of a single piece attached to the fuselage to as many as four pieces (on one side).

The ailerons control movement around the longitudinal axis, known as roll. The ailerons are attached to the outboard trailing edge of each wing and move in opposite directions.

Moving the aileron controls with the control stick to the right causes the right aileron to deflect upward and the left aileron to deflect downward. The upward deflection of the right aileron decreases the effective camber (curvature of the wing surface), resulting in decreased lift on the right wing. *[Figure 2-8]* The corresponding downward deflection of the left aileron increases the effective camber, resulting in increased lift on the left wing. Thus, the increased lift on the left wing and decreased lift on the right wing causes the glider to roll to the right.

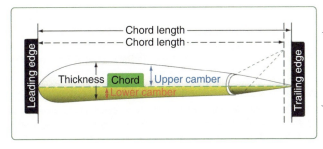

Figure 2-8. *The wing camber remains the same physically, but the ailerons change the "effective" camber of the wing and increase or decrease lift to change lift vectors to affect turns.*

Lift/Drag Devices

Gliders are equipped with devices that modify the lift/drag of the wing. These high drag devices include spoilers, dive brakes, and flaps. Spoilers extend from the upper surface of the wing, interrupting or spoiling the airflow over the wings. This action causes the glider to descend more rapidly. Dive brakes extend from both the upper and lower surfaces of the wing and help to increase drag.

Flaps are located on the trailing edge of the wing, inboard of the ailerons, and can be used to increase lift, drag, and descent rate. *[Figure 2-9]* Each flap type has a use depending on aircraft design. When the glider is cruising at moderate airspeeds in wings-level flight, the flaps can sometimes be set to a negative value (up from trail or level) for high speed cruising in some high efficiency gliders. When the flap is extended downward, wing camber is increased, and the lift and the drag of the wing increase.

Gliders are generally equipped with simple flaps and these flaps can generally be set in three different positions which are trail, down or negative. *[Figure 2-10]* When deflected downward, it increases the effective camber and changes the wing's chord line, which is an imaginary straight line drawn from the leading edge of an airfoil to the trailing edge. Both of these factors increase the lifting capacity of the wing.

Negative flap is used at high speeds at which wing lift reduction is desired to reduce drag. When the flaps are

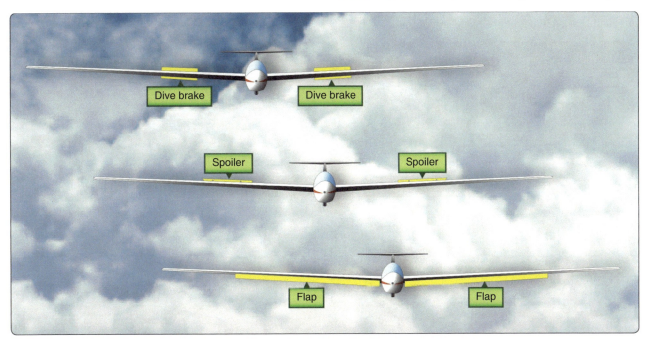

Figure 2-9. *Types of lift/drag devices.*

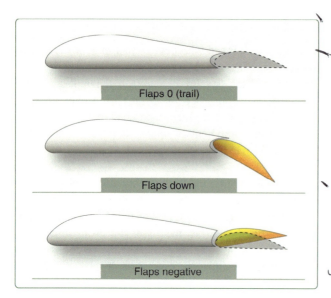

Figure 2-10. *Flap positions.*

extended in an upward direction, or negative setting, the effective camber of the wing is reduced, resulting in a reduction of lift produced by the wing at a fixed angle of attack and airspeed. This action reduces the down force, or balancing force, required from the horizontal stabilizer.

Empennage

The empennage includes the entire tail section, consisting of the fixed surfaces, such as the horizontal stabilizer and vertical fin, and moveable surfaces such as the elevator or stabilizer, rudder and any trim tabs. These two fixed surfaces act like the feathers on an arrow to steady the glider and help maintain a straight path through the air. *[Figure 2-11]*

The elevator is attached to the back of the horizontal stabilizer. The elevator controls movement around the lateral axis. This is known as pitch. During flight, the elevator is used to move the nose up and down, which controls the pitch attitude of the glider. The horizon is the primary pitch reference for a glider pilot. The elevator is primarily used to change or hold the same angle of attack of the glider. The trim tab, normally located on the elevator of the glider, lessens the resistance felt on the flight controls due to the airflow over the associated control surface.

The rudder is attached to the back of the vertical stabilizer. The rudder controls movement about the vertical axis. This is known as yaw. The rudder is used in combination with the ailerons and elevator to coordinate turns during flight.

Some gliders use a stabilator, which is used in lieu of an elevator and horizontal stabilizer. The stabilator pivots up and down on a central hinge point. When pulling back on the control stick, the nose of the glider moves up; when pushing forward, the nose moves down. Stabilators sometimes employ an anti-servo trim tab to achieve pitch trim. The anti-servo tab provides a control feel comparable to that of an elevator.

Trim devices reduce pilot workload by relieving the pressure required on the controls to maintain a desired airspeed. One type of trim device found on gliders is the elevator trim tab, a small, hinged, cockpit-adjustable tab on the trailing edge of the elevator. *[Figure 2-12]* Other types of elevator trim device include bungee spring systems and ratchet trim systems. In these systems, fore and aft control stick pressure is applied by an adjustable spring or bungee cord.

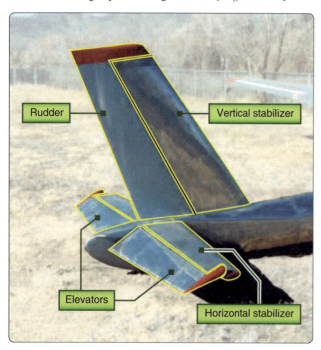

Figure 2-11. *Empennage components.*

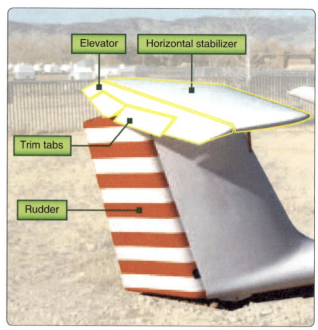

Figure 2-12. *Additional empennage components.*

Primary flight controls (aileron, elevator, and rudder), assisted by the trim devices, reduce control loading and provide positive feed to the pilot. The trim tab is either servo or anti-servo. *[Figure 2-13]* Anti-servo tab movement is opposite to the control surface providing a positive feedback (or feel) to the pilot. Servo tabs move in the same direction as the control surface and allow the pilot to remove (or lighten) control load, reducing fatigue during flight and providing aerodynamic trim.

The glider may have a towhook located on or under the nose and/or under the center of gravity (CG), near the main landing gear. The forward towhook is used for aerotow. The CG hook is used for ground launch. A glider with only a CG hook may be approved for aerotow in accordance with the Glider Flight Manual/Pilot's Operating Handbook. *[Figure 2-14]*

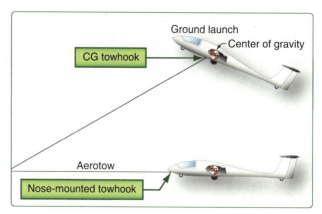

Figure 2-14. *Towhook locations.*

Powerplant

Self-Launching Gliders

Self-launching gliders are equipped with engines powerful enough to enable them to launch without external assistance. The engines may also be used to sustain flight if the soaring conditions deteriorate. Self-launching gliders differ widely in terms of engine location and type of propeller. There are two types of self-launching gliders: touring motor gliders and high-performance self-launching gliders.

Figure 2-13. *Additional empennage components.*

Over the years, the shape of the empennage has taken different forms. Early gliders were most often built with the horizontal stabilizer mounted at the bottom of the vertical stabilizer. This type of tail arrangement is called the conventional tail. Other gliders were designed with a T-tail, and still others were designed with V-tail. T-tail gliders have the horizontal stabilizer mounted on the top of the vertical stabilizer, forming a T. V-tails have two tail surfaces mounted to form a V. V-tails combine elevator and rudder movements. This combination of elevator and rudder are referred as ruddervators.

Towhook Devices

An approved towhook is a vital part of glider equipment. The towhook is designed for quick release when the pilot exerts a pulling force on the release handle. As a safety feature (on most of the bellyhooks (CG hook)), if back pressure occurs from either getting out of position during the tow or overrunning the towrope, the release automatically opens. Part of the glider pilot's preflight is ensuring that the towhook releases properly with applied forward and back pressure.

Touring motor gliders are equipped with a fixed, nose-mounted engine and a full feathering propeller. *[Figure 2-15]* Touring motor gliders resemble an airplane to the untrained eye. They do have some basic airplane characteristics but are not certified as an airplane. On other types of self-launching gliders, the engine and propeller are located aft of the cockpit. High-performance self-launching gliders generally are seen with engines and propellers mounted behind the cockpit that completely retract into the fuselage for minimal drag in the soaring mode. *[Figure 2-16]* Propellers may fold or may simple align with the engine and retract completely. This configuration preserves the smooth low drag nose configurations important for good soaring efficiencies. When the engine and propeller are not in use, they are retracted into the fuselage, reducing drag and increasing soaring performance. These types of self-launch engines are usually coupled to a folding propeller, so the entire powerplant can be retracted and the bay doors are closed and sealed.

Figure 2-15. *A Grob G109B touring motor glider.*

Sustainer Engines

Some gliders are equipped with sustainer engines to assist in remaining aloft long enough to return to an airport. However, sustainer engines do not provide sufficient power to launch the glider from the ground without external assistance. These sailplanes are launched by either aerotow or ground launch. *[Figure 2-17]* A more detailed explanation of engine operations can be found in Chapter 7, Launch and Recovery Procedures and Flight Maneuvers.

Landing Gear

Glider landing gear usually includes a main wheel, a front skid or wheel and a tail wheel or skid, and often wing tip wheels or skid plates. Gliders designed for high speed and low drag often feature a fully retractable main landing gear and a small breakaway tailwheel or tail skid. Breakaway tail skids are found on high-performance gliders, and are designed to break off when placed under side loads. *[Figure 2-18]*

For safety reasons, the main landing gear remains extended during the launch process. If there is a tow break or early release, the pilot needs to focus on a safe return. The pilot's

Figure 2-17. *A Schleicher ASH 26e motor glider with the sustainer engine mast extended.*

normal landing checklist provides a landing gear check, but during a low-altitude emergency, important items could be skipped on any checklist. Therefore, it is good practice to leave the main gear extended until reaching a safe altitude.

Wheel Brakes

The wheel brake, mounted on the main landing gear wheel, helps the glider slow down or stop after touchdown. The type of wheel brake used often depends on the design of the glider. Many early gliders relied on friction between the nose skid and the ground to come to a stop. Current glider models are fitted with drum brakes, disk brakes, and friction brakes. The most common type of wheel brake found in modern gliders is the disk brake, which is very similar to the disk brake on the front wheels of most cars. Most glider disk brakes are hydraulically operated to provide maximum braking capability. Wheel brake controls vary from one glider type to another.

Figure 2-16. *A DG-808B 18-meter high-performance glider in self-launch.*

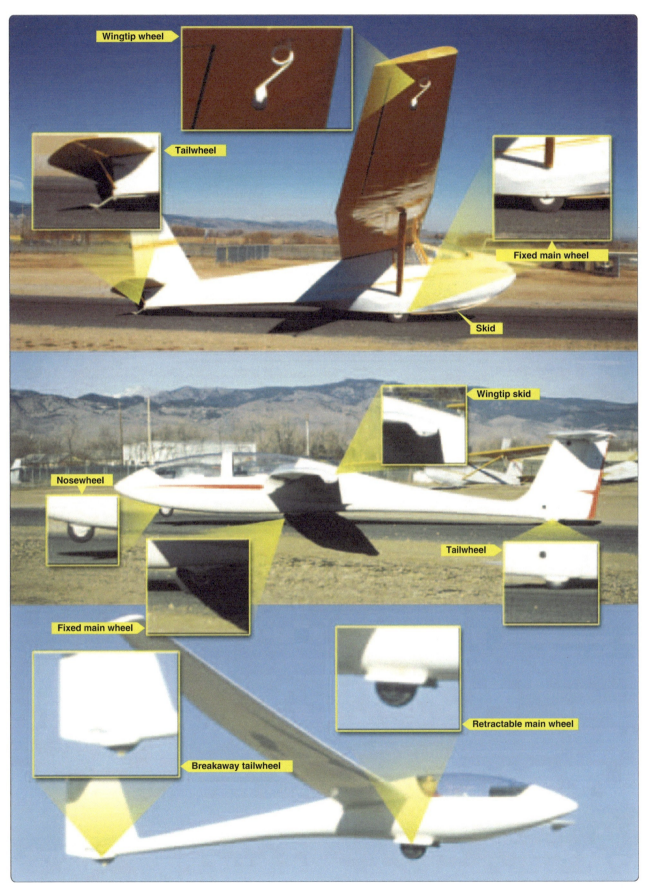

Figure 2-18. *Landing gear wheels on a glider.*

Chapter 3
Aerodynamics of Flight

Introduction

To understand what makes a glider fly, pilots must first have an understanding of aircraft aerodynamics and how flight is possible. An understanding of aerodynamics and how it affects takeoffs, flight maneuvers, and landings allows pilots to be more skillful and aware of the capabilities of the glider. A thorough discussion about aeronautical terminology and concepts related to aircraft in flight can be found in the Pilot's Handbook of Aeronautical Knowledge (FAA-H-8083-25), which new pilots should review before learning about the aerodynamics specific to gliders. This chapter discusses the fundamentals of aerodynamics as it relates to gliders and glider performance. The study of aerodynamics is a complicated science, and pilots should consider the task of learning aerodynamics as critical as learning how to land safely.

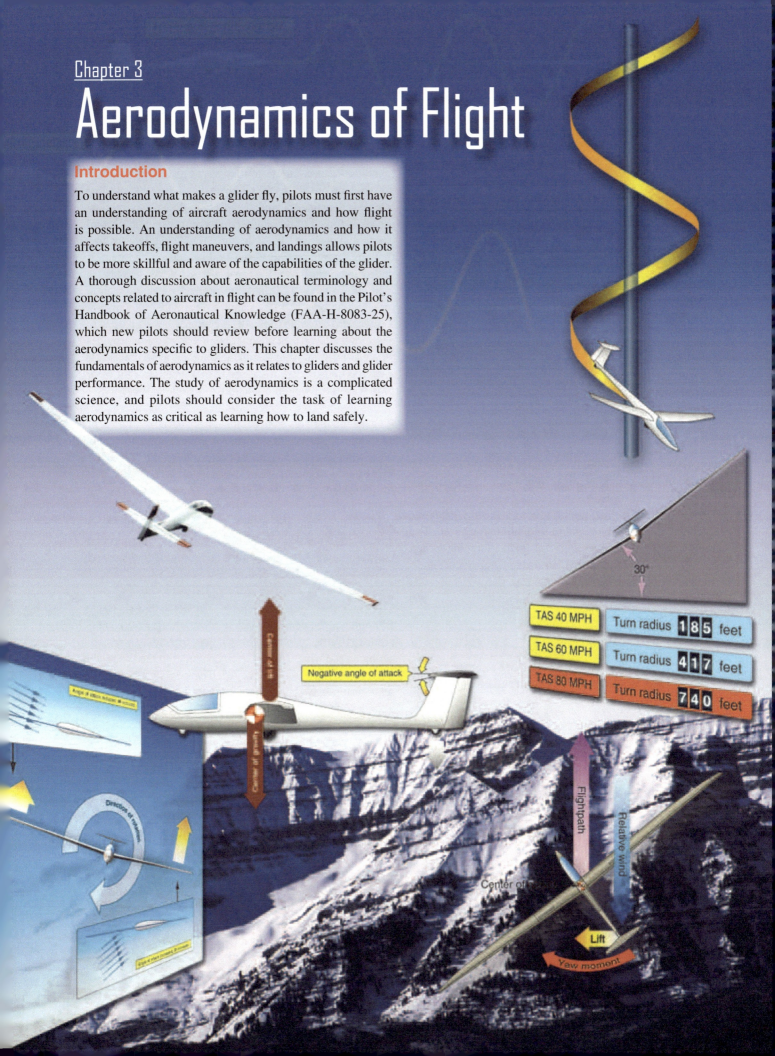

Forces of Flight

There are four forces that act upon an aircraft during straight-and-level flight. They are lift, gravity, thrust, and drag. Lift counters gravity, and drag counters thrust. When all four forces are in balance, straight-and-level flight is sustained. Engine-powered gliders obtain thrust from the engine. Once in flight and the engine has been shut off, or the glider has been launched, towed, or winched, the need to obtain thrust is still there. The glider does this by converting the potential energy that it has accumulated into kinetic energy as it glides downward, trading height for distance. In essence, the gravity vector becomes the horizontal forward thrust vector component. We measure the force of gravity as the weight in pounds or kilograms. This explains why the faster the glider flies, the faster it also descends.

Figure 3-1 shows a basic vector diagram for an unpowered glider with all forces in equilibrium. The lift vector is effectively split into two components: one part is opposing the weight force (gravity in straight-and-level flight), and the other component of the lift vector opposes drag by supplying thrust by the conversion of potential energy of the elevated weight of the glider into kinetic energy. This conversion continues until the airframe comes to rest on the surface. A glider is always descending in the air. This allows development of thrust by the energy conversion process. The objective of a glider pilot is to remain in air rising faster than the glider must descend to maintain flying speed. The same is true for a powered aircraft with its engine turned off. These forces are explained in greater detail in the Pilot's Handbook of Aeronautical Knowledge (FAA-H-8083-25) and by examining Newton's laws of motion.

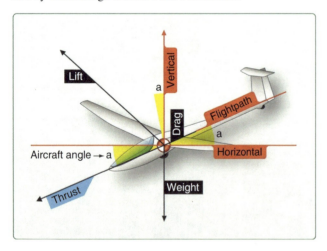

Figure 3-1. *Vector components of lift, drag, and weight (gravity).*

Newton's Third Law of Motion

According to Newton's Third Law of Motion, for every action there is an equal and opposite reaction. Thus, the air that is deflected downward also produces an upward (lifting) reaction. The wing's construction is designed to take advantage of certain physical laws that generate two actions from the air mass. One is a positive pressure lifting action from the air mass below the wing, and the other is a negative pressure lifting action from the lowered pressure above the wing.

As the airstream strikes the relatively flat lower surface of the wing when inclined at a small angle to its direction of motion, the air is forced to rebound downward, causing an upward reaction in positive lift. At the same time, airstream striking the upper curve section of the leading edge of the wing is deflected upward, over the top of the wing. The increase in airspeed on the top of the wing produces a sharp drop in pressure. Associated with the lowered pressure is downwash, a downward backward flow. In other words, a wing shaped to cause an action on the air, and forcing it downward, provides an equal reaction from the air, forcing the wing upward. If a wing is constructed in such form that it causes a lift force greater than the weight of the glider, the glider flies.

If all the required lift were obtained from the deflection of air by the lower surface of the wing, a glider would need only a flat wing like a kite. This, of course, is not the case at all. The balance of the lift needed to support the glider comes from the flow of air above the wing. Herein lies the key to flight. Lift is the result of the airflow above and over the wing lowering the air pressure above the wing, which pull the wing upwards and the downwash from below the wing pushing the wing upward. This fact must be thoroughly understood to continue in the study of flight.

Lift

Lift opposes the downward force of weight (gravity) and is produced by the dynamic effects of the surrounding airstream acting on the wing. Lift acts perpendicular to the flightpath through the wing's center of lift. There is a mathematical relationship between lift, angle of attack (AOA), airspeed, altitude, and the size of the wing. In the lift equation, these factors correspond to the coefficient of lift, velocity, air density, and wing surface area. These relationships are expressed in *Figure 3-2*. For a complete explanation of the lift formula and terms refer to the Pilots Handbook of Aeronautical Knowledge.

This shows that for lift to increase, one or more of the factors on the other side of the equation must increase. Lift is proportional to the square of the velocity, or airspeed; therefore, doubling airspeed quadruples the amount of lift if everything else remains the same. Likewise, if other factors remain the same while the coefficient or lift increases, lift also increases. The coefficient of lift goes up as the AOA is increased. As air density increases, lift increases. However,

$$L = C_L V^2 \frac{\rho}{2} S$$

L = Lift
C_L = Coefficient of lift
(This dimensionless number is the ratio of lift pressure to dynamic pressure and area. It is specific to a particular airfoil shape, and, below the stall, it is proportional to angle of attack.)
V = Velocity (feet per second)
ρ = Air density (slugs per cubic foot)
S = Wing surface area (square feet)

Figure 3-2. *Equation of the factors of lift.*

glider pilots are usually more concerned with how lift is diminished by reductions in air density on a hot day, or as they climb higher.

The Effects of Drag on a Glider

The force that resists the movement of the glider through the air is called drag. Two different types of drag combine to form total drag: parasite and induced. The various types of drag are explained in greater detail in the Pilot's Handbook of Aeronautical Knowledge (FAA-H-8083-25).

Parasite Drag

Parasite drag is the resistance offered by the air to anything moving through it. The aircraft surface deflects or interferes with the smooth airflow around the glider. The wing of the sailplane alone has very low parasite drag, but when the total drag of the glider is added to it, the amount of drag becomes significant. This is apparent particularly at high speeds since parasite drag increases with the square of speed. Simply put, if the speed of the glider is doubled, parasite drag increases four times. *[Figure 3-3]* Parasite drag is divided into three types: form drag, skin friction, and interference drag.

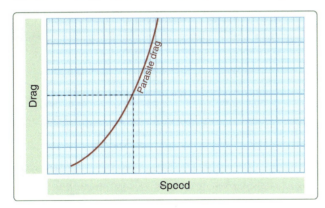

Figure 3-3. *Drag versus speed.*

Form Drag

Form drag results from the turbulent wake caused by the separation of airflow from the surface of a structure. *[Figure 3-4]* Any object moving through the air has to push

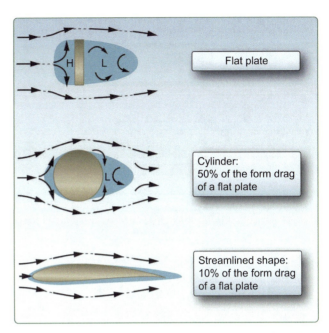

Figure 3-4. *Streamlined airfoil designs greatly reduce form drag by reducing the amount of airflow separation.*

the air in front of it out of the way. This causes a buildup of pressure in front of the object. Similarly, the object leaves a low-pressure void in its wake. This difference in pressure between the front and back surfaces of the object results in the force called form drag. Form drag can be reduced by reducing the object's cross-sectional area or by streamlining it.

Skin Friction Drag

Skin friction drag is caused by the roughness of the glider's surfaces. Even though the surfaces may appear smooth, they may be quite rough when viewed under a microscope. This roughness allows a thin layer of air to cling to the surface and create small eddies or areas of lower pressure that contribute to drag. As air flows across a wing, friction brings the layer of air molecules directly in contact with the surface to a standstill. Air is a viscous fluid, hence the stationary layer of air on the wing's surface slows the layer above it, but not as much as the layer above. This layer then slows the layer above it, but again not as much, and so on. Therefore, the velocity of the flow increases with distance from the surface until the full speed of the flow is reached. This layer of decelerated air is called the boundary layer. The frictional forces that create the boundary layer *[Figure 3-5]* create an equal and opposite skin friction force on the glider. When the surface area is reduced, the amount of skin friction is reduced.

The boundary layer can take on two distinct forms: the laminar boundary layer and the turbulent boundary layer.

- Laminar boundary layer—each layer of air molecules slides smoothly over its neighbors. *[Figure 3-6]*

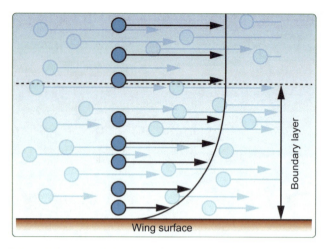

Figure 3-5. *Layer of decelerated air called the boundary layer.*

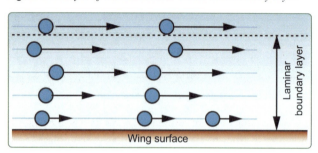

Figure 3-6. *Laminar boundary layer.*

- Turbulent boundary layer—dominated by eddies and irregular turbulent flow. *[Figure 3-7]*

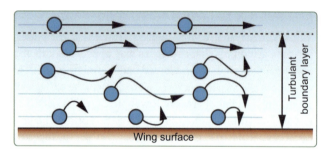

Figure 3-7. *Turbulent boundary layer.*

Turbulent boundary layers generate 5 to 10 times more skin friction drag than the equivalent laminar boundary layer. *[Figure 3-8]* Therefore, glider designers try to maintain laminar flow across as much of the aircraft as possible. *Figure 3-9* shows why this turbulent transition occurs.

There is a point that is referred to as the separation point, in which the boundary layer breaks away from the surface of the wing due to the magnitude of the positive pressure gradient. Beneath the separated layer, bubbles of stagnant air form, creating additional drag because of the lower pressure in the wake behind the separation point.

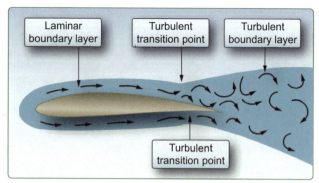

Figure 3-8. *Skin friction increases due to the turbulent boundary layer.*

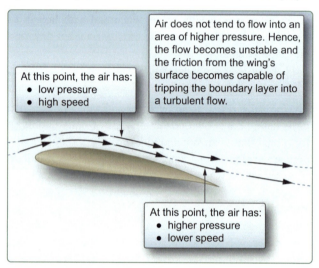

Figure 3-9. *Combinations of low and high pressure on the airfoil causing a turbulent flow of air.*

These bubbles can be reduced or even eliminated by shaping the airfoil to move the separation point downstream or by adding a turbulator. Turbulators are aerodynamically positioned in a spanwise line along the wing and are used to trip laminar flow air into turbulent flow air at a desired location on the wing. This is beneficial because the turbulent boundary layer contains more energy, which will delay separation until a greater magnitude of negative pressure gradient is reached, effectively moving the separation point further aft on the airfoil and possible eliminating separation completely. A consequence of the turbulent boundary layer is increased skin friction relative to a laminar boundary layer, but this is very small compared to the increase in drag associated with separation.

In gliders, the turbulator is often a thin zig-zag strip that is placed on the underside of the wing and sometimes on the fin. *[Figure 3-10]* For a glider with low Reynolds numbers (i.e., where minimizing turbulence and drag is a major concern), the small increase in drag from the turbulator at higher speeds is minor compared with the larger improvements at best glide speed, at which the glider can fly the farthest for a given height.

Figure 3-10. *Glider wing on the left shows the airflow with a turbulator installed and the glider wing on the right shows how the airflow is disturbed without the turbulator installed.*

The boundary layer can also be tripped into a turbulent flow at any point by discontinuities on the wing's surface. It is important to keep wings clean and avoid rain and icing to prevent premature transition, and the increase in drag that it causes. As the boundary layer is only 1.0 millimeter thick at the leading edge, objects, such as rivets, splattered insects, rain drops, ice crystals, and dust, are all large enough to cause localized turbulent transition to occur. *[Figure 3-11]*

Interference Drag

Interference drag occurs when varied currents of air over a glider meet and interact. Placing two objects adjacent to one another may produce turbulence 50–200 percent greater than the parts tested separately. An example of interference drag is the mixing of air over structures, such as the wing, tail surfaces, and wing struts. Interference drag can be reduced on gliders with fairings to streamline the intersection of air.

Induced Drag

Induced drag is generated as the wing is driven through the air to develop the difference in air pressures that we call lift. As the higher pressure air on the lower surface of the airfoil curves around the end of the wing and fills in the lower pressure area on the upper surface, the lift is lost, yet the energy to produce the different pressures is still expended. The result is drag because it is wasted energy. The more energy the glider requires to fly, the greater the required rate of descent is to supply sufficient energy to convert into thrust

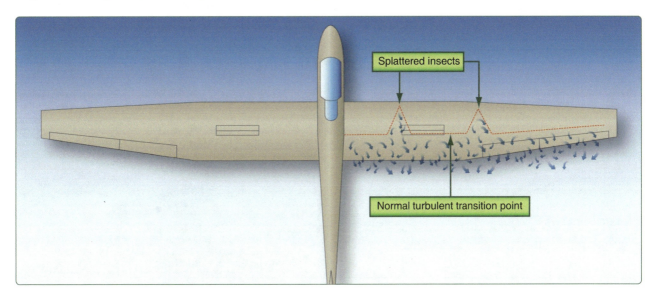

Figure 3-11. *Turbulence due to insects, ice crystals, and dust.*

to overcome that unnecessary drag. The energy that produces the vortices is wasted energy. The object of glider design is to convert all of the energy into useful lift and the necessary thrust. Any wasted energy translates into poorer performance. *[Figure 3-12]* Glider designers attempt to reduce drag by increasing the aspect ratio of the glider. The greater the aspect ratio of the wing is, the lower the induced drag is. Wingtip devices, or winglets, are also used to improve the efficiency of the glider. There are several types of wingtip devices and, though they function in different manners, the intended effect is always to reduce the aircraft's drag by altering the airflow near the wingtips. Such devices increase the effective aspect ratio of a wing, without materially increasing the wingspan.

Total Drag

Total drag on a glider is the sum of parasite and induced drag. The total drag curve represents these combined forces and is plotted against airspeed. *[Figure 3-13]*

L/D_{MAX} is the point at which the lift-to-drag ratio is greatest. At this speed, the total lift capacity of the glider, when compared to the total drag of the glider, is most favorable. In calm air, this is the airspeed used to obtain maximum glide distance.

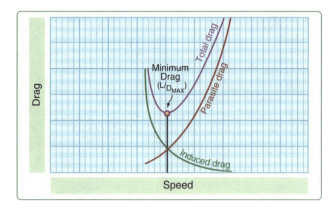

Figure 3-13. *Total drag from the sum of parasite and induced drag.*

Wing Planform

The shape, or planform, of the wings also has an effect on the amount of lift and drag produced. The four most common wing planforms used on gliders are elliptical, rectangular, tapered, and swept forward. *[Figure 3-14]*

Elliptical Wing

An elliptical wing is a wing planform shape that minimizes induced drag. Elliptical taper shortens the chord near the wingtips in such a way that all parts of the wing experience equivalent downwash, and lift at the wing tips is essentially

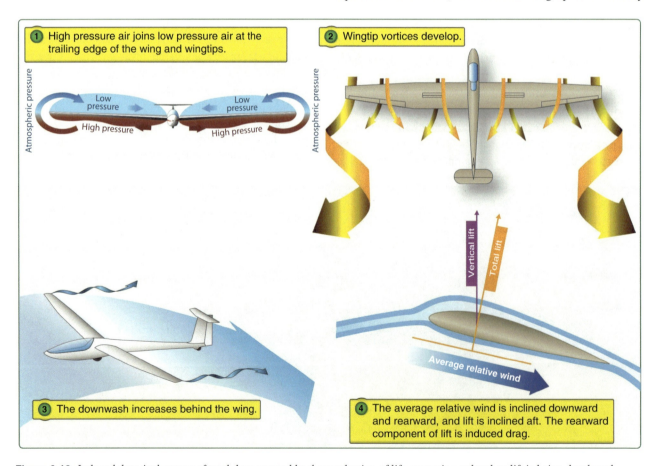

Figure 3-12. *Induced drag is that part of total drag created by the production of lift, occurring only when lift is being developed.*

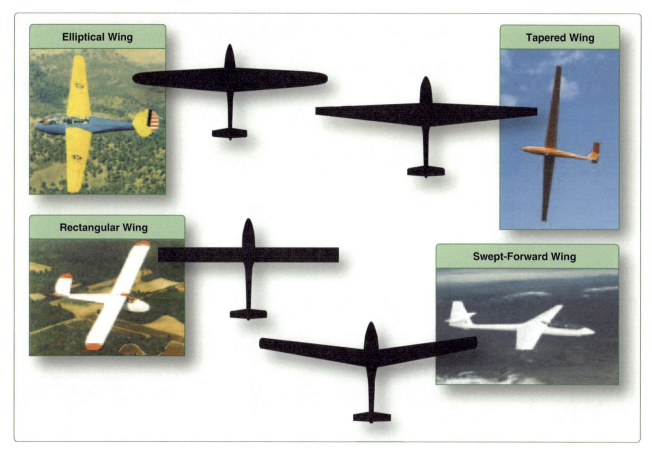

Figure 3-14. *Planforms of glider wings.*

zero, improving aerodynamic efficiency. This wing design is difficult and costly to manufacture because of the compound curves in its design. The elliptical wing is more efficient in terms of L_D, but the wing's uniform lift distribution causes the entire span of the wing to stall simultaneously, potentially causing loss of control with little warning.

Rectangular Wing

The rectangular wing is similar in efficiency to the elliptical wing, but is much easier to build. Rectangular wings have very gentle stall characteristics with a warning buffet prior to stall, and are easier to manufacture than elliptical wings. One drawback to this wing design is that rectangular wings create more induced drag than an elliptical wing of comparable size.

Tapered Wing

The tapered wing is the planform found most frequently on gliders. Assuming equal wing area, the tapered wing produces less drag than the rectangular wing, because there is less area at the tip of the tapered wing. If speed is the primary consideration, a tapered wing is more desirable than a rectangular wing, but a tapered wing with no twist (also called washout) has undesirable stall characteristics.

Swept-Forward Wing

A swept-forward planform is a wing configuration in which the quarter-chord line of the wing has a forward sweep. Swept-forward wings are used to allow the lifting area of the wing to move forward, while keeping the mounting point aft of the cockpit. This wing configuration is used on some tandem two-seat gliders to allow for a small change in center of gravity (CG) with the rear seat occupied, or while flying solo. This type of planform design gives the glider increased maneuverability due to airflow from wing tip to wing root, preventing a stall of the wing tips and ailerons at high angles of attack. Instead, the stall occurs in the region of the wing root.

Washout

Washout is built into wings by putting a slight twist between the wing root and wing tip. When washout is designed into the wing, the wing displays very good stall characteristics. Moving outward along the span of the wing, the trailing edge moves up in reference to the leading edge. This twist causes the wing root to have a greater AOA than the tip, and as a result, stall first. This provides ample warning of the impending stall and, at the same time, allows continued aileron control.

Glide Ratio

Glide ratio is the number of feet a glider travels horizontally in still air for every foot of altitude lost. If a glider has a 50:1 glide ratio, then it travels 50 feet for every foot of altitude lost.

$$\text{Glide ratio} = \frac{\text{Lift}}{\text{Drag}} : 1$$

This explains why minimizing drag is so critically important. Because drag varies with airspeed, the glide ratio must also vary with airspeed. A glide polar shown in *Figure 3–15* is a graph, normally provided in a glider's flight manual, that details the glider's still air sink rate at airspeeds within its flight envelope. The glide ratio at a particular airspeed can be estimated from the glide polar using:

$$\text{Glide ratio} = \frac{\text{Airspeed}}{\text{Sink rate}} : 1$$

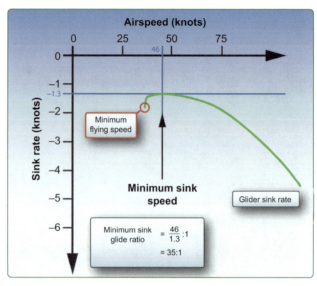

Figure 3-16. *Minimum sink speed can be found using the glide polar graph.*

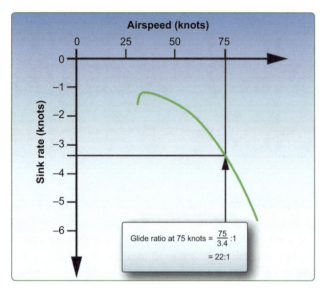

Figure 3-15. *Glide polar graph.*

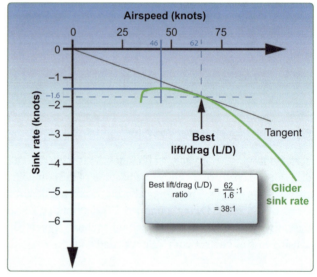

Figure 3-17. *The glider polar graph helps determine the glider's best glide speed.*

Airspeed and sink rate must both be in the same units. The example in *Figure 3-14* uses knots. The minimum sink speed is the airspeed at which the glider loses altitude at the lowest rate. It can be determined from the polar by locating the point on the graph with the lowest sink rate and reading off the corresponding airspeed. *[Figure 3-16]*

The best glide speed is the airspeed at which, in still air, the glider achieves its best glide ratio. It is also known as the best lift/drag (L/D) speed. This can be determined from the polar by drawing a line from the origin that is tangential to the curve (e.g., just touching). *[Figure 3-17]* The point of contact is the best glide speed; the glide ratio at this speed can be calculated as previously described. In still air, the glider should be flown at this speed to get from A to B with minimum height loss.

Increasing the mass of a glider by adding water ballast, for example, shifts the glide polar down and to the right. *[Figure 3-18]* The minimum sink rate is therefore increased, so as expected, the extra weight makes it harder to climb in thermals. However, the best glide ratio remains approximately the same, but now occurs at a higher airspeed. Therefore, if the thermals are strong enough to compensate for the poor climb performance, then water ballast allows a faster inter-thermal cruise. This results in greater distances being traveled per time interval.

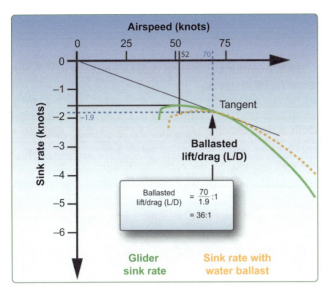

Figure 3-18. *Calculating glide speed with water ballast.*

Aspect Ratio

The aspect ratio is another factor that affects the lift and drag created by a wing. Aspect ratio is determined by dividing the wingspan (from wingtip to wingtip), by the average wing chord.

Glider wings have a high aspect ratio, as shown in *Figure 3-19*. High aspect ratio wings produce a comparably high amount of lift at low angles of attack with less induced drag.

Weight

Weight is the third force that acts on a glider in flight. Weight opposes lift and acts vertically through the CG of the glider. Gravitational pull provides the force necessary to move a glider through the air since a portion of the weight vector of a glider is directed forward.

Thrust

Thrust is the forward force that propels a self-launching glider through the air. Self-launching gliders have engine-driven propellers that provide this thrust. Unpowered gliders have an outside force, such as a towplane, winch, or automobile, to launch the glider. Airborne gliders obtain thrust from conversion of potential energy to kinetic energy.

Three Axes of Rotation

The glider is maneuvered around three axes of rotation: yaw (vertical), lateral, and longitudinal. They rotate around one

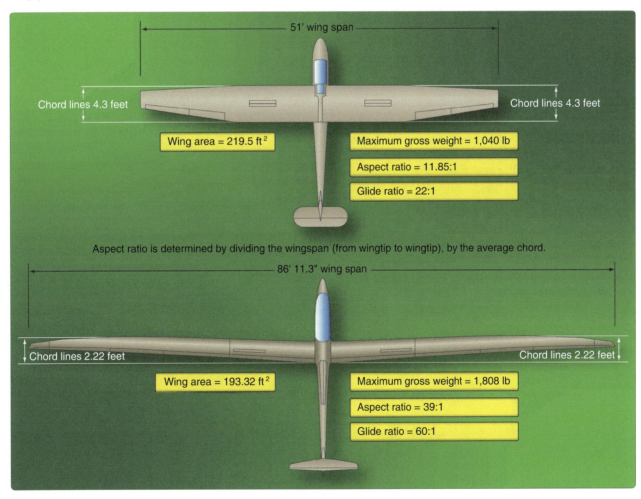

Figure 3-19. *Aspect ratio.*

central point in the glider called the CG. This point is the center of the glider's total weight and varies with the loading of the glider.

Yaw is movement around the vertical axis, which can be represented by an imaginary straight line drawn vertically through the CG. Moving the rudder left or right causes the glider to yaw the nose to the left or right. Moving the ailerons left or right to bank moves the glider around the longitudinal axis. This axis would appear if a line were drawn through the center of the fuselage from nose to tail. Pulling the stick back or pushing it forward, raising or lowering the nose, controls the pitch of the glider or its movement around the lateral axis. The lateral axis could be seen if a line were drawn from one side of the fuselage to the other through the CG. *[Figure 3-20]*

Stability

A glider is in equilibrium when all of its forces are in balance. Stability is defined as the glider's ability to maintain a uniform flight condition and return to that condition after being disturbed. Often during flight, gliders encounter equilibrium-changing pitch disturbances. These can occur in the form of vertical gusts, a sudden shift in CG, or deflection of the controls by the pilot. For example, a stable glider would display a tendency to return to equilibrium after encountering a force that causes the nose to pitch up.

Static stability and dynamic stability are two types of stability a glider displays in flight. Static stability is the initial tendency to return to a state of equilibrium when disturbed from that state. The three types of static stability are positive, negative, and neutral. When a glider demonstrates positive static stability, it tends to return to equilibrium. A glider demonstrating negative static stability displays a tendency to increase its displacement. Gliders that demonstrate neutral static stability have neither the tendency to return to equilibrium nor the tendency to continue displacement.

Dynamic stability describes a glider's motion and time required for a response to static stability. In other words, dynamic stability describes the manner in which a glider oscillates when responding to static stability. A glider that displays positive dynamic and static stability reduces its oscillations with time. A glider demonstrating negative dynamic stability is the opposite situation; its oscillations increase in amplitude with time following a displacement. A glider displaying neutral dynamic stability experiences oscillations, which remain at the same amplitude without increasing or decreasing over time. *Figure 3-21* illustrates the various types of dynamic stability.

Both static and dynamic stability are particularly important for pitch control about the lateral axis. Measurement of stability about this axis is known as longitudinal stability. Gliders are designed to be slightly nose heavy in order to improve their longitudinal stability. This causes the glider to tend to nose down during normal flight. The horizontal stabilizer on the tail is mounted at a slightly negative AOA to offset this tendency. When a dynamically stable glider oscillates, the amplitude of the oscillations should reduce through each cycle and eventually settle down to a speed at which the downward force on the tail exactly offsets the tendency to dive. *[Figure 3-22]*

Adjusting the trim assists in maintaining a desired pitch attitude. A glider with positive static and dynamic longitudinal stability tends to return to the trimmed pitch attitude when the force that displaced it is removed. If a glider displays negative stability, oscillations increase over time. If uncorrected, negative stability can induce loads exceeding the design limitations of the glider.

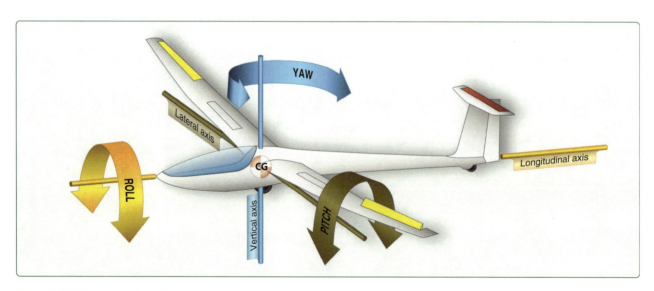

Figure 3-20. *Three axes of rotation.*

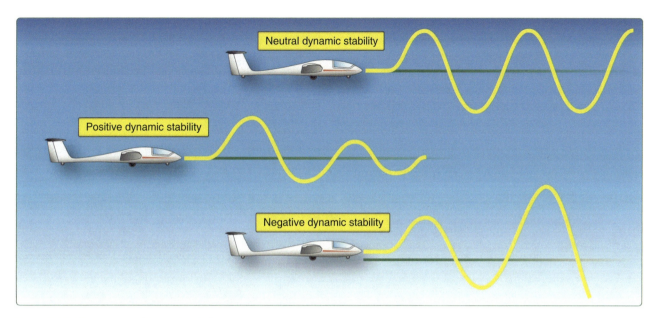

Figure 3-21. *Three types of dynamic stability.*

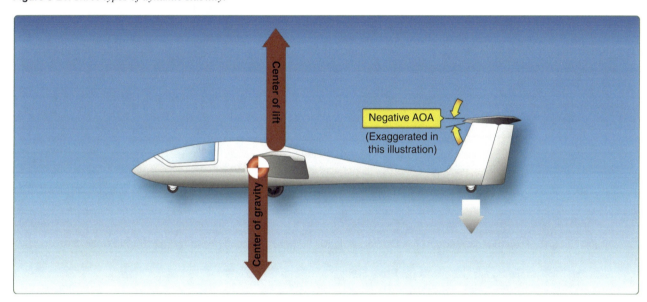

Figure 3-22. *Use of the horizontal stabilizer angle to offset the natural tendency of a glider to nose down.*

Another factor that is critical to the longitudinal stability of a glider is its loading in relation to the CG. The CG of the glider is the point at which the total force of gravity is considered to act. When the glider is improperly loaded so it exceeds the aft CG limit, it loses longitudinal stability. As airspeed decreases, the nose of a glider rises. To recover, control inputs must be applied to force the nose down to return to a level flight attitude. It is possible that the glider could be loaded so far aft of the approved limits that control inputs are not sufficient to stop the nose from pitching up. If this were the case, the glider could enter a spin from which recovery would be impossible. Loading a glider with the CG too far forward is also hazardous. In extreme cases, the glider may not have enough pitch control to hold the nose up during an approach to a landing. For these reasons, it is important to ensure that the glider is within weight and balance limits prior to each flight. Proper loading of a glider and the importance of CG is discussed further in Chapter 5, Performance Limitations.

Flutter

Another factor that can affect the ability to control the glider is flutter. Flutter occurs when rapid vibrations are induced through the control surfaces while the glider is traveling at high speeds. Looseness in the control surfaces can result in flutter while flying near maximum speed. Another factor that can reduce the airspeed at which flutter can occur is a disturbance to the balance of the control surfaces. If vibrations are felt in the control surfaces, reduce the airspeed.

Lateral Stability

Another type of stability that describes the glider's tendency to return to wings-level flight following a displacement is lateral stability. When a glider is rolled into a bank, it has a tendency to sideslip in the direction of the bank. For example, due to a gust of wind, the glider wing is lifted and the glider starts to roll. The angle of attack on the downward going wing is increased because the wing is moving down and now the air is moving up past it. This causes the lift on this wing to increase. On the upward going wing, the opposite is occurring. The angle of attack is reduced because the wing is moving up and the air is moving down past it. Lift on this wing is therefore reduced. This does produce a countertorque that damps out the rolling motion, but does not roll the glider back to wings level as the effect stops when the glider stops. *[Figure 3-23]* To obtain lateral stability, dihedral is designed into the wings.

Dihedral is the upward angle of the wings from a horizontal (front/rear view) axis of the plane. As a glider flies along

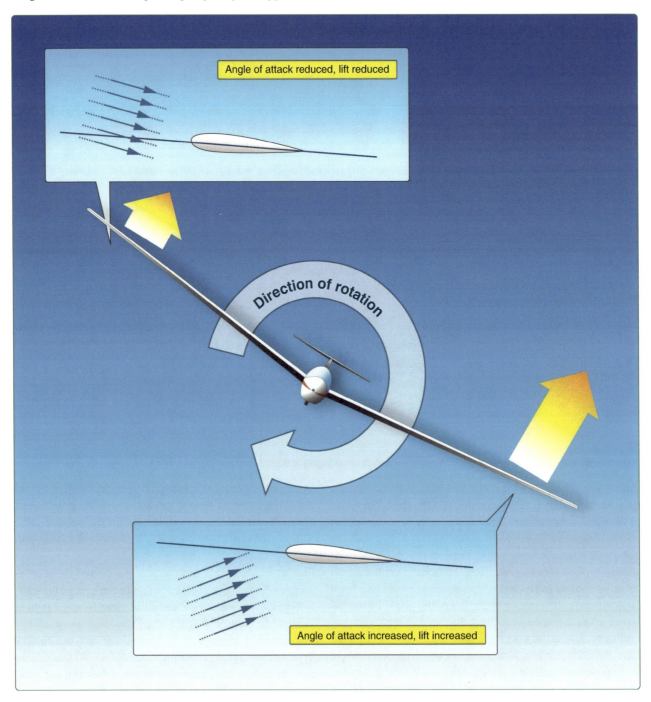

Figure 3-23. *Lateral stability.*

and encounters turbulence, the dihedral provides positive lateral stability by providing more lift for the lower wing and reducing the lift on the raised wing. As one wing lowers, it becomes closer to perpendicular to the surface and level. Because it is closer to level and perpendicular to the weight force, the lift produced directly opposes the force of weight. This must be instantly compared to the higher and now more canted wing referenced to the force of weight. The higher wing's lift relative to the force of weight is now less because of the vector angle. This imbalance of lift causes the lower wing to rise as the higher descends until lift equalizes, resulting in level flight. *[Figure 3-24]*

Turning Flight

Before a glider turns, it must first overcome inertia, or its tendency to continue in a straight line. A pilot creates the necessary turning force by using the ailerons to bank the glider so that the direction of total lift is inclined. This divides the force of lift into two components; one component acts vertically to oppose weight, while the other acts horizontally to oppose centrifugal force. The latter is the horizontal component of lift. *[Figure 3-25]*

To maintain attitude with the horizon during a turn, glider pilots need to increase back pressure on the control stick. The horizontal component of lift creates a force directed inward toward the center of rotation, which is known as centripetal force. *[Figure 3-26]* This center-seeking force causes the glider to turn. Since centripetal force works against the tendency of the aircraft to continue in a straight line, inertia tends to oppose centripetal force toward the outside of the turn. This opposing force is known as centrifugal force. In reality, centrifugal force is not a true aerodynamic force; it is an apparent force that results from the effect of inertia during the turn.

Load Factors

The preceding sections only briefly considered some of the practical points of the principles of turning flight. However, with the responsibilities of the pilot and the safety of passengers, the competent pilot must have a well-founded concept of the forces that act on the glider during turning flight and the advantageous use of these forces, as well as the operating limitations of the particular glider. Any force applied to a glider to deflect its flight from a straight line produces a stress on its structure; the amount of this force is called load factor.

Figure 3-24. *Dihedral angle.*

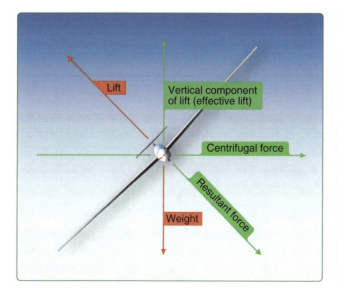

Figure 3-25. *Forces in a banked turn.*

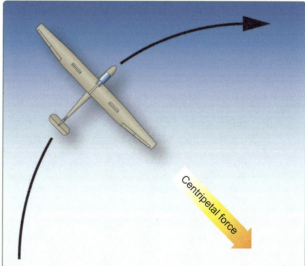

Figure 3-26. *Centripetal force is a force that makes a body follow a curved path.*

A load factor is the ratio of the total air load acting on the glider to the gross weight of the glider. A glider in flight with a load factor of one does not mean the glider is accelerating; it means the lift on the aircraft is the same as in straight-and-level flight. Load factor may be positive or negative, dependent on the current flightpath.

A load factor of three means that the total load on a glider's structure is three times its gross weight. Gravity load factors are usually expressed in terms of "G"—that is, a load factor of three may be spoken of as three Gs, or a load factor of four as four Gs. A load factor of one, or 1 G, represents conditions in straight-and-level flight, in which the lift is equal to the weight. Therefore, two Gs would be two times the normal weight. Gliders may be designed to withstand stress of up to nine Gs.

It is interesting to note that in subjecting a glider to three Gs in a pullup from a dive, the pilot is pressed down into the seat with a force equal to three times the person's weight. Thus, an idea of the magnitude of the load factor obtained in any maneuver can be determined by considering the degree to which the pilot is pressed down into the seat. Since the operating speed of modern gliders has increased significantly, this effect has become so pronounced that it is a primary consideration in the design of the structure for all gliders.

If attempting to improve turn performance by increasing angle of bank while maintaining airspeed, pay close attention to glider limitations due to the effects of increasing the load factor. Load factor is defined as the ratio of the load supported by the glider's wings to the actual weight of the aircraft and its contents. A glider in stabilized, wings-level flight has a load factor of one. Load factor increases rapidly as the angle of bank increases due to increase wing loading. *[Figure 3-27]* With the structural design of gliders planned to withstand only a certain amount of overload, knowledge of load factors has become essential for all pilots. Load factors are important to the pilot for two distinct reasons:

1. It is possible for a pilot to impose an obviously dangerous overload on the glider structures.
2. Increased load factor increases the stalling speed, making stalls possible at seemingly safe flight speeds due to increased wing loading.

In a turn at constant speed, the AOA must be increased to furnish the extra lift necessary to overcome the centrifugal force and inertia opposing the turn. As the bank angle increases, AOA must also increase to provide the required lift. The result of increasing the AOA is a stall when the critical AOA is exceeded in a turn. *[Figure 3-28]*

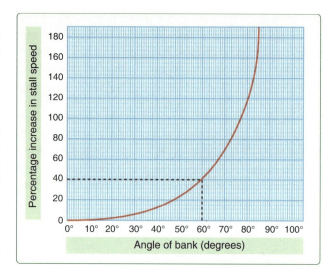

Figure 3-27. *A glider's stall speed increases as the bank angle increases. For example, a 60° angle of bank causes a 40 percent increase in the glider's stall speed.*

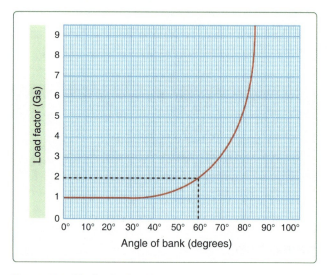

Figure 3-28. *The loads placed on a glider increase as the angle of bank increases.*

Rate of Turn
Rate of turn refers to the amount of time it takes for a glider to turn a specified number of degrees. If flown at the same airspeed and angle of bank, every glider turns at the same rate. If airspeed increases and the angle of bank remains the same, the rate of turn decreases. Conversely, a constant airspeed coupled with an angle of bank increase results in a higher rate of turn.

Radius of Turn
The amount of horizontal distance an aircraft uses to complete a turn is referred to as the radius of turn. The radius of turn at any given bank angle varies directly with the square of the airspeed. Therefore, if the airspeed of the glider were doubled,

the radius of the turn would be four times greater. Although the radius of turn is also dependent on a glider's airspeed and angle of bank, the relationship is the opposite of rate of turn. As the glider's airspeed is increased with the angle of bank held constant, the radius of turn increases. On the other hand, if the angle of bank increases and the airspeed remains the same, the radius of turn is decreased. *[Figure 3-29]* When flying in thermals, the radius of turn is an important factor as it helps to gain the maximum altitude. A smaller turn radius enables a glider to fly closer to the fastest rising core of the thermal and gain altitude more quickly.

Turn Coordination

It is important that rudder and aileron inputs are coordinated during a turn so maximum glider performance can be maintained. If too little rudder is applied, or if rudder is applied too late, the result is a slip. Too much rudder, or rudder applied before aileron, results in a skid. Both skids and slips swing the fuselage of the glider into the relative wind, creating additional parasite drag, which reduces lift and airspeed. Although this increased drag caused by a slip can be useful during approach to landing to steepen the approach path and counteract a crosswind, it decreases glider performance during other phases of flight.

When rolling into a turn, the aileron on the inside of the turn is raised and the aileron on the outside of the turn is lowered. The lowered aileron on the outside wing increases lift by increasing wing camber and produces more lift for that wing. Since induced drag is a byproduct of lift, the outside wing also produces more drag than the inside wing. This causes adverse yaw, a yawing tendency toward the outside of the turn. Coordinated use of rudder and aileron corrects for adverse yaw and aileron drag. Adverse yaw in gliders can be more pronounced due to the much longer wings as compared to an airplane of equal weight. The longer wings constitute longer lever arms for the adverse yaw forces to act on the glider. Therefore, more rudder movement is necessary to counteract the adverse yaw and have a coordinated turn.

Slips

A slip is a descent with one wing lowered and the glider's longitudinal axis at an angle to the flightpath. It may be used for one or both of two purposes: to steepen the approach path without increasing the airspeed, as would be the case if a dive were used, or used to make the glider move sideways through the air to counteract the drift that results from a crosswind.

Formerly, slips were used as a normal means of controlling landing descents to short or obstructed fields, but they are now primarily used in the performance of crosswind and short-field landings. With the installation of wing flaps and effective spoilers on modern gliders, the use of slips to steepen or control the angle of descent is no longer the only procedure available. However, pilots still need skill in the performance of forward slips to correct for possible errors in judgment of the landing approach.

The shape of the glider's wing planform can greatly affect the slip. If the glider has a rectangular wing planform, the slip has little effect on the lift production of the wing other than the wing area being obscured by the fuselage vortices. The direction of the relative wind to the wing has the same effect on both wings so no inequalities of lift form. However, if the wing is tapered or has leading edge aft sweep, then the relative wind has a large effect on the production of lift.

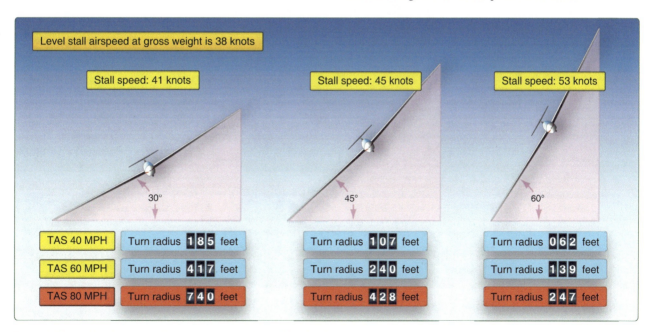

Figure 3-29. *A glider's radius of turn as compared to angle of bank.*

If a glider with tapered wings, as shown in *Figure 3-14*, were to begin a slip to the left with the left wing lower, the left wing will have a relative wind more aligned with its chord line and effectively higher airflow (airspeed) that generates more lift as compared to the higher right wing with angled relative wind, resulting in lower effective airflow (airspeed) over that wing. This differential in airflow or relative airspeed of the wings when taken to the extremes of the flight envelope results in the higher wing stalling and often an inverted spin.

Depending on the exact wing shape, an elliptical wing can have characteristics more like a tapered wing. *[Figure 3-14]* Pilots should always consult the GFM and know what the gliders limitations are concerning slips.

The use of slips has limitations. Some pilots may try to lose altitude by violent slipping, rather than by smoothly maneuvering, exercising good judgment, and using only a slight or moderate slip. In short-field landings, this erratic practice invariably leads to trouble since enough excess speed may prevent touching down anywhere near the proper point, and very often results in overshooting the entire field.

If a slip is used during the last portion of a final approach, the longitudinal axis of the glider must be aligned with the runway just prior to touchdown so that the glider touches down headed in the direction in which it is moving over the runway. This requires timely action to modify the slip and align the glider's longitudinal axis with its direction of travel over the ground at the instant of touchdown. Failure to accomplish this imposes severe sideloads on the landing gear and imparts violent ground looping tendencies.

Discontinuing the slip is accomplished by leveling the wings and simultaneously releasing the rudder pressure, while readjusting the pitch attitude to the normal glide attitude. If the pressure on the rudder is released abruptly, the nose swings too quickly into line and the glider tends to acquire excess speed.

Because of the location of the pitot tube and static vents, airspeed indicators in some gliders may have considerable error when the glider is in a slip. The pilot must be aware of this possibility and recognize a properly performed slip by the attitude of the glider, the sound of the airflow, and the feel of the flight controls.

Forward Slip

The forward slip is a slip in which the glider's direction of motion is the same as before the slip was begun. *[Figure 3-30]* The primary purpose of a forward slip is to dissipate altitude without increasing the glider's speed, particularly in gliders not equipped with flaps, or if the spoilers are inoperative. There are many circumstances requiring the use of forward slips, such as a landing approach over obstacles and short-field landings, in which it is always wise to allow an extra margin of altitude for safety in the original estimate of the approach. In the latter case, if the inaccuracy of the approach is confirmed by excess altitude when nearing the boundary of the selected field, slipping can dissipate the excess altitude. If there is any crosswind, the slip is much more effective if made toward the wind.

Assuming the glider is originally in straight flight, the wing on the side toward which the slip is to be made should be lowered by use of the ailerons. Simultaneously, the airplane's nose must be yawed in the opposite direction by applying opposite rudder so that the glider's longitudinal axis is at an angle to its original flightpath. The degree to which the nose is yawed in the opposite direction from the bank should be such that the original ground track is maintained. The nose should also be raised as necessary to prevent the airspeed from increasing.

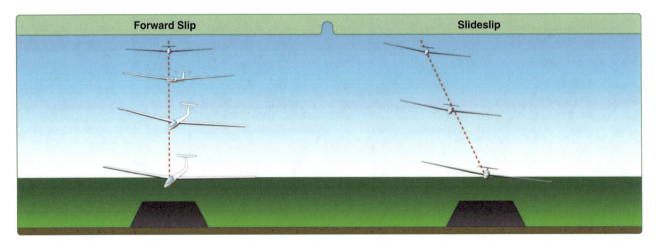

Figure 3-30. *A comparison of a forward slip to a sideslip.*

Note: Forward slips with wing flaps extended should not be done in gliders wherein the manufacturer's operating instructions prohibit such operation.

Sideslip

A sideslip, as distinguished from a forward slip, is one during which the glider's longitudinal axis remains parallel to the original flightpath, but in which the flightpath changes direction according to the steepness of the bank. To perform a sideslip, the upwind wing is lowered, and simultaneously the opposite rudder is applied to maintain the landing area alignment. The sideslip is important in counteracting wind drift during crosswind landings and is discussed in a later chapter.

The dihedral angle of the wings works to add lateral stability to the airframe and ease the pilot's tasking to correct for upsets. As the glider flies along, turbulence may upset the balance and raise one wing and roll the glider about the longitudinal axis. As the wing rises, the vertical lift vector decreases while the horizontal component of the wing's lifting force increases. As the other wing descends, the lifting force vertical component increases while the horizontal component decreases. This imbalance is designed so the airframe returns to level without pilot input. Depending on the airflows, the AOA on the wings may or may not be a factor. If the air on one wing is descending (sink) and the air on the other wing is ascending (lift) both wings will have different relative winds, thus different AOAs and developed lift.

Stalls

It is important to remember that a stall can occur at any airspeed and at any flight attitude. A stall occurs when the critical AOA is exceeded. *[Figure 3-31]* During a stall, the wings still support some of the aircraft's weight. If the wings did not, it would accelerate according to Newton's Second Law. The stall speed of a glider can be affected by many factors, including weight, load factor due to maneuvering, and environmental conditions. As the weight of the glider increases, a higher AOA is required to maintain flight at the same airspeed since more lift is required to support the increase in weight. This is why a heavily loaded glider stalls at a higher airspeed than when lightly loaded. The manner in which this weight is distributed also affects stall speed. For example, a forward CG creates a situation that requires the tail to produce a greater downforce to balance the aircraft. The result of this configuration requires the wings to produce more lift than if the CG were located further aft. Therefore, a more forward CG also increases stall speed.

Environmental factors also can affect stall speed. Snow, ice, or frost accumulation on the wing's surface can increase the weight of the wing, in addition to changing the wing shape and disrupting the airflow, all of which increase stall speed. Turbulence is another environmental factor that can affect a glider's stall speed. The unpredictable nature of turbulence can cause a glider to stall suddenly and abruptly at a higher airspeed than it would in stable conditions. Turbulence has a strong impact on the stall speed of a glider because the vertical gusts change the direction of the relative wind and abruptly increase the AOA. During landing in gusty conditions, it is important to increase the approach airspeed by half of the gust spread value in order to maintain a wide margin above stall. For example, if the winds were 10 knots gusting to 15 knots, it would be prudent to add 2.5 knots ((15 − 10) ÷ 2 = 2.5) to the approach speed. This practice usually ensures a safe margin to guard against stalls at very low altitudes.

Spins

If the aircraft is not stalled, it cannot spin. A spin can be defined as an aggravated stall that results in the glider descending in a helical, or corkscrew, path. A spin is a complex, uncoordinated flight maneuver in which the wings are unequally stalled. Upon entering a spin, the wing that is more completely stalled drops before the other, and the nose of the aircraft yaws in the direction of the low wing. *[Figure 3-32]*

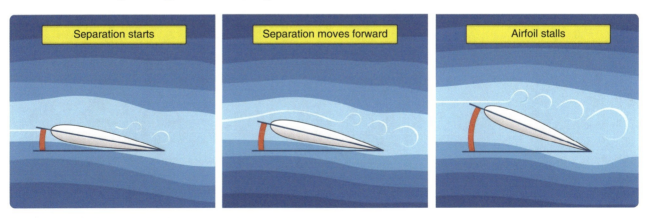

Figure 3-31. *A stall occurs when the critical angle of attack is exceeded.*

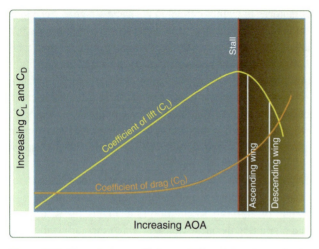

Figure 3-32. *The relative coefficients of lift and drag for each wing during a spin. Note that the ascending wing experiences more lift and less drag. The opposite wing is forced down and back due to less lift and increased drag.*

The cause of a spin is stalled airflow over one wing before airflow stalling over the other wing. This is a result of uncoordinated flight with unequal airflows over the wings.

Spins occur in uncoordinated slow flight and high rate turns (overbanking for airspeed). The lack of coordination is normally caused by too much or not enough rudder control for the amount of aileron being used. If the stall recovery is not promptly initiated, the glider is likely to enter a full stall that may develop into a spin. Spins that occur as the result of uncoordinated flight usually rotate in the direction of the rudder being applied, regardless of the raised wing. When entering a slipping turn, holding opposite aileron and rudder, the resultant spin usually occurs in the direction opposite of the aileron already applied. In a skidding turn in which both aileron and rudder are applied in the same direction, rotation is also in the direction of rudder application. Glider pilots should always be aware of the type of wing forms on their aircraft and the stall characteristics of that wing in various maneuvers.

Spins are normally placed in three categories, as shown in *Figure 3-33*. The most common is the upright, or erect, spin, which is characterized by a slightly nose-down rolling and yawing motion in the same direction. An inverted spin involves the aircraft spinning upside down with the yaw and roll occurring in opposite directions. A third type of spin, the

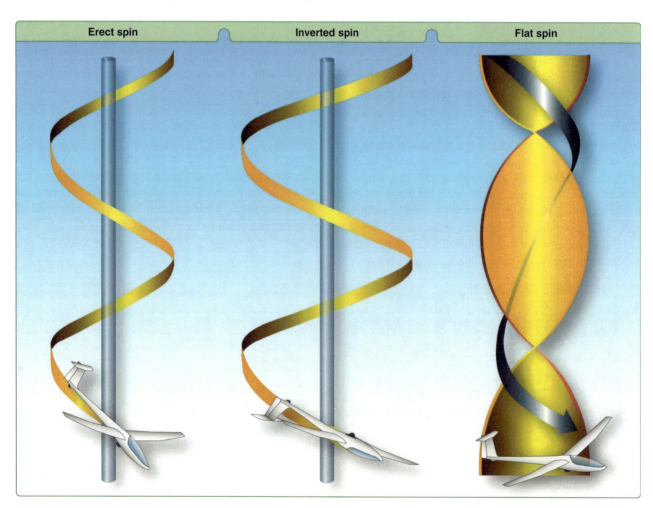

Figure 3-33. *A glider's stall speed increases as the bank angle increases. In a spin, one wing is more deeply stalled than the other.*

flat spin, is the most hazardous of all spins. In a flat spin, the glider yaws around the vertical axis at a pitch attitude nearly level with the horizon. A flat spin often has a very high rate of rotation; the recovery is difficult, and sometimes impossible. If a glider is properly loaded within its CG limits, entry into a flat spin should not occur. Erect spins and flat spins can also be inverted. The entry, wing form, and CG usually determine the type of spin resulting from an uncoordinated wing stall.

Since spins normally occur when a glider is flown in an uncoordinated manner at lower airspeeds, coordinated use of the flight controls is important. It is critical that pilots learn to recognize and recover from the first sign of a stall or spin. Entering a spin near the ground, especially during the landing pattern, is usually fatal. *[Figure 3-33]* A pilot must learn to recognize the warning signs, especially during the approach and landing phase in a crosswind. A crosswind resulting in a tailwind on the base leg may lead the pilot to tighten the turn using rudder, or too steep a turn for the airspeed. An uncoordinated turn could lead to the upper wing exceeding its critical AOA before the lower wing, which could result in a very high rate of roll towards the upper wing as the upper wing stalls. If an excessive steep turn is attempted, the glider may roll towards the inside wing or the outside wing depending on the exact trim state at the instant of the stall. Situational awareness of position to final approach should be part of a before-landing routine.

Ground Effect

Ground effect is a reduction in induced drag for the same amount of lift produced. Within one wingspan above the ground, the decrease in induced drag enables the glider to fly at a lower airspeed. In ground effect, a lower AOA is required to produce the same amount of lift. Ground effect enables the glider to fly near the ground at a lower airspeed and causes the glider to float as it approaches the touchdown point.

During takeoff and landing, the ground alters the three-dimensional airflow pattern around the glider. The result is a decrease in downwash and a reduction in wingtip vortices. Upwash and downwash refer to the effect an airfoil has on the free airstream. Upwash is the deflection of the oncoming airstream upward and over the wing. Downwash is the downward deflection of the airstream as it passes over the wing and past the trailing edge.

During flight, the downwash of the airstream causes the relative wind to be inclined downward in the vicinity of the wing. This is called the average relative wind. The angle between the free airstream relative wind and the average relative wind is the induced AOA. In effect, the greater the downward deflection of the airstream, the higher the induced AOA and the higher the induced drag. Ground effect restricts the downward deflection of the airstream, decreasing both induced AOA and induced drag.

Ground effect, in addition to the decrease in wind due to surface friction and other terrain features upwind of the landing area, can greater increase the landing distance of a glider. A glider pilot, especially a visiting pilot, should inquire about local effects from local pilots to enhance flight planning and safe landings.

Chapter 4
Flight Instruments

Introduction

Flight instruments in the glider cockpit provide information regarding the glider's direction, altitude, airspeed, and performance. The categories include pitot-static, magnetic, gyroscopic, electrical, electronic, and self-contained. This categorization includes instruments that are sensitive to gravity (G-loading) and centrifugal forces. Instruments can be a basic set used typically in training aircraft or a more advanced set used in the high performance sailplane for cross-country and competition flying. To obtain basic introductory information about common aircraft instruments, please refer to the Pilot's Handbook of Aeronautical Knowledge (FAA-H-8083-25).

Instruments displaying airspeed, altitude, and vertical speed are part of the pitot-static system. Heading instruments display magnetic direction by sensing the earth's magnetic field. Performance instruments, using gyroscopic principles, display the aircraft attitude, heading, and rates of turn. Unique to the glider cockpit is the variometer, which is part of the pitot-static system. Electronic instruments using computer and global positioning system (GPS) technology provide pilots with moving map displays, electronic airspeed and altitude, air mass conditions, and other functions relative to flight management. Examples of self-contained instruments and indicators that are useful to the pilot include the yaw string, inclinometer, and outside air temperature gauge (OAT).

Pitot-Static Instruments

There are two major divisions in the pitot-static system:

1. Impact air pressure due to forward motion (flight) captured in the pitot tube transferred to instruments by way of air pressure lines or tubing.

2. Static or free air pressure sensed at static air ports designed to be free of motion induced pressure variations. This reference pressure is necessary because the free pressure of the atmosphere decreases as altitude increases and changes due to the current weather (barometric) pressure variations. This static or free air pressure is transferred to instruments by way of the static pressure lines or tubing.

Impact and Static Pressure Lines

The impact air pressure (air striking the glider because of its forward motion) is taken from the pitot tube, which is mounted on either the nose or the vertical stabilizer. *[Figure 4-1]* Pitot tubes are aligned with the relative wind. These locations minimize air disturbance or turbulence during glider flight through the air.

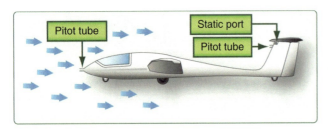

Figure 4-1. *A pitot tube is often mounted in the glider's nose or the vertical fin, the open end of which is exposed directly to the oncoming airflow.*

When a glider is in flight, the oncoming air tries to flow into the open end of the pitot tube. *[Figure 4-2]* Connecting a diaphragm to the back end of the pitot tube means that the air flowing in has nowhere to go. The pressure in the diaphragm rises until it is high enough to prevent any further air from entering. Increasing the airspeed of the glider causes the force exerted by the oncoming air to rise. More air is able to push its way into the diaphragm and the pressure within the diaphragm increases. The pressure inside the diaphragm to oncoming airflow increases as airspeed increases.

The static pressure (pressure of the still air) is taken from the static line that is attached to a port, or ports, mounted flush with the side of the fuselage or tube mounted on the vertical stabilizer. *[Figure 4-3]* Gliders using a fuselage flush mounted static source have two vents, one on each side of the fuselage. This compensates for variation of static pressure due to changes in glider attitude and air turbulence.

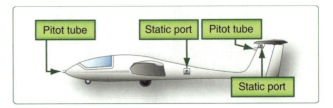

Figure 4-3. *Static ports mounted flush with the side of the fuselage or tube mounted on the vertical stabilizer.*

The openings of both the pitot tube and the static port(s) should be checked during the preflight inspection to ensure they are free from obstructions. Clogged, or partially clogged, openings should be cleaned by a certificated mechanic. Blowing into these openings is not recommended, because this could damage flight instruments.

Airspeed Indicator

The airspeed indicator displays the indicated airspeed (IAS) of the glider through the air. *[Figure 4-4]* Some airspeed indicator dials provide color-coded arcs that depict permissible airspeed ranges for different phases of flight. The

Figure 4-4. *Airspeed indicator.*

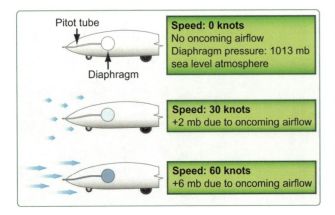

Figure 4-2. *Pressure inside the capsule increases as airspeed increases.*

upper (top) and lower (bottom) limits of the arcs correspond to airspeed limitations for specific gliders configurations which are discussed later in this chapter. These speed limitations are set by the manufacturer. *Figure 4-5* shows the anatomy of the airspeed indicator and where the pitot and static pressure inlets are located.

The airspeed indicator depends on both pitot pressure and static pressure. *[Figure 4-6]* When pitot pressure and static pressure are the same, zero airspeed is indicated. As pitot pressure becomes progressively greater than static pressure, airspeed is indicated by the needle pointing to the speed scale. The airspeed instrument contains a diaphragm that senses differential pitot and static pressure. The diaphragm expands or contracts according to the difference of static and pitot pressures; this movement drives the needle (airspeed needle pointer) on the face of the instrument. *[Figure 4-7]*

The Effects of Altitude on the Airspeed Indicator
Like pressure, air density also decreases with altitude. The airspeed indicator's diaphragm is calibrated to correctly display airspeed when the air through which the aircraft is moving is of average sea level density. Above sea level, due to the lower air density, the buildup of pressure in the diaphragm is lower, and the airspeed indicator reads artificially low. The higher the altitude above sea level, the more erroneous the airspeed indicator value. *[Figure 4-8]*

Types of Airspeed
There are three kinds of airspeed that the pilot should understand: IAS, calibrated airspeed (CAS), and true airspeed (TAS). *[Figure 4-9]*

Indicated Airspeed (IAS)
IAS is the direct instrument reading obtained from the airspeed indicator, uncorrected for variations in atmospheric density, installation error, or instrument error. *Figure 4-10*

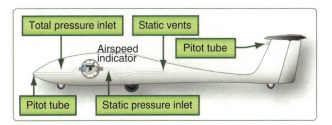

Figure 4-6. *The functionality of the airspeed indicator depends on both pitot and static pressure.*

shows that the IAS at which a glider stalls in steady wings-level flight does not vary with altitude. However, pilots must remember that different gliders stall at different speeds. The IAS shown in *Figure 4-10* may not be the stall speed for each particular glider.

The IAS at which never exceed speed (V_{NE}) is reached decreases with altitude. The glider flight manual (GFM) should include a table, such as the one shown in *Figure 4-11*, that details how V_{NE} should be reduced with altitude. These figures vary from glider to glider; therefore, pilots should always refer to the manual specific to the glider they are flying, which should show a chart similar to the one in *Figure 4-11*.

Calibrated Airspeed (CAS)
CAS is IAS corrected for installation and instrument error. Although manufacturers attempt to keep airspeed errors to a minimum, it is impossible to eliminate all errors throughout the airspeed operating range. At certain airspeeds and with certain flap/spoiler settings, the installation and instrument error may be significant. The error is generally greatest at low airspeeds. In the cruising and higher airspeed ranges, IAS and CAS are approximately the same.

It is important to refer to the airspeed calibration chart to correct for possible airspeed errors because airspeed limitations, such as those found on the color-coded face of the airspeed indicator, on placards in the cockpit, or in

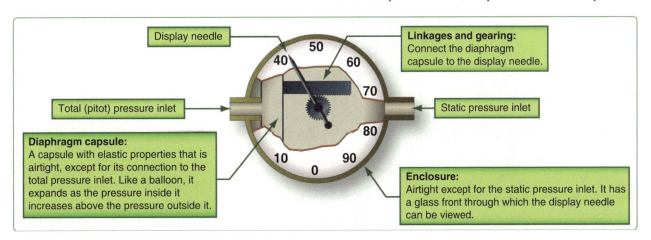

Figure 4-5. *Anatomy of the airspeed indicator.*

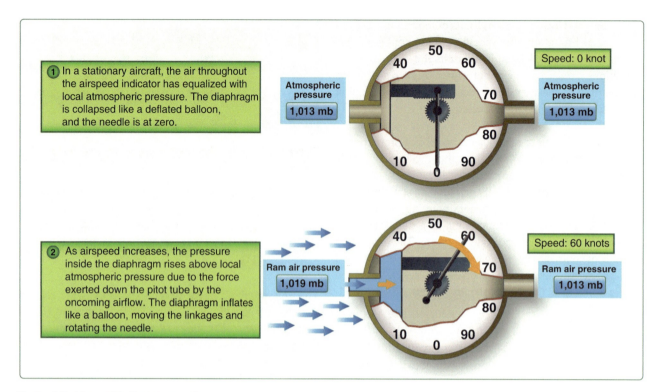

Figure 4-7. *Airspeed indicator operation.*

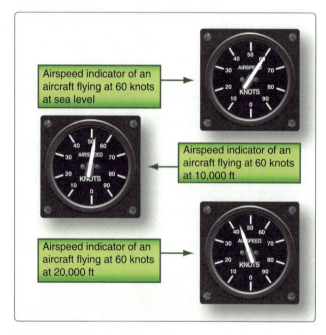

Figure 4-8. *Effects of altitude on the airspeed indicator.*

the GFM or Pilot's Operating Handbook (GFM/POH), are usually CAS. Some manufacturers use IAS rather than CAS to denote the airspeed limitations mentioned. The airspeed indicator should be calibrated periodically.

Dirt, dust, ice, or snow collecting at the mouth of the pitot tube may obstruct air passage and prevent correct indications. Vibrations may also destroy the sensitivity of the diaphragm.

True Airspeed (TAS)

TAS is the true speed at which the aircraft is moving through the air. The airspeed indicator is calibrated to indicate TAS only under standard atmospheric conditions at sea level (29.92 inches of mercury ("Hg) and 15 °C or 59 °F). Because air density decreases with an increase in altitude, the glider must be flown faster at higher altitudes to cause the same pressure difference between pitot impact pressure and static pressure. Therefore, for a given TAS, IAS decreases as altitude increases; for a given IAS, TAS increases with an increase in altitude.

Fortunately for the pilot, the amount by which the airspeed indicator underreads approximately cancels out the air density related changes to the glider's flight dynamics. This means that if the IAS at the point of stall at 1,000 feet in steady wings-level flight is 40 knots, then the IAS at 20,000 feet at the point of the stall is also 40 knots, despite the fact that the stall is actually occurring at a TAS that is 14 knots higher. Therefore, the pilot needs to remember only one set of numbers that work at all altitudes. A decrease in air density with altitude also affects a glider's flight dynamics. For example, a glider that stalls at a TAS of 40 knots in steady wings-level flight at 1,000 feet stalls at a TAS of 54 knots at 20,000 feet. Consider the inconvenience that this would cause if the airspeed indicator did actually display TAS. The pilot would need to use quick reference cards continuously to look up the stall speed, best L/D speed, and minimum sink speed for the current altitude—not a

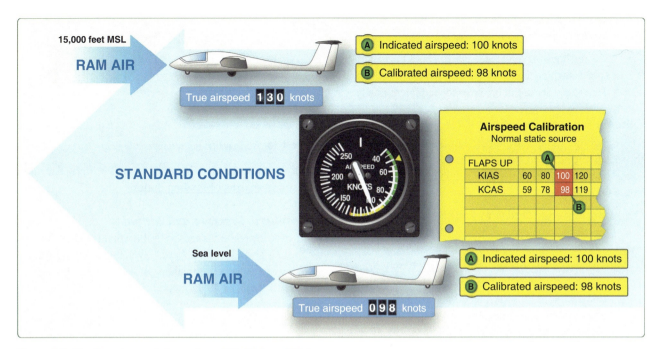

Figure 4-9. *The three types of airspeed are IAS, CAS, and TAS.*

Altitude center vertically	IAS at which stall occurs in steady wings-level flight	True airspeed (TAS)
1,000 feet	40 knots	41 knots
10,000 feet	40 knots	48 knots
20,000 feet	40 knots	56 knots
30,000 feet	40 knots	64 knots
40,000 feet	40 knots	72 knots

Figure 4-10. *In steady wings-level flight, IAS does not vary with altitude.*

Altitude (in feet)	V_{NE} (IAS in knots)
Up to 6,500	135
10,000	128
13,000	121
16,500	115

Figure 4-11. *IAS at which V_{NE} is reached decreases with altitude.*

particularly convenient thing to do while trying to fly. *Figure 4-10* shows how steady, wings-level flight stall speed is affected by different altitudes. *Figure 4-10* is only an example, and the figures used in it do not pertain to all gliders. For specific stall speeds, always refer to the POH of the glider that is being flown.

A pilot can find TAS by two methods. The first method, which is more accurate, involves using a flight computer. In this method, the CAS is corrected for temperature and pressure variation by using the airspeed correction scale on the computer. A second method, which is a rule of thumb, can be used to compute the approximate TAS. This is done by adding to the IAS 2 percent of the IAS for each 1,000 feet of altitude.

Airspeed Indicator Markings

Aircraft weighing 12,500 pounds or less, manufactured after 1945 and certificated by the Federal Aviation Administration (FAA), are required to have airspeed indicators that conform to a standard color-coded marking system. *[Figure 4-4]* This system enables the pilot to determine, at a glance, certain airspeed limitations that are important to the safe operation of the aircraft. For example, if during the execution of a maneuver, the pilot notes that the airspeed needle is in the yellow arc and is rapidly approaching the red line, immediate corrective action to reduce the airspeed should be taken. It is essential that the pilot use smooth control pressure at high airspeeds to avoid severe stressors upon the glider structure.

The following is a description of what the standard color-code markings are on an airspeed indicator and how they correspond to maneuvers and airspeeds.

- The white arc—flap operating range
- The lower limit of the white arc—stalling speed with the wing flaps and landing gear in the landing position.
- The upper limit of the white arc—maximum flaps-extended speed. This is the highest airspeed at which the pilot should extend full flaps. If flaps are operated at higher airspeeds, severe strain or structural failure could result.
- The lower limit of the green arc—stalling speed with the wing flaps and landing gear retracted.
- The upper limit of the green arc—maximum structural cruising speed. This is the maximum speed for normal operations.

- The yellow arc—caution range. The pilot should avoid this area unless in smooth air.
- The red line—never-exceed speed. This is the maximum speed at which the glider can be operated in smooth air. This speed should never be exceeded intentionally.

Other Airspeed Limitations

There are other important airspeed limitations not marked on the face of the airspeed indicator. These speeds are generally found on placards *[Figure 4-12]* in the view of the pilot and in the GFM/POH.

- Maneuvering speed (Va)—maximum speed at which the limit load can be imposed (either by gusts or full defection of the control surfaces for one cycle) without causing structural damage. If rough air or severe turbulence is encountered during flight, the airspeed should be reduced to maneuvering speed or less to minimize the stress on the glider structure. Maneuvering speed is not marked on the airspeed indicator. For gliders, if there is a rough airspeed (V_b) limitation published the pilot should be below that speed for maximum gust intensity.
- Landing gear operating speed—maximum speed for extending or retracting the landing gear if using glider equipped with retractable landing gear.
- Minimum sink speed—important when thermalling.
- Best glide speed—airspeed that results in the least amount of altitude loss over a given distance, not considering the effects of wind.
- Maximum aerotow or ground launch speed—maximum airspeed that the glider may safely be towed without causing structural damage.

Altimeter

The altimeter measures the static air pressure of the surrounding air mass. A flexible plastic tube connects the altimeters static pressure inlet to the static port holes located on the side of the glider. *[Figure 4-13]* If set to the proper local pressure, the altimeter needles and dial indicate heights above mean sea level (MSL). *[Figures 4-14 and 4-17]* Glider pilots must be fully aware of the ground elevations on

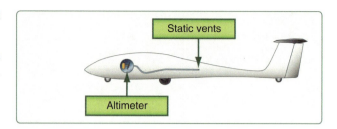

Figure 4-13. *Static vents and altimeter plumbing.*

the flight route or area in order to make flight decisions concerning soaring or landing options.

Atmospheric Pressure and Altitude

Atmospheric pressure is caused by the weight of the column of air above a given location. At sea level, the overlying column of air exerts a force equivalent to 14.7 pounds per square inch, 1013.2 mb, or 29.92 inches of mercury. The higher the altitude is, the shorter the overlying column of air is and the lower the weight of that column is. Therefore, atmospheric pressure decreases with altitude. At 18,000 feet, atmospheric pressure is approximately half that at sea level. *[Figure 4-16]*

Principles of Operation

The pressure altimeter is simply an aneroid barometer that measures the pressure of the atmosphere at the level at which the altimeter is located and presents an altitude indication in feet. The altimeter uses static pressure as its source of operation. Air is denser at the surface of the earth than aloft; as altitude increases, atmospheric pressure decreases. This difference in pressure at various levels causes the altimeter to indicate changes in altitude. *Figures 4-15 and 4-17* illustrate how the altimeter functions. The presentation of altitude varies considerably between different types of altimeters. Some have one pointer while others have more.

The dial of a typical altimeter is graduated with numerals arranged clockwise from 0 to 9 inclusive, as shown in *Figure 4-14*. Movement of the aneroid element is transmitted through a gear train to the three hands, which sweep the calibrated dial to indicate altitude. The shortest hand indicates altitude in tens of thousands of feet; the intermediate hand in thousands of feet; and the longest hand in hundreds of feet, subdivided into 20-foot increments.

Valid when **lower or side hook** is installed:				
Maximum winch-launching speed	65 KIAS		Maximum winch-launching speed	120 km/hr IAS
Maximum aerotowing speed	81 KIAS	OR	Maximum aerotowing speed	150 km/hr IAS
Maximum maneuvering speed	81 KIAS		Maximum maneuvering speed	150 km/hr IAS

Valid when **front hook only** is installed:				
Maximum aerotowing speed	81 KIAS	OR	Maximum aerotowing speed	150 km/hr IAS
Maximum maneuvering speed	81 KIAS		Maximum maneuvering speed	10 km/hr IAS

Figure 4-12. *Speed limitation placards placed in the glider and in view of the pilot.*

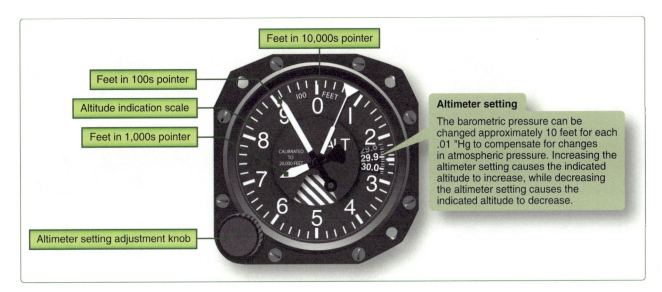

Figure 4-14. *Altimeter.*

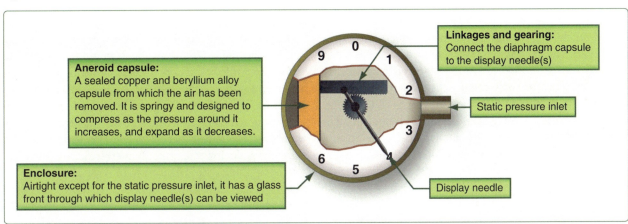

Figure 4-15. *Inside the altimeter.*

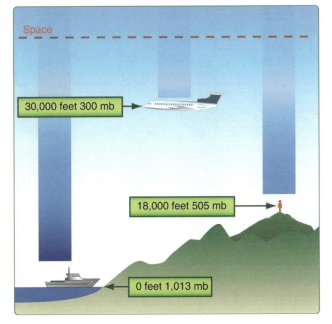

Figure 4-16. *Atmospheric pressure and altitude.*

The altitude indicated on the altimeter is correct only if the sea level barometric pressure is standard (29.92 "Hg), the sea level free air temperature is standard (+15 °C or 59 °F), and the pressure and temperature decreases at a standard rate with an increase in altitude. Since atmospheric pressure continually changes, a means is provided to adjust the altimeter to compensate for nonstandard conditions. This is accomplished through a system by which the altimeter setting (local station barometric pressure reduced to sea level) is set to a barometric scale located on the face of the altimeter. Only after the altimeter is set properly will it indicate the correct altitude.

Effect of Nonstandard Pressure and Temperature

If no means were provided for adjusting altimeters to nonstandard pressure, flight could be hazardous. For example, if a flight is made from a high-pressure area to a low-pressure area without adjusting the altimeter, the actual altitude of the glider is lower than indicated altitude. When flying from a low-pressure area to a high-pressure area, the actual altitude

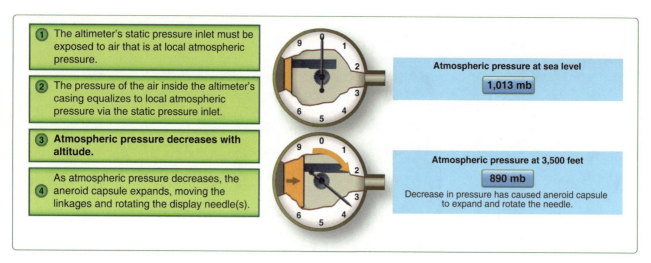

Figure 4-17. *How the altimeter functions.*

of the glider is higher than the indicated altitude. Fortunately, this error can be corrected by setting the altimeter properly. When flying in the local area and communication with ATC is not available to provide the current altimeter setting, there is an alternative procedure. Set the altimeter on zero while on the ground to directly read AGL referenced to the landing zone. However, for cross-country flights and flights from higher elevation airports, that procedure may not be an option due to the excessive Kollsman window setting instrument required. In those instances, the altimeter can be set to read the field elevation and either disregard the Kollsman window setting or applying a correction factor, or set in the barometric altimeter setting and remember if it reads high or low.

Variations in air temperature also affect the altimeter. On a warm day, the expanded air is lighter in weight per unit volume than on a cold day, and consequently the pressure levels are raised. For example, the pressure level at which the altimeter indicates 10,000 feet is higher on a warm day than under standard conditions. On a cold day, the reverse is true, and the 10,000-foot level would be lower. The adjustment made by the pilot to compensate for nonstandard pressures does not compensate for nonstandard temperatures. Therefore, if terrain or obstacle clearance is a factor in the selection of a cruising altitude, particularly at higher altitudes, remember to anticipate that colder than standard temperature places the glider lower than the altimeter indicates. Therefore, a higher altitude should be used to provide adequate terrain clearance. A memory aid in applying the above is "from a high to a low or hot to cold, look out below." *[Figure 4-18]*

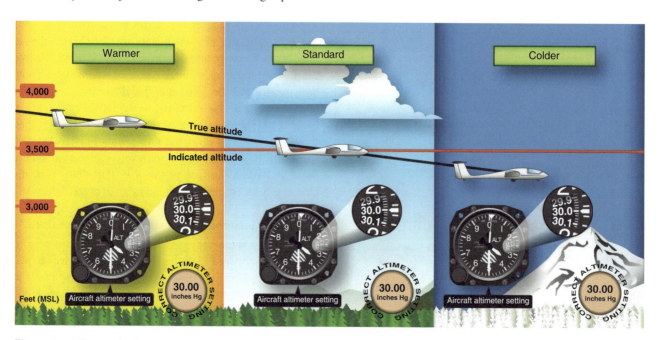

Figure 4-18. *Nonstandard pressure and temperature.*

Setting the Altimeter (Kollsman Window)

To adjust the altimeter for variation in atmospheric pressure, the pressure scale in the altimeter setting window (Kollsman Window), calibrated in inches of mercury ("Hg), is adjusted to correspond with the given altimeter setting. Altimeter settings can be defined as station pressure reduced to sea level, expressed in inches of mercury. Pilots should be aware of three altimeter setting acronyms: QNH, QFE, and QNE. The pilot sets QNH to read MSL, sets QFE to read the altitude above ground level (AGL), and QNE when flying above the transition level (18,000 feet in the United States). A glider pilot would use this setting when wave flying and is above 18,000 feet or flight level 180 (FL180). To read QNH, pilots should set the current altimeter setting into the altimeter's barometric setting window. The altimeter should read what the approximate field elevation is, which is a good way to check if it is working properly. A good memory aid for this step is to think of "H" (QNH) for home. QFE is set at zero when on the field. As a memory aid, think of the F in QFE as "field." Many altimeters cannot be set to read zero when operating from the higher elevation airports.

The station reporting the altimeter setting takes an hourly measurement of the station's atmospheric pressure and corrects this value to sea level pressure. These altimeter settings reflect height above sea level only in the vicinity of the reporting station. Aircraft flying above the transition level (in the United States, FL180), must use the standard altimeter setting of 29.92 "Hg (QNE). When flying below 18,000 feet MSL, it is necessary to adjust the altimeter setting as the flight progresses from one station to the next.

When flying over high mountainous terrain, certain atmospheric conditions can cause the altimeter to indicate an altitude of 1,000 feet, or more, higher than the actual altitude. For this reason, a generous margin of altitude should be allowed—not only for possible altimeter error, but also for possible downdrafts that are particularly prevalent if high winds are encountered.

To illustrate the use of the altimeter setting system, follow a cross-country flight from TSA Gliderport, Midlothian, Texas, to Winston Airport, Snyder, Texas, via Stephens County Airport, Breckenridge, Texas. Before takeoff from TSA Gliderport, the pilot receives a current local altimeter setting of 29.85 from the Fort Worth automated flight service station (AFSS). This value is set in the altimeter setting window of the altimeter. The altimeter indication should then be compared with the known airport elevation of 660 feet. Since most altimeters are not perfectly calibrated, an error may exist. VFR flights altimeters do not need to be calibrated but if an altimeter indication differs from the field elevation by more than 75 feet, the accuracy of the instrument is questionable, and it should be referred to an instrument repair station.

When over Stephens County Airport, assume the pilot receives a current area altimeter setting of 29.94 and applies this setting to the altimeter. Before entering the traffic pattern at Winston Airport, a new altimeter setting of 29.69 is received from the Automated Weather Observing System (AWOS), and applied to the altimeter. If the pilot desires to enter the traffic pattern at approximately 1,000 feet above terrain, and the field elevation of Winston Airport is 2,430 feet, an indicated altitude of 3,400 feet should be used.

2,430 feet + 1,000 feet = 3,430 feet, rounded to 3,400 feet

The importance of properly setting and reading the altimeter cannot be overemphasized. Let us assume that the pilot neglected to adjust the altimeter at Winston Airport to the current setting, and uses the Stephens County area setting of 29.94. If this occurred, the glider would be approximately 250 feet below the airport downwind entry altitude of 3,200 feet when entering the Winston Airport traffic pattern, and the altimeter would indicate approximately 250 feet higher than the field elevation (2,430 feet) upon landing.

This altitude error is another reason for a glider pilot to always fly a safe visual approach angle to the landing zone and not solely depend on instrument readings or past selection of turn points for the traffic pattern. The visual angle to the landing zone is the one item of information that will always be true. Reports of wind and barometric pressure if available may still be suspect. The glider pilot must always ensure sufficient altitude is available for expected or possible winds to allow landing in the landing zone.

   Actual altimeter setting = 29.94

   Correct altimeter setting = 29.69

   Difference = .25

One inch of pressure is equal to approximately 1,000 feet of altitude.

.25 × 1,000 feet = 250 feet

The previous calculation may be confusing, particularly in determining whether to add or subtract the amount of altimeter error. The following additional explanation is offered and can be helpful in finding the solution to this type of problem.

There are two means by which the altimeter pointers can be moved. One utilizes changes in air pressure, while the other utilizes the mechanical makeup of the altimeter setting system.

When the glider altitude is changed, the changing pressure within the altimeter case expands or contracts the aneroid barometer that, through linkage, rotates the pointers. A decrease in pressure causes the altimeter to indicate an increase in altitude, and an increase in pressure causes the altimeter to indicate a decrease in altitude. If the glider is flown from a pressure level of 28.75 "Hg to a pressure level of 29.75 "Hg, the altimeter would show a decrease of approximately 1,000 feet in altitude.

The other method of moving the pointers does not rely on changing air pressure, but on the mechanical construction of the altimeter. When the knob on the altimeter is rotated, the altimeter setting pressure scale moves simultaneously with the altimeter pointers. This may be confusing because the numerical values of pressure indicated in the window increase while the altimeter indicates an increase in altitude, and decrease while the altimeter indicates a decrease in altitude. This is contrary to the reaction on the pointers when air pressure changes and is based solely on the mechanical makeup of the altimeter. To further explain this point, assume that the correct altimeter setting is 29.50, or a .50 difference. This would cause a 500 foot error in altitude. In this case, if the altimeter setting is adjusted from 30.00 to 29.50, the numerical value decreases and the altimeter indicates a decrease of 500 feet in altitude. Before this correction was made, the glider was actually flying at an altitude of 500 feet lower than was shown on the altimeter. It is important to calibrate the altimeter for all VFR flights because if they are off by more than a comfortable margin, calibration or repair is advisable.

Types of Altitude

Knowing the glider's altitude is vitally important to the pilot for several reasons. The pilot must be sure that the glider is flying high enough to clear the highest terrain or obstruction along the intended route. To keep above mountain peaks, the pilot must be aware of the glider's altitude and elevation of the surrounding terrain at all times. Knowledge of the altitude is necessary to calculate TAS.

Altitude is vertical distance above some point or level used as a reference. There may be as many kinds of altitude as there are reference levels from which altitude is measured, and each may be used for specific reasons.

The following are the four types of altitude that affect glider pilots. *[Figure 4-19]*

- Indicated altitude—altitude read directly from the altimeter (uncorrected) after it is set to the current altimeter setting (QNH) in the Kollsman window. Indicated altitude can be used for maintaining terrain/obstacle clearance and estimating distance to glide over the terrain without benefit of lift.

- True altitude—true vertical distance of the glider above sea level (known as MSL). This altitude is measured above a standard datum due to the shape of the earth (often expressed in this manner: 10,900 feet MSL, 5,280 feet MSL, or 940 feet MSL). Airport, terrain, and obstacle elevations found on aeronautical charts are expressed as MSL (true altitudes). With

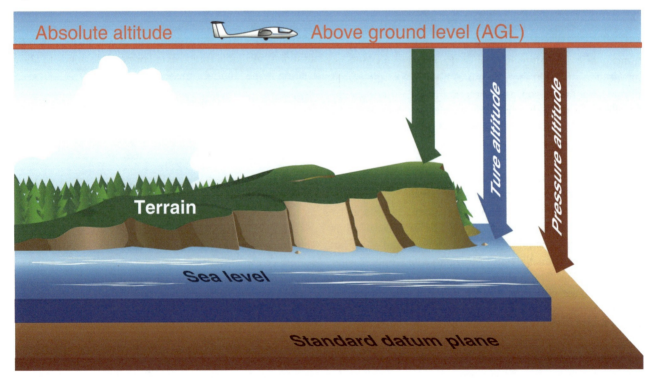

Figure 4-19. *Types of altitude.*

proper local altimeter setting (QHN), indicated and true altitude are synonymous.

- Absolute altitude—vertical distance above the terrain, above ground level (AGL). An altimeter set to the proper pressure reading (QFE setting) indicates zero feet at touchdown. It is referred to as QFE. The METAR weather report in the remarks section lists this setting as sea level pressure (SLP) and is expressed in millibars (mb). Absolute altitude is very important when flying low and determining when an out landing must be accomplished. An out landing is a glider landing not at the intended airfield but required when lift is insufficient to remain aloft.

- Pressure altitude—altitude indicated at which the altimeter setting window (barometric scale) is adjusted to 29.92 is the standard datum plane, a theoretical plane where air pressure (corrected to 15 °C or 59 °F) is equal to 29.92 "Hg. Pressure altitude is used for computer solutions to determine density altitude, true altitude, TAS, etc.

- Density altitude—pressure altitude corrected for nonstandard temperature variations. Density altitude is a yardstick by which we can reference the density of air. The wings of the glider are affected by the density of air because they use air molecules to generate lift. Thinner air restricts fuel burn and lowers compression in the engine thereby reducing the power output. Thinner air necessitates an increased AOA to generate the same amount of lift. High density altitudes decrease towplane (and self-launching combustion powerplant) power, so expect much longer takeoff runs during tows, slower climbs, and the higher TAS results in longer landing rollouts due to higher ground speeds.

When conditions are standard, pressure altitude and density altitude are the same. Consequently, if the temperature is above standard, the density altitude is higher than pressure altitude. If the temperature is below standard, the density altitude is lower than pressure altitude. The density altitude determines the gliders performance and greatly affects the performance of towplanes and powerplants in self-launching gliders.

Variometer

Variometer instruments measure the vertical ascent or descent of the local air mass and glider combined and displays that information as speed. The principles of operation are similar to the altimeter. The variometer is viewed as a critical part of the glider's instrument display, giving the pilot information on performance of the glider while flying through the atmosphere. The variometer depends upon the pressure lapse rate in the atmosphere to derive information about rate of climb or rate of descent. A non-electric variometer uses a separate insulated tank (thermos or capacity flask) as a reference chamber. The tubing is plumbed from the reference chamber through the variometer instrument to an outside static port. *[Figure 4-20]*

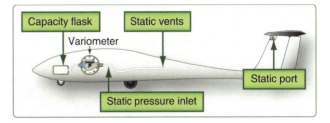

Figure 4-20. *Uncompensated variometer plumbing.*

A variometer with tubing is connected to an outside static port is uncompensated. The internal hairspring mechanism determines sensitivity of the variometer. The variometer has a very rapid response due to the small mass and lightweight construction of the moving parts. *[Figure 4-21]*

Pressure differences between the air inside the variometer/reference chamber system and the air outside of the system tend to equalize as air flows from high pressure areas to low pressure areas. When pressure inside the reference chamber is greater than the pressure outside, air flows out of the reference chamber through the mechanical variometer to the outside environment. When air pressure outside the reference chamber is greater than pressure inside, air flows through the variometer and into the reference chamber until pressure is equalized. The variometer needle indicates a vertical descending air mass or sink which is falling air that forces the glider to lose height. *Figures 4-22* and *4-23* illustrate how the variometer works in level flight and while the glider is ascending. In addition, *Figure 4-24* illustrates certain flight maneuvers that cause the variometer to display changes in altitude.

Electric-powered variometers offer several advantages over the non-electric variety. These advantages include more rapid response rates and separate audible signals for climb and descent.

Some electric variometers operate by the cooling effect of airflow on an element called a thermistor, a heat-sensitive electrical resistor. The electrical resistance of the thermistor changes when temperature changes. As air flows into or out of the reference chamber, it flows across two thermistors in a bridge circuit. An electrical meter measures the imbalance across the bridge circuit and calculates the rate of climb or descent. It then displays the information on the variometer.

Newer electric variometers operate on the transducer principle. A tiny vacuum cavity on a circuit board is sealed with a flexible membrane. Variable resistors are embedded in the membrane. When pressure outside the

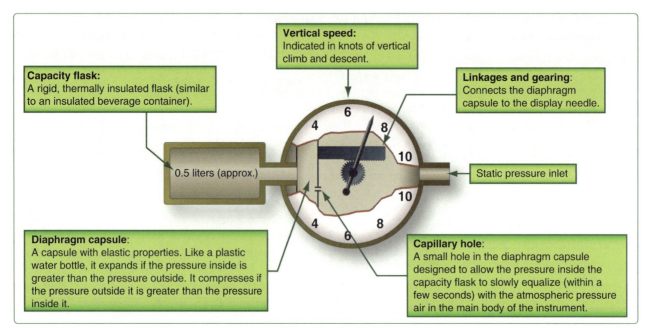

Figure 4-21. *A variometer diaphragm anatomy.*

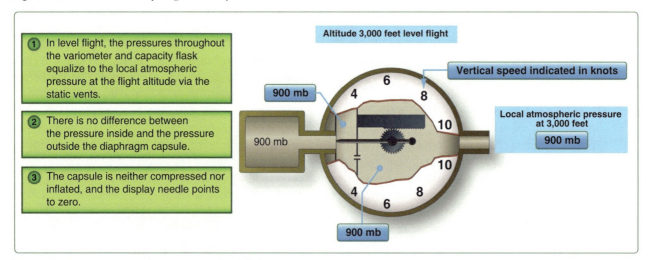

Figure 4-22. *Uncompensated variometer in level flight.*

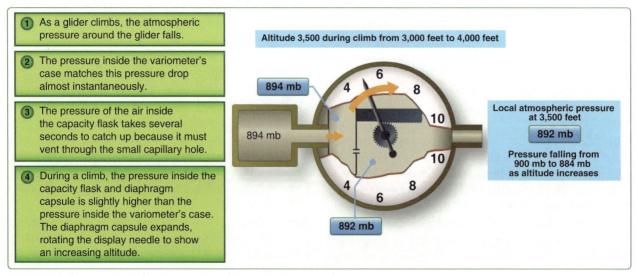

Figure 4-23. *Uncompensated variometer in a climb.*

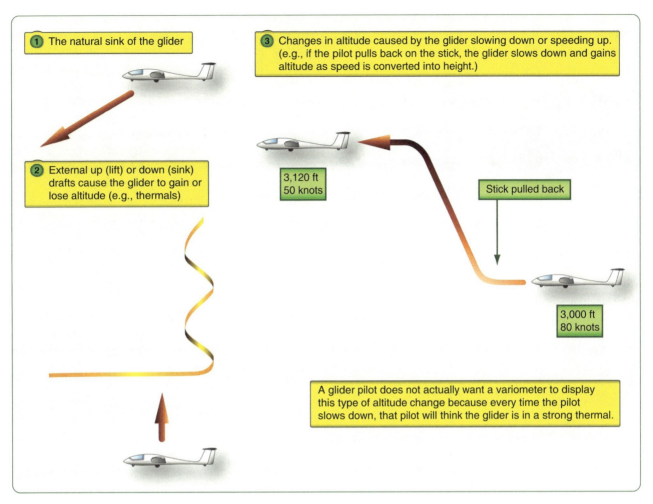

Figure 4-24. *Flight maneuvers that display altitude changes on an uncompensated variometer.*

cavity changes, minute alterations in the shape of the membrane occur. As a result, electrical resistance in the embedded resistors changes. These changes in electrical resistance are interpreted by a circuit board and indicated on the variometer dial as climb or descent.

Many electrical variometers provide audible tones, or beeps, that indicate the rate of climb or rate of descent of the glider. Audio variometers enhance safety of flight because they make it unnecessary for the glider pilot to look at the variometer to discern the rate of climb or rate of descent. Instead, the pilot can hear the rate of climb or rate of descent. This allows the pilot to minimize time spent looking at the flight instruments and maximize time spent looking outside for other air traffic. [Figure 4-25]

Some variometers are equipped with a rotatable rim speed scale called a MacCready ring. This scale indicates the optimum airspeed to fly when traveling between thermals for maximum cross-country performance. During the glide between thermals, the index arrow is set at the rate of climb expected in the next thermal. On the speed ring, the

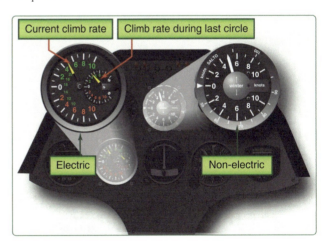

Figure 4-25. *When an electric variometer is mounted to the glider, a non electric variometer is usually installed as a backup.*

variometer needle points to the optimum speed to fly (STF) between thermals. If expected rate of climb is low, optimum interthermal cruise airspeed is relatively low. When expected lift is strong, however, optimum interthermal cruise airspeed is much faster. [Figure 4-26] A MacCready ring has single pilot values in front and dual pilot values for the second seat instrument. Marked for specific aircraft, some may have empty ballast and full ballast values.

Figure 4-26. *The MacCready ring.*

Variometers are sensitive to changes in pressure altitude caused by airspeed. In still air, when the glider dives, the variometer indicates a descent. When the glider pulls out of the dive and begins a rapid climb, the variometer indicates an ascent. This indication is sometimes called a stick thermal. A glider lacking a compensated variometer must be flown at a constant airspeed to receive an accurate variometer indication.

Total Energy System

A variometer with a total energy system senses changes in airspeed and tends to cancel out the resulting climb and dive indications (stick thermals). This is desirable because the glider pilot wants to know how rapidly the air mass is rising or descending despite changes in airspeed.

A popular type of total energy system consists of a small venturi mounted in the air stream and connected to the static outlet of the variometer or simply as a slot or pair of holes on the back side of a quarter inch vertical tube. When airspeed increases, more suction from the venturi moderates (offsets) the pressure at the static outlet of the variometer. Similarly, when airspeed decreases, reduced suction from the venturi moderates (offsets) the pressure at the static outlet of the variometer. If the venturi is properly designed and installed, the net effect is to reduce climb and dive indications caused by airspeed changes. To maximize the precision of this compensation effect, the total energy probe needs to be in undisturbed airflow ahead of the aircraft nose or tail fin (the "Braunschweig tube", the long cantilevered tube with a kink in the end that can be seen projecting from the leading edge of the tail fin on most modern sailplanes.) *[Figure 4-27]*

Another type of total energy system is designed with a diaphragm-type compensator placed in line from the pitot tube to the line coming from the reference chamber (thermos or capacity flask). Deflection of the diaphragm is proportional to the effect the airspeed change has on pitot pressure. In effect, the diaphragm modulates pressure changes in the capacity flask. When properly adjusted, the diaphragm compensator does an adequate job of masking stick thermals. *[Figure 4-28]*

Netto

A variometer that indicates the vertical movement of the air mass, regardless of the glider's climb or descent rate, is called a Netto variometer system. Some Netto variometer systems employ a calibrated capillary tube that functions as a tiny

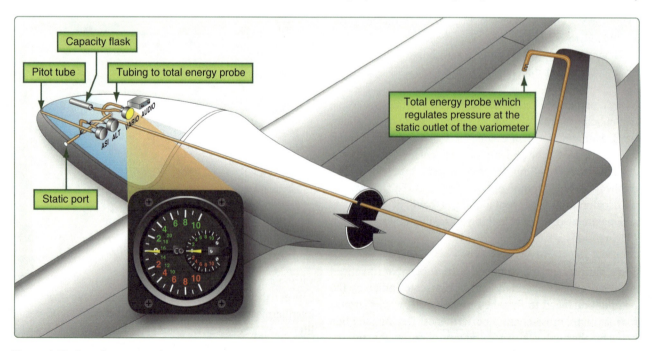

Figure 4-27. *A total energy variometer system.*

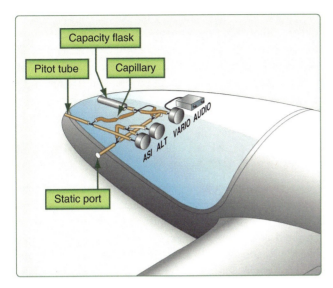

Figure 4-28. *An example of a Netto variometer system.*

Figure 4-29. *High end flight computer system.*

valve. Pitot pressure pushes minute quantities of air through the valve and into the reference chamber tubing. The effect is to remove the glider's sink rate at various airspeeds from the variometer indication (polar sink rate). *[Figure 4-28]*

Computerized (electronic) Netto variometers employ a different method to remove the glider performance polar sink rate from the variometer indication. In this type of system, sensors for both pitot pressure and static pressure provide airspeed information to the computer. The sink rate of the glider at every airspeed is stored in the computer memory. At any given airspeed, the sink rate of the glider is mathematically removed, and the variometer displays the rate of ascent or descent of the air mass itself.

Electronic Flight Computers

Electronic flight computers are found in the cockpits of gliders that are flown in competition and cross-country soaring. Since nonpowered gliders lack a generator or alternator, electrical components, such as the flight computer and very high frequency (VHF) transceiver, draw power from the glider battery or batteries. The battery is usually a 12- or 14-volt sealed battery. Solar cells are sometimes arrayed behind the pilot, or on top of the instrument panel cover, to supply additional power to the electrical system during flight in sunny conditions.

The primary components of most flight computer systems are an electric variometer, a coupled GPS receiver, and a microprocessor. The variometer measures rate of climb and descent. The GPS provides position information. The microprocessor interprets altitude, speed, and position information. The microprocessor output aids the pilot in cross-country decision-making. Shown in *Figure 4-29* is a high end glider flight computer.

The GPS-coupled flight computer can provide the following information:

- Where you are
- Where you have been
- Distance to planned destination
- How fast you are going there
- How high you need to be to glide there
- How fast you are climbing or descending
- The optimum airspeed to fly to the next area of anticipated lift
- The optimum airspeed to fly to a location on the ground, such as the finish line in a race or the airport of intended landing at the end of a cross-country flight

The primary benefits of the flight computer can easily be divided into two areas: navigation assistance and performance (speed) enhancement.

Fundamental to the use of the flight computer is the concept of waypoint. A waypoint is simply a point in space. The three coordinates of the point are latitude, longitude, and altitude. Glider races and cross-country glider flights frequently involve flight around a series of waypoints called turnpoints. The course may be an out-and-return course, a triangle, a quadrilateral or other type of polygon, or a series of waypoints laid out more or less in a straight line. The glider pilot must navigate from point to point, using available lift sources to climb periodically so that flight can continue to the intended goal. The GPS-enabled flight computer aids in navigation and in summarizing how the flight is going. When strong lift is encountered, and if the pilot believes it is likely that the strong lift source may be worth returning to after rounding a turnpoint, the flight computer can mark the location of the thermal. Then, the glider pilot can round a nearby turnpoint and use the flight computer to guide the return to the marked thermal in the hopes of making a rapid climb and heading out on course toward the next turnpoint.

During the climb portion of the flight, the flight computer's variometer constantly updates the achieved rate of climb. During cruise, the GPS-coupled flight computer aids in navigating accurately to the next turnpoint. The flight computer also suggests the optimum cruise airspeed for the glider to fly, based on the expected rate of climb in the next thermal. During final glide to a goal, the flight computer can display glider altitude, altitude required to reach the goal, distance to the goal, the strength of the headwind or tailwind component, and optimum airspeed to fly.

Most flight computers incorporate an electronic audiovisual variometer. The rate of climb or descent can be viewed on the computer's visual display. The variometer also provides audible rate of climb information through a small loudspeaker. The loudspeaker allows the pilot to hear how fast the glider is climbing or descending. Because this information is received through hearing, the pilot's vision can be constantly directed outside the glider to enhance safety of flight and cross-country performance.

Flight computers also provide information to help the pilot select and fly the optimum airspeed for the weather conditions being encountered. When lift is strong and climbs are fast, higher airspeeds around the course are possible. The flight computer detects the rapid climbs and suggests very high cruise airspeeds to enhance performance. When lift is weak and climbs are slow, optimum airspeed is significantly lower than when conditions are strong. The flight computer, sensing the relatively low rate of climb on a difficult day, compensates for the weaker conditions, and suggests optimum airspeeds that are lower than they would be if conditions were strong. The flight computer relieves the pilot of the chore of making numerous speed-to-fly calculations during cross-country flight. This freedom allows the pilot to look for other air traffic, look for sources of lift, watch the weather ahead, and plot a strategy for the remaining portion of the flight.

The presence of water ballast alters the performance characteristics of the glider. In racing, the ability to make faster glides without excess altitude penalty is very valuable. The additional weight of water in the glider's ballast tanks allows flatter glides at high airspeeds. The water ballast glider possesses the strongest advantage when lift conditions are strong and rapid climbs are achievable. The flight computer compensates for the amount of water ballast carried, adjusting speed-to-fly computations according to the weight and performance of the glider. Some flight computers require the pilot to enter data regarding the ballast condition of the glider. Other flight computers automatically compensate for the effect of water ballast by constantly measuring the performance of the glider and deducting the operating weight of the glider from these measurements. If the wings of the glider become contaminated with bugs, glider performance declines. The glide computer can be adjusted to account for the resulting performance degradation.

Magnetic Compass

Some gliders do not have compass deviation cards because they are not required instrumentation per the Type Certificate Data Sheets (TCDS). Most gliders are not considered powered aircraft as referenced in Title 14 of the Code of Federal Regulations (14 CFR) part 91, section 91.205, and are only subject to regulations specifying "civil aircraft." Two examples that show these are 14 CFR part 91, section 91.209 and 91.211.

Yaw String

The most effective, yet least expensive, slip/skid indicator is made from a piece of yarn mounted in the free airstream in a place easily visible to the pilot, as shown in *Figure 4-30*. The yaw string indicates whether the pilot is using the rudder and aileron inputs together in a coordinated fashion. When the controls are properly coordinated, the yarn points straight back, aligned with the longitudinal axis of the glider. During a slipping turn, the tail of the yaw string is offset toward the outside of the turn. In flight, the rule to remember is simple: step on the head of the yaw string. If the head of the yaw string is to the right of the tail, then the pilot needs to apply right pedal. If the head of the yaw string is to the left of the tail, then the pilot should apply left pedal.

Inclinometer

Another type of slip/skid indicator is the inclinometer. Like the magnetic compass, this instrument requires no electrical power or input from other aircraft systems. The inclinometer is influenced by centrifugal force and gravity. Mounted in the bottom of a turn-and-bank indicator or mounted separately in the instrument panel, the inclinometer consists of a metal ball in an oil-filled, curved glass tube. When the glider is flying in coordinated fashion, the ball remains centered at the bottom of the glass tube. The inclinometer differs from the yaw string during uncoordinated flight. The ball moves to the inside of the turn to indicate a slip and to the outside of the turn to indicate a skid. Remember the phrase, "step on the ball" in reference to the inclinometer; it helps coordinate the turn using rudder inputs. The long glider wing tends to increase the adverse yaw effects from the ailerons and requires more rudder control than many aircraft.

Figure 4-30. *Left turn condition indications of a yaw string and inclinometer.*

Gyroscopic Instruments

Gyroscopic instruments are found in virtually all modern airplanes but are infrequently found in gliders. Self-launching gliders often have one or more gyroscopic instruments on the panel. Gliders without power rarely have gyroscopic instruments installed. The three gyroscopic instruments found most frequently in a glider are the heading indicator, attitude indicator, and turn coordinator.

G-Meter

Another instrument that can be mounted in the instrument panel of a glider is a G-meter. G-meters register positive G forces from climbs and turns, as well as negative G forces when diving down or pushing over from a climb. The G-meter measures and displays the load imposed on the glider during flight. During straight, unaccelerated flight in calm air, a glider experiences a load factor of 1 G (1.0 times the force of gravity). During aerobatics or during flight in turbulent air, the glider and pilot experience G-loads greater than 1 G. These additional loads result from accelerations imposed on the glider. Some of these accelerations result from external sources, such as flying into updrafts or downdrafts. Other accelerations arise from pilot input on the controls, such as pulling back or pushing forward on the control stick. G-loads are classified as positive or negative.

Positive G is felt when increasing pitch rapidly for a climb. Negative G is felt when pushing over into a dive or during sustained inverted flight. Each glider type is designed to withstand a specified maximum positive G-load and a specified maximum negative G-load. The GFM/POH is the definitive source for this information. Exceeding the allowable limit loads may result in deformation of the glider structure. In extreme cases, exceeding permissible limit loads may cause structural failure of the glider. The G-meter allows the pilot to monitor G-loads from moment to moment. This is useful in aerobatic flight and during flight in rough air. Most G-meters also record and display the maximum positive G-load and the maximum negative G-load encountered during flight. The recorded maximum positive and negative G-loads can be reset by adjusting the control knob of the G-meter. *[Figure 4-31]*

Figure 4-31. *The G-meter.*

FLARM Collision Avoidance System

Mid-air collisions are a long standing danger in aviation and glider pilots have additional mid-air threats due to thermalling, cloud-street flying, and ridge running. All of these can put the glider in close proximity to other gliders and other aircraft. No matter how vigilant pilots are, too many stories of "near misses" exist. There are mid-air collisions or near misses each year in both club flying and in competition and between gliders and towplanes.

As a way to mitigate mid-air collisions, the FLARM collision avoidance system was developed for glider pilots by glider pilots. FLARM warns FLARM-equipped pilots of impending collisions and gives the location of non-threatening nearby FLARM-equipped gliders. *Figure 4-32* shows the interior of an ASW 19 glider with a FLARM unit on top of the instrument panel. It only works if both gliders have FLARMs. FLARM knows about the unique flight characteristics of gliders and stays quiet unless there is a real hazard.

Figure 4-32. *FLARM unit on top of the instrument panel.*

FLARM (the name being inspired from 'flight alarm') obtains its position from an internal global positioning system (GPS) and a barometric sensor and then broadcasts this with forecast data about the future 3D flight track. Its receiver listens for other FLARM devices within typically 3-5 kilometers and processes the information received. Motion-prediction algorithms predict potential conflicts for up to 50 other signals and warn the pilot using sound and visual means. FLARM can also store information about static aerial obstacles, such as cables, into a database.

Unlike conventional transponders in aircraft, FLARM has a low-power consumption and is relatively inexpensive to buy and to install. Furthermore, conventional Airborne Collision Avoidance Systems (ACAS) are of little use in preventing gliders from colliding with each other because gliders are frequently close to each other without being in danger of collision. ACAS would provide continuous and unnecessary warnings about all aircraft in the vicinity, whereas FLARM only gives selective alerts to aircraft posing a collision risk. Versions are sold for use in light aircraft and helicopters, as well as gliders. However, the short range of the signal makes FLARM unsuitable for avoiding collisions with fast moving aircraft, such as commercial and military jets.

Outside Air Temperature Gauge

The outside air temperature gauge (OAT) is a simple and effective self-contained device mounted so that the sensing element is exposed to the outside air. The sensing element consists of a bimetallic-type thermometer in which two dissimilar metals are welded together into a single strip and twisted into a helix. One end is anchored into a protective tube, and the other end is affixed to the pointer that reads against the calibration on a circular face. OAT gauges are calibrated in degrees Celsius, degrees Fahrenheit, or both. An accurate air temperature provides the glider pilot with useful information about temperature lapse rate with altitude change. A very fast reading OAT gauge can give glider pilots another indication of the hottest center portion of thermals for maximum loft and where the edge of the lifting currents are located.

When flying a glider loaded with water ballast, knowledge of the height of the freezing level is important to safety of flight. Extended operation of a glider loaded with water ballast in below-freezing temperatures may result in frozen drain valves, ruptured ballast tanks, and structural damage to the glider. *[Figure 4-33]*

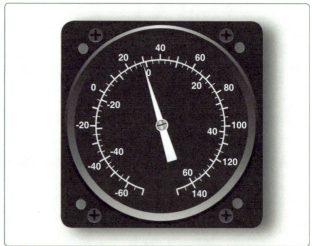

Figure 4-33. *Outside air temperature (OAT) gauge.*

Chapter 5
Glider Performance

Introduction
Glider performance during launch phase, landing, and free flight phase depends on many factors: design, weather, wind, and other atmospheric phenomena.

Factors Affecting Performance

Glider performance during launch depends on the power output of the launch mechanism and on the aerodynamic efficiency of the glider itself. The four major factors that affect performance are density altitude, weight, design, and wind.

High and Low Density Altitude Conditions

Every pilot must understand the terms "high density altitude" and "low density altitude." In general, high density altitude refers to thin air, while low density altitude refers to dense air. Those conditions that result in a high density altitude (thin air) are high elevations, low atmospheric pressure, high temperatures, high humidity, or some combination thereof. Lower elevations, high atmospheric pressure, low temperatures, and low humidity are more indicative of low density altitude (dense air). However, high density altitudes may be present at lower elevations on hot days, so it is important to calculate the density altitude and determine performance before a flight.

One way to determine density altitude is to use charts designed for that purpose. *[Figure 5-1]* For example, you plan to depart an airport where the field elevation is 1,600 feet MSL. If the altimeter setting is 29.80, and the temperature is 85 °F, what is the density altitude? First, correct for nonstandard pressure (29.8 "Hg) by referring to the right side of the chart and adding 112 feet to the field elevation. The result is a pressure altitude of 1,712 feet. Then, enter the chart at the bottom, just above the temperature of 85 °F (29.4 °C). Proceed up the chart vertically until intercepting the diagonal 1,712-foot pressure altitude line, then move horizontally to the left and read the density altitude of approximately 3,500 feet. This means a self-launching glider or towplane will perform as if it were at 3,500 feet MSL on a standard day.

Most performance charts do not require a pilot to compute density altitude. Instead, the computation is built into the performance chart itself. A pilot needs only the correct pressure altitude and the temperature. Some charts, however, may require computing density altitude before entering them. Density altitude may be computed using a density altitude chart or by using a flight computer.

Atmospheric Pressure

Due to changing weather conditions, atmospheric pressure at a given location changes from day to day. The following is the METAR report for Love Field observed on the 23rd at 21:53Z (GMT) which indicates a local pressure of A2953, or altimeter setting of 29.53 "Hg. When barometric pressure drops, air density decreases. The reduced density of the air results in an increase in density altitude and decreased glider performance. This reduces takeoff and climb performance and increases the length of runway needed for landing.

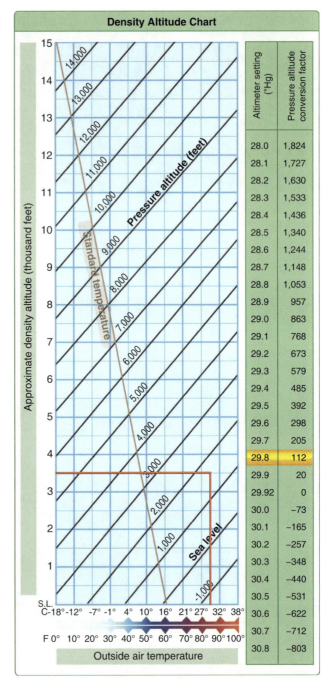

Figure 5-1. *Density altitude chart.*

KDAL 232153Z 21006KT 7SM -RA BKN025 BKN060 OVC110 12/11 A2953 RMK AO2 PRESFR SLP995 P0005 T01220106

The 12/11 notation of this report indicates the reported temperature and dewpoint for Love Field.

When barometric pressure rises, air density increases. The greater density of the air results in lower density altitude. Thus, takeoff and climb performance improves, and the length of runway needed for landing decreases.

Altitude

As altitude increases, air density decreases. At altitude, the atmospheric pressure that acts on a given volume of air is less, allowing the air molecules to space themselves further apart. The result is that a given volume of air at high altitude contains fewer air molecules than the same volume of air at lower altitude. As altitude increases, density altitude increases, and glider takeoff and climb performance is reduced.

Temperature

Temperature changes have a large effect on density altitude. When air is heated, it expands—the molecules move farther apart, making the air less dense. Takeoff and climb performance is reduced, while the length of runway required for landing is increased.

Consider the following METAR for two airports with same altimeter setting, temperature, and dewpoint. Love Field (KDAL) airport elevation of 487 feet versus Denver International (KDEN) at 5,431 feet.

KDAL 240453Z 21007KT 10SM CLR 25/15 A3010 RMK AO2…
KDEN 240453Z 24006KT 10SM FEW120 SCT200 25/15 A3010 RMK AO2…

The computed density altitude for Love Field is 1,774 feet; for Denver, 7,837 feet—almost twice the density altitude increase compared to the increase for Love Field. The effects of attitude and temperature are significant, a fact pilots must consider when computing aircraft performance.

Wind

Wind affects glider performance in many ways. Headwind during launch results in shorter ground roll, while tailwind causes longer ground roll before takeoff. *[Figure 5-2]* Crosswinds during launch require proper crosswind procedures or control input to track along the runway.

During cruising flight, headwinds reduce the groundspeed of the glider. A glider flying at 60 knots true airspeed into a headwind of 25 knots has a groundspeed of only 35 knots. Tailwinds, on the other hand, increase the groundspeed of the glider. A glider flying at 60 knots true airspeed with a tailwind of 25 knots has a groundspeed of 85 knots.

Crosswinds during cruising flight cause glider heading (the direction in which the glider nose is pointed) and glider track (the path of the glider over the ground) to diverge. In a glider, it must be remembered that crosswinds have some head or tailwind component that results in a lower or higher true groundspeed. When planning the landing, the wind effects must be factored into the landing pattern sight picture

Figure 5-2. *Apparent wind effect on takeoff distance and climb out angle.*

and allowances must be made for the winds, indicated or expected. It is a lot easier to lose altitude than it is to make up altitude when the glider is down low. When gliding toward an object on the ground in the presence of crosswind, such as on final glide at the end of a cross-country flight, the glider pilot should keep the nose of the glider pointed somewhat upwind of the target on the ground. For instance, if the crosswind is from the right during final glide, the nose of the glider is pointed a bit to the right of the target on the ground. The glider's heading is upwind (to the right, in this case) of the target, but if the angle of crab is correct, the glider's track is straight toward the target on the ground. *[Figure 5-3]*

Headwind during landing results in a shortened ground roll, and tailwind results in a longer ground roll. Crosswind landings require the pilot to compensate for drift with the proper flight control input, such as a sideslip or a crab. Glider pilots must be aware of the apparent angle versus the rate of descent. The glider descends at a constant rate, but the different groundspeeds will result in different approach angles. These different approach angles require specific techniques to ensure safe touchdowns in the landing zone. For example, if landing in a strong headwind, the glider pilot should plan for a closer base leg to allow for the apparent steeper approach due to the slower ground speed. Another technique would be the delayed extension of spoilers or drag brakes and accepting the faster airspeed to counter the headwind component. In the case of a tailwind and an apparent lower angle of approach, the glider pilot can use more spoiler or drag brake extension or slipping or a combination as allowed by the GFM to touchdown in the landing zone. In any condition, the glider pilot must make allowances for the current conditions of wind and density altitude to ensure a safe landing in the landing area. A glider pilot must respond to the current conditions and amend the traffic pattern and/or modify their procedures to compensate

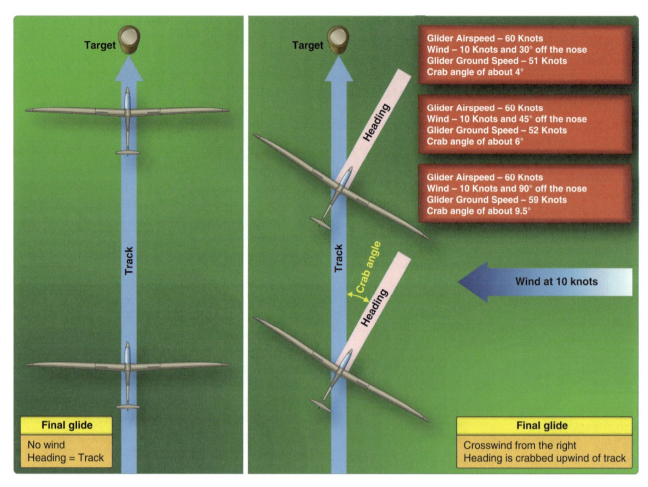

Figure 5-3. *Crosswind effect on final glide.*

for the conditions and land safely. The different groundspeeds also result in different touchdown points unless the pilot takes some kind of action. In any case, the pilot should aim for the touchdown zone markers and not for the end of the runway. *[Figure 5-4]*

During landing in windy/gusty conditions, there is a tendency to lose airspeed (flying speed) and increase sink. The friction between the ground and the air mass reduces the wind strength. The glider may be flying into a strong headwind at one moment; a few seconds later, the windspeed diminishes to nearly zero. The pilot landing into a headwind can usually expect to lose some of that headwind while approaching the surface due to surface friction slowing the wind. When the change is abrupt, the pilot experiences a loss of airspeed because it requires some small time and loss of altitude to accelerate the inertia of the glider up to the airspeed previously displayed when into the stronger headwind. This takes on the appearance of having to dive at the ground to maintain flying speed. Fly a faster approach to ensure staying above stalling speed. Depending on the wind change, a longer ground roll may be the result. If this occurs near the ground, the glider loses speed, and there may be insufficient altitude to recover the lost speed. This is called "wind gradient." Consideration

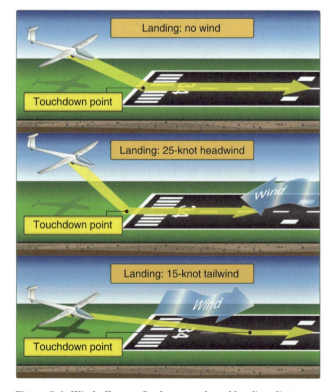

Figure 5-4. *Wind effect on final approach and landing distance.*

of wind gradient during a ground launch is important, as a sudden increase in windspeed could result in exceeding the designed launch speed. *[Figure 5-5]*

The pilot landing with a tail wind has a higher groundspeed for an indicated airspeed. As the surface friction slows the winds, the pilot may see an increase in airspeed before the higher inertia-induced airspeed is dissipated, which may increase the ground roll distance to touchdown. This may be experienced with a downdraft in the vicinity of obstructions upwind of the runway as the winds curl down and wrap under the obstructions. This effect can lead to major undershoots of the approach path and landing short if the winds are strong enough. Local pilots can be a rich source of information about local wind currents and hazards.

Glider pilots must understand that wind near the ground behaves differently higher up. Atmospheric conditions, such as thermal formation, turbulence, and gust and lulls, change the in-flight behavior of the glider significantly. As the wind flows over the ground, ground obstructions, such as buildings, trees, hills, and irregular formations along the ground, interfere with the flow of the wind, decreasing its velocity and breaking up its smooth flow as occurs in wave and ridge flying.

Wind gradient affects a pilot turning too steeply on final approach at a very low airspeed and at low altitudes near to the surface. There is less wind across the lower wing than across the higher wing. The rolling force created by the wind gradient affects the entire wing area. This can prevent the pilot from controlling the bank with the ailerons and may roll the glider past a vertical bank. *[Figure 5-6]* Be cautious with any bank angle and at any airspeed while close to the ground when transitioning a wind gradient.

When approaching to land during windy and gusty conditions, add half of the wind velocity to the approach speed to ensure adequate speed for a possible encounter with a wind gradient. During landing under these conditions, it is acceptable to allow the glider to touch down a little faster than normal instead of holding the glider off the ground for a low kinetic energy landing. Upon touchdown during these landings, extending the air brakes fully prevents the glider from becoming airborne through a wind gust during the landing roll.

Some self-launching gliders are designed for extended periods of powered cruising flight. For these self-launching gliders, maximum range (distance) for powered flight and maximum duration (elapsed time aloft) for powered flight are primarily limited by the self-launching glider's fuel capacity. Wind has no effect on flight duration but does have a significant effect on range. During powered cruising flight, a headwind reduces range, and a tailwind increases range. The Glider Flight Manual/Pilot's Operating Handbook (GFM/POH) provides recommended airspeeds and power settings to maximize range when flying in no-wind, headwind, or tailwind conditions.

Weight

Glider lift, drag, and glide ratio characteristics are governed solely by its design and construction, and are predetermined at takeoff. The only characteristic the pilot controls is the weight of the glider. In some cases, pilots may control glider configurations, as some high-performance gliders may have a wing extension option not available on other models. Increased weight decreases takeoff and climb performance, but increases high-speed cruise performance. During launch, a heavy glider takes longer to accelerate to flying speed. The heavy glider has more inertia, making it more difficult to accelerate the mass of the glider to flying speed. After takeoff, the heavier glider takes longer to climb out because

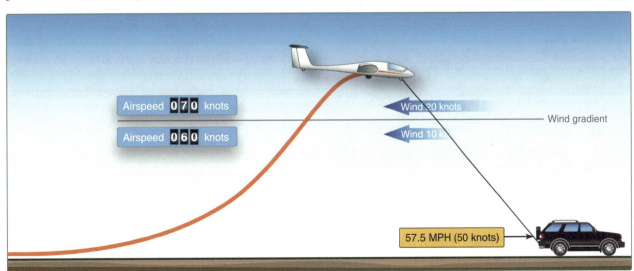

Figure 5-5. *During gusting conditions, the pilot must monitor the pitch during the tow.*

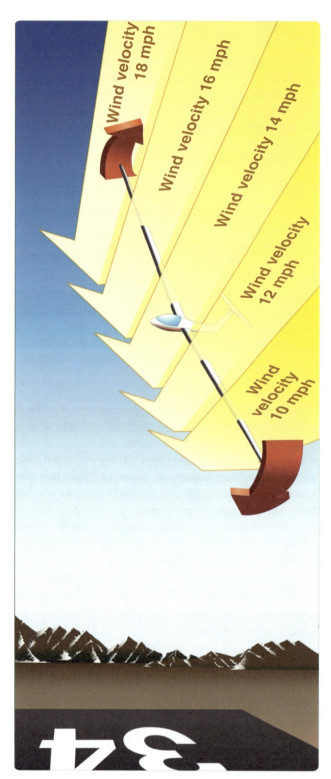

Figure 5-6. *Effect of wind velocity gradient on a glider turning into the wind. Stronger airflow over higher wing causes bank to steepen when close to the surface where surface friction slows winds.*

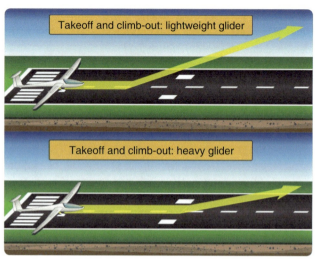

Figure 5-7. *Effect of weight on takeoff distance and climb-out rate and angle.*

The heavy glider has a higher stall speed and a higher minimum controllable airspeed than an otherwise identical, but lighter, glider. The stall speed of a glider increases with the square root of the increase in weight. If the weight of the glider is doubled (multiplied by 2.0), then the stall speed increases by more than 40 percent (1.41 is the approximate square root of 2; 1.41 times the old stall speed results in the new stall speed at the heavier weight). For example, a 540-pound glider has a stalling speed of 40 knots. The pilot adds 300 pounds of water ballast making the new weight 840 pounds. The new stalling speed is approximately 57 knots (square root of $\sqrt{300} + 40 = 57$).

When circling in thermals to climb, the heavy glider is at a disadvantage relative to the light glider. The increased weight of the heavy glider means stall airspeed and minimum sink airspeed are greater than they would be if the glider were operating at a light weight. At any given bank angle, the heavy glider's higher airspeeds mean the pilot must fly larger diameter thermalling circles than the pilot of the light glider. Since the best lift in thermals is often found in a narrow cylinder near the core of the thermal, larger diameter circles generally mean the heavy glider is unable to exploit the strong lift of the thermal core, as well as the slower, lightweight glider. This results in the heavy glider's inability to climb as fast in a thermal as the light glider. *[Figure 5-8]*

The heavy glider can fly faster than the light glider while maintaining the same glide ratio as the light glider. The advantage of the heavier weight becomes apparent during cruising flight. The heavy glider can fly faster than the light glider and still retain the same lift-to-drag (L/D) ratio.

the heavier glider has more mass to lift to altitude than does the lighter glider (whether ground launch, aerotow launch, or self-launch). *[Figure 5-7]*

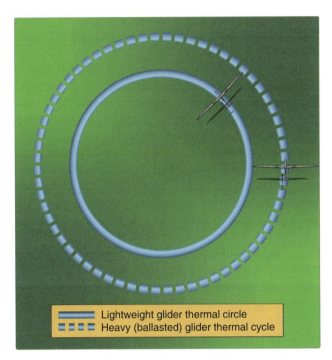

Figure 5-8. *Effect of added weight on thermaling turn radius.*

If the operating weight of a given glider is increased, the stall airspeed, minimum controllable airspeed, minimum sink airspeed, and the best L/D airspeed are increased by a factor equal to the square root of the increase in weight. *[Figure 5-9]* Glide ratio is not affected by weight because, while a heavier glider sinks faster, it does so at a greater airspeed. The glider descends faster, but covers the same horizontal distance (at a higher speed) as a lighter glider with the same glide ratio and starting altitude.

Operating Weight	Stall Airspeed	Minimum Sink	Best L/D Airspeed
800 pounds	36 knots	48 knots	60 knots
1,200 pounds	44 knots	58 knots	73 knots
1,600 pounds	50 knots	68 knots	83 knots

Figure 5-9. *Effect of added weight on performance airspeeds.*

To help gliders fly faster, some gliders have tanks that can hold up to 80 gallons of water. Higher speeds are desirable for cross-country flying and racing. The disadvantages of these ballasted gliders include reduced climb rates in thermals and the possibility that suitable lift cannot be located after tow release. To prevent this, the water ballast can be jettisoned at any time through dump valves, allowing the pilot to reduce the weight of the glider to aid in increased climb rates.

The addition of ballast to increase weight allows the glider to fly at increased airspeeds while maintaining its L/D ratio. *Figure 5-9* shows that adding 400 pounds of water ballast increases the best L/D airspeed from 60 knots to 73 knots. The heavy glider has more difficulty climbing in thermals than the light glider, but if lift is strong enough for the heavy glider to climb reasonably well, the heavy glider's advantage during the cruising portion of flight outweighs the heavy glider's disadvantage during climbs.

Water is often used as ballast to increase the weight of the glider. However, the increased weight requires a higher airspeed during the approach and a longer landing roll. Once the cross-country phase is completed, the water ballast serves no further purpose. The pilot should jettison the water ballast prior to entering the traffic pattern. Reducing the weight of the glider prior to landing allows the pilot to make a normal approach and landing. The lighter landing weight also reduces the loads that the landing gear of the glider must support.

With the glide ratio data available to the pilot, provided by the charts/graphs located in the GFM/POH for the glider, the pilot can review or plot any specific combination of airspeed and glide ratio/lift to drag ratio (L/D). The resulting plot of L/D with airspeed (angle of attack) shows that glide ratio increases to some maximum at the lowest airspeed. Maximum lift-to-drag ratio (L/D_{MAX})/glide ratio, occurs at one specific airspeed (angle of attack and lift coefficient). If the glider is operated in a steady flight condition, total drag is at a minimum. This is solely based on airspeed. Any airspeed (angle of attack lower or higher) than that for L/D_{MAX}/glide ratio reduces the L/D_{MAX}/glide ratio and consequently increases the total drag for a given glider's lift.

Note that a change in gross weight would require a change in airspeed to support the new weight at the same lift coefficient and angle of attack. This is why the glider GFM/POH has different speeds for flying with or without ballast. The configuration of a glider during flight has a great effect on the L/D. One of the most important of which is the glider's best L/D/glide ratio.

Rate of Climb

Rate of climb for the ground-launched glider primarily depends on the strength of the ground-launching equipment. When ground launching, rates of climb generally are quite rapid, and can exceed 2,000 feet per minute (fpm) if the winch or tow vehicle is very powerful. When aerotowing, rate of climb is determined by the power of the towplane. It is important when selecting a towplane to ensure that it is capable of towing the glider, considering the existing conditions and glider weight.

Self-launching glider rate of climb is determined by design, powerplant output, and glider weight. The rate of climb of self-launching gliders may vary from as low as 200 fpm to as much as 800 fpm or more in others. The pilot should consult the GFM/POH to determine rate of climb under the existing conditions.

Flight Manuals and Placards

The GFM/POH provides the pilot with the necessary performance information to operate the glider safely. A GFM/POH may include the following information:

- Description of glider primary components
- Glider assembly
- Weight and balance data
- Description of glider systems
- Glider performance
- Operating limitations

Placards

Cockpit placards provide the pilot with readily available information that is essential for the safe operation of the glider. All required placards are located in the GFM/POH.

The amount of information that placards must convey to the pilot increases as the complexity of the glider increases. High performance gliders may be equipped with wing flaps, retractable landing gear, a water ballast system, drogue chute for use in the landing approach, and other features that are intended to enhance performance. These gliders may require additional placards. *[Figure 5-10]*

Performance Information

The GFM/POH is the source provided by the manufacturer for glider performance information. In the GFM/POH, glider performance is presented in terms of specific airspeed, such as stall speed, minimum sinking airspeed, best L/D airspeed, maneuvering speed, rough air speed, and the never exceed speed (V_{NE}). Some performance airspeeds apply only to particular types of gliders. Gliders with wing flaps, for instance, have a maximum permitted flaps extended airspeed (V_{FE}).

Manuals for self-launching gliders include performance information about powered operations. These include rate of climb, engine and propeller limitations, fuel consumption, endurance, and cruise.

Glider Polars

In addition, the manufacturer provides information about the rate of sink in terms of airspeed, which is summarized in a graph called a polar curve, or simply a polar. *[Figures 5-11]*

The vertical axis of the polar shows the sink rate in knots (increasing sink downwards), while the horizontal axis shows airspeed in knots. Every type of glider has a characteristic polar derived either from theoretical calculations by the designer or by actual in-flight measurement of the sink rate at different speeds. The polar of each individual glider varies (even from other gliders of the same type) by a few percent depending on relative smoothness of the wing surface, the amount of sealing around control surfaces, and even the number of bugs on the wing's leading edge. The polar forms the basis for speed to fly and final glide tools that will be discussed in Chapter 11, Cross-Country Soaring.

Minimum sink rate is determined from the polar by extending a horizontal line from the top of the polar to the vertical axis. *[Figure 5-12]* In this example, a minimum sink of 1.9 knots occurs at 40 knots. Note that the sink rate increases between minimum sink speed and the stall speed (the left end point of the polar). The best glide speed (best L/D) is found by drawing a tangent to the polar from the origin. The best L/D speed is 50 knots with a sink speed of 2.1 knots. The glide ratio at best

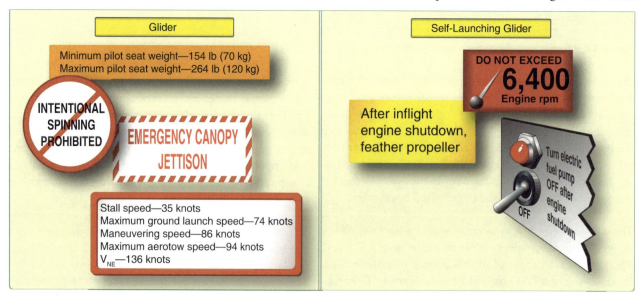

Figure 5-10. *Typical placards for nonmotorized and self-launching gliders.*

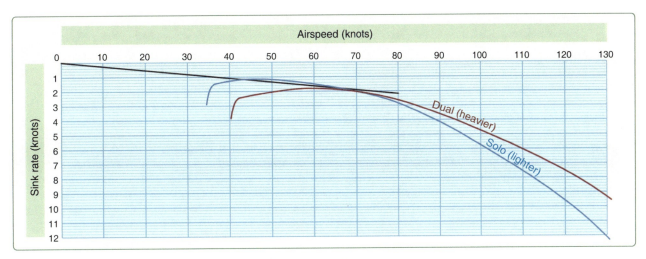

Figure 5-11. *Dual and solo polar performance curves for a two-seat glider.*

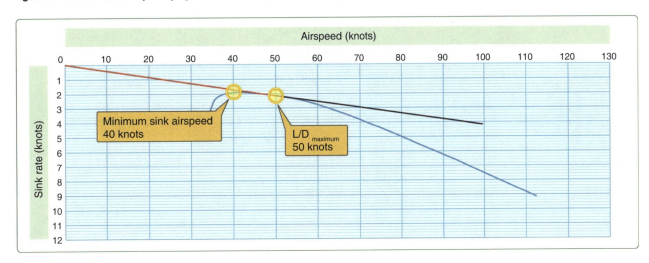

Figure 5-12. *Minimum sink airspeed and maximum L/D speed.*

L/D speed is determined by dividing the best L/D speed by the sink rate at that speed, or 50/2.1, which is approximately 24. Thus, this glider has a best glide ratio in calm air (no lift or sink and no headwind or tailwind) of 24:1 at 50 knots.

The best speed to fly for distance in a headwind is easily determined from the polar. To do this, shift the origin to the right along the horizontal axis by the speed of the headwind and draw a new tangent line to the polar.

From the new tangent point, read the best speed to fly. An example for a 20-knot headwind is shown in *Figure 5-13*. The speed to fly in a 20-knot headwind is found to be 60 knots. By repeating the procedure for different headwinds, it is apparent that flying a faster airspeed as the headwind increases results in the greatest distance over the ground. If this is done for the polar curves from many gliders, a general rule of thumb is found: add half the headwind component to the best L/D for the maximum distance. For tailwinds, shift the origin to the left of the zero mark on the horizontal axis.

The speed to fly in a tailwind lies between minimum sink and best L/D, but is never lower than minimum sink speed.

Sinking air usually exists between thermals, and it is most efficient to fly faster than best L/D in order to spend less time in sinking air. How much faster to fly can be determined by the glider polar, as illustrated in *Figure 5-14* for an air mass that is sinking at 3 knots. The polar graph in this figure has its vertical axis extended upwards. Shift the origin vertically by 3 knots and draw a new tangent to the polar. Then, draw a line vertically to read the best speed to fly. For this glider, the best speed to fly is found to be 60 knots. Note, the variometer shows the total sink of 5 knots (3 knots for sink and 2 knots for the aircraft) as illustrated in the figure.

If the glider is equipped with water ballast, wing flaps, or wingtip extensions, the performance characteristics of the glider is depicted in multiple configurations. *[Figures 5-15, 5-16, and 5-17]* Comparing the polar with and without ballast, it is evident that the minimum sink is higher

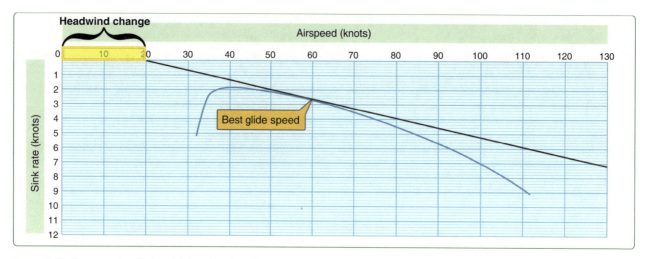

Figure 5-13. *Best speed to fly in a 20-knot headwind.*

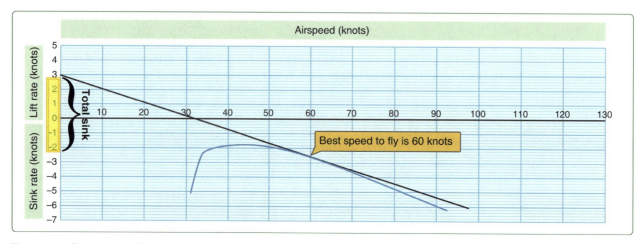

Figure 5-14. *Best speed to fly in sink.*

and occurs at a higher speed. *[Figure 5-15]* With ballast, it would be more difficult to work small, weak thermals. The best glide ratio is the same, but it occurs at a higher speed. In addition, the sink rate at higher speeds is lower with ballast. From the polar, then, ballast should be used under stronger thermal conditions for better speed between thermals. Note that the stall speed is higher with ballast as well.

Flaps with a negative setting as opposed to a 0 degree setting during cruise also reduce the sink rate at higher speeds, as shown in the polar. *[Figure 5-16]* Therefore, when cruising at or above 70 knots, a –8° flap setting would be advantageous for this glider. The polar with flaps set at –8° does not extend to speeds lower than 70 knots since the negative flap setting loses its advantage there.

Wingtip extensions also alter the polar, as shown in *Figure 5-17*. The illustration shows that the additional 3 meters of wingspan is advantageous at all speeds. In some gliders, the low-speed performance is better with the tip extensions, while high-speed performance is slightly diminished by comparison.

Weight and Balance Information

The GFM/POH provides information about the weight and balance of the glider. This information is correct when the glider is new as delivered from the factory. Subsequent maintenance and modifications can alter weight and balance considerably. Changes to the glider that affect weight and balance should be noted in the airframe logbook and on appropriate cockpit placards that might list, for example, "Maximum Fuselage Weight: 460 pounds."

Weight is a major factor in glider construction and operation; it demands respect from all pilots. The pilot should always be aware of proper weight management and the consequences of overloading the glider.

Limitations

Whether the glider is very simple or very complex, designers and manufacturers provide operating limitations to ensure the safety of flight. The VG diagram provides the pilot with information on the design limitations of the glider, such as limiting airspeeds and load factors (L.F. in *Figure 5-18*).

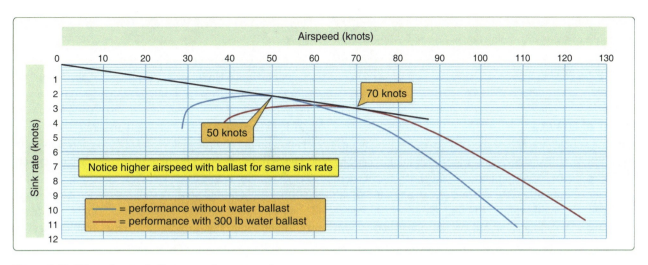

Figure 5-15. *Effect of water ballast on performance polar.*

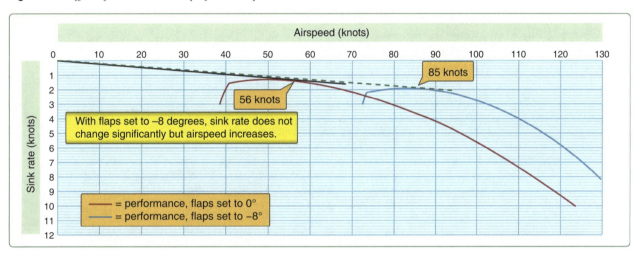

Figure 5-16. *Performance polar with flaps at 0° and –8°.*

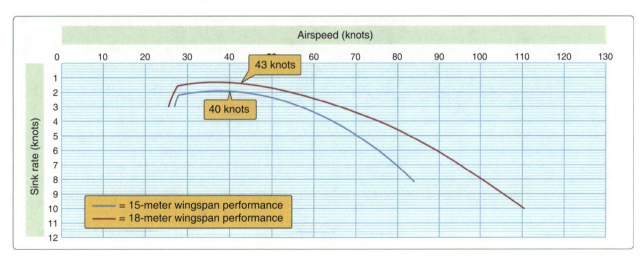

Figure 5-17. *Performance polar with 15-meter and 18-meter wingspan configurations.*

Pilots should become familiar with all the operating limitations of each glider being flown. *Figure 5-18* shows four different possible conditions and the basic flight envelope for a high performance glider.

Weight and Balance
Center of Gravity
Longitudinal balance affects the stability of the longitudinal axis of the glider. To achieve satisfactory pitch attitude handling in a glider, the CG of the properly loaded glider is forward of the center of pressure (CP). When a glider is produced, the manufacturer provides glider CG limitations, which require compliance. These limitations are generally found in the GFM/POH and may also be found in the glider airframe logbook. Addition or removal of equipment, such as radios, batteries, or flight instruments, or airframe repairs can have an effect on the CG position. Aviation maintenance technicians (AMTs) must record any changes in the weight and balance data in the GFM/POH or glider airframe logbook. Weight and balance placards in the cockpit must also be updated.

Problems Associated With CG Forward of Forward Limit
If the CG is within limits, pitch attitude control stays within acceptable limits. However, if the glider is loaded so the CG is forward of the forward limit, handling is compromised. The glider is said to be nose heavy. Nose heaviness makes it difficult to raise the nose on takeoff and considerable back pressure on the control stick is required to control the pitch attitude. Tail stalls occur at airspeeds higher than normal and are followed by a rapid nose-down pitch tendency. Restoring a normal flight attitude during stall recoveries takes longer. The landing flare is more difficult than normal, or perhaps even impossible, due to nose heaviness. Inability to flare could result in a hard nose-first landing.

The following are the most common reasons for CG forward of forward limit:

- Pilot weight exceeds the maximum permitted pilot weight.
- Seat or nose ballast weights are installed but are not required due to the weight of the pilot.

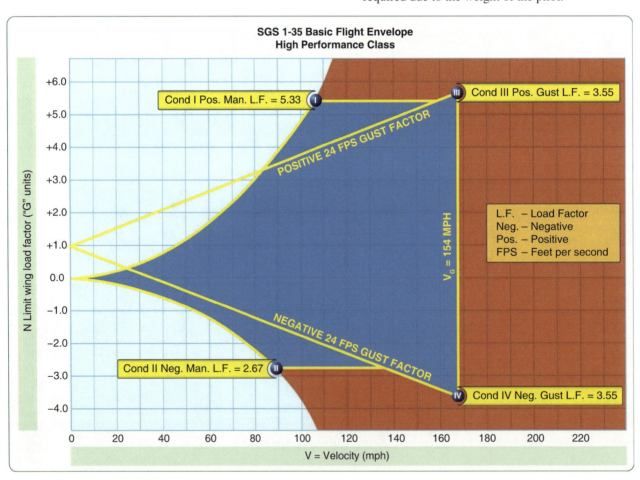

Figure 5-18. *Typical example of basic flight envelope for a high-performance glider.*

Problems Associated With CG Aft of Aft Limit

If the glider is loaded so the CG location is behind the aft limit, handling is compromised. The glider is said to be tail heavy. Tail heaviness can make pitch control of the glider difficult or even impossible.

The fundamental problem with a CG aft of the aft limit is the designed function of the horizontal stabilizer and elevator. Fixed wing aircraft are generally designed so that the horizontal stabilizer and elevator provide a down force to counter the slightly nose forward CG such that the aircraft tend to resume a level pitch attitude after an upset about the lateral axis. As the airspeed changes, the pilot changes the trim or trims the aircraft so the down force exactly balances the forward CG within limits. Should the aircraft be upset and the nose pitches upward, the resultant slower airspeed results in less down force produced by the horizontal stabilizer and elevator. This decreased down force lets the nose lower so the airspeed retains to the pre-upset value. This is called positive stability. Conversely, if the upset places the aircraft in a nose down attitude, the increased airspeed will increase the down force and raise the nose to the pre-upset balanced condition. However, if the control surface is in a stalled condition, this stabilizing action will not begin until the control surface regains un-stalled airflow and begins producing down force again.

The following are the most common reasons for flight with CG located behind permissible limits:

- Pilot weight is less than the specified minimum pilot seat weight and trim ballast weights necessary for the lightweight pilot are not installed in the glider prior to flight.

- Tailwheel dolly is still attached, far aft on the tailboom of the glider.

- Foreign matter or debris (water, ice, mud, sand, and nests) has accumulated in the aft fuselage of the glider and was not discovered and removed prior to flight.

- A heavy, non-approved tailwheel or tail skid was installed on the aft tail boom of the glider.

Sample Weight and Balance Problems

Some glider manufacturers provide weight and balance information in a graphic presentation. A well designed graph provides a convenient way to determine whether the glider is within weight and balance limitations.

In *Figure 5-19*, the chart indicates that the minimum weight for the front seat pilot is 125 pounds, and that the maximum is 250 pounds. It also indicates that the maximum rear seat pilot weight is 225 pounds. If each pilot weighs 150 pounds, the intersection of pilot weights falls within the envelope;

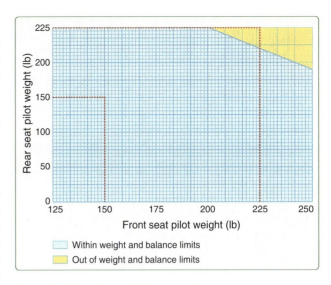

Figure 5-19. *Weight and balance envelope.*

the glider load is within the envelope and is safe for flight. If each pilot weighs 225 pounds, the rear seat maximum load is exceeded, and the glider load is outside the envelope and unsafe for flight.

The CG position can also be determined by calculation using the following formulas:

- Weight × Arm = Moment
- Total Moment ÷ Total Weight = CG Position (in inches aft of the reference datum)

The computational method involves the application of basic math functions. The following is an example of the computational method.

Given:

Maximum gross weight.....................1,100 lb

Empty weight......................................600 lb

CG range....................................14.8–18.6 in

Front seat occupant..............................180 lb

Rear seat occupant..............................200 lb

To determine the loaded weight and CG, follow these steps.

1. List the empty weight of the glider and the weight of the occupants.

2. Enter the moment for each item listed. Remember, weight × arm = moment. To simplify calculations, the moments may be divided by 100.

3. Total the weight and moments.

4. To determine the CG, divide the moments by the weight.

NOTE: The weight and balance records for a particular glider provide the empty weight and moment, as well as the information on the arm distance. *[Figure 5-20]*

Item	Weight (pounds)	Arm (inches)	Moment (inch·pounds)
Empty weight	600	+20	12,000
Front seat pilot	180	+30	+5,400
Rear seat pilot	200	−5	−1,000
	980 total weight	+16.73	+16,400 total moment

Figure 5-20. *Weight and balance: front and rear seat pilot weights and moments.*

In *Figure 5-20*, the weight of each pilot has been entered into the correct block in the table. For the front seat pilot, multiplying 180 pounds by +30 inches yields a moment of +5,400 inch·pounds. For the rear seat pilot, multiplying 200 pounds by −5 inches yields a moment of −1,000 inch·pounds. The next step is to find the sum of all weights (980 pounds) and record it. Then, find the sum of all moments (+16,400 inch·pounds) and record it. Now, find the arm (the CG position) of the loaded glider. Divide the total moment by the total weight to discover the CG of the loaded aircraft glider in inches from the datum:

+16,400 inch·pounds ÷ 980 pounds = +16.73 inches

The final step is to determine whether total weight and CG location values are within acceptable limits. The GFM/POH lists the maximum gross weight as 1,100 pounds. The operating weight of 980 pounds is less than the 1,100 pounds maximum gross weight. The GFM/POH lists the approved CG range as between +14.80 inches and +18.60 inches from the datum. The operating CG is +16.73 inches from the datum and is within these limits. The weight and balance are within operating limits.

Ballast

Ballast is nonstructural weight that is added to a glider. In soaring, ballast weight is used for two purposes. Trim ballast is used to adjust the location of the CG of the glider so handling characteristics remain within acceptable limits. Performance ballast is loaded into the glider to improve high-speed cruise performance.

Removable trim ballast weights are usually made of metal and are bolted into a ballast receptacle incorporated in the glider structure. The manufacturer generally provides an attachment point well forward in the glider cabin for trim ballast weights. These weights are designed to compensate for a front seat pilot who weighs less than the minimum permissible front seat pilot weight. The ballast weight mounted well forward in the glider cabin helps place the CG within permissible limits, which allows the maximum shift in CG with the minimum addition of weight.

Some trim ballast weights are in the form of seat cushions, with sand or lead shot sewn into the unit to provide additional weight. This type of ballast, which is installed under the pilot's seat cushion, is inferior to bolted-in ballast because seat cushions tend to shift position. Seat cushion ballast should never be used during acrobatic or inverted flight.

Sometimes trim ballast is water placed in a tail tank in the vertical fin of the fuselage. The purpose of the fin trim ballast tank is to adjust CG location after water is added to, or drained from, the main wing ballast tanks. Unless the main wing ballast tanks are precisely centered on the CG of the loaded aircraft glider, CG location shifts when water is added to the main ballast tanks. CG location shifts again when water is dumped from the main ballast tanks. Adjusting the amount of water in the fin tank compensates for CG shifts resulting from changes in the amount of water ballast carried in the main wing ballast tanks. Water weighs 8.35 pounds per gallon. Because the tail tank is located far aft, it does not take much water to have a considerable effect on CG location. For this reason, tail tanks do not need to contain a large volume of water. Tail tank maximum water capacity is generally less than two gallons of water.

Although some older gliders employed bags of sand or bolted-in lead weights as performance ballast, water is used most commonly to enhance high-speed performance in modern sailplanes. Increasing the operating weight of the glider increases the optimum speed to fly during wings-level cruising flight. The resulting higher groundspeed provides a very desirable advantage in cross-country soaring and in sailplane racing.

Water ballast tanks are located in the main wing panels. Clean water is added through fill ports in the top of each wing. In most gliders, the water tanks or bags can be partially or completely filled, depending on the pilot's choice of operating weight. After water is added, the filler caps are replaced to prevent water from sloshing out of the filler holes.

Drain valves are fitted to the bottom of each tank. The valves are controlled from inside the cockpit. The tanks can be fully or partially drained while the glider is on the ground to reduce the weight of the glider prior to launch, if the pilot so desires. The ballast tanks also can be partially or completely drained in flight—a process called dumping ballast. The long streaks of white spray behind a speeding airborne glider are dramatic evidence that the glider pilot is dumping water ballast, most likely to lighten the glider prior to landing. The filler caps are vented to allow air to enter the tanks to replace the volume of water draining from the tanks. It is important to ensure that the vents are working properly to prevent wing damage when water ballast is drained or jettisoned. *[Figures 5-21 and 5-22]*

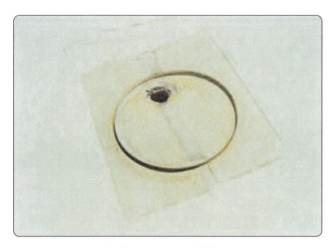

Figure 5-21. *Water ballast tank vented filler cap.*

It is important to check the drain valves for correct operation prior to flight. Water ballast should drain from each wing tank at the same rate. Unequal draining leads to a wing-heavy condition that makes in-flight handling, as well as landings, more difficult. If the wing-heavy condition is extreme, it is possible the pilot will lose control of the glider.

Ballast drains should also be checked to ensure that water ballast drains properly into the airstream, rather than leaking into the fuselage and pooling in the bottom of the fuselage. Water that is trapped in the fuselage may flow through or over bulkheads, causing dislocation of the CG of the glider. This CG dislocation can lead to loss of control of the glider.

The flight manual provides guidance regarding the length of time it takes for the ballast tanks to drain completely. For modern gliders, it takes about 3 to 5 minutes to drain a full tank. When landing is imminent, dump ballast early enough to give the ballast drains sufficient time to empty the tanks.

Use of water ballast when ambient temperatures are low can result in water freezing the drain valve. If the drain valve freezes, dumping ballast is difficult or impossible. If water in the wings is allowed to freeze, serious wing damage is likely to occur. Damage occurs because the volume of water expands during the freezing process. The resulting increased volume can deform ribs and other wing structures or cause glue bonds to delaminate. When weather or flight conditions are very cold, do not use water ballast unless antifreeze has been added to the water. Prior to using an antifreeze solution, consult the GFM to ensure that antifreeze compounds are approved for use in the glider.

A glider carrying large amounts of water ballast has noticeably different handling characteristics than the same glider without water ballast. Water ballast:

- Reduces the rate of acceleration of the glider at the beginning of the launch due to the increased glider weight.
- Increases the length of ground roll prior to glider liftoff.
- Increases stall speed.
- Reduces aileron control during the takeoff roll, increasing the chance of uncontrolled wing drop and resultant ground loop.
- Reduces rate of climb during climb-out.
- Reduces aileron response during free flight. The addition of large amounts of water increases lateral stability substantially. This makes quick banking maneuvers difficult or impossible to perform.

Water ballast is routinely dumped before landing to reduce the weight of the glider. Dumping ballast:

- Decreases stall speed.
- Decreases the optimum airspeed for the landing approach.
- Shortens landing roll.

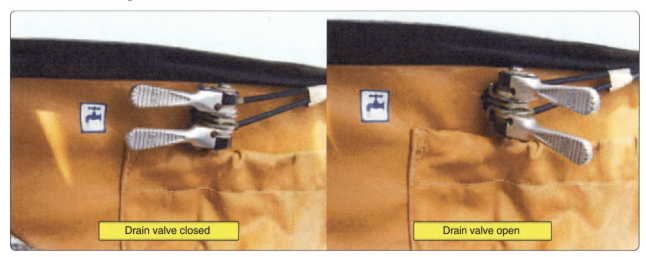

Figure 5-22. *Water ballast drain valve handles.*

- Reduces the load that glider structures must support during landing and rollout.

The performance advantage of water ballast during strong soaring conditions is considerable. However, there is a down side. The pilot should be aware that water ballast degrades takeoff performance, climb rate, and low-speed handling. Before committing to a launch with water ballast aboard, the pilot should review operating limitations to ensure that safety of flight is not compromised.

Chapter 6
Preflight and Ground Operations

Introduction

Operating a glider requires meticulous assembly and preflight. Proper assembly techniques, followed by a close inspection of the glider using checklists contained in the Glider Flight Manual/Pilot's Operating Handbook (GFM/POH), are essential for flight safety. In order to ensure correct and safe procedures for assembly of a glider, students and pilots unfamiliar with glider assembly should seek instruction from a knowledgeable glider flight instructor or certificated private or higher glider pilot. Safely launching a glider requires careful inspection, appropriate use of checklists, and quality teamwork. Launch procedures should be carried out systematically and consistently for each flight.

- A) Altimeter set to correct elevation.
- B) Seat belts and shoulder harnesses fastened and tightened.
- C) Controls checked for full and free movement.
- C) Cable or towrope properly connected to the correct hook.
- C) Canopy closed, locked, and checked.
- D) Dive brakes closed and locked.
- D) Direction of wind checked and emergency plan reviewed.

Assembly and Storage Techniques

The assembly of a glider to include the installation of glider wings and tail surfaces is classified as operations functions not preventative maintenance. This information can be found in Amendment 43-27, published in 52 FR 17276, May 6, 1987 which is an amendment to 14 CFR part 43. Prior to assembling the glider, the pilot must check the required documentation that must be on board the glider for flight as required by Title 14 of the Code of Federal regulations (14 CFR) parts 21 and 91. Required documentation includes:

- Airworthiness certificate
- Registration
- Required placards
- GFM/POH

While preparing to assemble a glider, consider the following elements: location, number of crewmembers, tools and parts necessary, and checklists that detail the appropriate assembly procedures. Glider pilots should also develop and follow a procedure, or procedures, to deal with distractions that may occur during the glider assembly. Something as simple as rechecking the previous two steps and then continuing the checklist steps might be sufficient. The GFM/POH should contain checklists for assembling and preflighting a glider. If not, develop one and follow it every flight. Haphazard assembly and preflight procedures can lead to unsafe conditions.

Before assembling a glider, ensure that the glider trailer is secured with the wheel brake on and the wheels chocked. Adjust the leveling of the trailer as needed according to the GFM/POH so the glider can be removed without damaging items, such as the antenna and other glider components (e.g., wings, tips, horizontal elevator). If using a single rigging device, ensure that the wing holder is adjusted so the wing does not slide out of the holder and become damaged by striking or falling to the ground.

Find a location that shields the project from the elements and offers enough room for completion. Wind is an important factor to consider during an outdoor assembly. Each wing is an airfoil whether or not it is connected to the fuselage; even a gentle breeze is enough to produce lift on the wings, making them cumbersome or impossible to handle. If assembling the glider in a spot unshielded from the wind, great care must still be taken when handling the wings.

When performing the assembly inside a hangar, ensure there is enough room to maneuver the glider's components throughout the process. Also, consider the length of time anticipated to complete the entire procedure, and choose an area that allows complete undisturbed assembly. Moving the glider during assembly may cause parts or tools to be misplaced.

Wing stands or a wing dolly, the proper tools, wing tape, and lubricants should be on hand when assembling the glider. *[Figure 6-1]* To stay organized, use a written assembly checklist, and keep an inventory of parts and tools. Some organizations track tools and components by placing all of the necessary components and hardware used with necessary tools on a piece of canvas or material and outlining each tool. This facilitates a quick inventory before assembly and afterwards. Once glider assembly is complete, pilots should account for all parts and tools used during assembly. Objects inadvertently misplaced in the glider could become jammed in the flight controls, making control difficult, if not impossible. In addition, when taping the wing roots, turtle deck (cover where the flight controls are attached) elevator and other areas, ensure the tape is placed properly and is secure. If the seal tape comes off in flight, the tape may cause control issues with the glider.

Figure 6-1. *Wing stands and wing dollies are used as support when assembling the glider.*

Depending on the type of glider, two or more people may be required for assembly. It is important for everyone involved to maintain focus throughout the assembly process to avoid missed steps. Outside disturbances should also be avoided. Once the assembly is finished, a thorough inspection of all attach points ensures that bolts and pins were installed and secured properly. Do not use a hammer to tap wing bolts or other glider components in their place. The main wing pins should slide into the socket with minimum application of force. If the wing bolts require such force, a mechanic should be retained to ensure that the main wing spar is not bent or damaged.

On most gliders, the wing can be completely removed from the fuselage area. On some motor gliders, the wing can be folded up for ease of storage. *[Figures 6-2]* This allows the glider to be placed in a normal size hangar. Hangars are usually between 35 and 45 feet in width. Because most glider wings are a minimum of 40 feet (12 meters) total length, a larger hangar is usually desirable.

Once the gliders wings have been folded, the glider can easily be moved in and around the hangar area. On some gliders, operators may elect to leave the wings attached for quick access. This is usually the practice at larger glider operations. These gliders can be fitted or rolled onto a small dolly that has castering wheels. The glider's main wheel fits into a slot, and the entire glider can be pivoted and moved to accommodate other gliders.

Once the glider has been completely assembled, the pilot then inspects all critical areas to ensure all flight controls are attached. The pilot should refer to a written checklist either provided by the manufacturer or a commercial source that prints glider checklists.

This final check is very critical and usually takes time to complete. Pilots should not be interrupted when they are attempting to check the glider. The Soaring Society of America (SSA) and one of its affiliates, the Soaring Safety Foundation (SSF), have developed a checklist for preparing a glider, which is Safety Advisory 00-1, Glider Critical Assembly Procedures, and can be found in Appendix A of this handbook.

Many manufacturers provide a critical assembly checklist (CAC) to be completed after assembly, which is the preferred method of ensuring a proper assembly has been completed. When provided by the manufacturer, it is mandatory. A positive control check (PCC) is not a CAC, but an additional means of verification. If a CAC is provided, it must be used as is any other checklist a manufacturer provides. A PCC is not regulatory, but it is a good idea whether or not you just completed the required CAC.

Trailering

Specially designed trailers are used to transport, store, and retrieve gliders. *[Figure 6-3]* The components of the glider should fit snugly without being forced, be guarded against chafing, and be well secured within the trailer. Once the loading is completed, take a short drive, stop, and check for rubbing or chafing of components. Ensure that any items carried inside the trailer are secure from movement. For example, jacks, ramps, wing stands, and ground dollies must be secured so that these items do not damage the glider.

Figure 6-3. *Components of a glider stored and transported in a trailer.*

Figure 6-2. *The wings of the glider can be folded in order to conveniently store the glider.*

Prior to taking the trailer on the road, complete a thorough inspection. Ensure:

- Proper inflation of and adequate tread on trailer tires,
- Trailer tires are rated for Special Trailer (ST) duty, which are rated only to 65 miles per hour (mph) towing speed. The maximum speed of 65 mph can be exceeded safely if the air pressure is increased by 10 psi for every 10 mph over 65 that it is pulled and the maximum load is decreased 10 percent for every 10 mph over 65 mph of towing speed,
- Operation of all lights,
- Free movement and lubrication of hitch,
- Appropriate rating of vehicle attachment for the weight of the trailer,
- Proper operation of vehicle and trailer brakes,
- Adequate wheel bearing lubrication, and
- Proper tow vehicle mirror adjustment.

When using a trailer, there are other precautions to note. First, avoid towing with too much or too little tongue weight as either causes the trailer to fishtail at certain speeds, possibly rendering it uncontrollable. Towing a long glider trailer requires good driving skills and a good sense of road and weather conditions. Take care in heavy crosswinds because a long trailer can be affected by windy conditions. Also, take care when unloading the glider to avoid damage. Practice and planning are key to a successful operation.

Tiedown and Securing

Anytime the glider is left unattended, it should be tied down with the canopy closed and latched. When selecting a tiedown location, choose a spot that faces into the wind if possible. Permanent tiedowns are often equipped with straps, ropes, or chains for the wings and tail. Having the proper tie down kit is recommended for a cross-country trip. Check tiedown conditions before using to ensure the safety of the glider. When tying down on airports shared by powered aircraft, propeller wash can cause damage to an improperly secured glider.

If strong winds are expected, tie the spoilers open with seat belts, or place a padded stand under the tail to reduce the angle of attack of the wings. This reduces the pull of the glider against the tiedowns. When securing the glider outside for an extended period of time, install gust locks on the control surfaces to prevent them from banging against their stops in the wind. Cover the pitot tube and the total energy probe to prevent spiders, wasps, and other insects or debris from getting inside. *[Figure 6-4]*

Figure 6-4. *Protecting the pitot tube and total energy probe.*

Always use a cover to protect the glider canopy. It can be damaged by blowing dust and sand or scratched by apparel, such as watches or belt buckles. A cover protects the canopy from damage while shielding the interior of the cockpit from ultraviolet (UV) rays. *[Figure 6-5]*

Figure 6-5. *Protecting the canopy.*

Water Ballast

When transporting a glider or parking the glider for long periods of time, especially overnight the water ballast should be emptied due to the danger of freezing. This is usually done while in flight before landing. When de-rigging, the water ballast tanks will empty themselves through the wing root connecting pipes. If the glider has to be towed for a long way it is best to empty the water tanks. If that is not an option, ensure that antifreeze is added to prevent freezing when traveling in cold temperatures.

Ground Handling

Moving a glider on the ground requires special handling procedures, especially during high winds. Normally, gliders are pushed or pulled by hand or towed with a vehicle. When moving a glider, ensure that all appropriate personnel have been briefed on procedures and signals.

When using a vehicle to tow a glider, use a towline that is more than half the wingspan of the glider. If one wingtip stops moving for any reason, this towline length prevents the glider from pivoting and striking the tow vehicle with the opposite wingtip. Full wingspan length is desirable; however, half the wingspan plus 10 feet provides safe operation. Ensure that the glider canopy is always closed if no one is around the glider. This prevents the wind, or turbulence from a taxiing towplane, to cause the canopy to close abruptly, which could damage the canopy frame or even crack the canopy glass.

When starting, slowly take up slack in the line with the vehicle to prevent sudden jerking of the glider. The towing speed should be no faster than a brisk walk. When towing a glider, always use at least one wing walker. The wing walker and the driver of the tow vehicle function as a team, alert for obstacles, wind, and any other factor that may affect the safety of the glider. The driver should always stay alert for any signals from the wing walkers. *[Figure 6-6]*

If it is necessary to move the glider during high winds, use two or more crewmembers placed at the wingtips and tail. Also, have a pilot in the cockpit, with the spoilers deployed, holding the controls appropriately to reduce lift on the glider. Strong winds and gusts can cause damage to the glider during ground handling, so exercise care during these conditions.

Another method of towing uses specially designed towing gear similar to a trailer tow bar that attaches directly to a vehicle towing a trailer. The tow bar makes guiding the glider much easier and allows the wing walkers to concentrate on ensuring wingtip clearances. *[Figure 6-7]*

Launch Equipment Inspection

Prior to making a flight, it is important to inspect the condition of the towline/towrope. The glider pilot is primarily responsible for inspection and selection of the proper towrope. However, the tow pilot has a responsibility to ensure that the towrope selection meets the criteria stated in 14 CFR part 91 and is acceptable for use. This inspection is the responsibility of the tow pilot. The towline should be free from excess wear; all strands should be intact, and the line should be free from knots. Towropes should be inspected prior to every flight. Consideration should be given in replacing the towrope after a period of time due to usage and ultraviolet (UV) exposure from being in the sun and exposed to the elements. *[Figure 6-8]* 14 CFR part 91, section 91.309, requires that the strength of the towline be within a range of 80 to 200 percent of the maximum certificated weight of the glider. If the towrope is more than twice the maximum strength, a safety link is required between the tow rope and glider rated at not less than 80 percent of the maximum certified operating weight of the glider but not greater than twice the operating weight. Also, a safety link must be installed between the towing aircraft and towrope with breaking strength greater than the glider safety link, but no more than 25 percent greater, and not greater than twice the maximum certificated weight of the glider. *Figure 6-9* shows the strength of some ropes typically used.

Figure 6-6. *Positioning the glider for the tow vehicle.*

Figure 6-7. *A wing dolly (left) ready for attachment and a tail dolly (right) being used for glider transport.*

6-5

Figure 6-8. *Inspecting the towline.*

Diameter	Nylon	Dacron	Polyethylene Hollow braid	Polypropylene Monofilament	Polypropylene Multifilament
3/16"	960	720	700	800	870
1/4"	1,500	1,150	1,200	1,300	1,200
5/16"	2,400	1,750	1,750	1,900	2,050

Figure 6-9. *Rope strengths.*

A knot in the towline reduces its strength by up to 50 percent, and causes a high spot in the rope that is more susceptible to wear. Pay particular attention to the ring area to which the glider attaches because this is also a high-wear area.

The safety link is constructed of towline with a towring on one end and the other end spliced into a loop. The weak link at the glider attach end of the towline must be 80 to 200 percent of the maximum certificated operating weight of the glider. The safety link at the towplane attach end must be of greater strength than the safety link at the glider attach end of the towline, but not more than 25 percent greater, nor greater than 200 percent of the maximum certificated weight of the glider. Towlines and weak links are assembled using a towring that is appropriate for the operation. Lightweight balls are attached to the towline to help protect the towline, prevent line rash, and prevents the line from whipping. *[Figure 6-10]*

The tow hooks on both the glider and the towplane need to be inspected. The two most common types of tow hook are an over-the-top design, such as a Schweizer hook, or a grasping style, such as a Tost hook. Any tow hook must be freely operating, and free from damage. *[Figures 6-11 and 6-12]*

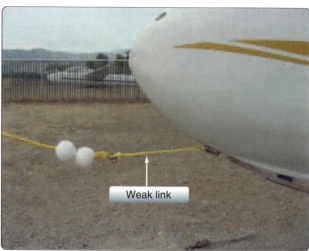

Figure 6-10. *The weak link.*

Figure 6-11. *Schweizer-type tow hook.*

Figure 6-12. *Tost hook.*

Glider Preflight Inspection

A thorough inspection of the glider should be accomplished before launch. A preflight checklist for a glider should be in the GFM/POH. If not, develop a checklist using the guidelines contained in *Figure 6-13.*

- Begin by assessing the overall condition of the fiberglass or fabric.
- Be alert for signs of damage or excessive wear.
- Ensure that the canopy is clean and free from damage.
- Verify the interior wing and control connections are safe and secure.
- If a battery is used, ensure that it is charged and safely fastened in the proper spot.
- Ensure that seat harnesses are free from excessive wear.
- Buckle and tighten any harness that will not be used to prevent it from inadvertently interfering with controls.
- Test the tow hook to ensure it is operating correctly.
- Inspect top, bottom, and leading edge of wings, ensuring they are free from excess dirt, bugs, and damage.
- Inspect spoilers/dive brakes for mechanical damage. They should be clear of obstructions.
- Inspect the wingtip and wingtip skid or wheel for general condition.
- Inspect ailerons for freedom of movement, the condition of hinges and connections, and the condition of the gap seal.
- Check the condition of flaps for freedom from damage and for appropriate range of motion.
- Inspect the general condition of the empennage.
- Check static ports, pitot tube, and total energy probe to ensure they are free from obstruction.
- Check top, bottom, and leading edge of tailplane for of bugs, dirt, and damage.
- Check the landing gear for signs of damage or excessive wear. The brake pads should be checked if they are visible; otherwise, the brakes can be checked by pulling the glider forward and applying the brakes. Note that the landing gear is frequently a problem area for gliders used in training.
- Check elevator and trim tab for condition of connections, freedom of movement, and condition of gap seal.
- Check rudder freedom of movement and condition of connections.

Figure 6-13. *A glider preflight inspection checklist.*

Prelaunch Checklist

Adjustments to the pilot or passenger seats, as well as adjustable controls, such as rudder pedals, should be made prior to buckling the seat belt and shoulder harness. Caution should be exercised to avoid crimping or clamping the oxygen supply. At this point, especially if the glider has just been assembled, it is appropriate to do a positive control check with the help of one crewmember. While the pilot moves the control stick, the crewmember alternately holds each aileron and the elevator to provide resistance. This also applies to the spoilers and flaps, and ensures the control connections are correct and secure. If the stick moves freely while the control surfaces are being restricted, the connections are not secure, and the glider is not airworthy. *[Figure 6-14]*

If the GFM/POH does not provide a specific prelaunch checklist, then some good generic checklists are CB SWIFT CBE and ABCCCDD, which are explained in *Figure 6-15*. Regardless of which checklist you elect to use, have a plan. Stay with that checklist and ensure that each step is being carefully followed.

Glider Care

Depending on the type of glider, different cleaning methods should be employed. After all flights, wipe down the glider with a soft cloth or a wet chamois. This removes any debris

Figure 6-14. *Positive control check of spoilers.*

or bugs. This should be done in a timely manner because waiting too long allows bugs to dry making removal difficult.

Training gliders made of fabric should be cleaned with spray-on and wash-off products. Avoid using large amounts of water as the water may penetrate cracks and holes, especially on earlier wooded or vintage gliders, which damages and reduces the life of the fabric or wood. Moisture damages any glider if allowed to stay wet. On metal gliders, a low-pressure hose and mild detergent is used for cleaning. For

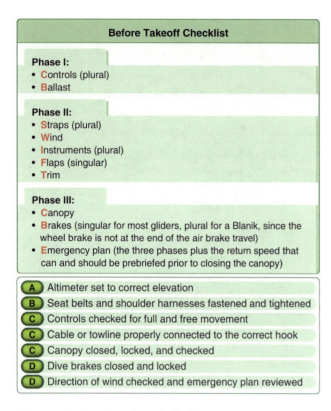

Figure 6-15. *Generic prelaunch checklists.*

high performance fiberglass gliders, use a special spray or cleaning paste. Consult the GFH/POH, or a glider supply store, for proper materials based on the type of glider. Care must be taken when cleaning high performance and fiberglass gliders. The use of buffers should be avoided, as the buffer may burn the fiberglass if not done in a proper manner.

After cleaning, a coat of wax or a sealer is usually applied to fabric, metal, and fiberglass gliders. When applying wax to fiberglass gliders, it is recommended to use a silicon-free wax. Silicon adheres to the pores in the fiberglass and makes any type of future repairs extremely difficult. After applying any wax, use a clean, soft cloth to wipe off excess wax and buff the area by hand. For the cleaning of the canopy, care must be taken and only recommended cleaners for the specific type of canopy should be used.

Minor repairs on fiberglass gliders can be performed by the owner/pilot. Consult a fiberglass expert prior to making any minor repair, such as a scratch or chip. Always use approved parts and materials when conducting these repairs. All certifications of gliders, either standard or experimental, should be repaired in accordance with the manufacturer's recommended procedures and 14 CFR part 43. Pilots should always refer to the specific GFM/POH for any additional care and cleaning of the glider.

Preventive Maintenance

Preventive maintenance is limited to the following work, provided it does not involve complex assembly operations. For more information on preventive maintenance, refer to Appendix A to Part 43, Major Alterations, Major Repairs, and Preventive Maintenance.

- Removing, installing, and repairing of landing gear tires
- Replacing elastic shock absorber cords on landing gear
- Servicing landing gear shock struts by adding oil, air, or both
- Servicing landing gear wheel bearings, such as cleaning and greasing
- Replacing defective safety wiring or cotter keys
- Lubricating cover plates, cowlings, fairings, etc., that do not require disassembly other than removal of nonstructural items
- Making simple fabric patches not requiring rib stitching or the removal of structural parts or control surfaces
- Replenishing hydraulic fluid in the hydraulic reservoir
- Refinishing decorative coating of fuselage, wings, tail group surfaces (excluding balanced control surfaces), fairings, cowlings, landing gear, cockpit interior when removal or disassembly of any primary structure or operating system is not required
- Applying preservative or protective material to components for which no disassembly of any primary structure or operating system is involved and on which such coating is not prohibited or is not contrary to good practices
- Repairing upholstery and decorative furnishings of the cockpit when the repairing does not require disassembly of any primary structure or operating system or interfere with an operating system or affect the primary structure of the aircraft
- Making small, simple repairs to fairings, nonstructural cover plates, cowlings, and small patches and reinforcements that do not change the contour enough to interfere with proper air flow
- Replacing side windows where that work does not interfere with the structure or any operating system, such as controls, electrical equipment, etc.
- Replacing safety belts
- Replacing seats or seat parts with replacement parts approved for the aircraft not involving disassembly of any primary structure or operating system

- Troubleshooting and repairing broken circuits in landing light wiring circuits
- Replacing bulbs, reflectors, and lenses of position and landing lights
- Replacing wheels for which no weight and balance computation is involved
- Replacing any cowling not requiring removal of the propeller or disconnection of flight controls
- Replacing or cleaning spark plugs and setting spark plug gap clearance
- Replacing any hose connection, except hydraulic connections
- Replacing prefabricated fuel lines
- Cleaning or replacing fuel and oil strainers or filter elements
- Replacing and servicing batteries
- Replacing or adjusting nonstructural standard fasteners incidental to operations
- Removing, checking, and replacing magnetic chip detectors

Chapter 7
Launch and Recovery Procedures and Flight Maneuvers

Introduction

In the early days of soaring, gliders were launched from the top of a hill into the wind by means of bungee cord, a stretchable cord made of rubber bands. The tail of the glider was held back or tied down, and the bungee was attached at its midpoint to a hook on the nose of the glider. Then, a group of people took each end and, when the signals were given, they walked, then ran with the bungee as hard as they could. When the tension became quite high, the tail tie-down was severed, or released, and the glider shot ahead as though it had been launched from a slingshot.

As gliders got heavier and better, pilots began to look for improved ways to launch. It was not long before enthusiasts began to use cars to pull shock cords and then to pull the gliders by the long wire or rope. Once again, improvements in technology and equipment were introduced and powered winches and airplane towing became the preferred method of launching gliders.

This chapter discusses several glider launch techniques and procedures along with takeoff procedures, traffic patterns, flight maneuvers, and landing and recovery procedures. Additional information may be found at the Soaring Society of America (SSA) website at www.ssa.org and the Soaring Safety Foundation website at www.soaringsafety.org.

Aerotow Takeoff Procedures
Signals
Launching a nonpowered glider requires the use of visual signals for communication and coordination between the glider, towing aircraft, and the ground crew. Ground launching signals consist of prelaunch signals and in-flight signals.

Prelaunch Signals
Aerotow prelaunch signals facilitate communication between pilots and launch crewmembers/wing runners preparing for the launch. These signals are shown in *Figure 7-1*.

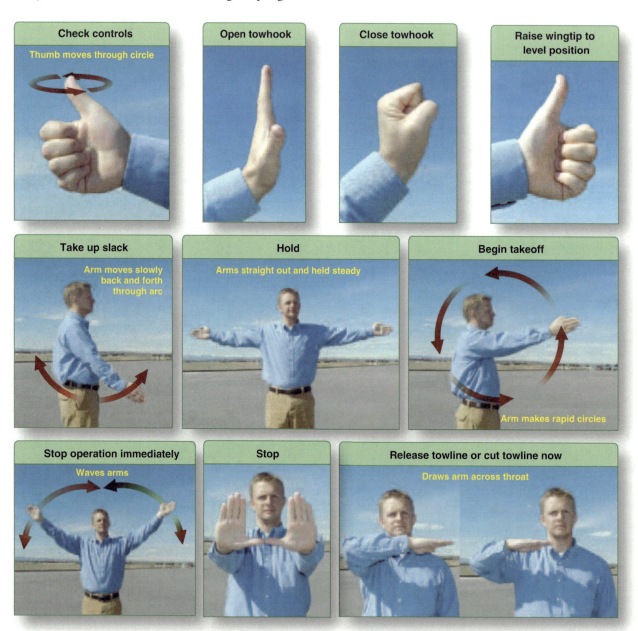

Figure 7-1. *Aerotow prelaunch signals.*

Inflight Signals

Visual signals allow the tow pilot and the glider pilot to communicate with each other. The signals are divided into two types: those from the tow pilot to the glider pilot and signals from the glider pilot to the tow pilot. These signals are shown in *Figure 7-2*.

Takeoff Procedures and Techniques

Takeoff procedures for gliders require close coordination between launch crewmembers, wing runners, and pilots. Both the glider pilot and tow pilot must be familiar with the appropriate tow procedures. The assisted takeoff includes a wing runner that holds the wing in a level position. An unassisted takeoff does not include a wing runner or other ground crew. The unassisted launch requires good procedures and should only be attempted by highly experienced glider and tow pilots. It is recommended that all takeoffs include a ground crewmember for traffic scanning and general assistance during the takeoff.

It is very important to never connect a glider to a towplane or towline unless the pilot is aboard and ready for flight. If the pilot exits the glider for any reason, the towline should be released and disconnected because some hitches like a Tost hitch require slight pressure for the tow ring to actually move from the jaws. If no tension is applied, the ring stays in place and connected when the jaws close.

Normal takeoffs are made into the wind. Prior to takeoff, the tow pilot and glider pilot must reach an agreement on the plan for the aerotow. The glider pilot should ensure that the launch crewmember is aware of safety procedures concerning the tow. Some of these items would be proper runway and pattern clearing procedures and glider configuration checks (spoilers closed, tailwheel dolly removed, canopy secured).

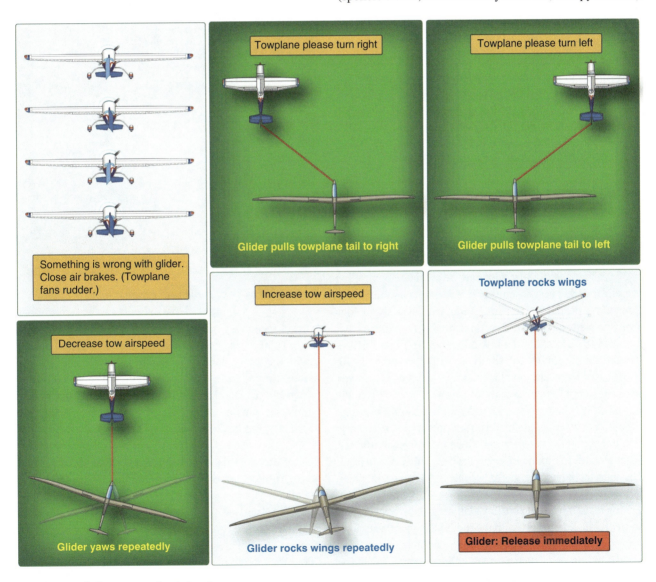

Figure 7-2. *Inflight aerotow visual signals.*

When the required checklists have been completed and both the glider and towplane are ready for takeoff, the glider pilot signals the launch crewmember/wing runner to hook the towline to the glider.

Normal Assisted Takeoff

The towrope hookup should be done deliberately and correctly, and the release mechanism should be checked for proper operation. The launch crewmember/wing runner applies tension to the towline and signals the glider pilot to activate the release. The launch crewmember should verify that the release works properly and signal the glider pilot. When the towline is hooked up to the glider again, the launch crewmember repositions to the wing that is down. When the glider pilot signals "ready for takeoff," the launch crewmember/wing runner clears both the takeoff and landing area, and then signals the tow pilot to "take up slack" in the towline. Once the slack is out of the towline, the launch crewmember verifies that the glider pilot is ready for takeoff; this may include a "thumbs up" by the glider pilot. The crewmember/wing runner does a final traffic pattern check, and then raises the wings to a level position. With the wings raised, the crewmember/wing runner then signals the tow pilot for takeoff. At the same time, the glider pilot signals the tow pilot by wagging the rudder back and forth, concurring with the launch crewmember's/wing runner's takeoff signal. If a radio is used, the glider pilot advises the tow pilot that he or she is ready for takeoff, stating "Canopy and dive/air brakes closed and locked."

As the launch begins and the glider accelerates, the launch crewmember/wing runner runs alongside the glider, holding the wing level. When the glider achieves lift-off speed, the glider pilot should allow the glider to become just barely airborne and level behind the towplane's tail, as it accelerates to climb speed. The glider pilot must be precise in controlling the glider at this very low altitude of 2 to 4 feet, more or less depending on the aircraft involved. Any large excursions from the position of level directly behind the towplane's tail can lead to disaster for the tow pilot and the glider pilot(s). The glider pilot must not climb above the towplane's tail, as this can force the towplane's propeller into the runway surface. Lateral glider deviations side to side can drive the towplane off the runway. The glider pilot should maintain this altitude by applying forward stick pressure, as necessary, while the glider is accelerating. Once the towplane lifts off, it accelerates in ground effect to the desired climb airspeed, and then the climb begins for both the glider and towplane.

During takeoff while at very low altitudes, it may be necessary to steer the glider solely with the rudder due to the very long wings of most gliders. The long wings, combined with very short landing gear stances, make gliders prone to hitting runway lights and signage. Keeping the glider's wings level helps prevent collisions with obstructions but restricts aileron usage close to the surface. Control the bank angle of the wings with the ailerons. Full deflection of the flight controls may be necessary at low airspeeds, but the flight controls become more effective as airspeed increases. *[Figure 7-3]*

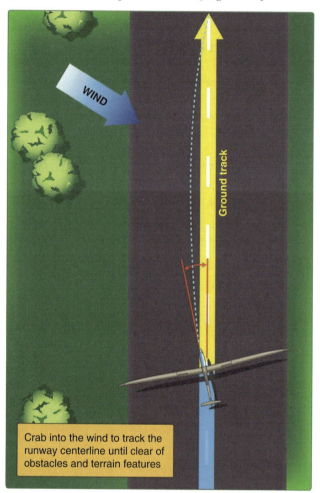

Figure 7-3. *Tracking the runway centerline.*

In most takeoffs, the glider achieves flying airspeed before the towplane. However, if the glider is a heavily ballasted glider, the towplane may be able to achieve liftoff airspeed before the glider. In such a situation, the towplane should remain in ground effect until the glider is off the ground. Climb-out must not begin until the previously determined climb airspeed has been achieved.

One of the most dangerous occurrences during aerotow is allowing the glider to fly high above and losing sight of the towplane. The tension on the towline caused by the glider pulls the towplane tail up, lowering its nose. If the glider continues to rise, pulling the towplane tail higher, the tow pilot may not be able to raise the nose. Ultimately, the tow pilot may run out of up elevator authority.

In some towhook systems, the high pressure loading on the towhook causes towhook seizure, and the tow pilot may not be able to release the towline from the towplane. This situation can be critical if it occurs at altitudes below 500 feet above ground level (AGL). Upon losing sight of the towplane, the glider pilot must release immediately.

Unassisted Takeoff

The unassisted takeoff is basically conducted in the same manner as a normal takeoff, but the glider is positioned slightly off the runway heading (runway centerline) by approximately 10–20° with one wing on the ground. If the glider is canted to the right, then the right wing would be resting on the ground. To the left, the left wing would be resting on the ground. When the glider pilot is ready for takeoff, he or she advises the tow pilot either by radio, which is the preferred method, or by signaling the tow pilot with the "ready for takeoff" rudder waggle signal, as in the assisted takeoff. As the towplane accelerates, the wing on the ground (trailing wing) accelerates at a slightly faster rate as it is pulled in a slight arc, allowing that wing to rise quickly with little dragging.

If the glider is aligned with the towplane during the takeoff, the wing that is on the ground has a tendency to be dragged and a ground loop may occur (or severe swerving). After the wings are level, proceed as in the normal takeoff configuration.

Crosswind Takeoff

Crosswind takeoff procedures are a modification of the normal takeoff procedure. The following are the main differences in crosswind takeoffs:

- The glider tends to weathervane into the wind any time the main wheel is touching the ground. The stronger the crosswind is, the greater the tendency of the glider is to turn into the wind.

- After lift-off, the glider tends to drift downwind off the runway centerline. The stronger the crosswind is, the greater the tendency of the glider is to drift downwind.

Assisted

Prior to takeoff, the glider pilot should coordinate with the launch crewmember to hold the upwind wing slightly low during the initial takeoff roll. If a crosswind is indicated, full aileron should be held into the wind as the takeoff roll is started. This control position should be maintained while the glider is accelerating and until the ailerons become effective for maneuvering the glider about its longitudinal (roll) axis. With the aileron held into the wind, the takeoff path must be held straight with the rudder. This requires application of downwind rudder pressure, since the glider tends to weathervane into the wind while on the ground. *[Figure 7-4]* As the glider's forward speed increases, the crosswind

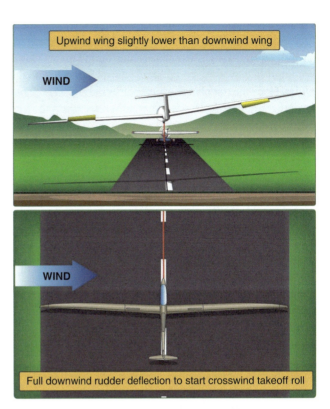

Figure 7-4. *Crosswind correction for takeoff.*

becomes more of a relative headwind; the mechanical application of full aileron into the wind should be reduced. It is when increasing pressure is being felt on the aileron control that the ailerons are becoming more effective. Because the crosswind component effect does not completely dissipate, some aileron pressure must be maintained throughout the takeoff roll to prevent the crosswind from raising the upwind wing. If the upwind wing rises, exposing more wing surface to the crosswind, a skipping action may result, as indicated by a series of small bounces occurring when the glider attempts to fly and then settles back onto the runway. This side skipping imposes side loads on the landing gear. Keeping the upwind wingtip slightly lower than the downwind wingtip prevents the crosswind from getting underneath the upwind wing and lifting it. If the downwind wingtip touches the ground, the resulting friction may cause the glider to yaw in the direction of the dragging wingtip. This yaw could lead to a loss of directional control and runway departure.

While on the runway throughout the takeoff, the glider pilot uses the rudder to maintain directional control and alignment behind the towing aircraft. Yawing back and forth behind the towplane should be avoided, as this affects the ability of the towplane pilot to maintain control. If glider controllability becomes a problem, the glider pilot must release and stop the glider on the remaining runway. Remember, as the glider slows, the crosswind may cause it to weathervane into the wind.

Prior to the towplane becoming airborne, and after the glider lifts off, the glider pilot should turn into the wind and establish a wind correction angle to remain behind the towplane. This is accomplished by using coordinated control inputs to turn the glider. Once the towplane becomes airborne and establishes a wind correction angle, the glider pilot repositions to align behind the towplane.

Unassisted

Just as in the unassisted takeoff with no wind, the unassisted crosswind takeoff is conducted slightly differently with regard to wing positioning and glider alignment. The glider should be placed on the upwind side of the runway or take area; if unable, the towplane should try to angle into the wind as best as possible to reduce the crosswind component for the glider. Most gliders have a crosswind limit up to approximately 10–12 knots. See the Glider Flight Manual/Pilot's Operating Handbook (GFM/POH) for information specific to your glider. Again, the unassisted launch should be attempted only by highly experienced pilots.

The glider should be placed with the upwind wing on the ground and the glider angled approximately 20–30° into the wind. *[Figure 7-5]* If the upwind wing is permitted to be up during the takeoff run, the glider pilot finds it very difficult to level the wings. A ground loop usually results since the downwind wing is being dragged along the ground. With the upwind wing on the ground during the early stages of the takeoff, the glider pilot finds it easier to level the wings early in the takeoff. As in the unassisted takeoff, the upwind wing is swung forward at a faster rate than the downwind wing, aiding the pilot in leveling the wings. The crosswind strikes the fuselage of the glider, tending to push it downwind, making it necessary to place the glider on the upwind side of the runway. Execute a crosswind takeoff from this point after both wings are level.

Common errors in aerotow takeoffs include:

- Improper glider configuration for takeoff,
- Improper initial positioning of flight controls,
- Improper alignment of the glider (unassisted takeoff),
- Improper use of visual launch signals,
- Failure to maintain alignment behind towplane before towplane becomes airborne,
- Improper alignment with the towplane after becoming airborne, and
- Climbing too high after lift-off and causing a towplane upset.

Aerotow Climb-Out

Once airborne and climbing, the glider can fly one of two tow positions. High tow is aerotow flight with the glider positioned slightly above the wake of the towplane. Low tow is aerotow flight with the glider positioned just below the wake of the towplane. *[Figure 7-6]* Climbing turns are made with shallow bank angles and the glider in the high tow position. Pilots are trained using these positions to learn coordinated towing procedures and understanding the dynamics of the aerotow. In training, glider pilots are advised to control vertical position relative to the towplane using the horizon.

The glider pilot's sight picture depends on the type of towplane being used for the launch. The instructor, through flight experience, can determine the particular towplane's vertical wake boundaries and describe the positions. Sometimes, the glider may use the picture of the towplane's wings on the horizon. On another type of towplane, maintaining the towplane's rudder centered over the fuselage of the towplane ensures the glide is directly behind the towplane in straight flight. Any excessive deviation from the low or high tow position by the glider requires abnormal control inputs by the tow pilot, which always generates more drag and degrades climb performance during the tow.

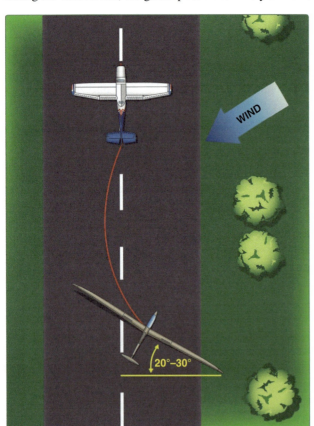

Figure 7-5. *When setting up for a crosswind takeoff, the glider should be placed on the upwind side of the runway.*

The towplane's wake drifts down behind the towing aircraft. Straight ahead climbs are made with the glider in the level or

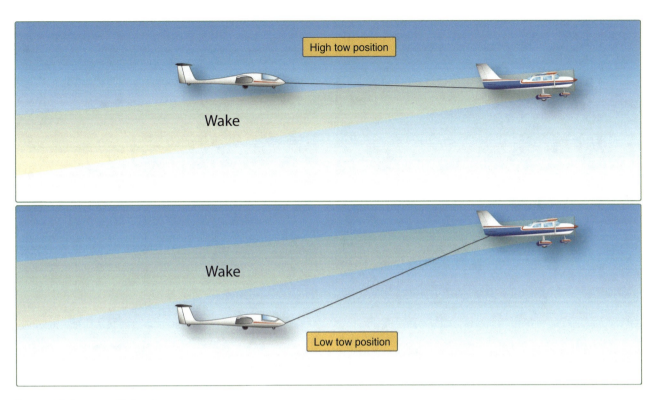

Figure 7-6. *Aerotow climb-out.*

high tow position. The tow pilot strives to maintain a steady pitch attitude and a constant power setting for the desired climb airspeed. The glider pilot uses visual references on the towplane to maintain a proper lateral and vertical position.

In a level flight tow, the pilot should position the glider above the wake of the towplane. Low tow offers the glider pilot a better view of the towplane and provides for a more aerodynamically efficient tow, especially during climb, as the towplane requires less upward elevator deflection due to the downward pull of the glider. However, because of the risk of towline fouling if the towline breaks or is released by the towplane, low tow should be mainly used for level flight aero-tows such as for a cross-country flight.

Climbing turns are made with shallow bank angles in the high tow position. During turns, the glider pilot observes and matches the bank angle of the towplane. In order to stay in the same flightpath of the towplane, the glider pilot must aim the nose of the glider at the outside wingtip of the towplane. This allows the glider's flightpath to coincide with the flightpath of the towplane. *[Figure 7-7]*

If the glider's bank is steeper than the towplanes bank, the glider's turn radius is smaller than the towplane turn radius. *[Figure 7-8]* If this occurs, the reduced tension on the towline causes it to bow and slack, allowing the glider's airspeed to slow. As a result, the glider begins to sink relative to the towplane. The correct course of action is to reduce the

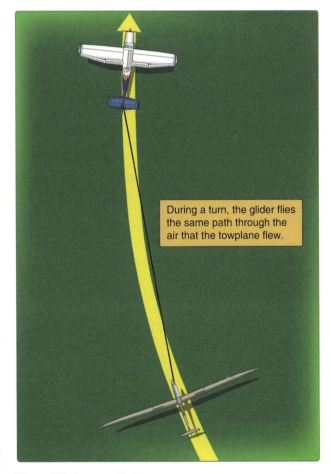

Figure 7-7. *Aerotow climbing turns.*

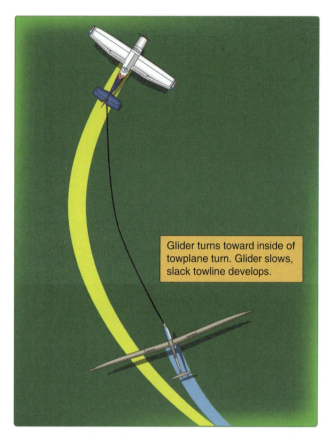

Figure 7-8. *Glider bank is steeper than that of towplane, causing slack in towline.*

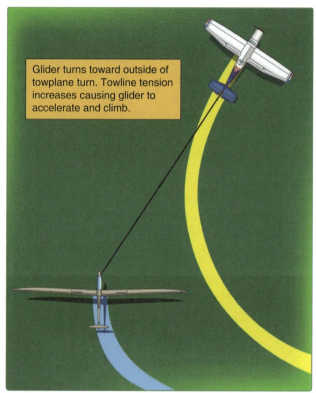

Figure 7-9. *Glider bank too shallow, causing turn outside towplane turn.*

glider's bank angle so the glider flies the same radius of turn as the towplane. If timely corrective action is not taken and the glider slows and sinks below the towplane, the towplane may rapidly pull the towline taut and possibly cause it to fail and/or cause structural damage to both aircraft.

If the glider's bank is shallower than the towplane, the glider's turn radius is larger than the towplane's turn radius. *[Figure 7-9]* If this occurs, the increased tension on the towline causes the glider to accelerate and climb. The correct course of pilot action when the glider is turning outside the towplane radius of turn is to increase glider bank angle. As the glider moves back into position behind the towplane, the glider corrects to the same radius of turn as the towplane. If timely corrective action is not taken and the glider accelerates and climbs above the towplane, the towplane may lose rudder and elevator control. In this situation, the glider pilot should release the towline and turn to avoid the towplane.

Common errors in aerotow climb-out include:

- Faulty procedures by not maintaining proper vertical and lateral position during high or low tow.
- Inadvertent entry into towplane wake.
- Failure to maintain glider alignment during turns on aerotow causing towplane upset.

Aerotow Release

Standard aerotow release procedures provide safety benefits for both the glider and the towing aircraft. When the aerotow reaches release position, the glider pilot should clear the area for other aircraft in all directions, especially to the right. Prior to release, the towline should be under normal tension for a normal release. Depending on the hook, some tension is required to extract the ring from the hook. The hook-type towing attachments may need pressure to make the hook swing open to release the hook. When ready to release, the glider pilot pulls the release handle completely out to ensure the towline hook is fully open to allow the release of the towline and hold the hook release open until it is verified that the towline is free of the glider. Generally, the release of the towline is felt as the forward motion begins to decelerate, but the glider pilot should always visually confirm the towline release prior to the 90° right clearing turn. *[Figure 7-10A]* Next, the glider pilot banks to the right, accomplishing 90° of heading change, then in level flight flies away from the release point while observing the towplane actions.

Shown in *Figure 7-10B*, this 90° change of heading achieves maximum separation between towplane and glider in minimum time. After confirming glider release and 90° turn away from the towplane, the tow pilot turns left away from the release point, achieving safe maximum separation.

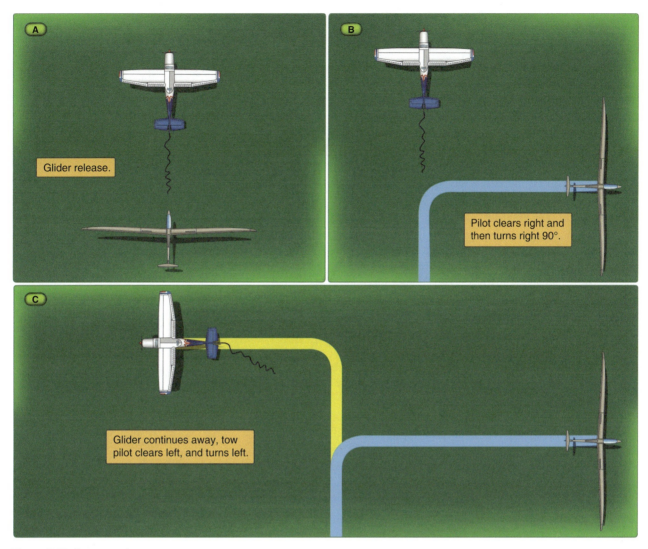

Figure 7-10. *Aerotow release.*

Shown in *Figure 7-10C*, once clear of the glider and other aircraft, the tow pilot then begins a descent. The tow pilot should continue to observe the glider's actions as the glider pilot may have started his/hers thermalling procedure with the possibility of the glider pilot losing sight of the towing aircraft. Common errors in aerotow release include:

- Lack of normal tension on towline or slack in towline.
- Failure to clear the area prior to release.
- Failure to make a 90° right turn after release.
- Release in close proximity of other aircraft.
- Glider pilot and tow pilot losing sight of each other's aircraft.

Maintaining proper release procedures is important to ensure proper aircraft separation in case pilots lose sight of each other's aircraft. It is imperative for the tow pilot to exit the immediate area of the glider release. If the glider releases in a thermal or other lift, the glider must stay in that lift to gain altitude, whereas the tow pilot has the ability to completely clear the glider's area before returning to the airport. Both the tow pilot and glider pilot should be aware of other gliders near areas of lift.

Slack Line

Slack line is a reduction of tension in the towline. If the slack is severe enough, it might entangle the glider or cause damage to the glider or towplane. The following situations may result in a slack line:

- Abrupt power reduction by the towplane
- Aerotow descents
- Glider turns inside the towplane turn radius *[Figure 7-8]*
- Updrafts and downdrafts
- Abrupt recovery from a wake box corner position *[Figure 7-11]*

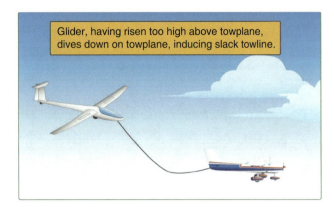

Figure 7-11. *Diving on towplane.*

When the towplane precedes the glider into an updraft, the glider pilot first perceives that the towplane is climbing much faster and higher than it actually is. Then, as the glider enters the updraft, it is lighter and more efficient than the towplane. It climbs higher and faster than the towplane did in the same updraft. As a result, the glider pilot pitches the glider over to regain the proper tow altitude but gains airspeed more quickly than the towplane, hence the slack towline. The glider pilot must be ready to control the descent and closure rate to the towplane.

Slack line recovery procedures should be initiated as soon as the glider pilot becomes aware of the situation. The glider pilot should try slipping back into alignment with the towplane. In the event that slipping fails to reduce the slack sufficiently, careful use of spoilers/dive brakes can decelerate the glider and take up the slack. When the towline tightens, stabilize the tow and gradually resume the desired aerotow position. When slack in the towline is excessive, or beyond the pilot's capability to safely recover, the glider pilot should immediately release from the aerotow.

Common errors regarding a slack line include:

- Failure to take corrective action at the first indication of a slack line.
- Use of improper procedure to correct slack line causing excessive stress on the towline, towplane, and the glider.

Boxing the Wake

Boxing the wake is a training and performance maneuver designed to demonstrate a pilot's ability to accurately maneuver the glider around the towplanes wake during aerotow. This maneuver is used by flight instructors to teach students how to find the towing aircraft wake; then, safely maneuver around the wake during the aerotow. *[Figure 7-12]*

Boxing the wake requires flying a rectangular pattern around the towplane's wake and not the towplane. Prior to takeoff, the glider pilot should advise the tow pilot that he or she is planning to box the wake. Boxing the wake should commence outside of the traffic pattern area and at no lower than 1,000 feet AGL.

Before starting the maneuver, the glider should descend through the wake to the center low tow position as a signal to the tow pilot that the maneuver is about to begin. The pilot uses coordinated control inputs to move the glider level to one side of the wake and holds that lower corner of the rectangle momentarily with rudder pressure.

Applying back pressure to the control stick starts a vertical ascent using rudder pressure to maintain equal distance from the wake. The pilot holds the wings almost level with the ailerons to parallel the towplane. When the glider has attained high corner position, the pilot momentarily maintains this position.

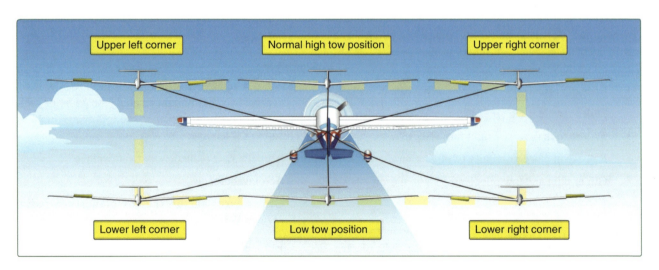

Figure 7-12. *Boxing the wake.*

As the maneuver continues, the pilot reduces the rudder pressure and uses coordinated flight controls to slightly bank the glider to fly along the top side of the box. The glider proceeds to the opposite corner using aileron and rudder pressure, as appropriate. The pilot maintains this position momentarily with rudder pressure, then begins a vertical descent by applying forward pressure to the control stick. Rudder pressure is used to maintain glider position at an equal distance from the wake.

The pilot holds the wings level with the ailerons to parallel the towplane. When the glider has attained low corner position, the pilot momentarily maintains this position. The pilot releases the rudder pressure and, using coordinated flight controls, slightly banks the glider to fly along the bottom side of the box until reaching the original center low tow position.

From center low tow position, the pilot maneuvers the glider through the wake to the center high tow position, completing the maneuver.

Common errors when boxing the wake include:

- Performing an excessively large rectangle around the wake. *Figure 7-12* has exaggerated positions and is not to scale.
- Improper control coordination and procedure.
- Abrupt or rapid changes of position.
- Allowing or developing unnecessary slack during position changes.

Ground Launch Takeoff Procedures

When ground launching, it is essential to use a center of gravity (CG) towhook that has an automatic back release feature. This protects the glider if the pilot is unable to release the towline during the launch. The failure of the tow release could cause the glider to be pulled to the ground as it flies over the launching vehicle or winch. Since the back release feature of the towhook is so important, it should be tested prior to every flight. *[Figure 7-13]*

CG Hooks

Some training and high-performance gliders have only a CG towhook. CG towhooks are necessary for ground launch operations so the glider is not pulled into the ground. Attachment at the center of gravity allows the glider pilot to have full control of the glider without undue influence from the ground pull. Attachment of a ground launch towline to the nose hook would tend to pull the glider into the ground and would overload the horizontal stabilizer and elevator. Conversely, depending on design, the CG hook may not have sufficient movement to fully release an aerotow line under pressure. If the hook only swings about 90° down, the towline may stay hung on the gliders hook until the pressure is released and slack allows the towline to simply fall off. It may be located either ahead of the landing gear, in the landing gear well, or the glider may utilize a bracket that attaches outside on the fuselage near the cockpit.

If the CG hook is in the landing gear well, retracting the gear on tow interferes with the towline. Even if the glider has a nose hook, retracting the gear on tow is not recommended until the aircraft is safely airborne and an immediate or emergency return is not necessary. Leaving the gear down allows the glider pilot more time to assess the best landing options.

A CG hook, as compared to a nose hook, makes a crosswind takeoff more difficult since the glider can weathervane into the wind more easily. In addition, a CG hook makes the glider more susceptible to kiting on takeoff, especially if the CG is near the aft limit. This can present a serious danger to the towplane during the aerotow.

Signals
Prelaunch Signals (Winch/Automobile)

Prelaunch visual signals for a ground launch operation allow the glider pilot, the wing runner, the safety officer, and the

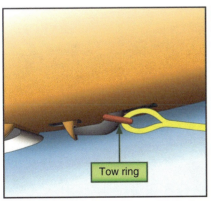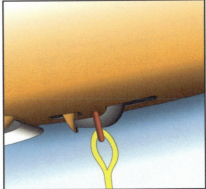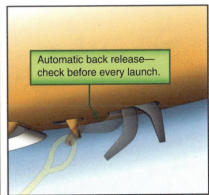

Figure 7-13. *Testing the towhook.*

launch crew to communicate over considerable distances. When launching with an automobile, the glider and launch automobile may be 1,000 feet or more apart. When launching with a winch, the glider may start the launch 4,000 feet or more from the winch. Because of the great distances involved, members of the ground launch crew use colored flags or large paddles to enhance visibility, as shown in *Figure 7-14*. When complex information must be relayed over great distances, visual prelaunch signals can be augmented with direct voice communications between crewmember stations. Hard-wired ground telephones, two-way radios, or wireless telephones can be used to communicate between stations, adding protection against premature launch and facilitating an aborted launch if an unsafe condition arises. The towline should never be attached to the glider until the crew is onboard and ready to launch.

Inflight Signals

Since ground launches are of short duration, inflight signals for ground launches are limited to signals to the winch operator or ground vehicle driver to increase or decrease speed. *[Figure 7-15]*

Tow Speeds

Proper ground launch tow speed is critical for a safe launch. *Figure 7-16* compares various takeoff profiles that result when tow speeds vary above or below the correct speed.

Figure 7-14. *Winch and aerotow prelaunch signals.*

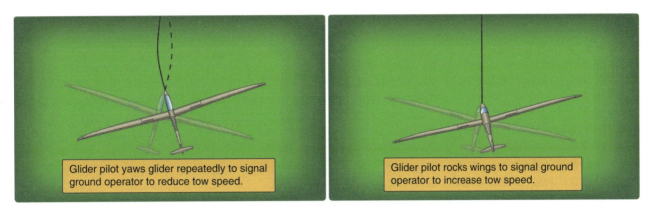

Figure 7-15. *Inflight signals for ground launch.*

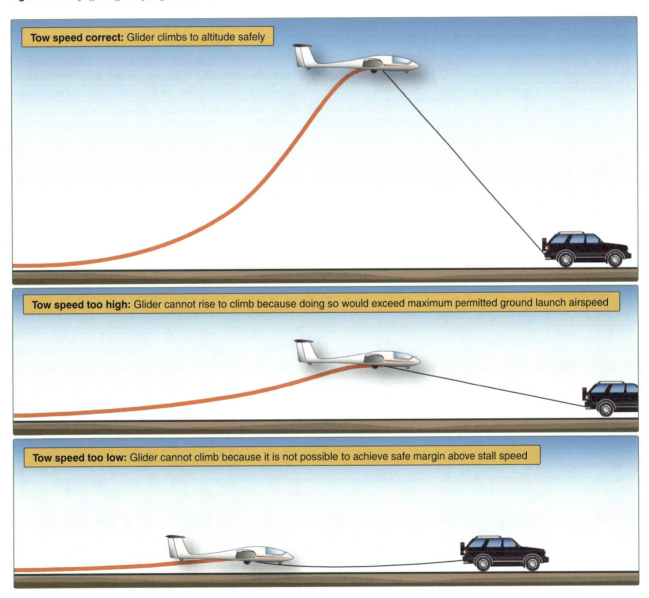

Figure 7-16. *Ground launch tow speed.*

7-13

Each glider certified for ground launch operations has a placarded maximum ground launch tow speed. This speed is normally the same for automobile or winch launches. The glider pilot should fly the launch staying at or below this speed to prevent structural damage to the glider during the ground tow.

Automobile Launch

Automobile launches today are very rare. During automobile ground launches, the glider pilot and driver should have a thorough understanding of the groundspeeds to be used prior to any launch. Before the first launch, the pilot and vehicle driver should determine the appropriate vehicle ground tow speeds, considering the surface wind velocity, the glider speed increase during launch, and the wind gradient encountered during the climb. They should include a safety factor to avoid exceeding this maximum vehicle ground tow speed.

If a crosswind condition is present, the glider should be positioned slightly downwind of the takeoff heading and angled into the wind to help eliminate control problems until sufficient airspeed is obtained. Due to the slow acceleration of the glider during an automobile ground launch, the towline should be laid out to allow the glider to obtain sufficient speed for control while still in a headwind. *[Figure 7-17]*

The tow speed can be determined by using the following calculations:

1. Subtract the surface winds from the maximum placarded ground launch tow speed for the particular glider.
2. Subtract an additional five miles per hour (mph) for the airspeed increase during the climb.
3. Subtract the estimated wind gradient increase encountered during the climb.
4. Subtract a 5 mph safety factor.

Maximum ground launch tow speed .... 75 mph
1. Surface winds 10 mph .... –10 mph
2. Airspeed increase during climb 5 mph .... –5 mph
3. Estimated climb wind gradient 5 mph .... –5 mph
4. Safety factor of 5 mph .... –5 mph
Automobile tow speed .... 50 mph

During winch launches, the winch operator applies full power smoothly and rapidly until the glider reaches an angle of 30° above the horizon. At this point, the operator should start to reduce the power until the glider is about 60° above the horizon where approximately 20 percent power is needed. As the glider reaches the 70° point above the horizon, power is reduced to idle. The winch operator monitors the glider continuously during the climb for any signals to increase or decrease speed from the glider pilot. *[Figure 7-18]*

Crosswind Takeoff and Climb

The following are the main differences between crosswind takeoffs and climb procedures and normal takeoff and climb procedures:

- During the takeoff roll, the glider tends to weathervane into the wind.
- After liftoff, the glider drifts toward the downwind side of the runway.
- In strong crosswinds there is a greater tendency for the glider to drift downwind.
- If space is available in the takeoff area, the towline or cable should be laid out in a manner that the initial takeoff roll is slightly into the wind to reduce the crosswind component of the glider. *[Figure 7-19]*

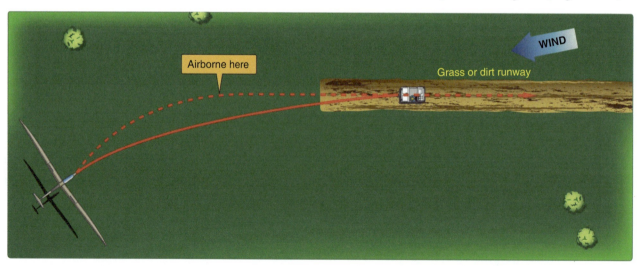

Figure 7-17. *Ground launch procedures.*

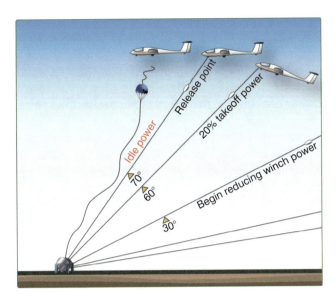

Figure 7-18. *Winch procedures.*

After lift-off, the glider pilot should establish a wind correction angle toward the upwind side of the runway to prevent drifting downwind. This prevents downwind drift and allows the glider to work upwind of the runway during the climb-out. When the towline is released at the top of the climb, it tends to drift back toward the centerline of the launch runway, as shown in *Figure 7-20*. This helps keep the towline from fouling nearby wires, poles, fences, aircraft, and other obstacles on the side of the launching runway. Should the glider drift to the downwind side of the runway, the towline could damage other aircraft, runway lights, nearby fences, structures, obstacles, etc.

Normal Into-the-Wind Launch

Normal takeoffs are made into the wind. Prior to launch, the glider pilot, ground crew, and launch equipment operator must be familiar with the launch signals and procedures. When the required checklists for the glider and ground launch equipment have been completed and the glider pilot, ground crew, and launch equipment operator are ready for takeoff, the glider pilot should signal the ground crewmember to hook the towline to the glider. The hookup must be done deliberately and correctly. The release mechanism should be checked for proper operation. To accomplish this, the ground crewmember should apply tension to the towline and signal the glider pilot to activate the release. The ground crewmember should verify that the release has worked properly and signal the glider pilot. When the towline is hooked up to the glider again, the ground crewmember takes a position at the wingtip of the down wing. When the glider pilot signals "ready for takeoff," the ground crewmember clears both takeoff and landing areas. When the ground crewmember has ensured the traffic pattern is clear, the ground crewmember then

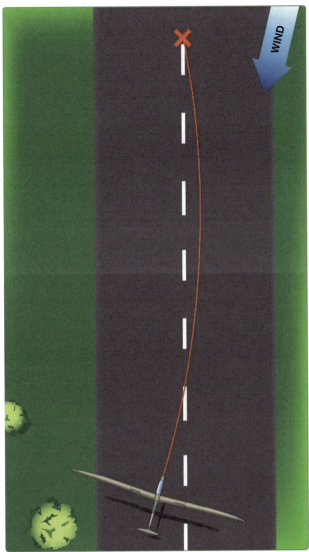

Figure 7-19. *Wind correction angle for winch procedures.*

signals the launch equipment operator to "take up slack" in the towline. Once the slack is removed from the towline, the ground crewmember again verifies that the glider pilot is ready for takeoff. Then, the ground crewmember raises the wings to a level position, does a final traffic pattern check, and signals to the launch equipment operator to begin the takeoff.

CAUTION: Never connect a glider to a towplane or towline unless the pilot is aboard and ready for flight. If the pilot exits the glider for any reason, the towline should be released and disconnected. Glider pilots should be prepared for a takeoff anytime the towline is attached to the glider.

The length, elasticity, and mass of the towline used for ground launching have several effects on the glider being launched. First, it is difficult or impossible to prevent the glider from

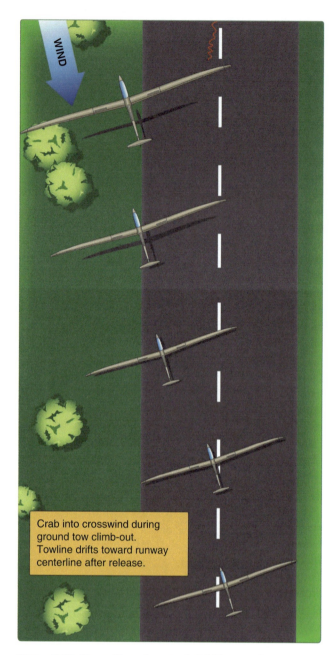

Figure 7-20. *Ground launch crosswind drift correction.*

moving forward as the long towline is tautened. Elasticity in the towline causes the glider to creep forward as the towline is tightened. For this reason, the towline is left with a small amount of slack prior to beginning the launch. It is important for the pilot to be prepared for the launch prior to giving the launch signal. If the launch is begun before the pilot gives the launch signal, the glider pilot should pull the towline release handle promptly. In the first several seconds of the launch, the glider pilot should hold the stick forward to avoid kiting. During the launch, the glider pilot should track the runway centerline and monitor the airspeed. *[Figure 7-21, position A]*

When the glider accelerates and attains lift-off speed, the glider pilot eases the glider off the ground. The time interval from standing start to lift-off may be as short as 3 to 5 seconds. After the initial lift-off, the pilot should smoothly raise the nose to the proper pitch attitude, watching for an increase in airspeed. If the nose is raised too soon or too steeply, the pitch attitude is excessive while the glider is still at low altitude. If the towline breaks or the launching mechanism loses power, recovery from such a high pitch attitude may be difficult or impossible. Conversely, if the nose is raised too slowly, the glider may gain excessive airspeed and may exceed the maximum ground launch tow speed. The shallow climb may result in the glider not attaining planned release altitude. If this situation occurs, the pilot should pull the release and land straight ahead, avoiding any obstacles and equipment.

As the launch progresses, the pilot should ease the nose up gradually *[Figure 7-21, position B]* while monitoring the airspeed to ensure that it is adequate for launch but does not exceed the maximum permitted ground launch tow airspeed. When optimum pitch attitude for climb is attained, *[Figure 7-21, position C]* the glider should be approximately 200 feet AGL. The pilot must monitor the airspeed during this phase of the climb-out to ensure the airspeed is adequate to provide a safe margin above stall speed but below the maximum ground launch airspeed. If the towline breaks, or if the launching mechanism loses power at or above this altitude, the pilot has sufficient altitude to release the towline and lower the nose from the climb attitude to the approach attitude that provides an appropriate airspeed for landing straight ahead.

As the glider nears its maximum altitude *[Figure 7-21, position D]*, it begins to level off above the launch winch or tow vehicle to reduce the rate of climb. In this final phase of the ground launch, the towline is pulling steeply down on the glider. The pilot should gently lower the nose of the glider to reduce tension on the towline and then pull the towline release two to three times to ensure the towline releases. The pilot feels the release of the towline as it departs the glider. The pilot should enter a turn to visually confirm the fall of the towline. If only a portion of the towline is seen falling to the ground, it is possible that the towline is broken and a portion of the towline is still attached to the glider.

If pulling the tow release handle fails to release the towline, the back release mechanism of the towhook should automatically release the towline as the glider overtakes and passes the launch vehicle or winch.

Climb-Out and Release Procedures

The pitch attitude/airspeed relationship during ground launch is a unique flight experience. During the launch, pulling back on the stick tends to increase airspeed, and pushing forward tends to reduce airspeed. This is opposite of the

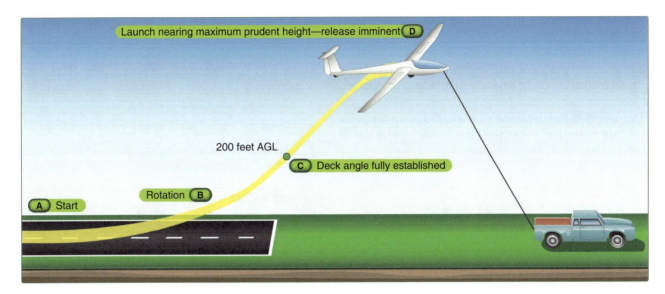

Figure 7-21. *Ground launch takeoff profile.*

normal pitch/airspeed relationship. The wings of the glider divert the towing force of the launch vehicle in an upward direction, enabling rapid climb. The greater the diversion is from horizontal pulling power to vertical lifting power, the faster the airspeed is. This is true if the tow vehicle is powerful enough to meet the energy demands the glider is making on the launch system.

Common errors in ground launching include:

- Improper glider configuration for takeoff.
- Improper initial positioning of flight controls.
- Improper use of visual launch signals.
- Improper crosswind procedure.
- Improper climb profile.
- Faulty corrective action for adjustment of airspeed and pitch.
- Exceeding maximum launch airspeed.
- Improper towline release procedure.

Self-Launch Takeoff Procedures
Preparation and Engine Start

The self-launching glider *[Figure 7-22]* has many more systems than a nonmotorized glider, so glider preflight inspection is more complex. A positive control check is just as critical as it is with any aircraft. Ailerons, elevator, rudder, elevator trim tab, flaps, and spoiler/dive brakes must all be checked. In addition, numerous other systems must be inspected and readied for flight. These include the fuel system, electrical system, engine, propeller, cooling system, and any mechanisms and controls associated with extending or retracting the engine or propulsion system. Instruments, gauges, and all engine and propulsion system controls must be inspected for proper operation.

After preflighting the self-launching glider and clearing the area, start the engine in accordance with the manufacturer's instructions. Hearing protection may be needed and is advisable when using combustion engines in self-launching or sustaining gliders. Typical items on a self-launching glider engine-start checklist include fuel mixture control, fuel tank

Figure 7-22. *Types of self-launching gliders.*

selection, fuel pump switch, engine priming, propeller pitch setting, throttle setting, magneto or ignition switch setting, and electric starter activation. After starting, the oil pressure, oil temp, alternator/generator charging, and flight instruments should be checked. If the engine and propulsion systems are operating within normal limits, taxi operations can begin. These types of gliders often feature a retractable powerplant for drag reduction. After the launch, the powerplant is retracted into the fuselage and stowed.

Common errors in preparation and engine start include:

- Failure to use or improper use of checklist.
- Improper or unsafe starting procedures.
- Excessively high revolutions per minutes (rpm) after starting.
- Failure to ensure proper clearance of propeller.

Taxiing

Self-launching gliders are designed with a variety of landing gear systems, including tricycle or tailwheel landing gear configurations. Other types of self-launching gliders rest primarily on the main landing gear wheel in the center of the fuselage and depend on outrigger wheels or skids to prevent the wingtips from contacting the ground.

Due to the long wingspan and low wingtip ground clearance of gliders, the self-launching glider pilot needs to consider airport layout and runway configuration. Some taxiways and airport ramps may not accommodate the long wingspan of the glider or limit maneuvering. Additionally, the pilot must consider the glider's crosswind capability during taxi operations. Taxiing on soft ground requires additional power. Self-launching gliders with outrigger wingtip wheels may lose directional control if a wingtip wheel bogs down. Well-briefed wing walkers should hold the wings level during low-speed taxi operations on soft ground.

Common errors in taxiing a self-launching glider include:

- Improper use of brakes.
- Failure to comply with airport markings, signals, and clearances.
- Taxiing too fast for conditions.
- Improper control positioning for wind conditions.
- Failure to consider wingspan and space required to maneuver during taxiing.

Pretakeoff Check

The manufacturer provides a takeoff checklist. As shown in *Figure 7-23*, the complexity of many self-launching gliders makes a written takeoff checklist an essential safety item. Pretakeoff items on a self-launching glider may include fuel quantity check, fuel pressure check, oil temperature check, oil pressure check, engine runup, throttle/rpm check, propeller pitch setting, cowl flap setting, and vacuum check. Other items that also must be completed include ensuring seat belts and shoulder harnesses are latched or secured, doors and windows are closed and locked, canopies are closed and locked, air brakes are closed and locked, altimeter is set, communication radio set to the proper frequency for traffic advisory, and flight instruments are adjusted for takeoff.

Common errors in the before takeoff check include:

- Improper positioning of the self-launching glider for runup.
- Failure to use or improper use of checklist.
- Improper check of flight controls.
- Failure to review takeoff emergency procedures.
- Improper radio and communications procedures.

Figure 7-23. *Self-launching glider instrument panels.*

Normal Takeoff

When the pretakeoff checklist is complete, the pilot should check for traffic and prepare for takeoff. If operating from an airport with an operating control tower, request and receive an air traffic control (ATC) clearance prior to taxi. The pilot should make a final check for conflicting traffic, then taxi out onto the active runway and align the glider with the centerline.

The pilot should smoothly apply full throttle and begin the takeoff roll while tracking the centerline of the runway and then fly the self-launching glider off the runway at the recommended lift-off airspeed, allowing the glider to accelerate in ground effect (IGE) until reaching the appropriate climb airspeed. If the runway has an obstacle ahead, the preferred airspeed is best angle of climb airspeed (V_X) until the obstacle is cleared. If no obstacle is present, the preferred airspeed is either best rate of climb airspeed (V_Y) or the airspeed for best engine cooling during climb. The pilot should monitor the engine and instrument systems during climb-out. If the self-launching glider has a time limitation on full throttle operation, the throttle should be adjusted as necessary during the climb.

Crosswind Takeoff

The long wingspan and low wingtip clearance of the typical self-launching glider make it vulnerable to wingtip strikes on runway signage and airport runway and taxiway lights. The takeoff roll should be started with the upwind wing on the ground with the aileron and rudder controls coordinated for the pilots current wind situation. For example, in a right crosswind, the control stick should be held to the right and the rudder held to the left. The aileron input keeps the crosswind from lifting the upwind wing, and the downwind rudder minimizes the weathervaning tendency of the self-launching glider in a crosswind. As airspeed increases, control effectiveness improves and the pilot can gradually decrease the control setting to coordinated flight. The self-launching glider should be lifted off at the appropriate lift-off airspeed and accelerate to climb airspeed. During the climb, a wind correction angle should be established so that the self-launching glider tracks the extended centerline of the takeoff runway. *[Figure 7-24]*

Common errors in crosswind takeoff include:

- Improper initial positioning of flight controls.
- Improper power application.
- Inappropriate removal of hand from throttle.
- Poor directional control.
- Improper use of flight controls.
- Improper pitch attitude during takeoff.

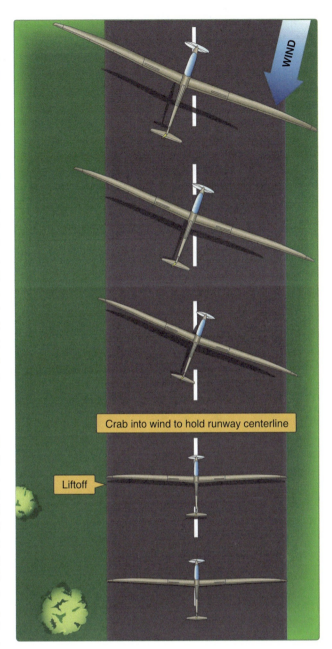

Figure 7-24. *Self-launching gliders—crosswind takeoff.*

- Failure to establish and maintain proper climb attitude and airspeed.
- Maintaining takeoff slip instead of transitioning to crab to achieve more climb efficiency.

Climb-Out and Shutdown Procedures

Self-launching gliders have powerplant limitations, as well as aircraft performance and handling limitations. Powerplant limitations include engine and oil temperatures, engine rpm limits, and other engine/aircraft limitations listed in the GFM/POH.

The GFM or POH provides useful information about recommended power settings and target airspeed for best angle of climb, best rate of climb, best cooling performance climb, and cruise performance while in powered flight. If full throttle operation is time limited to reduce engine wear, the GFM/POH describes the recommended operating procedures. Aircraft performance includes weight and balance limits, minimum and maximum front seat weight restrictions, maximum permitted airspeed with engine extended, maximum airspeed to extend or retract the engine, flap operating airspeed range, air brake operating airspeed range, maneuvering speed, rough air speed limitations, and never-exceed speed.

The engine heats up considerably during takeoff and climb, so cooling system mismanagement can lead to dangerously high temperatures in a short time. An overheated engine cannot supply full power, meaning climb performance is reduced. Extended overheating can cause an inflight fire. To minimize the chances of engine damage or fire, monitor engine temperatures carefully during high power operations, observing engine operating limitations described in the GFM/POH.

Many self-launching gliders have a time limitation on full throttle operation to prevent overheating and premature engine wear. If the self-launching glider is equipped with cowl flaps for cooling, make certain the cowl flaps are set properly for high power operations. In some self-launching gliders, operating at full power with cowl flaps closed can result in overheating and damage to the engine in as little as 2 minutes. If abnormally high engine system temperatures are encountered, follow the procedures described in the GFM/POH. Typically, these require reduced power with higher airspeed to enhance engine cooling. Cowl flap instructions may be provided as well. If these measures are ineffective in reducing high temperatures, the safest course of action may be to shut down the engine and make a precautionary landing. A safe landing, whether on or off the airport, is always preferable to an inflight fire.

Handling limitations for a given self-launching glider may be quite subtle and may include minimum controllable airspeed with power on, minimum controllable airspeed with power off, and other limitations described in the GFM/POH. Self-launching gliders come in many configurations. Those with a top-mounted retractable engine and/or propeller have a thrust line that is quite distant from the longitudinal axis of the glider. The result is that significant changes of power settings tend to cause substantial pitch attitude changes. For instance, full power setting in these self-launching gliders introduces a nose-down pitching moment because the engine thrust line is high above the longitudinal axis of the glider. To counteract this pitching moment, the pilot holds the control stick back pressure and trim. If power is quickly reduced from full power to idle power while holding an control up stick force, the glider tends to pitch up with the power reduction. This nose-pitching moment may be vigorous enough to induce aircraft stall. Smooth and coordinated management of power and flight control provides the safest procedure under these conditions.

During climb-out, the pilot should hold a pitch attitude that results in climbing out at the desired airspeed, adjusting elevator trim as necessary. As previously stated, climbs in self-launching gliders are best managed with smooth control inputs; when power changes are necessary, make smooth and gradual throttle adjustments.

When climbing under power, most self-launching gliders exhibit a left or right turning tendency (depending on whether the propeller is turning clockwise or counterclockwise) due to P-factor. P-factor is caused by the uneven distribution of thrust caused by the difference in the angle of attack (AOA) of the ascending propeller blade and the descending propeller blade. Use the rudder to counteract P-factor during climbs with power. *[Figure 7-25]*

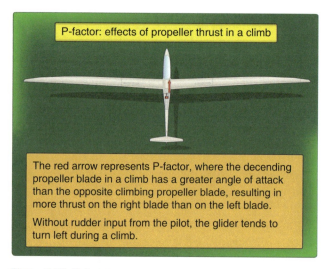

Figure 7-25. *P-factor.*

Turns are accomplished with a shallow bank angle because steep banks result in a greatly reduced rate of climb. As with all turns, properly coordinated aileron and rudder movement result in a more efficient flight and faster climb rate. The pilot should scan for other aircraft traffic before making any turn. Detailed engine shutdown procedures are described in the GFM/POH. A guide to shutdown procedures is described below, but the GFM/POH is the authoritative source for any self-launching glider.

Engines reach high operating temperatures during extended high-power operations. To reduce or eliminate shock cooling caused by a sudden reduction of engine power setting, reduce power slowly. Shock cooling is generally considered to be the outside components of an engine cooling much faster than the truly hot parts inside the engine not directly exposed to cooling airflow. This shock cooling allows the external parts to cool faster and shrink more than the interior components resulting in binding and scuffing of moving parts such as piston rings and valves.

To reduce the possibility of inflight fire, the manufacturer provides engine cool-down procedures for reducing engine system temperatures prior to shutdown. Reducing throttle setting allows the engine to begin a gradual cool down. The GFM/POH may also instruct the pilot to adjust propeller pitch at this time. Lowering the nose to increase airspeed provides faster flow of cooling air to the engine cooling system. Several minutes of reduced throttle and increased cooling airflow are enough to allow the engine to be shut down.

If the engine is retractable, additional time after engine shutdown may be necessary to reduce engine temperature to acceptable limits prior to retracting and stowing the engine in the fuselage. Consult the GFM/POH for details. *[Figure 7-22]*

Retractable-engine self-launching gliders are aerodynamically more efficient when the engine is stowed, but produce high drag when the engine is extended and not providing thrust. Stowing the engine is critical to efficient soaring flight. Prior to stowing, the propeller must be aligned with the longitudinal axis of the glider, so the propeller blades do not interfere with the engine bay doors.

Since the engine/propeller installation in these gliders is aft of the pilot's head, these gliders usually have a mirror, enabling the pilot to perform a visual propeller alignment check prior to stowing the engine/propeller pod. Detailed instructions for stowing the engine and propeller are found in the GFM/POH for the particular glider. If a malfunction occurs during engine shutdown and stowage, the pilot cannot count on being able to get the engine restarted. The pilot should have a landing area within power-off gliding distance in anticipation of this eventuality.

Some self-launching gliders use a nose-mounted engine/propeller installation that resembles the typical installation found on single-engine airplanes. In these self-launching gliders, the shutdown procedure usually consists of operating the engine for a short time at reduced power to cool the engine down to acceptable shutdown temperature. After shutdown, the cowl flaps (if installed) should be closed to reduce drag and increase gliding efficiency. The manufacturer may recommend a time interval between engine shutdown and cowl flap closure to prevent excess temperatures from developing in the confined, tightly cowled engine compartment. These temperatures may not be harmful to the engine itself, but may degrade the structures around the engine, such as composite engine mounts or installed electrical components. Excess engine heat may result in fuel vapor lock.

If the propeller blade pitch can be controlled by the pilot while in flight, the propeller is usually set to coarse pitch. Some installations have a propeller feathering system that reduces propeller drag to a minimum for use during non-powered flight. Some self-launching gliders require the pilot to set the propeller to coarse pitch prior to engine shutdown. Other self-launching gliders require the pilot to shut down the engine first and then adjust propeller blade pitch to coarse pitch or setting to a feathered position. As always, pilots must follow the recommended shutdown procedures described in their GFM/POH.

Common errors during climb-out and shutdown procedures include:

- Failure to follow manufacturer's recommended procedure for engine shutdown, feathering, and stowing (if applicable).
- Failure to maintain positive aircraft control while performing engine shutdown procedures.
- Failure to follow proper engine extension and restart procedures.

Landing

If the self-launching glider is to land under power, the pilot should perform the engine restart procedures at an altitude that allows time to reconfigure. The pilot should follow the manufacturer's recommended engine start checklist. Once the engine is started, the pilot should allow time for it to warm up. After the engine is started, the pilot should ensure that all systems necessary for landing are operational, such as the electrical system and landing gear.

Caution: Follow the manufacturer's recommended engine extension and restart procedures or a loss of situational awareness could result in attempting a landing with the glider a high drag configuration. The pilot of a sustainer or self-launching glider should plan for the engines to fail to start and not have sufficient power to retract the engine and exhibit a much higher drag coefficient. Should the engine not start and retract, a glider pilot should have an alternate landing area available with the decreased performance available in the higher drag configuration.

The pilot should fly the traffic pattern to land into the wind and plan the approach path to avoid all obstacles. The landing area should be of sufficient length to allow for touchdown and roll-out within the performance limitations of the particular self-launching glider. The pilot should also take into consideration any crosswind conditions and the landing surface. After touchdown, the pilot should maintain direction control and slow the self-launching glider to clear the landing area. The after-landing checklist should be completed when appropriate.

Common errors during landing include:

- Poor judgment of approach path.
- Improper use of flaps, spoilers, and/or dive brakes.
- Improper approach and landing speed.
- Improper crosswind correction.
- Improper technique during flare and touchdown.
- Poor directional control after landing.
- Improper use of brakes.
- Failure to use the appropriate checklist.
- Failure to use proper radio communication procedures.

Gliderport/Airport Traffic Patterns and Operations

The pilot must be familiar with the approach and landing traffic pattern to a gliderport or airport because the approach actually starts some distance away. Gliderports and airport operators should comply with Federal Aviation Administration (FAA) recommended procedures established in Advisory Circulars (AC), the Aeronautical Information Manual (AIM), and current FAA regulations for operating in United States airspace. If glider operation is conducted in other countries, the air regulations for those countries would apply. These publications also serve as good references to ensure safe glider operations.

Pilots need to determine a proper visual reference point as an initial point (IP) from which to begin the approach for each landing area. The IP may be located over the center of the gliderport/airport or at a remote location near the traffic pattern. As shown in *Figure 7-26,* the sequence of a normal approach is from over the IP to the downwind leg, base leg, final approach, flare, touchdown, rollout, and stop. Some gliderports and airports have established procedures to follow when conducting flight operations in and out of their airfield. It is good pilot practice to review existing approach and departure procedures so as to always follow safe established procedures. Be aware that compensation for winds often requires modifying the traffic pattern to retain a safe approach angle.

Determining the IP comes with good training and experience. The IP should only be used as a visual reference point for proper positioning into the traffic pattern. Do not rely on these visual points, as when landing at a different gliderport/airports these points will change. Pilots should develop proper placement, altitude, and distances based on current conditions. Use proper alignment for winds and always consider other environmental factors. Flying the glider traffic pattern is basically the same as a power pattern; however, the glider pilot must consider other environmental factors that affect the landing.

Once over the IP, the pilot flies along the downwind leg of the planned landing pattern. The pilot should plan to be over the IP at an altitude of 800 to 1,000 feet AGL or as recommended by the local field operating procedures. During this time, it is important to look for other aircraft and, if installed, listen to the radio for other aircraft in the vicinity of the gliderport/airport. Glider pilots should plan to make any radio calls early in the pattern, so the pilot can concentrate and on the landing task without being distracted. Glider pilots should be aware of other activities located at the gliderport/airport, and it is important that they are familiar with good operating practices. Glider operations usually establish the patterns for their operation with other activities in mind. Pilots new to a gliderport/airport should obtain a thorough checkout before conducting any flights.

Pilots should complete the landing checklist prior to the downwind leg. A good landing checklist is known as FUSTALL. This checklist can be modified as necessary for any glider.

- **F**laps—set (if applicable)
- **U**ndercarriage—down and locked (if applicable)
- **S**peed—normal approach speed established (as recommended by the GFM/POH)
- **T**rim—set
- **A**ir brakes (spoilers/dive brakes)—checked for correct operation
- **L**anding area—look for wind, other aircraft, and personnel
- **L**and the glider

Normal Approach and Landing

Prior to entering the downwind leg and accomplishing the landing checklist, concentrate on judging the approach angle, distance from the landing area, and staying clear of other aircraft while monitoring approach airspeed. The normal approach speed, as recommended by the GFM/POH, is the speed for ideal flight conditions. Medium turns can be used in the traffic pattern, but do not exceed a 45° bank angle. The approach should be made using spoilers/dive brakes as necessary to dissipate excess altitude. Use the elevator to

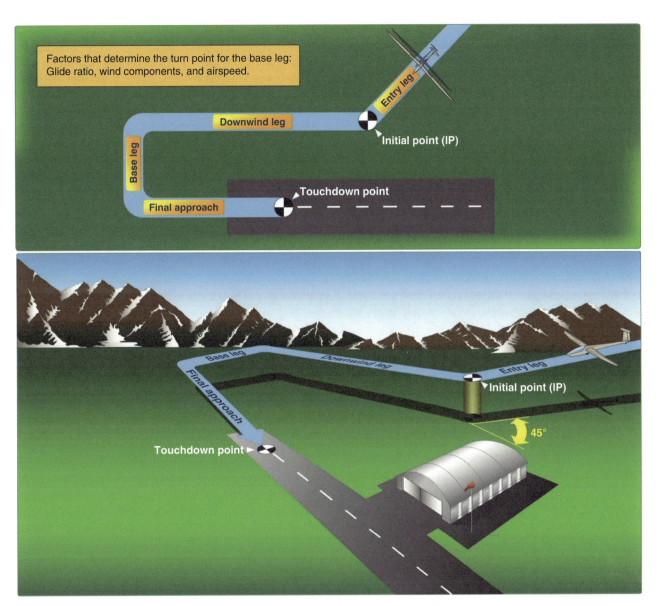

Figure 7-26. *Traffic pattern.*

maintain the recommended approach airspeed established by the manufacturer. If no approach speed is recommended by the manufacturer, use 1.5 V_{SO}. Establishing a proper pattern entry and normal approach speed is a foundation for a good approach to landing. During the entry into the traffic pattern, pilots need to ensure that the glider is in trim and keep the yaw string straight during these turns while maneuvering in the traffic pattern at all times.

Strong crosswinds, tailwinds, or high sink rates that are encountered in the traffic pattern require the pilot to modify the individual pattern leg (downwind, base, or final) and to adjust the approach speed as appropriate. It is recommended that half of the gust factor be added to the normal approach speed to compensate for wind gusts and sink. A strong tailwind or headwind requires a respective shortening or lengthening of the leg. A sudden encounter with a high sink rate may require the pilot to turn toward the landing area sooner than normal. The pilot should not conduct a 360° turn once established on the downwind leg. Throughout the traffic pattern, the pilot should be constantly aware of the approach speed and plan ahead by keeping the glider in trim and the yaw string straight.

When at an appropriate distance from the IP, the pilot should maneuver the glider to enter the downwind leg. The distance for a normal pattern from downwind leg to the landing area should be approximately one quarter to one half of a mile. Of course, this depends on current conditions and the type of glider. This varies at different locations. On the downwind leg, the glider should descend to arrive abeam the touchdown point at an altitude between 500 and 600 feet AGL. On the downwind leg, the groundspeed is higher if a tailwind is present. The pilot should use the spoilers/dive brakes as necessary to arrive at this altitude. The pilot should also monitor the glider's position with reference to the touchdown area. If the wind pushes the glider away from or toward the touchdown area, the pilot should stop the drift by establishing a wind correction angle into the wind. Failure to do so affects the point where the base leg should be started.

The base leg should not be started any later than when the touchdown point is approximately 45° over the pilot's shoulder looking back at the touchdown area, under a no-wind condition. Newer, higher glide ratio, faster gliders may need to extend the downwind leg somewhat, whereas lower ratio, slower gliders may need to turn to the base leg much sooner. Each glider pilot must determine the landing conditions and configure the glider for that landing under those conditions. Slip and drag devices can dissipate excess altitude, but nothing on a glider can make up for insufficient altitude to glide to the landing area. Base altitude should be no lower than approximately 500 feet AGL.

Once established on the base leg, the pilot should scan the extended final approach path to detect any aircraft that might be on long final approach to the landing area in use. If a radio is installed in the glider, this would be a good time to broadcast position for turn to final. The turn to the base leg should be timely enough to keep the point of intended touchdown area within easy gliding range. The pilot should adjust the turn to correct for wind drift encountered on the base leg and, if needed, make correction turns to ensure maintainance of the proper glide angle to the landing area. The pilot should also adjust the spoilers/dive brakes, as necessary, to position the glider at the desired glide angle.

NOTE: New pilots should learn to properly scan for another aircraft operating in the traffic pattern. Pilots should also review FAA AC 90-48C, Pilot's Role in Collision Avoidance.

The turn onto the final approach should not exceed a 45° bank and the glider should be on the appropriate approach angle to start the descent. The pilot should ensure that the yaw string is straight. Complete the turn to final to line up with the centerline of the touchdown area. The pilot should adjust the spoilers/dive brakes, as necessary, to fly the desired approach angle to the aim point and establish a stabilized approach at the recommended approach speed.

The stabilized approach is when the glider is at the proper glider path/angle with minimal spoilers/dive brakes deployed/extended, at the recommended approach speed for the current conditions (winds, gust, sink, etc.) and able to make the intended landing spot. The stabilized approach should be established no lower than 100 feet AGL. The final approach with spoilers/dive brakes extended approximately half open (not half travel of the spoiler/dive brake control handle) is ideal for most gliders. Avoid using full spoilers/dive brakes because this use causes a higher descent rate and increase in stall speed.

Minor adjustments in the spoilers/dive brakes may be needed to ensure proper glidepath control. Avoid pumping the spoilers/dive brakes from full open to full close. Under some conditions, the spoilers/dive brakes may have to be closed momentarily to correct the glidepath. The selected aim point should be prior to the touchdown point to accommodate the landing flare. The pilot may flare the glider at or about three to five feet AGL. The glider may float some distance until it touches down. If excess speed is used, the glider floats a considerable distance. Avoid using this technique as it uses a large amount of the intended landing area. Do not try to force the glider onto the ground at excessive speeds. This may introduce oscillations, such as porpoising and overcontrolling.

When within three to five feet of the landing surface, begin the flare with slight back elevator. As the airspeed decreases, the pilot holds the glider in a level or tail-low attitude to touchdown at the lowest possible speed for existing conditions, while the glider is still under aerodynamic control.

Pilots should avoid driving the glider into the ground by little or no flare. This type of landing puts excessive loads on the landing gear and wings. The pilot should hold the glider off as possible, but ensuring the touchdown is on the main wheel as stated in the GFM. In some gliders, the pilot can increase pitch attitude with slight back pressure to dissipate as much energy as possible prior to touchdown. The pilot should ensure that the glider touches down with a nose-high attitude, but not high enough to land tail first. A good glider landing in most gliders with a main wheel and tail wheel, or skid, is on the main wheel with the tail wheel just slightly touching or the tail wheel just barely off the surface. The main wheel is designed to withstand the shock of landings but the tail wheel is not. In some instances, the attach points or structure just in front of the empennage is the weakest point and may fail first. Pilots should always follow the GFM/POH recommendations of the manufacturer.

After touchdown, the pilot should concentrate on rolling out straight along the the centerline of the touchdown area, keeping full back stick on the elevator and the glider wings level. If an obstacle is detected (possible in an off-airport landing or landing out), a coordinated turn on the ground is needed to avoid the obstacle. Ensure that a wing is not allowed to contact the ground until the glider is at its lowest speed or stopped.

Tracking along a centerline of the touchdown area is an important consideration in gliders. The long, low wingtips of the glider are susceptible to damage from runway signage and runway lighting. Turning off the runway should be done only if and when the pilot has the glider under control.

Landing in high, gusty winds or turbulent conditions may require higher approach airspeed to improve controllability and provide a safer margin above stall airspeed. As a rule of thumb, pilots add one-half the reported gust factor to the normal recommended approach airspeed. This increased approach airspeed provides a safety margin and affords better penetration into the headwind on final approach.

Crosswind Landing

Crosswind landings require a crabbing, or slipping method, to correct for the effects of the wind on the final approach. Additionally, the pilot must land the glider without placing any unnecessary side load on the landing gear.

The crab method requires the pilot to point the nose of the glider into the wind and fly a straight track along the desired groundpath. The stronger the wind is, the greater the crab angle needs to be. The glider is in coordinated flight and tracking the extended centerline of the landing area. *[Figure 7-27A]* Prior to flare, the pilot must be prepared to align the glider with the landing direction. *[Figure 7-27B]* The pilot should use the rudder to align the glider prior to touchdown and deflect the ailerons into the wind to control the side drift caused by the crosswind.

In the slip method, the pilot uses rudder and ailerons to slip the glider into the wind to prevent drifting downwind of the touchdown area. The disadvantage of the slip method is that the sink rate of the glider increases, forcing the pilot to adjust the spoilers/dive brakes, as necessary, to compensate for this additional sink rate. Glider pilots should be ready to apply brakes to avoid leaving the runway or landing area as control authority is lost. The slip should be established no lower than 100 feet to ensure a stable approach.

Pilot selection of the slip or crab method for crosswind landing is personal preference and/or related to glider size and wingspan. The important action is to stabilize the approach early enough on final to maintain a constant approach angle and airspeed to arrive at the selected touchdown point.

Common errors during approach and landing include:

- Improper glidepath control.
- Improper use of flaps, spoilers/dive brakes.
- Improper airspeed control.
- Improper stabilize approach.
- Improper correction for crosswind.
- Improper procedure for touchdown/landing.
- Poor directional control during/after landing.
- Improper use of wheel brakes.

Slips

A slip is a descent with one wing lowered. It may be used for either of two purposes or both of them combined. A slip may be used to steepen the approach path without increasing the airspeed, as would be the case if the spoilers/dive brakes were inoperative, or to clear an obstacle. It can also be used to make the glider move sideways through the air to counteract the drift that results from a crosswind. Formerly, slips were used as a normal means of controlling landing descents to short or obstructed fields, but they are now primarily used in the performance of crosswind landings and short/off-field landings.

With the installation of effective spoilers/dive brakes on modern gliders, the use of slips to steepen or control the angle of descent is no longer the only procedure available

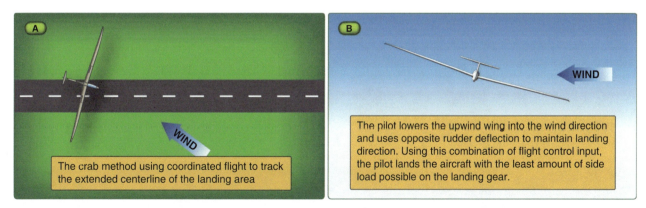

Figure 7-27. *Using the crab method to track the extended centerline of the landing area (A). Controlling side drift by adjusting the glider into the wind before landing (B).*

to the glider pilot. However, the pilot still needs proficiency in performance of forward slips to correct for possible errors in judgment of the landing approach.

The forward slip is a slip in which the glider's direction of motion remains the same as before the slip was begun. If there is any crosswind, the slip is much more effective if made into the wind. If the glider is originally in straight flight, the wing on the side that the slip is to be made should be lowered by using the ailerons. Simultaneously, the glider's nose must be yawed in the opposite direction by applying opposite rudder so the glider's longitudinal axis is at an angle to its original flightpath. The degree to which the nose is yawed in the opposite direction from the bank should be such that the original ground track is maintained. The nose should also be raised as necessary to prevent the airspeed from increasing.

The primary purpose of forward slips is to dissipate altitude without increasing the glider's airspeed, particularly in gliders not equipped with flaps or those with inoperative spoilers/dive brakes. There are many circumstances requiring the use of forward slips, such as in a landing approach over obstacles and in making off-field landings. It is always wise to allow an extra margin of altitude for safety in the original estimate of the approach. In the latter case, if the inaccuracy of the approach is confirmed by excess altitude when nearing the boundary of the selected field, slipping may dissipate the excess altitude.

The use of slips has definite limitations. Some pilots may try to lose altitude by violent slipping rather than by smoothly maneuvering, exercising good judgment, and using only a slight or moderate slip. In off-field landings, this erratic practice invariably leads to trouble since enough excess speed may result in preventing touchdown anywhere near the touchdown point, and very often results in overshooting the entire field.

A sideslip, as distinguished from a forward slip, is one during which the glider's longitudinal axis remains parallel to the original flightpath, but in which the flightpath changes direction according to the steepness of the bank. *[Figure 7-28]* The sideslip is important in counteracting wind drift during crosswind landings and is discussed in the crosswind landing section of this chapter.

Sideslip is used during the last portion of a final approach. The longitudinal axis of the glider must be aligned with the runway just prior to touchdown so the glider touches down in the direction in which it is moving. This requires timely action to decrease the slip to maintain ground track alignment with the landing zone. Failure to accomplish this alignment imposes severe sideloads on the landing gear and imparts violent ground looping tendencies.

Decreasing the slip is accomplished by leveling the wings and simultaneously releasing the rudder pressure while readjusting the pitch attitude to the normal glide attitude. If the pressure on the rudder is released abruptly, the nose swings too quickly into line and the glider tends to acquire excess airspeed.

Because of the location of the pitot tube and static vents, airspeed indicators in some gliders may have considerable error when the glider is in a slip. The pilot must be aware of this possibility and recognize a properly performed slip by the attitude of the glider, the sound of the airflow, and the feel of the flight controls.

Common errors when performing a slip include:
- Improper glidepath control.
- Improper use of slips.
- Improper airspeed control.
- Improper correction for crosswind.

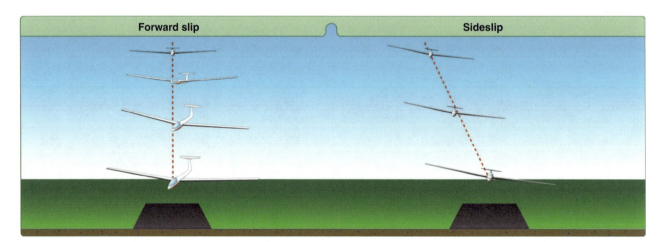

Figure 7-28. *Forward slip and sideslip.*

- Improper procedure for touchdown/landing.
- Poor directional control during/after landing.
- Improper use of spoilers, air brakes or dive brakes.

Downwind Landing

Downwind landings present special hazards and should be avoided when an into-the-wind landing is available. However, factors like gliderport/airport design, obstacles, or high terrain at one end of the runway, and runway slope may dictate a downwind procedure takeoff and landing procedures. Emergencies or a launch failure at low altitude can also require a downwind landing. The pilot must use the normal approach airspeed during a downwind landing. Any airspeed in excess only causes the approach area and runway needed for approach and landing to increase.

A tailwind increases the touchdown groundspeed and lengthens the landing roll. The increased distance for landing can be determined by dividing the actual touchdown speed by the normal touchdown speed, and squaring the result. For example, if the tailwind is 10 knots and the normal touchdown speed is 40 knots, the actual touchdown speed is 50 knots. This touchdown speed is 25 percent higher than the normal speed (10 divided by 40 = .25 × 100 = 25 percent), a factor of 1.25. A factor of 1.25 squared is approximately 1.56; the landing distance increases 56 percent over the normal landing distance.

On downwind approaches, a shallower approach angle should be used, depending on obstacles in the approach path. Use the spoilers/dive brakes and perhaps a forward slip, as necessary, to achieve the desired glidepath.

After touchdown, use the wheel brake and all available drag devices to reduce groundspeed and stop as soon as is practical. This is necessary to maintain control of the glider. Landing with a tail wind means a loss of control at a much higher ground speed and requires more braking action.

Common errors during downwind landing include:
- Improper glidepath control.
- Improper use of slips.
- Improper airspeed control.
- Improper correction for wind.
- Improper procedure for touchdown/landing.
- Poor directional control during/after landing.
- Improper use of wheel brakes.

After Landing and Securing

After landing, move or taxi the glider clear of all runways. If the glider is to be parked for a short interval between flights, choose a spot that does not inconvenience other gliderport/airport users. Protect the glider from wind by securing a wingtip with a weight or by tying it down. Consult the manufacturer's handbook for the recommended methods for securing the glider. Remember that even light winds can cause gliders to move about, turn sideways, or cause the higher wing in a parked glider to slam into the ground. Because gliders are particularly vulnerable to wind effects, the glider should be secured any time it is unattended.

When the glider has finished flying for the day, move it to the tiedown area. Secure the glider in accordance with the recommendation in the GFM/POH. The tiedown anchors should be strong and secure. Apply external control locks to the glider flight control surfaces. Control locks should be large, well marked, and brightly painted. If a cover is used to protect the pitot tube, the cover should be large and brightly colored. If a canopy cover is used, secure it so that the canopy cover does not scuff or scratch the canopy in windy conditions.

If the glider is stored in a hangar, be careful while moving the glider to avoid damaging it or other aircraft in the hangar. Chock the main wheel and tailwheel of the glider when it is in position in the hangar. If stored in a wings-level position, put a wing stand under each wingtip. If stored with one wing high, place a weight on the lowered wing to hold it down.

If the glider is to be disassembled and stored in a trailer, tow the glider to the trailer area and align the fuselage with the long axis of the trailer. Collect all tools and dollies required to disassemble and stow the glider. Secure the trailer so that loading the glider aboard does not move or upset the trailer or trailer doors. Follow the disassembly checklist in the GFM/POH. Stow the glider components securely in the trailer. When the glider has been stowed and secured, collect all tools and stow them properly. Close trailer doors and hatches. Secure the trailer against wind and weather by tying it down properly.

Performance Maneuvers

Straight Glides

To perform a straight glide, the glider pilot must hold a constant heading and airspeed. The heading reference should be some prominent point in front of the glider on the ground. The pilot also notes that, during a straight glide, each wingtip should be an equal distance above the ground. With the wings level, the pitch attitude is established with reference to a point on or below the horizon to establish a specified airspeed. Any change in pitch attitude results in a change in airspeed. There is a pitch attitude reference for best glide speed, another for the minimum sink speed, and another for slow flight. The pitch attitude is adjusted with the elevator to hold the specific airspeed. The glider elevator trim control allows the pilot to trim the glider to hold a constant pitch attitude and, therefore, a constant airspeed. Straight glides should be coordinated as indicated by a centered yaw string or slip-skid ball.

The glider pilot should also stay alert to airflow noise changes. At a constant airspeed in coordinated flight, wind noise should be constant. Any changes in airspeed or coordination cause a change in the wind noise. Gusts that cause the airspeed to change momentarily can be ignored. Holding the glider at a constant pitch attitude results in maintaining the desired airspeed control.

The glider pilot should learn to fly throughout a wide range of airspeeds, from minimum controllable airspeed to maximum allowable airspeed. This enables the pilot to learn the feel of the controls of the glider throughout its speed range. If the glider is equipped with spoilers/dive brakes and/or flaps, the glider pilot should become familiar with the changes that occur in pitch attitude and airspeed when these controls are used.

Common errors during straight glides include:

- Rough or erratic pitch attitude and airspeed control.
- Rough, uncoordinated, or inappropriate control applications.
- Failure to use trim or improper use of trim.
- Improper use of controls when using spoilers, dive brakes, and/or flaps.
- Prolonged uncoordinated flight—yaw or ball not centered.

Turns

The performance of turns involves coordination of all three flight controls: ailerons, rudder, and elevator. For purposes of this discussion, turns are divided into the following three classes as shown in *Figure 7-29*.

- Shallow turns are those in which the bank (less than approximately 20°) is so shallow that the inherent lateral stability of the glider levels the wings unless some aileron is applied to maintain the bank.
- Medium turns are those resulting from a degree of bank (approximately 20° to 45°) at which lateral stability is overcome by the overbanking tendency, resulting in no control inputs (other than elevator) being required to maintain the angle.

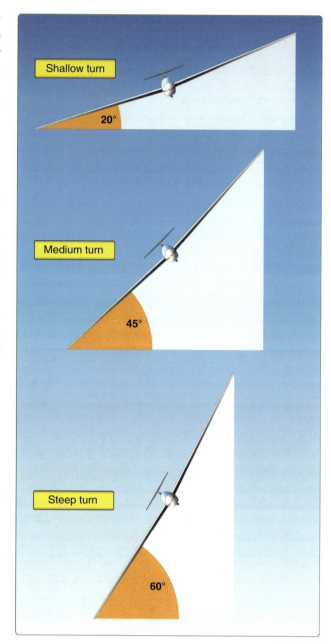

Figure 7-29. *Shallow, medium, and steep turns.*

- Steep turns are those resulting from a degree of bank (45° or more) at which the overbanking tendency of a glider overcomes stability, and the bank increases unless aileron is applied to prevent it.

Before starting any turn, the pilot must clear the airspace in the direction of the turn. A glider is turned by banking (lowering the wing in the direction of the desired turn, thus raising the other). When the glider is flying straight, the total lift is acting perpendicular to the wings and to the earth. As the glider is banked into a turn, total lift becomes the resultant of two components: 1) the vertical lift component continues to act perpendicularly to the earth and opposes gravity and 2) the horizontal lift component (centripetal) acts parallel to the earth's surface and opposes inertia (apparent centrifugal force). These two lift components act at right angles to each other, causing the resultant total lifting force to act perpendicular to the banked wing of the glider. It is the horizontal lift component that actually turns the glider, not the rudder.

Roll-In

When applying aileron to bank the glider, the aileron on the rising wing is lowered, producing a greater drag than the raised aileron on the lowering wing. This increased drag causes the glider to yaw toward the rising wing or opposite the direction of turn. To counteract this adverse yawing moment, rudder pressure must be applied in the desired direction of turn simultaneously with aileron pressure. This action is required to produce a coordinated turn.

After the bank has been established in a medium banked turn, all pressure applied to the aileron may be relaxed. The glider remains at the selected bank with no further tendency to yaw since there is no longer a deflection of the ailerons. As a result, pressure may also be relaxed on the rudder pedals, and the rudder is allowed to streamline itself with the direction of the slipstream. Rudder pressure maintained after establishing the turn causes the glider to skid to the outside of the turn. If a definite effort is made to center the rudder rather than let it streamline itself to the turn, it is probable that some opposite rudder pressure will be exerted inadvertently. This forces the glider to yaw opposite its turning path, causing the glider to slip to the inside of the turn. The yaw string or ball in the slip indicator is displaced off center whenever the glider is skidding or slipping sideways. In proper coordinated flight, there is no skidding or slipping.

In constant airspeed turns, it is necessary to increase the AOA of the wing as the bank progresses by adding nose-up elevator pressure. This is required because the total lift must be equal to the vertical component of lift plus the horizontal lift component. To stop the turn, coordinated use of the aileron and rudder pressure are added to bring the wings back to level flight as elevator pressure is relaxed.

There is a direct relationship between airspeed, bank angle, and rate and radius of turn. The rate of turn at any given true airspeed depends on the horizontal lift component. The horizontal lift component varies in proportion to the amount of bank. Therefore, the rate of turn at a given true airspeed increases as the angle of bank is increased. On the other hand, when a turn is made at a higher true airspeed at a given bank angle, the inertia is greater and the horizontal lift component required for the turn is greater, causing the turning rate to become slower. Therefore, at a given angle of bank, a higher true airspeed makes the radius of turn larger because the glider is turning at a slower rate.

As the angle of bank is increased from a shallow bank to a medium bank, the airspeed of the wing on the outside of the turn increases in relation to the inside wing. The additional lift developed by the bank balances the lateral stability of the glider. No aileron pressure is required to maintain the bank. At any given airspeed, aileron pressure is not required to maintain the bank. If the bank is increased from a medium bank to a steep bank, the radius of turn decreases even further. The greater lift of the outside wing then causes the bank to steepen, and opposite aileron is necessary to keep the bank constant.

As the radius of the turn becomes smaller, a significant difference develops between the speed of the inside wing and the speed of the outside wing. The wing on the outside of the turn travels a longer circuit than the inside wing, yet both complete their respective circuits in the same length of time. Therefore, the outside wing travels faster than the inside wing, and as a result, it develops more lift. This creates an overbanking tendency that must be controlled by the use of the ailerons. Because the outboard wing is developing more lift, it also has more induced drag. This causes a slip during steep turns that must be corrected by rudder usage.

To establish the desired angle of bank, the pilot should use visual reference points on the glider, the earth's surface, and the natural horizon. The pilot's posture while seated in the glider is very important, particularly during turns. It affects the interpretation of outside visual references. The beginning pilot may lean away from or into the turn rather than ride with the glider. This should be corrected immediately if the pilot is to properly learn to use visual references.

Applications of large aileron and rudder produces rapid roll rates and allow little time for corrections before the desired bank is reached. Slower (small control displacement) roll rates provide more time to make necessary pitch and bank corrections. As soon as the glider rolls from the wings-level attitude, the nose starts to move along the horizon, increasing its rate of travel proportionately as the bank is increased.

As the desired angle of bank is established, aileron and rudder pressures should be relaxed. This prevents increase in bank because the aileron and rudder control surfaces are neutral in their streamlined position. The up-elevator pressure should not be relaxed, but should be held constant to maintain the desired airspeed. Throughout the turn, the pilot should cross-check the airspeed indicator to verify the proper pitch is being maintained. The cross-check and instrument scan should include outside visual references. If the glider is gaining or losing airspeed, the pitch attitude should be adjusted in relation to the horizon. During all turns, aileron, rudder, and elevator are used to correct minor variations in pitch and bank just as they are in straight glides.

Roll-Out

The roll-out from a turn is similar to the roll-in except that coordinated flight controls are applied in the opposite direction. Aileron and rudder are applied in the direction of the roll-out or toward the high wing. As the angle of bank decreases, the elevator pressure should be relaxed, as necessary, to maintain airspeed.

Since the glider continues turning as long as there is any bank, the roll-out must be started before reaching the desired heading. The amount of lead required to roll out on the desired heading depends on the degree of bank used in the turn. Normally, the lead is one half the degrees of bank. For example, if the bank is 30°, lead the roll-out by 15°. As the wings become level, the control pressures should be smoothly relaxed so the controls are neutralized as the glider returns to straight flight. As the roll-out is being completed, attention should be given to outside visual references, as well as the airspeed and heading indicators to determine that the wings are being leveled and the turn stopped.

Common errors during a turn include:

- Failure to clear turn.
- Nose movement before the bank starts—rudder is being applied too soon.
- Commencement of bank before the nose starts turning, or nose movement in the opposite direction—the rudder is being applied too late.
- Up or down nose movement when entering a bank—excessive or insufficient elevator is being applied.
- Rough or uncoordinated use of controls during the roll-in and roll-out.
- Failure to establish and maintain the desired angle of bank.
- Overshooting/undershooting the desired heading.

In a slipping turn, the glider is not turning at the rate appropriate to the bank being used, since the glider is yawed toward the outside of the turning flightpath. The glider is banked too much for the rate of turn, so the horizontal lift component is greater than the centrifugal force. Equilibrium between the horizontal lift component and centrifugal force is reestablished either by decreasing the bank (ailerons), increasing yaw (rudder), or a combination of the two. *[Figure 7-30]*

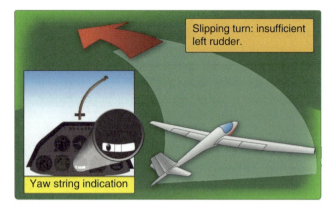

Figure 7-30. *Slipping turn.*

A skidding turn results from an excess of centrifugal force over the horizontal lift component, pulling the glider toward the outside of the turn. The rate of turn is too great for the angle of bank. Correction of a skidding turn thus involves a decrease in yaw (rudder), an increase in bank (aileron), or a combination of the two changes. *[Figure 7-31]*

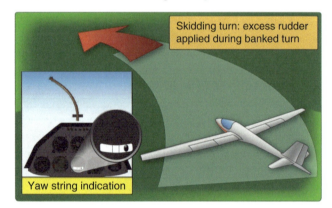

Figure 7-31. *Skidding turn.*

The yaw string identifies slips and skids. In flight, the rule to remember is simple: step on the head of the yaw string. If the head of the yaw string is to the right of the tail, then the pilot needs to apply right pedal. If the head of the yaw string is to the left of the tail, then the pilot should apply left pedal. *[Figure 7-32]*

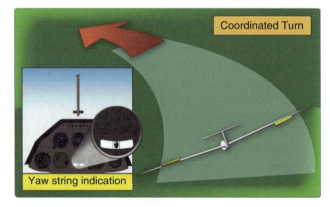

Figure 7-32. *Coordinated turn.*

The ball in the slip/skid indicator also indicates slips and skids. When using this instrument for coordination, apply rudder pressure on the side that the ball is offset (step on the ball). Correction for uncoordinated condition should be accomplished by using appropriate rudder and aileron control pressures simultaneously to coordinate the glider.

Steep Turns

Soaring flight requires competence in steep turns. In thermalling flight, small-radius turns are often necessary to keep the glider in or near the core of the thermal updraft where lift is usually strongest and rapid climbs are possible. At any given airspeed, increasing the angle of bank decreases the radius of the turn and increases the rate of turn. The radius of a turn at any given bank angle varies directly with the square of the airspeed at which the turn is made; therefore, the lower the airspeed is, the smaller the turn radius is. To keep the radius of turn small, it is necessary to bank steeply while maintaining an appropriate airspeed, such as minimum sink or best glide speed. The pilot must be aware that as the bank angle increases, the stall speed increases.

Before starting the steep turn, the pilot should ensure that the area is clear of other traffic since the rate of turn is quite rapid. After establishing the appropriate airspeed, the glider should be smoothly rolled into a coordinated steep turn with at least 45° of bank. The pilot should use outside visual reference to establish and maintain the desired bank angle. If the pilot does not add back pressure to maintain the desired airspeed after the bank is established, the glider has a tendency to enter a spiral. To counteract the overbanking tendency caused by the steep turn, the pilot should apply top aileron pressure. Because the top aileron pressure pulls the nose away from the direction of the turn, the pilot also must apply bottom rudder pressure. A coordinated (no slip or skid) steep turn requires back pressure on the elevator for airspeed control, top aileron pressure for bank control, and bottom rudder pressure to streamline the fuselage with the flightpath.

Common errors during steep turns include:

- Failure to clear turn.
- Uncoordinated use of controls.
- Loss of orientation.
- Failure to maintain airspeed within tolerance.
- Unintentional stall or spin.
- Excessive deviation from desired heading during roll-out.

Maneuvering at Minimum Controllable Airspeed

Maneuvering during slow flight demonstrates the flight characteristics and degree of controllability of a glider at minimum speeds. By definition, the term "flight at minimum controllable airspeed" means a speed at which any further increase in AOA or load factor causes an immediate stall. Pilots must develop an awareness of the particular glider flight characteristics in order to recognize and avoid stalls that may inadvertently occur during the low airspeeds used in takeoffs, climbs, thermaling, and approaches to landing.

The objective of maneuvering at minimum controllable airspeed is to develop the pilot's sense of feel and ability to use the controls correctly, and to improve proficiency in performing maneuvers that require low airspeeds. Maneuvering at minimum controllable airspeed should be performed using outside visual reference. It is important that pilots form the habit of frequently referencing the pitch attitude of the glider for airspeed control while flying at low speeds.

The maneuver is started from either best glide speed or minimum sink speed. The pitch attitude is smoothly and gradually increased. While the glider is losing airspeed, the position of the nose in relation to the horizon should be noted and should be adjusted as necessary until the minimum controllable airspeed is established. During these changing flight conditions, it is important to retrim the glider, as necessary, to compensate for changes in control pressures. Back pressure that is excessive or too aggressive on the elevator control may result in an abrupt increase in pitch attitude and a rapid decrease in airspeed, which lead to a higher AOA and a possible stall. When the desired pitch attitude and airspeed have been established, it is important to continually cross-check the pitch attitude on the horizon and the airspeed indicator to ensure accurate control is being maintained.

When minimum controllable airspeed is established in straight flight, turns should be practiced to determine the glider's controllability characteristics at this selected airspeed. During the turns, the pitch attitude may need to be decreased in order to maintain the airspeed. If a steep turn is encountered, and the pitch attitude is not decreased, the increase in load factor may result in a stall. A stall may also occur as a result of abrupt or rough control movements resulting in momentary increases in load factor. Abruptly raising the flaps during minimum controllable airspeed results in sudden loss of lift and possibly causing a stall.

Minimum controllable airspeed should also be practiced with extended spoilers/dive brakes. This provides additional understanding of the changes in pitch attitude caused by the increase in drag from the spoilers/dive brakes.

Actual minimum controllable airspeed depends upon various conditions, such as the gross weight and CG location of the glider and the maneuvering load imposed by turns and pull-ups. Flight at minimum controllable airspeed requires positive use of rudder and ailerons. The diminished effectiveness of the flight controls during flight at minimum controllable airspeed helps pilots develop the ability to estimate the margin of safety above the stalling speed.

Common errors during maneuvers at minimum controllable airspeed include:

- Failure to establish or to maintain minimum controllable airspeed.
- Improper use of trim.
- Rough or uncoordinated use of controls.
- Failure to recognize indications of a stall.

Stall Recognition and Recovery

All pilots must be proficient in stall recognition and recovery. A stall can occur at any airspeed and at any attitude. In the case of the self-launching glider under power, a stall can also occur with any power setting. A stall occurs when the smooth airflow over the glider's wing is disrupted and the wings stop producing enough lift. This occurs when the wing exceeds its critical AOA.

The practice of stall recovery and the development of stall awareness are of primary importance in pilot training. The objectives in performing intentional stalls are to familiarize the pilot with the conditions that produce stalls, to assist in recognizing an approaching stall, and to develop the habit of taking prompt preventive or corrective action.

Intentional stalls should be performed so the maneuver is completed by 1,500 feet above the ground with a landing area within gliding distance, in the event lift cannot be found. Although it depends on the degree to which a stall has progressed, most stalls require some loss of altitude during recovery. The longer it takes to recognize the approaching stall, the more complete the stall is likely to become, and the greater the loss of altitude to be expected.

Pilots must recognize the flight conditions that are conducive to stalls and know how to apply the necessary corrective action since most gliders do not have an electrical or mechanical stall warning device. Pilots should learn to recognize an approaching stall by sight, sound, and feel. The following cues may be useful in recognizing the approaching stall.

1. Vision—useful in detecting a stall condition by noting the attitude of the glider versus the horizon.
2. Hearing—also helpful in sensing a stall condition. In the case of a glider, a change in sound due to loss of airspeed is particularly noticeable. The lessening of the noise made by the air flowing along the glider structure as airspeed decreases is quite noticeable, and when the stall is almost complete, the pilot starts to feel airframe buffeting or aerodynamic vibration as the stall occurs.
3. Feeling
    a. Kinesthesia, or the sensing of changes in direction or speed of motion, is an important intuitive indicator to the trained and experienced pilot. If this sensitivity is properly developed, it warns of a decrease in speed or the beginning of a settling, or mushing, of the glider.
    b. The feel of control pressures is also very important. As speed is reduced, the resistance to pressure on the controls becomes progressively less. Pressures exerted on the controls tend to become movements of the control surfaces. As the airflow slows and stalls, the aerodynamic controls (ailerons, elevator, and rudder) have significantly less authority and require much more movement to create the same amount of directional change as compared to the normal flight regime responses. As the wing airflow stalls and the stalling strongly affects the controls, the controllability of the glider can become questionable. Properly designed and certificated gliders should retain marginal control authority when the wing is stalled. The lag between these movements and the response of the glider becomes greater until in a complete stall.

Signs of an impending stall include the following:

- Nose-high attitude for higher wing loading with possible increasing trend.
- Low airspeed indication with a decreasing trend.
- Low airflow noise and decreasing.
- Back pressure increasing, requiring more elevator trimming and/or not having anymore aft trim.
- Poor control responses from the glider and decreasing feedback pressures from control movements.
- Wing (airframe) buffeting as stalling begins.
- Yaw string (if equipped) movement from normal flight position.

Always make clearing turns before performing stalls. During the practice of intentional stalls, the real objective is not to learn how to stall a glider, but to learn how to recognize an approaching stall and take prompt corrective action. The recovery actions must be taken in a coordinated manner.

First, at the indication of a stall, the pitch attitude and AOA must be decreased positively and immediately. Since the basic cause of a stall is always an excessive AOA, the cause must first be eliminated by releasing the back-elevator pressure that was necessary to attain that AOA or by moving the elevator control forward. This lowers the nose and returns the wing to an effective AOA. The amount of elevator control pressure or movement to use depends on the design of the glider, the severity of the stall, and the proximity of the ground. In some gliders, a moderate movement of the elevator control—perhaps slightly forward of neutral—is enough, while others may require a forcible push to the full forward position. An excessive negative load on the wings caused by excessive forward movement of the elevator may impede, rather than hasten, the stall recovery. The object is to reduce the AOA, but only enough to allow the wing to regain lift. [Figure 7-33]

If stalls are practiced or encountered in a self-launching glider, the maximum allowable power should be applied during the stall recovery to increase the self-launching glider's speed and assist in reducing the wing's AOA. Generally, the throttle should be promptly, but smoothly, advanced to the maximum allowable power. Although stall recoveries should be practiced with and without power, in self-launching gliders during actual stalls, the application of power is an integral part of the stall recovery. Usually, the greater the applied power is, the less the loss of altitude is. Maximum allowable power applied at the instant of a stall usually does not cause overspeeding of an engine equipped with a fixed-pitch propeller, due to the heavy air load imposed on the propeller at low airspeeds. However, it is necessary to reduce the power as airspeed is gained after the stall recovery so the airspeed does not become excessive.

When performing intentional stalls, pilots should never allow the engine to exceed its maximum designed rpm limitation. The maximum rpm is marked by a red line on the engine tachometer gauge. Exceeding rpm limitations can cause damage to engine components.

Whether in a towed glider or self-launching glider, stall recovery is accomplished by leveling the wings and returning to straight flight using coordinated flight controls. The first few practice sessions should consist of approaches to stalls with recovery initiated at the first airframe buffet or when partial loss of control is noted. Using this method, pilots become familiar with the initial indications of an approaching stall without fully stalling the glider.

Stall accidents usually result from an inadvertent stall at a low altitude in which a recovery was not accomplished prior to contact with the surface. As a preventive measure, stalls should be practiced at an altitude that allows recovery at no lower than 1,500 feet AGL and within gliding distance of a landing area.

Different types of gliders have different stall characteristics. Most gliders are designed so the wings stall progressively outward from the wing roots (where the wing attaches to the fuselage) to the wingtips. This is the result of designing the wings so the wingtips have a smaller angle of incidence than the wing roots. When exceeding the critical angle of attack results in a stall, the inner wing does not support normal aerodynamic flight, but the outer part of the wing does retain some aerodynamic effectiveness. Wings are designed in this manner so aileron control is available at high AOA (low airspeed) and to give the glider more stable stalling characteristics. When the glider is in a stalled condition, the wingtips continue to provide some degree of lift, and the ailerons still have some control effect. During recovery from a stall, the return of lift begins at the tips and progresses toward the roots. Thus, the ailerons can be used to level the wings.

Using the ailerons requires finesse to avoid an aggravated stall condition. For example, if the right wing drops during the stall and excessive aileron control is applied to the left to raise the wing, the aileron that deflects downward (right wing) would produce a greater AOA (and drag). Possibly a more complete stall would occur at the tip, because the critical AOA would be exceeded. The increase in drag created by the

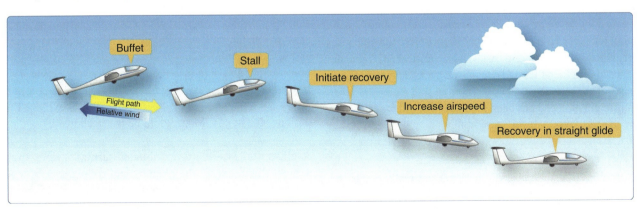

Figure 7-33. *Stall recovery.*

high AOA on that wing might cause the airplane to yaw in that direction. This adverse yaw could result in a spin unless directional control were maintained by rudder and/or aileron control is sufficiently reduced.

Even though excessive aileron pressure may have been applied, a spin does not occur if directional (yaw) control is maintained by timely application of coordinated rudder pressure. Therefore, it is important that the rudder be used properly during both entry and recovery from a stall. The primary use of the rudder in stall recovery is to counteract any tendency of the glider to yaw. The correct recovery technique would be to decrease the pitch attitude by applying forward elevator pressure to reduce the AOA while simultaneously maintaining directional control with coordinated use of the aileron and rudder.

Due to engineering design variations, the stall characteristics for all gliders cannot be specifically described; however, the similarities found in gliders are noteworthy enough to be considered. The factors that affect the stalling characteristics of the glider are weight and balance, bank and pitch attitude, coordination, and drag. The pilot should learn the stall characteristics of the glider being flown and the proper correction procedures. It should be reemphasized that a stall can occur at any airspeed, in any attitude, or at any power setting in the case of a self-launching or sustaining glider, depending on the total value of factors affecting the particular glider.

Whenever practicing stalls while turning, a constant bank angle should be maintained until the stall occurs. After the stall occurs, coordinated control inputs should be made to return the glider to wings-level flight.

Advanced stalls include secondary, accelerated, and crossed-control stalls. These stalls are extremely useful for pilots to expand their knowledge of stall/spin awareness.

Secondary Stalls
A secondary stall occurs after a recovery from a preceding stall. It is caused by attempting to hasten the completion of a stall recovery with abrupt control input before the glider has regained sufficient flying speed and the critical AOA is again exceeded. When this stall occurs, the back-elevator pressure should again be released as in a normal stall recovery. When sufficient airspeed has been regained, the glider can then be returned to wings-level, straight flight.

Accelerated Stalls
Although the stalls already discussed normally occur at a specific airspeed, the pilot must thoroughly understand that all stalls result solely from attempts to fly at excessively high angles of attack. During flight, the AOA of a glider wing is determined by a number of factors, the most important of which are airspeed, gross weight of the glider, and load factors imposed by maneuvering.

At gross weight, the glider consistently stalls at the same indicated airspeed if no acceleration is involved. However, the glider stalls at a higher indicated airspeed when excessive maneuvering loads are imposed by steep turns, pull-ups, or other abrupt changes in its flightpath. Stalls entered from such flight situations are called "accelerated maneuver stalls, a term that has no reference to the airspeeds involved. Stalls that result from abrupt maneuvers tend to be more rapid or severe than the unaccelerated or steady state stall. Accelerated stalls occur at higher-than-normal airspeeds and may be unexpected by pilots. These accelerated stalls result when the AOA exceeds the angle necessary to stall the airflow over the wing. The relative wind angle increases as the loads on the wings require more lift to change direction, either vertically or horizontally, and inertia pushes the wings into the airmass resulting in an increased AOA. Depending on the wing configuration and quality of coordination, one wing may stall prior to the other wing resulting in a wingover entry into a spiral or spin. If the wings have a slight or pronounced sweep, one wing can easily develop more lift than the other wing almost instantaneously resulting in a wingover before the pilot can react. This is the common killer scenario of a pilot turning too tightly in the traffic pattern and crashing upside down.

Accelerated maneuver stalls should not be performed in any glider in which this maneuver is prohibited by the GFM/POH. If they are permitted, they should be performed with a bank of approximately 45° and never at a speed greater than the glider manufacturer's recommended airspeeds or the design maneuvering speed specified for the glider. The design maneuvering speed is the maximum speed at which the glider can be stalled or the application of full aerodynamic control will not exceed the glider's limit load factor. At or below this speed, the glider is designed so that it stalls before the limit load factor can be exceeded. The objective of demonstrating accelerated stalls is not to develop competency in setting up the stall, but rather to learn how they may occur and to develop the ability to recognize a prestall situation immediately and then take the proper recovery action. It is important that recovery is made at the first indication of a stall, or immediately after the stall has fully developed; a prolonged stall condition should never be allowed.

A glider stalls during a coordinated turn as it does from straight flight, except the pitching and rolling actions tend to be more sudden. If the glider is slipping toward the inside of the turn at the time the stall occurs, it tends to roll rapidly toward the outside of the turn as the nose pitches down because the outside wing stalls before the inside wing. If the glider is skidding toward the outside of the turn, it has a tendency to roll to the inside of the turn because the inside wing stalls first. If the coordination of the turn at the time of the stall is accurate, the glider's nose pitches away from the pilot just as it does in a straight flight stall, since both wings stall simultaneously. The configuration of the wings has a strong influence on exactly how a glider reacts to different airflows. The safe approach is to fly the specific glider into these situations at higher altitudes to determine how that glider reacts. The glider pilot should commit those newly discovered prestall conditions and indications to memory to avoid those conditions at lower altitudes where recovery is improbable or impossible.

Glider pilots enter an accelerated stall demonstration by establishing the desired flight attitude and then, with smooth actions, firmly and progressively increasing the AOA until a stall occurs. Because of the rapidly changing flight attitude, sudden stall entry, and possible loss of altitude, it is extremely vital that the area be clear of other aircraft. Entry altitudes should be adequate for safe recovery.

Actual accelerated stalls occur most frequently during turns in the traffic pattern close to the ground while maneuvering the glider for the approach. The demonstration of an accelerated stall is accomplished by exerting excessive back elevator pressure. It usually occurs during improperly executed steep turns, stall and spin recoveries, and pullouts from steep dives. The objectives are to determine the stall characteristics of the glider and develop the ability to instinctively recover at the onset of a stall at other-than-normal stall speed or flight attitudes. An accelerated stall, although usually demonstrated in steep turns, may actually be encountered any time excessive back-elevator pressure is applied and/or the AOA is increased too rapidly.

From straight flight at maneuvering speed or less, the glider should be rolled into a steep banked (45° maximum) turn and back-elevator pressure gradually applied. After the bank is established, back-elevator pressure should be smoothly and steadily increased. The resulting apparent centrifugal force pushes the pilot's body down in the seat, increases the wing loading, and decreases the airspeed. Back-elevator pressure should be firmly increased until a definite stall occurs.

When the glider stalls, recovery should be made promptly by releasing back-elevator pressure. If the turn is uncoordinated, one wing may tend to drop suddenly, causing the glider to roll in that direction. If this occurs, the glider should be returned to wings-level, straight flight with coordinated control pressure.

A glider pilot should recognize when an accelerated stall is imminent and take prompt action to prevent a completely stalled condition. It is imperative that prolonged stalls, excessive airspeed, or loss of altitude, and spins be avoided.

Crossed-Control Stalls

The objective of a crossed-control stall demonstration maneuver is to show the effect of improper control technique and to emphasize the importance of using coordinated control pressures whenever making turns. This type of stall occurs with the controls crossed—aileron pressure applied in one direction and rudder pressure in the opposite direction—and the critical AOA is exceeded. [Figure 7-34]

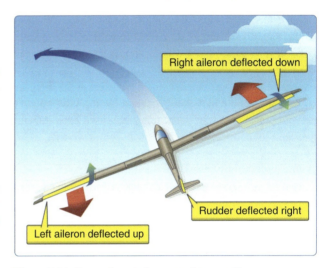

Figure 7-34. *Crossed-control approach to a stall.*

This is a stall that is most likely to occur during a poorly planned and executed base-to-final approach turn, and often is the result of overshooting the centerline of the runway during that turn. Normally, the proper action to correct for overshooting the runway is to increase the rate of turn by using coordinated aileron and rudder. At the relatively low altitude of a base-to-final approach turn, improperly trained pilots may be apprehensive of steeping the bank to increase the rate of turn.

The addition of rudder pressure on the inside of the turn causes the speed of the outer wing to increase, creating greater lift on that wing. To keep that wing from rising and to maintain a constant angle of bank, opposite aileron pressure is required. The added inside rudder pressure also causes the nose to lower in relation to the horizon. Consequently, additional back-elevator pressure would be required to maintain a constant pitch attitude. The resulting condition is a turn with rudder applied in one direction, aileron in the opposite direction, and excessive back-elevator pressure—a pronounced crossed-control condition.

Since the glider is in a skidding turn during the crossed-control condition, the wing on the outside of the turn increases speed and produces more lift than the inside wing, and the glider starts to increase its bank. The down aileron on the inside of the turn helps drag that wing back, slowing it and decreasing its lift. This further causes the glider to roll. The roll may be so fast that it is possible the bank will be vertical or past vertical before it can be stopped.

For the demonstration of the maneuver, it is important that it be entered at a safe altitude because of the possible extreme nose-down attitude and loss of altitude that may result. Before demonstrating this stall, the pilot should clear the area for other air traffic. While the gliding attitude and airspeed are being established, the glider should be retrimmed. When the glide is stabilized, the glider should be rolled into a medium banked turn to simulate a final approach turn that would overshoot the centerline of the runway. During the turn, excessive rudder pressure should be applied in the direction of the turn but the bank held constant by applying opposite aileron pressure. At the same time, increased back-elevator pressure is required to keep the nose from lowering.

All of these control pressures should be increased until the glider stalls. When the stall occurs, releasing the control pressures and simultaneously decreasing the AOA initiates the recovery. In a crossed-control stall, the glider often stalls with little warning. The nose may pitch down, the inside wing may suddenly drop, and the glider may continue to roll to an inverted position. This is usually the beginning of a spin. It is obvious that close to the ground is no place to allow this to happen.

Recovery must be made before the glider enters an abnormal attitude (vertical spiral or spin); it is a simple matter to return to wings-level, straight flight by coordinated use of the controls. The pilot must be able to recognize when this stall is imminent and must take immediate action to prevent a completely stalled condition. It is imperative that this type of stall not occur during an actual approach to a landing, since recovery may be impossible prior to ground contact due to the low altitude.

Common errors during advanced stalls include:

- Improper pitch and bank control during straight-ahead and turning stalls.
- Rough or uncoordinated control procedures.
- Failure to recognize the first indications of a stall.
- Failure to achieve a stall.
- Poor recognition and recovery procedures.
- Excessive altitude loss or airspeed or encountering a secondary stall during recovery.

Operating Airspeeds

Minimum Sink Airspeed

Minimum sink airspeed is defined as the airspeed at which the glider loses the least altitude in a given period of time. Minimum sink airspeed varies with the weight of the glider. Glider manufacturers publish altitude loss in feet per minute or meters per second (e.g., 122 ft/min or 0.62 m/sec) at a specified weight. Flying at minimum sink airspeed results in maximum duration in the absence of convection in the atmosphere.

The minimum sink airspeed given in the GFM/POH is based on the following conditions.

- The glider is wings level and flying a straight flightpath; load factor is 1.0 G.
- The glider flight controls are perfectly coordinated.
- Wing flaps are set to zero degrees and air brakes are closed and locked.
- The wings are free of bugs or other contaminants.
- The glider is at a manufacturer-specified weight.

While flying in a thermaling turn, the proper airspeed is the minimum sink airspeed appropriate to the load factor, or G-load, that the glider is undergoing. The glider's stall speed increases with load factor. The minimum sink speed needs to be increased with an increase in load factor. Another factor that always needs to be considered is that the gross weight and stall speed of the glider can vary if equipped with water ballast, which affects the minimum sink airspeed. For most gliders, the following weights will be of greatest interest:

1. Maximum gross weight with full water and both seats occupied
2. Maximum gross weight with both seats occupied and no water ballast
3. One pilot on board

The effect of only weight on stall speed can be expressed by using the basic lift formula that is manipulated and simplified to derive the necessary information. The modified lift formula is:

$$\frac{V_S 2}{V_S 1} = \frac{\sqrt{W2}}{W1}$$

$V_S 1$ = stall speed corresponding to some gross weight, W1
$V_S 2$ = stall speed corresponding to a different gross weight, W2

This can be manipulated into V_S times the square root of the load factor (which equals weight × G loading).

For example, if a glider stall speed is 34 knots, consider the following formula (34 × $\sqrt{1.2}$ (load factor) = 34 × 1.10 = 37 at 30°) for thermalling:

- In a 30° banked turn, load factor is 1.2 Gs. The approximate square root of 1.2 is 1.1. Now multiply 34 knots times 1.1 yields a 37-knot stall speed. Since the minimum sink speed is 40 which is still above the stall speed but by only approximately 3 knots, the margin of safety is decreasing and the pilot should consider increasing the minimum airspeed by a factor proportionate to the stall speed increase, in this case 44 knots (40 × $\sqrt{1.2}$ (load factor) = 40 × 1.10 = 44 at 30°).

- In a 45° banked turn, load factor is 1.18 (34 × $\sqrt{1.4}$ = 34 × 1.18 = 40.12 knots at 45°). Now multiply 34 knots times 1.18 which yields a 41-knot stall speed. The minimum sink speed of 40 knots is now below the stall speed. The pilot should increase the minimum airspeed proportionately to the stall airspeed, and the new speed would be 48 knots (40 × $\sqrt{1.4}$ (load factor) = 41 × 1.18 = 48 at 45°), a 7-knot safety factor.

- In a 60° banked turn, load factor is 2.0 Gs. The approximate square root of 2.0 is 1.4 (34 × $\sqrt{2.0}$ = 34 × 1.41 = 48 knots at 60°). Now multiply 34 knots times 1.4 which yields a 48-knot stall speed. The minimum sink speed of 40 knots is now below the stall speed. The pilot should increase the minimum airspeed proportionately to 57 knots, yielding an 9-knot safety (40 × $\sqrt{2.0}$ (load factor) = 40 × 1.41 = 56.4 at 60°).

Minimum sink airspeed is always lower than best L/D airspeed at any given operating weight. If the operating weight of the glider is noticeably less than maximum gross weight, then the actual minimum sink airspeed at that operating weight is lower than that published by the manufacturer.

Common errors regarding minimum sink airspeed include:

- Improper determination of minimum sink speed.
- Failure to maintain proper pitch attitude and airspeed control.

Best Glide Airspeed

Best glide (L/D) airspeed is defined as the airspeed that results in the least amount of altitude loss over a given distance. This allows the glider to glide the greatest distance in still air. This performance is expressed as glide ratio. The manufacturer publishes the best glide airspeed for specified weights and the resulting glide ratio. For example, a glide ratio of 36:1 means that the glider loses 1 foot of altitude for every 36 feet of forward movement in still air at this airspeed. The glide ratio decreases at airspeeds above or below best glide airspeed. The best glide speed can be found from the glider polars in Chapter 5, Performance Limitations.

Common errors regarding best glide airspeed include:

- Improper determination of best airspeed to fly and not factoring in lift and headwinds.
- Failure to maintain proper pitch attitude and airspeed control.

Speed to Fly

Much is said about the importance of maintaining the best gliding speed, but what is important is to maintain an optimum glide speed, a penetration speed that takes atmospheric conditions into account (e.g., sinking air or a headwind). The gliding community refers to this as the speed to fly. The normal recommendation for countering a headwind is to add one-third to one-half of the estimated wind speed to V_{BG}, which increases the rate of sink but also increases the ground speed. For a tailwind, deduct one-third to one-half the estimated wind speed from V_{BG}, which reduces both the rate of sink and the groundspeed. Bear in mind that, for safety, it is better to err towards higher rather than lower airspeeds.

To illustrate this, the polar curve in *Figure 7-35* indicates the optimum glide speed when adjusted for headwind, tailwind or sinking air. For a tailwind (A), the starting point on the horizontal scale has been moved a distance to the left corresponding to the tailwind velocity. Consequently, the black tangential line contacts the curve at an optimal glide speed that is lower than the best L/D no-wind glide (B), with a slightly lower rate of sink. This is the opposite for a headwind (C), shown by the purple line, and sinking air (D), shown

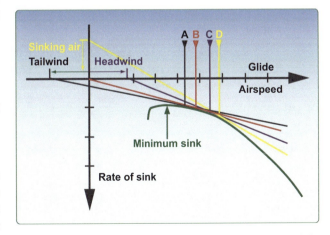

Figure 7-35. *Polar curve for optimum glide speed adjusted for headwind, tailwind, and sinking air.*

by the yellow line. For sinking air, the starting point on the vertical scale has been moved up a distance corresponding to the vertical velocity of the air. Consequently, the red tangential line contacts the curve at a glide speed higher than best glide speed.

Speed to fly depends on:

1. The rate of climb the pilot expects to achieve in the next thermal or updraft.
2. The rate of ascent or descent of the air mass through which the glider is flying.
3. The glider's inherent sink rate at all airspeeds between minimum-sink airspeed and never-exceed airspeed.
4. Headwind or tailwind conditions.

The object of speed to fly is to minimize the time and/or altitude required to fly from the current position to the next thermal and to minimize time in sink and maximize time in lift. Speed-to-fly information is presented to the pilot in one or more of the following ways:

- By placing a speed-to-fly ring (MacCready ring) around the variometer dial.
- Using the appropriate table or chart.
- Using an electronic flight computer that displays the current optimum speed to fly.

The pilot determines the speed to fly during initial planning and then constantly updates this information in flight. The pilot must be aware of changes in the flying conditions in order to be successful in conducting cross-country flights or during a soaring competition.

Common errors regarding speed to fly are:

- Improper determination of speed to fly.
- Failure to maintain proper pitch attitude and airspeed control.
- Not transitioning from cruise speed to climb speed in lift as needed and not changing to cruise speed when leaving lift in a prudent manner.

Chapter 8
Abnormal and Emergency Procedures

Introduction

Training for abnormal and emergency procedures is an essential element in becoming a glider pilot. Knowledge of procedures is required for coping with control problems, instrument failure, or equipment malfunction. This is especially important in soaring activities. Understanding how to use emergency equipment and survival gear is a practical necessity.

Yaw momentum of the mass of the glider's wings and fuselage contributes to overshooting the desired heading. This tendency is aggravated if the pilot holds corrective rudder too long.

Towline force

Towline

Center of mass

Premature takeoff resulting from mismanagement of elevator trim setting or wing flap position setting. Low airspeed at liftoff results in sluggish response to elevator. Startled pilot overcontrols the elevator and PIOs result.

Porpoising

Porpoising is a general term that refers to pitch oscillations that can occur in gliders and aircraft in general. In most cases, pilots induce these oscillations through overcontrolling the glider as they attempt to stop the oscillations from occurring in the first place.

Pilot-Induced Oscillations (PIOs)

The instability of a glider's attitude that arises when the pilot fails to recognize the lag time inherent in controlling the glider is known as a pilot-induced oscillation (PIO). Typically, PIOs occur when the glider fails to respond instantly to control input and the pilot quickly increases the pressure on the controls. By the time the pilot judges that the glider is responding satisfactorily, the extra control pressures have resulted in such a vigorous response that the glider overshoots the desired flight attitude. In an attempt to correct the situation, the pilot moves the controls rapidly in the opposite direction, overcompensating for the mistake. The undesired glider motion slows, stops for an instant, and then reverses. The alarmed pilot maintains significant control pressures to try to increase the rate of response. The glider, now in rapid motion in the desired direction in response to heavy-handed control inputs, again shoots past the desired attitude as the now thoroughly alarmed pilot jerks the flight controls in the opposite direction. Unless the pilot understands that these oscillations are the direct result of overcontrolling the glider, it is unlikely that the oscillations will cease. More likely, they increase in intensity until there is a complete loss of control.

Although PIOs can occur at anytime, these situations arise most commonly during primary training. Pitch instability is another result of center of gravity aft beyond limits. If a pilot encounters PIO, they should ensure the CG is within limits. Pitch instability tends to disappear as pilot experience grows because pilots gain familiarity with the lag time inherent in the flight controls. These types of oscillations may also occur when a pilot is making flights in unfamiliar types of gliders. For this reason, particular care must be taken when the pilot is preparing to fly a single-seat glider in which the pilot has no prior experience. When checking out a new make of single seat glider, the lag time of the flight controls must be learned without the obvious benefit of having an experienced glider flight instructor aboard during flight to offer advice or, if necessary, to intervene. While most PIO discussions are devoted to pitch oscillations, consideration should be given to roll-and-yaw induced oscillations.

The first step toward interrupting the PIO cycle is to recognize the lag time inherent in the glider's response. Any change in glider flight attitude takes an appreciable amount of time to accomplish as the flight controls take effect, and the mass of the glider responds to the pilot's control inputs. The second step is to modify control inputs to avoid overcontrolling the glider. The correct technique is to pressure the controls until the glider begins to respond in the desired direction, and then ease off the pressure. As the glider nears the desired attitude, center the appropriate flight control so that overshooting does not occur.

PIOs During Launch

PIOs are most likely to occur during launch because the glider's lag time changes rapidly as the glider accelerates. During the first moments of the takeoff roll, aerodynamic control is poor, the control feel of the glider is very sluggish, and lag time is great. Flight controls require a wide range of movement or input to have an effect on the glider's flightpath. As the glider gains speed, aerodynamic response improves, control feel becomes crisper, and lag time decreases. When the glider has acquired safe flying speed, lag time is short, the controls feel normal, and PIOs become much less likely.

Factors Influencing PIOs

The characteristics of the towhook/towline combination on pitch of the glider being flown may cause uncommanded pitch excursions if the pilot does not compensate for those effects. This can contribute to PIO during aerotow launch. In addition, the propwash and wing vortices of the towplane, through which the glider must pass if there is little or no crosswind, affect the flight attitude and control response of the glider, especially at low speeds during the start of the takeoff roll.

To minimize the influence of the towplane's wake, use a towline of adequate length—200 feet is the minimum length for normal towing operations. A longer towline provides more isolation from towplane wake during aerotow launch. Short towlines, on the other hand, keep the glider closer to the towplane and its turbulent wake, complicating the problem of controlling the glider.

There are several techniques that reduce the likelihood and severity of PIOs during aerotow launch. A pilot should not try to lift off until confident that flying speed and good aerodynamic control has been achieved. Also, just after the moment of lift-off, allow the glider to rise several feet above the runway before stabilizing the altitude of the glider. Two to three feet is high enough that minor excursions in pitch attitude, if corrected promptly, do not result in glider contact with the runway surface, but not high enough to lose sight of the towplane below the nose of the glider. Caution should be exercised if attempting to stabilize the glider just a few inches above the ground because it provides little margin for error if a PIO occurs.

Improper Elevator Trim Setting

The elevator trim control position also contributes to PIO in pitch attitude. The takeoff checklist includes a check to confirm the proper takeoff elevator trim setting. Trim set properly for takeoff results in normal elevator pressures felt through the control stick is normal, and the likelihood of PIO is reduced. If the elevator trim is set incorrectly, however, abnormal elevator pressure is felt through the control stick and may contribute to PIO.

Excessively nose-down trim requires the pilot to hold back pressure on the control stick to achieve and maintain the desired pitch attitude during launch and climb-out. If the trim is set excessively nose up, the pilot needs to hold forward pressure. The more pressure is needed, the more likely it is that the pilot overcontrols the glider.

Although all gliders exhibit these tendencies if the trim is improperly set, the effect is most pronounced on those gliders with an aerodynamic elevator trim tab or an antiservo tab on the elevator. The effect usually is less pronounced on those glider fitted with a simple spring system elevator trim. Regardless of the type of elevator trim installed in the glider, error prevention is superior to error correction. Use a comprehensive pretakeoff checklist and set the elevator trim in the appropriate position prior to launch to help prevent PIO attributable to elevator trim misuse. *[Figure 8-1]*

Improper Wing Flaps Setting

The likelihood of PIOs increases if the wing flaps are not correctly set in the desired takeoff position. For the majority of flap-equipped gliders, most Glider Flight Manuals/Pilot Operating Handbooks (GFM/POH) recommend that flaps be set at 0° for takeoff. Pilots should review their GFM/POH for the manufacturer recommendation for takeoff settings.

If the flaps are incorrectly set for takeoff, a positive flap setting increases wing camber and wing lift, the glider tends to rise off the runway prematurely, perhaps even before the elevator control is sufficient to control the pitch attitude. Attempting to prevent the glider from ballooning high above the runway, the pilot may exert considerable forward pressure on the control stick. As the glider continues to accelerate, this forward pressure on the control stick exerts a rapidly increasing nose-down force on the glider due to the increasing airflow over the elevator. When the glider eventually pitches down, the pilot may exert considerable back pressure on the stick to arrest the descent. Severe pitching or PIOs are likely to result. If allowed to continue, hard contact with the runway surface may result in glider damage and personal injury.

If the wing flaps are incorrectly set to a negative flap setting, decreasing wing camber and wing lift, then takeoff may be delayed so long that the towplane lifts off and begins to climb out while the glider is still rolling down the runway, unable to get airborne. Excessive back pressure on the control stick may eventually assist the glider in leaving the runway, but the relatively high airspeed at lift-off translates into a very effective elevator, and ballooning may occur as a result of the extreme elevator position. Overcorrecting for the ballooning with excessive forward pressure on the control stick increases the magnitude of this pitch excursion. A series of PIOs may result. If this condition is allowed to continue, the launch could lead to a premature termination of the tow.

Pilot-Induced Roll Oscillations During Launch

Pilot-induced roll oscillations occur primarily during launch, particularly via aerotow. As the tow pilot applies full power, the glider moves forward, balanced laterally on its main wheel by the wing-runner. After the wing-runner releases his or her balancing hold, aerodynamics or crosswind could cause a wing to drop. If a wingtip begins to drop toward the ground before the glider achieves significant speed, aileron control is marginal and considerable stick displacement must be applied to elicit a response from the glider's ailerons. As the glider accelerates, the control response improves and the latency of response from the glider shortens. As acceleration continues, the pilot must recognize the increased responsiveness of the glider to avoid overcontrolling the glider. *[Figure 8-2]*

Although roll oscillations can develop during ground launch operations, they occur less often than during aerotow operations because excellent aerodynamic control of the glider is quickly achieved due to the rapid acceleration. Since control improves as acceleration increases, operations that

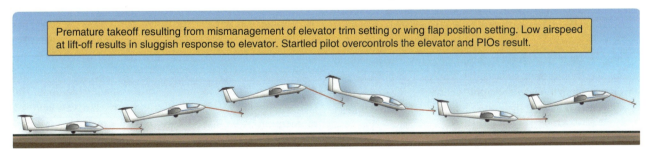

Figure 8-1. *Premature takeoffs and PIOs.*

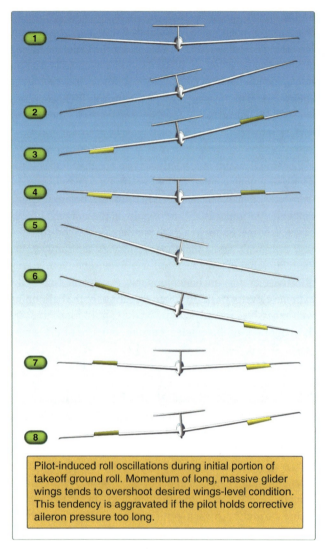

Figure 8-2. *Pilot-induced roll oscillations during takeoff roll.*

use a strong winch or launch vehicle are less likely to be hampered by oscillations.

Wing mass also affects roll oscillations. During low speeds, if the wings do not stay level, the pilot applies considerable aileron pressure to return the wings to level attitude. Because of the large mass and considerable aerodynamic damping that long-winged gliders exhibit, there is a considerable lag time from the moment pressure is applied until the moment the wings are level again. Inexperienced pilots maintain considerable pressure on the ailerons until the wings are level before releasing control pressure. The wings continue their rolling moment due to their mass, length, and momentum about the longitudinal axis of the glider. The pilot senses this momentum too late, and applies considerable pressure in the opposite direction in another attempt to level the wings.

After a time, the wings respond and roll back to level, whereupon the pilot centers the ailerons once again. As before, the momentum of the wings about the longitudinal axis is considerable, and the wings continue their motion in roll. This series of PIOs may continue until one wingtip contacts the ground, possibly with considerable force, causing wing damage or a ground loop and an aborted launch. To reduce the likelihood of this type of roll oscillation, anticipate the momentum of the glider wings about the longitudinal axis and reduce aileron control pressure as the wings approach the level position.

Pilot-Induced Yaw Oscillations During Launch

Pilot-induced yaw oscillations are usually caused by overcontrolling the rudder. As with roll oscillations, the problem is the failure of the pilot to recognize that the glider is accelerating and has considerable momentum. If the glider veers away from the towplane, rudder application in the appropriate direction helps correct the situation. If the rudder pressure is held too long, the large yaw momentum of the glider wings and fuselage results in overshooting the desired yaw position and veering off in the opposite direction. Overcompensating for large yaw, the pilot applies considerable rudder pressure in the direction opposite from the original rudder pressure. The alarmed pilot now applies considerable rudder pressure in the direction opposite the original rudder pressure. As the glider continues to accelerate, the power of the rudder increases and the lag time decreases. In extreme cases, the glider may veer off the runway and collide with runway border markers, airport lights, parked glider, or other obstacles. The cure for this type of yaw oscillation is anticipating the momentum of the glider wings and fuselage about the vertical axis and reduce rudder pedal pressure when the nose of the glider begins to yaw in the desired direction in response to rudder inputs. *[Figure 8-3]*

When a glider's wingtip contacts the ground during takeoff roll, an uncommanded yaw results. The drag of the wingtip on the ground induces a yaw in the direction of the grounded wingtip. The yaw usually is mild if the wingtip is on smooth pavement but much more vigorous if the wingtip is dragging through tall grass. If appropriate aileron pressure fails to raise the wingtip off the ground quickly, the only solution is to release the towline and abort the takeoff attempt before losing all control of the glider.

The greater the wing mass is and the longer the wingspan is, the more momentum the glider exhibits whenever roll or yaw oscillations arise. Some very high performance gliders feature remarkably long and heavy wings; once in motion, they tend to remain in motion for a considerable time. This is true not only of forward momentum, but yaw and roll momentum as well. The mass of the wings, coupled with the very long moment arm of large-span wings, results in substantial lag times in response to aileron and rudder inputs

Gust-Induced Oscillations

Gusty headwinds can induce pitch oscillations because the effectiveness of the elevator varies due to changes in the speed of the airflow over the elevator. Crosswinds also can induce yaw and roll oscillations. In gusty crosswinds, the effects on glider control change rapidly depending on the speed and rate of the crosswind component. A crosswind from the right, for instance, tends to weathervane the glider into the wind, causing an uncommanded yaw to the right. Crosswinds tend to lift the upwind wing of the glider and push the tail downwind.

Local terrain can have a considerable effect on the wind. Wind blowing over and around obstacles can be gusty and chaotic. Nearby obstacles, such as hangars, groves or lines of trees, hills, and ridges can have a pronounced effect on low altitude winds, particularly on the downwind side of the obstruction. In general, the effect of an upwind obstacle is to induce additional turbulence and gustiness in the wind. These conditions are usually found from the surface to an altitude of 300 feet or more. If flight in these conditions cannot be avoided, the general rule during takeoff is to achieve a faster-than-normal speed prior to lift-off.

The additional speed increases the responsiveness of the controls and simplifies the problem of correcting for turbulence and gusts. This provides a measure of protection against PIOs. The additional speed also provides a safer margin above stall airspeed. This is very desirable on gusty days because variations in the headwind component have a considerable effect on indicated airspeed.

Caution: Do not exceed the glider's tow speed limitations when adding safety speed margins for takeoff in windy conditions.

Vertical Gusts During High-Speed Cruise

Although PIOs occur most commonly during launch, they can occur during cruising flight, even when cruising at high speed. Turbulence usually plays a role in this type of PIO, as does the elasticity and flexibility of the glider structure. An example is an encounter with an abrupt updraft during wings-level high-speed cruise. The upward-blowing gust increases the angle of attack of the wings, which bend upward very quickly, storing elastic energy in the wing spars. For a moment, the G-loading in the cabin is significantly greater than one G. Like a compressed coil spring seeking release, the wing spars reflex downward, lofting the fuselage higher. When the fuselage reaches the top of this motion, the wing spars are storing elastic energy in the downward direction, and the fuselage is sprung downward in response to the release of elastic energy in the wing spars. The pilot then experiences reduced G-load, accompanied perhaps by a head bang against

Figure 8-3. *Pilot-induced yaw oscillations during takeoff roll.*

during the early portion of the takeoff roll and during the latter portion of the landing rollout. Even highly proficient glider pilots find takeoffs and landings in these gliders to be challenging. Many of these gliders are designed for racing or cross-country flights and have provisions for adding water ballast to the wings. Adding ballast increases mass, which results in an increase in lag time.

Low time pilots and pilots new to such high performance gliders should review the GFM/POH thoroughly prior to flight. It is also recommended to review normal procedures, emergency procedures, and the glider's fight characteristics with a qualified pilot or instructor pilot before attempting flight in any high performance glider.

the top of the canopy if the seat belt and shoulder harness are loosely fastened.

During these excursions, the weight of the pilot's hand and arm on the control stick may cause the control stick to move a significant distance forward or aft. During positive G-loading, the increased apparent weight of the pilot's arm tends to move the control stick aft, further increasing the angle of attack of the wing and G-load factor. During negative G-loading, the reduced apparent weight of the pilot's arm tends to result in forward stick motion, reducing the angle of attack and reducing the G-load factor still further. In short, this rapid cycle of induced flight control input affects load factor and increases the intensity of vertical gusts on the glider's airframe and the pilot. One protection against this is to reduce speed when cruising through turbulent air. Another protection is to brace both arms and use both hands on the control stick when cruising through turbulent air at high speed. It is worth noting that some glider designs incorporate a parallelogram control stick linkage to reduce the tendency toward PIO during high-speed cruise.

Pilot-Induced Pitch Oscillations During Landing

Instances of PIO may occur during the landing approach in turbulent air for the same reasons previously stated. Landing the glider involves interacting with ground effect during the flare and keeping precise control of the glider even as airspeed decays and control authority declines. A pilot can cause a PIO by overcontrolling the elevator during the flare, causing the glider to balloon well above the landing surface even as airspeed is decreasing. If the pilot reacts by pushing the stick well forward, the glider will quickly dive for the ground with a fairly rapid rate of descent. If the pilot pulls the control stick back to arrest this descent while still in possession of considerable airspeed, the glider balloons again and the PIO cycle continues. If airspeed is low when the pilot pulls back on the stick to avoid a hard landing, there will probably be insufficient lift available to arrest the descent. A hard or a nose-first landing may result.

To reduce ballooning during the flare, stabilize the glider at an altitude of 3 or 4 feet, and then begin the flare anew. Do not try to force the nose of the glider down on to the runway. If airspeed during the ballooning is low and the ballooning takes the glider higher than a normal flare altitude, it may be necessary to reduce the extension of the spoilers/dive brakes in order to moderate the descent rate of the glider. Care must be taken to avoid abrupt changes. Partial retraction of the spoilers/dive brakes allows the wing to provide a bit more lift despite decaying airspeed.

Another source of PIOs during the approach to landing is overly abrupt adjustment of the spoilers/dive brakes setting.

The spoilers/dive brakes on most modern gliders provide a very large amount of drag when fully deployed, and they reduce the lift of the wing considerably. Excessive use of the spoilers/dive brakes during the approach to land can easily lead to oscillations in pitch attitude and airspeed changes. The easiest way to guard against these oscillations is to make smooth adjustments in the spoilers/dive brakes setting whenever spoilers/dive brakes adjustment is necessary. This becomes particularly important during the landing flare just prior to touchdown. A sudden increase in spoilers/dive brakes extension results in a high sink rate and possible hard contact with the runway. This can lead to a rebound into the air, setting the stage for a series of PIOs. As before, the cure is to stabilize the glider, then resume the flare. If the spoilers/dive brakes are retracted abruptly during the flare, the glider will probably balloon into the air because of the increased lift provided by the wings. Remember, spoiler/dive brakes provide drag and reduce lift. This extra lift and pilot reaction may result in overcontrolling and PIOs. The use of spoiler/dive brakes should be determined by flight conditions. If a wind gust has caused the glider to balloon, then spoiler/dive brake use is an option for the pilot to reestablish the flare attitude. If the spoilers/dive brakes must be adjusted, do so with a smooth, gentle motion.

Glider-Induced Oscillations
Pitch Influence of the Glider Towhook Position

The location of the glider's aerotow towhook influences pitch attitude control of the glider during aerotow operations. During these operations, the towline is under considerable tension. If the towline is connected to a glider towhook located more or less directly on the longitudinal axis of the glider, the towline tension has little effect on the pitch attitude of the glider.

On many gliders, the tow hook is located below the cockpit or just forward of the landing gear. Many European gliders have the towhook located on the belly of the glider, just forward of the main landing gear and below the longitudinal axis of the glider. The glider's center of mass is above the location of the towhook in this position. In fact, virtually all of the glider's mass is above the towhook. The mass of the glider has inertia and resists acceleration when the towline tension increases. In these tow hook configurations, an increase in tension on the towline causes an uncommanded pitch-up of the glider nose as shown in *Figure 8-4*. Decrease in towline tension results in an uncommanded pitch-down.

Rapid changes in towline tension, most likely to occur during aerotow in turbulent air, cause these effects in alternation. Naturally, on days when good lift is available, the aerotow is conducted in turbulent air. The potential for inducing pitch

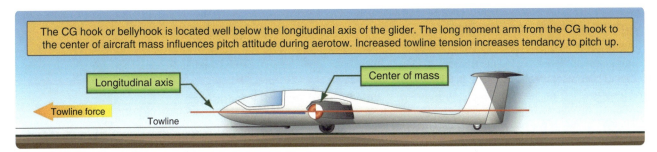

Figure 8-4. *Effects of increased towline tension on pitch altitude of bellyhook-equipped glider during aerotow.*

oscillations is obvious, as rapid alternations in towline tension induce rapid changes in the pitch attitude of the glider. To maintain a steady pitch attitude during aerotow, the pilot must be alert to variations in towline tension and adjust pressure on the flight controls to counteract the pitch effect of variations in towline tension.

Self-Launching Glider Oscillations During Powered Flight

In some self-launching gliders and gliders equipped with a sustainer engine, the engine is extended above the glider just behind the cockpit. The engine's propeller thrust vector is located above the glider's longitudinal axis and center of mass. *[Figure 8-5]* This combination of engine and airframe exhibits a complex relationship between power setting and pitch attitude. When power changes are made, the propeller's thrust line vector has a noticeable effect on the glider's pitch attitude. This includes the effects of propeller wash over the elevator causing variations in elevator effectiveness and adding to the complexities of flight. Prior to flight, study the GFM/POH carefully to discover what these undesired effects are and how to counteract them. When throttle settings must be changed, it is good practice to move the throttle control smoothly and gradually, coordinating with proper flight control input. This gives the pilot time to recognize and counteract the effect the power setting change has on pitch attitude. In most self-launching gliders, the effect is greatest when flying at or near minimum controllable airspeed (VMCA). Self-launching glider pilots should avoid slow flight when flying at low altitude under power. *[Figure 8-5]*

Self-launching gliders may also be susceptible to PIOs during takeoff roll, particularly those with a pylon engine mounted high above the longitudinal axis. *[Figure 8-5]* The high thrust vector and the propeller wash influence on the air flow over the self-launching glider's elevator may tend to cause considerable change in the pitch attitude of the glider when power changes are made.

Nosewheel Glider Oscillations During Launches and Landings

Many tandem two-seat fiberglass gliders, and some single-seat fiberglass gliders, feature a three-wheel landing gear configuration. The main wheel is equipped with a traditional large pneumatic tire; the tailwheel and the nosewheel are equipped with smaller pneumatic tires. During ground operations, if the pneumatic nosewheel remains in contact with the ground, any bump compresses the nosewheel tire. When the pneumatic nosewheel tire rebounds, an uncommanded pitch-up occurs. If the pitch-up is sufficient, as is likely to be the case after hitting a bump at fast taxi speeds, the tailwheel contacts the runway, compresses, and rebounds. This can result in porpoising, as the nosewheel and tailwheel alternate in hitting the runway, compressing, and rebounding. In extreme cases, the fuselage of the glider may be heavily damaged. During takeoff roll, the best way to avoid porpoising in a nosewheel-equipped glider is to use the elevator to lift the nosewheel off the runway as soon as practicable, then set the pitch attitude so the glider's main wheel is the only wheel in contact with the ground. To avoid porpoising during landing, hold the glider off during the flare until the main wheel and tailwheel touch simultaneously. During roll out, use the elevator to keep the nosewheel off the ground for as long as possible.

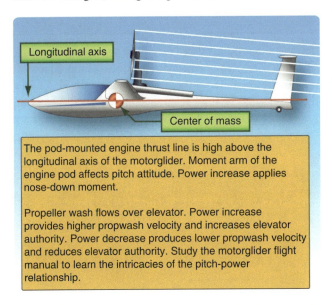

Figure 8-5. *Pitch attitude power setting relationships for self-launching glider with engine pod.*

Tailwheel/Tailskid Equipped Glider Oscillations During Launches and Landings

Most gliders have a tailwheel. When loaded and ready for flight, these gliders have the main wheel and the tailwheel or tailskid in contact with the ground. In these gliders, the center of gravity is aft of the main wheel(s). Because of this, any upward thrust on the main landing gear tends to pitch the nose of the glider upward unless the tailwheel or tailskid is in contact with the ground and prevents the change in pitch attitude.

Upward thrust on the main landing gear can occur in numerous circumstances. One cause is a bump in the runway surface during takeoff or landing roll. If the resultant pitch-up is vigorous enough, it is likely that the glider leaves the ground momentarily. If airspeed is slow, the elevator control is marginal. As the pilot reacts to the unexpected bounce or launch, overcontrolling the elevator results in a PIO. *[Figure 8-6]*

Improper landing technique in a tailwheel glider also can lead to upward thrust on the main landing gear and subsequent PIOs. Landing a tailwheel glider in a nose-down attitude, or even in a level pitch attitude, can lead to trouble. If the main wheel contacts the ground before the tailwheel or tailskid, the compression of the pneumatic tire and its inevitable rebound provides significant upward thrust. The glider nose may pitch up, the angle of attack increases, and the glider becomes airborne. As before, overcontrol of the elevator leads to PIOs.

To prevent this type of PIO, do not allow the glider to settle onto the landing surface with a nose-down attitude or with excess airspeed. During the landing flare, hold the glider a few inches above the ground with gentle backpressure on the control stick as necessary. The speed decays and the pitch attitude gradually changes to a slightly nose-up pitch attitude. The ideal touchdown is simultaneous gentle contact of main wheel and tailwheel or tailskid. Delaying the touchdown just a small amount results in the tailwheel or tailskid contacting the landing surface an instant before the mainwheel. This type of landing may be acceptable and desirable for many tailwheel gliders because it makes a rebound into the air very unlikely. Consult the GFM/POH for the glider being flown for further information about recommended procedure for touchdown.

Aerotow Abnormal and Emergency Procedures

Abnormal Procedures

Mechanical equipment failure, environmental factors, and pilot error can cause abnormal aerotow occurrences during climb-out. Mechanical equipment failures can be caused by towline and towhook failures, towplane mechanical failures, and glider mechanical failures. Towline failure (one that breaks unexpectedly) can result from using a weak or worn towline. Towline failures can be avoided by using appropriately rated towline material, weak links when necessary, proper tow rings, and proper towline maintenance.

Towhook system failures include uncommanded towline releases or the inability to release. These failures can occur in either the towplane or the glider towhook system. Proper preflight and maintenance of these systems should help to avoid these types of failures. Towplane mechanical failures can involve the powerplant or airframe. When the tow pilot or glider pilot encounters a mechanical failure, he or she should signal the glider pilot to release immediately. *[Figure 8-7]* This is one of many situations that make it vitally important that both the tow pilot and glider pilot have a thorough knowledge of aerotow visual signals.

Glider mechanical failure can include towhook system malfunctions, flight control problems, and improper assembly or rigging. If a mechanical failure occurs, the glider pilot must assess the situation to determine the best course of action. In some situations, it may be beneficial to remain on the aerotow, while other situations may require immediate release.

If the glider release mechanism fails, the tow pilot should be notified either by radio or tow signal and the glider should maintain the high tow position. The tow pilot should tow the glider over the gliderport/airport and release the glider from the towplane. The towline should fall back and below the glider. The design of the Schweizer towhook mechanism is such that the line pulls free from the glider by its own weight.

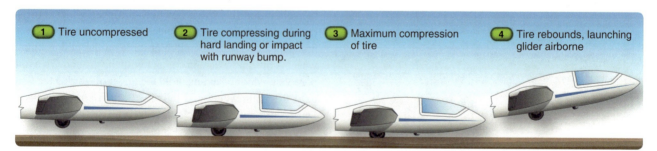

Figure 8-6. *Pneumatic tire rebound.*

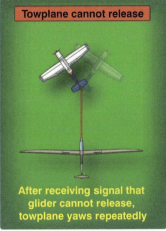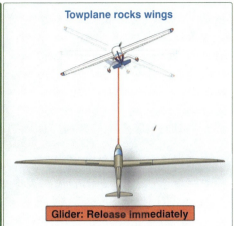

Figure 8-7. *Towplane and glider signal due to release mechanism failure.*

Since some gliders do not back release, the glider pilot should pull the release to ensure the towline is in fact released.

Towplanes are usually fitted with a variant of the Schweizer or Tost glider tow hitch. *[Figures 8-8 and 8-9]* The hitch is usually located at the extreme end of the rear fuselage below the rudder. The specific rings used to attach towlines to these hitch types can be seen in *Figure 8-10*. The wing runner must be familiar with the correct method of attachment. If the towplane has the Schweizer tow hitch, it is possible for the tow ring to rotate forward so that it traps the sleeve that locks the tow hitch in place. This may prevent the tow pilot from releasing the towline. *[Figure 8-11]*

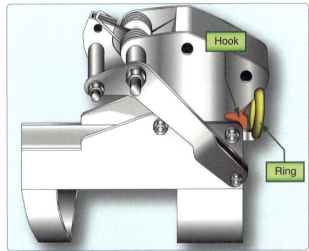

Figure 8-9. *A Tost tow hitch.*

Figure 8-8. *A Schweizer tow hitch.*

Failure of both towplane and glider release mechanisms is extremely rare. If it occurs, however, radio or tow signals between glider pilot and tow pilot should verify this situation. The glider pilot should move down to the low tow position

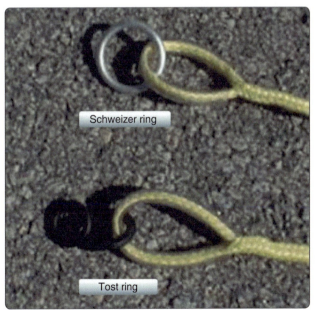

Figure 8-10. *Examples of Schweizer and Tost tow rings.*

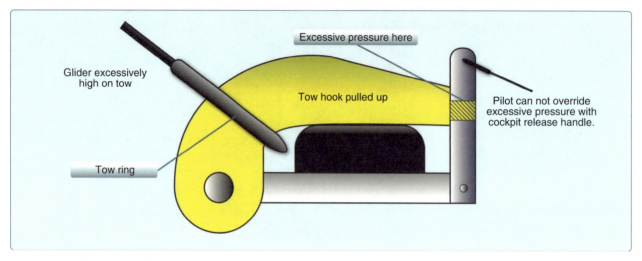

Figure 8-11 *A Schweizer tow hitch.*

once the descent has started to the gliderport/airport. The glider pilot needs to use spoilers/dive brakes to maintain the low tow position and to avoid overtaking the towplane. The tow pilot should plan the approach to avoid obstacles. The approach should be shallow enough for the glider to touch down first. The glider pilot should use the spoilers/dive brakes to stay on the runway, and use the wheel brake as necessary to avoid overtaking the towplane. Excessive use of the glider wheel brake may result in a hard landing for the towplane because the towline could slow the towplane below flying speed. Another valid method would be to stay on tow until well within gliding distance of the airport and then breaking the towline. The best experience to date suggests the procedure to break the towline would be by climbing above and diving down to develop slackline, then fully extending the dive brakes and/or spoilers to set up the overload condition as the towplane begins to accelerate without the load of the glider and the glider is decelerating due to the increase in drag. Once the towline breaks, the glider lands using the procedures of having the line attached, in case the line did not break at the gliders weak link.

Environmental factors for terminating the tow include encountering clouds, mountain rotors (area of turbulence created by wind and mountainous terrain), or restricted visibility. Any of these factors may require the glider pilot to release from the aerotow. During the aerotow, each pilot is responsible for avoiding situations that would place the other pilot at risk.

For the towplane pilot, examples of pilot error include deliberately starting the takeoff before the glider pilot has signaled the glider is ready for launch, using steep banks during the aerotow without prior consent of the glider pilot, or frivolous use of aerotow signals, such as "release immediately!" For the glider pilot, examples of pilot error include rising high above the towplane during takeoff and climb or leaving air brakes open during takeoff and climb.

The glider pilot may choose to deliberately terminate the tow/launch anytime it may appear to be a safer course of action. For example, the pilot discovers control binding once air pressure builds on the surfaces, releasing the towline is the better alternative than getting too high to stop and too low to bailout.

Towing Failures

Premature terminations of the tow have been a leading cause of glider accidents and incidents according to the Soaring Safety Foundation. Towing failure incidents related to rope breaks are not as common as other distractions in the glider cockpit. Extension of spoilers/dive brakes, unlocked canopies, and other distractions are major causes of the tow failure incidents leading to a towline break. Prevention is achieved with the proper use checklists and proper prelaunch discipline. There are five planning situations regarding in-motion towline breaks, uncommanded release, or power loss of the towplane and are listed below. While the best course of action depends on many variables, such as runway length, airport environment, density altitude, and wind, all tow failures or emergency release have one thing in common: the need to maintain control of the glider. Two possibilities are stalling the glider or dragging a wingtip on the ground during a low altitude turn.

On takeoff, all towplanes may plan to drift downwind if there is a wind present. If there is no wind or traffic, then the tow pilot should select an area on the take path/profile that has the fewest obstacles for both the towplane and glider. The tow pilot should plan to drift in that direction. This downwind drift does a few things for the glider pilot, the most important of which is that it ensures the glider has maneuverability if a tow failure occurs. This downwind drift allows the glider pilot to complete the course reversal without the need of extensive lower altitude turns to line up on the runway, reducing the possibility of dragging a glider wingtip on the ground during a low altitude turn. The tow pilot must initiate this drift. Remember, tow pilots need to know wind direction and plan accordingly to allow the glider pilot maneuverability options.

If the towplane proceeds straight out, the glider pilot may need to make the last alignment turn at a low altitude. The first turn is the course reversal; a second turn aligns the glider with the landing area. As mentioned, the low altitude turn may be difficult or impossible to complete. Winds may compound the situation if the turn is not planned properly. Pilots under these high-stress conditions sometimes cross-control the glider, compounding the issue. Remember, keep the yaw string or ball centered.

Tow Failure With Runway To Land and Stop

If a tow failure occurs or is inadvertently or deliberately released prior to towplane liftoff, the standard procedure is for the towplane either to continue the takeoff and clear the runway or abort the takeoff and remain on the left side of the runway. If the towplane loses power during the takeoff, the tow pilot should maneuver the towplane to the left side of the runway. If the glider is still on the runway, the glider pilot should pull the release, decelerate using the wheel brake, and be prepared to maneuver to the right side of the runway. If the line breaks, is inadvertently released, or the towplane loses power after the glider is airborne, the glider pilot should pull the towline release, land ahead, and be prepared to maneuver to the right side of the runway. *[Figure 8-12, panel 1]* Pulling the towline release in either case ensures that the rope is clear of the glider. Since local procedures vary, both glider pilot and tow pilot must be familiar with the specific gliderport/airport procedures.

Tow Failure Without Runway To Land Below Returning Altitude

If an inadvertent release, towline break, or a signal to release from the towplane occurs at a point at which the glider has insufficient runway directly ahead and has insufficient altitude (200 feet above ground level AGL) to make a safe turn, the best course of action is to land the glider ahead. *[Figure 8-12, panel 2]* When flying at higher elevations, a higher altitude return may be necessary to return to the runway due to increased ground speed and air density. After touchdown, use the wheel brake to slow and stop as conditions permit. Attempting to turn at low altitude prior to landing is very risky because of the likelihood of dragging a wingtip on the ground or stalling the glider. Landing ahead and slowing the glider as much as possible prior to touching down and rolling onto unknown terrain is usually the safest course of action. Low speed means low impact forces, which reduce both the likelihood of injury and risk of significant damage to the glider. Gliders pilots should always be looking on both sides and ahead trying to plan for the best area to land in the event of a premature landing. The greater amount of altitude the glider pilot has the greater number of options that are open to them during an emergency. Landing under control is always preferable to the "perfect" landing area almost within glide distance.

Tow Failure Above Return to Runway Altitude

A downwind landing on the departure runway may be attempted if an inadvertent release, towline break, or signal to release from the towplane occurs after the towplane and glider are airborne, and the glider possesses sufficient altitude to make a course reversal, which is determined by wind crab angle, wind velocity, and glider groundspeed. *[Figure 8-12, panel 3]*

The course reversal and downwind landing option should be used only if the glider is within gliding distance of the airport or landing area. In ideal conditions, a minimum altitude of 200 feet above ground level (AGL) is required to complete this maneuver safely. Such factors as a hot day, weak towplane, strong wind, or other traffic may require a greater altitude to make a return to the airport a viable option.

The responsibility of the glider pilot is to avoid the towplane, if the tow is terminated due to a towplane emergency; the tow pilot is also dealing with an emergency situation and may maneuver the aircraft abruptly. The glider pilot should never follow the towplane down if the towplane is experiencing engine problems or engine failure.

After releasing from the towplane at low altitude, if the glider pilot chooses to make a turn of approximately 180° and a downwind landing, the first responsibility is to maintain flying speed. The pilot must immediately lower the nose to achieve the proper pitch attitude necessary to maintain the appropriate approach airspeed. If a rope break occurred in the process, the glider pilot should release the rope portion still attached to the glider to avoid any entanglement on landing with the glider.

Make the initial turn into the wind. Use a 45° to 60° bank angle as necessary to make the course reversal to the departure. This provides a safe margin above stall speed and allows a course reversal turn to be completed in a timely manner. Using a bank angle that is too shallow may not allow enough time for the glider to align with the landing area. An excessively steep bank angle may result in an accelerated stall or wingtip ground contact. If the turn is made into the wind, only minor course corrections should be necessary to align the glider with the intended landing area

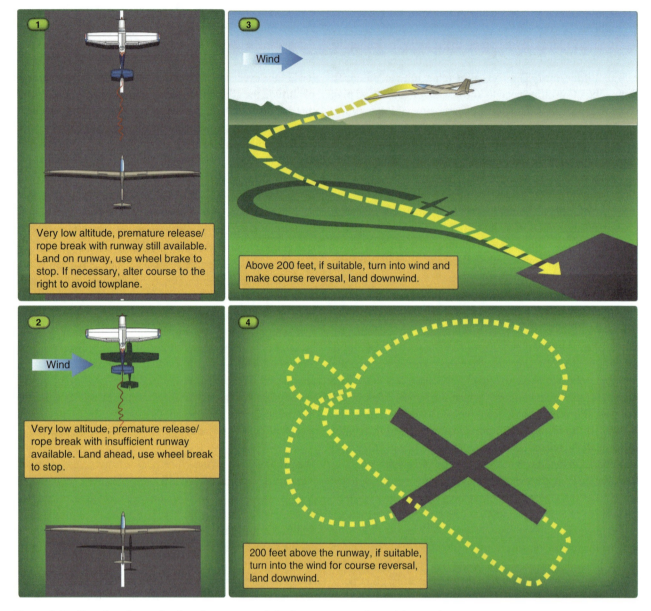

Figure 8-12. *Situations for towline break, uncommanded release, or power loss of the towplane.*

if the glider was allowed to drift downwind. Throughout the maneuver, the pilot must maintain the appropriate approach speed and proper coordination. Remember to keep the yaw string straight and ball centered (see Turns section for more information on the yaw string).

Downwind landings result in higher groundspeed due to the effect of tailwind. The glider pilot must maintain the appropriate approach airspeed. During the straight-in portion of the approach, spoilers/dive brakes should be used as necessary to control the descent path. Landing downwind results in a shallower than normal approach. Groundspeed is higher during a downwind landing and is especially noticeable during the flare. After touchdown, spoilers/dive brakes and wheel brakes should be used as necessary to slow and stop the glider as quickly as possible. During the later part of the rollout, the glider feels unresponsive to the controls despite the fact that it is rolling along the runway at a higher than normal groundspeed. It is important to stop the glider before any loss of directional control.

Tow Failure Above 800' AGL

When the emergency occurs at or above 800 feet above the ground, the glider pilot may have more time to assess the situation. Depending on the gliderport/airport environment, the pilot may choose to land on a cross runway, into the wind on the departure runway, or on a taxiway. *[Figure 8-12, panel 4]* In some situations, an off-gliderport/off-airport landing may be safer than attempting to land on the gliderport/airport.

Tow Failure Above Traffic Pattern Altitude

If an emergency occurs above the traffic pattern altitude, the glider pilot should maneuver away from the towplane, release the towline if still attached, and turn toward the gliderport/airport. The glider pilot should evaluate the situation to determine if there is sufficient altitude to search for lift or if it is necessary to return to the gliderport/airport for a landing. Pilots should remember their obligation when dropping objects from an aircraft according to Title 14 of the Code of Federal Regulations part 91, section 91.15, and not create a hazard to persons and property on the ground. *[Figure 8-12, panel 4]*

Slack Line

Slack line is a reduction of tension in the towline. If the slack is severe enough, it might entangle the glider or cause damage to the glider or towplane. The following situations may result in a slack line:

- Abrupt power reduction by the towplane
- Aerotow descents
- Glider turns inside the towplane turn radius *[Figure 8-13]*
- Updrafts and downdrafts
- Abrupt recovery from a wake box corner position *[Figure 8-14]*

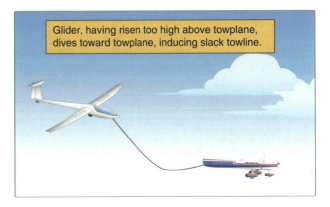

Figure 8-14. *One method of generating towline slack.*

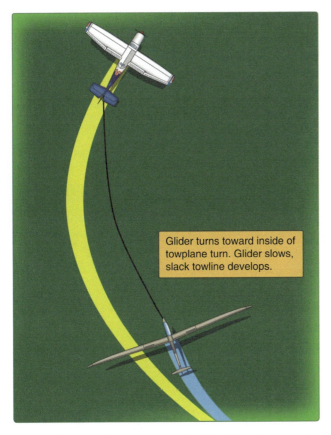

Figure 8-13. *Glider bank is steeper than that of towplane, causing slack in towline.*

When the towplane precedes the glider into an updraft, the glider pilot first perceives that the towplane is climbing much faster and higher than it actually is. Then, as the glider enters the updraft, it is lighter and more efficient than the towplane. It climbs higher and faster than the towplane did in the same updraft. As a result, the glider pilot pitches the glider over to regain the proper tow altitude but gains airspeed more quickly than the towplane, hence the slack towline. The glider pilot must be ready to control the descent and closure rate to the towplane by increasing drag.

Slack line recovery procedures should be initiated as soon as the glider pilot becomes aware of the situation. The glider pilot should try slipping back into alignment with the towplane. In the event that slipping motion fails to reduce the slack sufficiently, careful use of spoilers/dive brakes can decelerate the glider and take up the slack. As the towline begins to tighten, stabilize the tow and gradually resume the desired aerotow position. When slack in the towline is excessive, or beyond the pilot's capability to safely recover, the glider pilot should immediately release from the aerotow.

Common errors regarding a slack line include:

- Failure to take corrective action at the first indication of a slack line.
- Use of improper procedure to correct slack line causing excessive stress on the towline, towplane, and the glider.
- Failure to decrease drag as towline slack decreases.

Ground Launch Abnormal and Emergency Procedures

Abnormal Procedures

The launch equipment operator manages ground launch towline speed. Because the launch equipment operator is remote from the glider, it is not uncommon for initial tow to be too fast or too slow. If the towline speed is too great, the glider is not able to climb very high because of excessive airspeed. If the towline speed is too low, the glider may be incapable of lift-off or could stall after becoming airborne. Once airborne, the glider could be incapable of further climb. The pilot should use appropriate signals to direct the launch operator to increase or decrease speed. The pilot must anticipate and be prepared to deal with these situations. In the event these abnormal situations develop, the pilot's only alternative may be to release the towline and land ahead.

Wind gradient (a sudden increase in windspeed with height) can have a noticeable effect on ground launches. If the wind gradient is significant or sudden, or both, and the pilot maintains the same pitch attitude, indicated airspeed increases that could exceed the maximum ground launch tow speed could occur. The pilot must adjust the airspeed to deal with the effect of the gradient. When encountering a wind gradient, the pilot should push forward on the stick to reduce the indicated airspeed. *[Figure 8-15]* The only way for the glider to resume climb without exceeding the maximum ground launch airspeed is for the pilot to signal the launch operator to reduce tow speed. After the reduction of the towing speed, the pilot can resume normal climb. If the tow speed is not reduced, the glider may be incapable of climbing to safe altitude.

Ground launch may be interrupted by a ground launch mechanism malfunction. A gradual deceleration in rate of climb and/or airspeed may be an indication of such a malfunction. If a launch mechanism malfunction is suspected, release and land ahead.

Emergency Procedures

A broken towline is the most common type of problem when doing a ground launch. *[Figure 8-16]* When there is a towline failure, the glider pilot must pull the release handle and immediately lower the nose of the glider to achieve and maintain a safe airspeed. The distinguishing features of the ground launch are nose-high pitch attitude and a relatively low altitude for a significant portion of the launch and climb. If a towline break occurs and the glider pilot fails to respond promptly, the nose-high attitude of the glider may result in a stall. Altitude may be insufficient for recovery unless the pilot recognizes and responds to the towline break by lowering the nose.

If the glider tow release mechanism fails, the pilot should fly at airspeeds no lower than best lift over drag (L/D) airspeed. He or she should fly over and then past the ground launch equipment. This method allows the glider towhook back release to activate or the towline weak link to fail. The ground launch equipment is also equipped with an emergency release mechanism in the event the glider tow release fails. If a winch is used, it is equipped with a guillotine to cut the towline. If a motor vehicle is used as a ground launch, it should be equipped with some form of backup release mechanism.

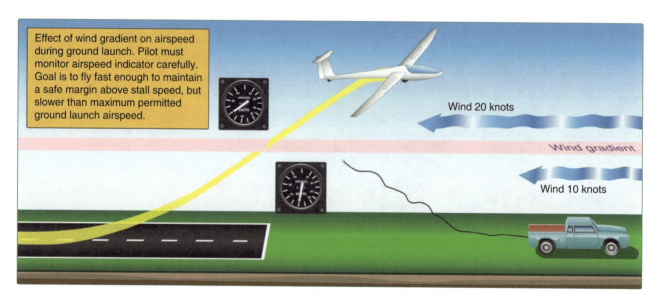

Figure 8-15. *Ground launch wind gradient.*

Tow Failure Above Traffic Pattern Altitude

If an emergency occurs above the traffic pattern altitude, the glider pilot should maneuver away from the towplane, release the towline if still attached, and turn toward the gliderport/airport. The glider pilot should evaluate the situation to determine if there is sufficient altitude to search for lift or if it is necessary to return to the gliderport/airport for a landing. Pilots should remember their obligation when dropping objects from an aircraft according to Title 14 of the Code of Federal Regulations part 91, section 91.15, and not create a hazard to persons and property on the ground. *[Figure 8-12, panel 4]*

Slack Line

Slack line is a reduction of tension in the towline. If the slack is severe enough, it might entangle the glider or cause damage to the glider or towplane. The following situations may result in a slack line:

- Abrupt power reduction by the towplane
- Aerotow descents
- Glider turns inside the towplane turn radius *[Figure 8-13]*
- Updrafts and downdrafts
- Abrupt recovery from a wake box corner position *[Figure 8-14]*

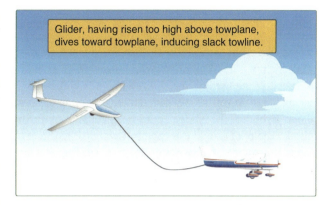

Figure 8-14. *One method of generating towline slack.*

When the towplane precedes the glider into an updraft, the glider pilot first perceives that the towplane is climbing much faster and higher than it actually is. Then, as the glider enters the updraft, it is lighter and more efficient than the towplane. It climbs higher and faster than the towplane did in the same updraft. As a result, the glider pilot pitches the glider over to regain the proper tow altitude but gains airspeed more quickly than the towplane, hence the slack towline. The glider pilot must be ready to control the descent and closure rate to the towplane by increasing drag.

Slack line recovery procedures should be initiated as soon as the glider pilot becomes aware of the situation. The glider pilot should try slipping back into alignment with the towplane. In the event that slipping motion fails to reduce the slack sufficiently, careful use of spoilers/dive brakes can decelerate the glider and take up the slack. As the towline begins to tighten, stabilize the tow and gradually resume the desired aerotow position. When slack in the towline is excessive, or beyond the pilot's capability to safely recover, the glider pilot should immediately release from the aerotow.

Common errors regarding a slack line include:

- Failure to take corrective action at the first indication of a slack line.
- Use of improper procedure to correct slack line causing excessive stress on the towline, towplane, and the glider.
- Failure to decrease drag as towline slack decreases.

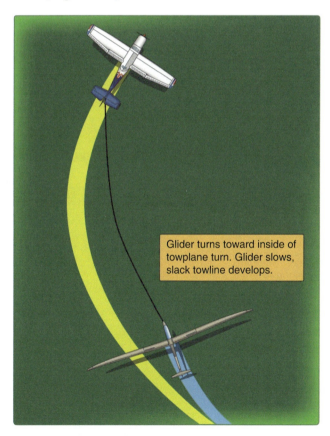

Figure 8-13. *Glider bank is steeper than that of towplane, causing slack in towline.*

Ground Launch Abnormal and Emergency Procedures

Abnormal Procedures

The launch equipment operator manages ground launch towline speed. Because the launch equipment operator is remote from the glider, it is not uncommon for initial tow to be too fast or too slow. If the towline speed is too great, the glider is not able to climb very high because of excessive airspeed. If the towline speed is too low, the glider may be incapable of lift-off or could stall after becoming airborne. Once airborne, the glider could be incapable of further climb. The pilot should use appropriate signals to direct the launch operator to increase or decrease speed. The pilot must anticipate and be prepared to deal with these situations. In the event these abnormal situations develop, the pilot's only alternative may be to release the towline and land ahead.

Wind gradient (a sudden increase in windspeed with height) can have a noticeable effect on ground launches. If the wind gradient is significant or sudden, or both, and the pilot maintains the same pitch attitude, indicated airspeed increases that could exceed the maximum ground launch tow speed could occur. The pilot must adjust the airspeed to deal with the effect of the gradient. When encountering a wind gradient, the pilot should push forward on the stick to reduce the indicated airspeed. *[Figure 8-15]* The only way for the glider to resume climb without exceeding the maximum ground launch airspeed is for the pilot to signal the launch operator to reduce tow speed. After the reduction of the towing speed, the pilot can resume normal climb. If the tow speed is not reduced, the glider may be incapable of climbing to safe altitude.

Ground launch may be interrupted by a ground launch mechanism malfunction. A gradual deceleration in rate of climb and/or airspeed may be an indication of such a malfunction. If a launch mechanism malfunction is suspected, release and land ahead.

Emergency Procedures

A broken towline is the most common type of problem when doing a ground launch. *[Figure 8-16]* When there is a towline failure, the glider pilot must pull the release handle and immediately lower the nose of the glider to achieve and maintain a safe airspeed. The distinguishing features of the ground launch are nose-high pitch attitude and a relatively low altitude for a significant portion of the launch and climb. If a towline break occurs and the glider pilot fails to respond promptly, the nose-high attitude of the glider may result in a stall. Altitude may be insufficient for recovery unless the pilot recognizes and responds to the towline break by lowering the nose.

If the glider tow release mechanism fails, the pilot should fly at airspeeds no lower than best lift over drag (L/D) airspeed. He or she should fly over and then past the ground launch equipment. This method allows the glider towhook back release to activate or the towline weak link to fail. The ground launch equipment is also equipped with an emergency release mechanism in the event the glider tow release fails. If a winch is used, it is equipped with a guillotine to cut the towline. If a motor vehicle is used as a ground launch, it should be equipped with some form of backup release mechanism.

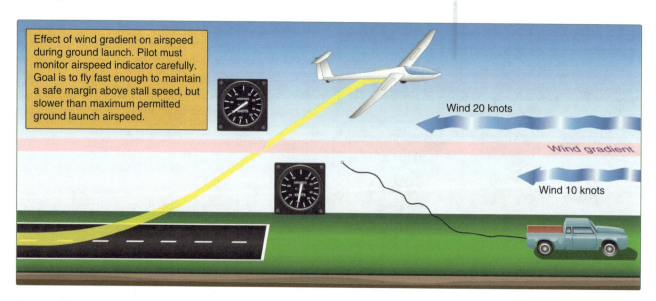

Figure 8-15. *Ground launch wind gradient.*

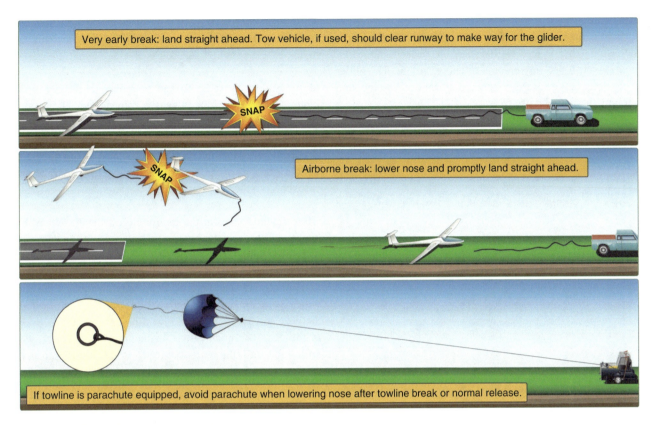

Figure 8-16. *Ground launch towline break.*

Self-Launch Takeoff Emergency Procedures

Emergency Procedures

The pilot of a self-launching glider should formulate emergency plans for any type of failure that might occur. Thorough knowledge of aircraft performance data, normal takeoff/landing procedures, and emergency procedures as outlined in the GFM/POH are essential to the successful management of any emergency situation.

Mismanagement of the aircraft systems through lack of knowledge may cause serious difficulty. For instance, if the spoilers/dive brakes are allowed to open during takeoff and climb, the self-launching glider may be incapable of generating sufficient power to continue climbing. Other emergency situations may include inflight fire, structural failure, encounters with severe turbulence/wind shear, canopy failure, and inadvertent encounter with instrument meteorological conditions (IMC).

Possible options for handling emergencies are influenced by the altitude above the terrain, wind, and weather conditions. As a part of preflight planning, pilots should review the effects of density altitude on glider performance. The takeoff runway length and landing areas near the gliderport and existing air traffic affect the pilot's approach and landing decision. Emergency options may include landing ahead on the remaining runway, landing off field, or returning to the gliderport to land on an available runway. The appropriate emergency procedures may be found in the GFM/POH for the specific self-launching glider.

Spiral Dives

Allowing the nose of the glider to get excessively low during a steep turn may result in a significant increase in airspeed and loss in altitude, creating a spiral dive. If the pilot attempts to recover from this situation by applying only back elevator pressure, the limiting load factor may be exceeded, causing structural failure. To recover from a spiral dive properly, the pilot should first reduce the angle of bank with coordinated use of the rudder and aileron, then smoothly increase pitch to the proper attitude.

Common errors during spiral dives include:

- Failure to recognize when a spiral dive is developing.
- Rough, abrupt, and/or uncoordinated control application during recovery.
- Improper sequence of control applications.

Spins

All flight instructor applicants must be proficient in spins. A spin may be defined as an aggravated stall that results in autorotation wherein the glider follows a downward corkscrew path. As the glider rotates around a vertical axis, the rising wing is less stalled than the descending wing, creating a rolling, yawing, and pitching motion. The glider is basically being forced downward by rolling, yawing, and pitching in a spiral path. *[Figure 8-17]*

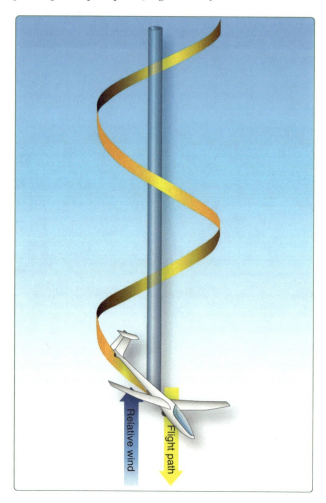

Figure 8-17. *Autorotation of spinning glider.*

The autorotation results from an unequal angle of attack on the glider's wings. The rising wing has a decreasing angle of attack in which the relative lift increases and the drag decreases. In effect, this wing is less stalled. Meanwhile, the descending wing has an increasing angle of attack, past the wing's critical angle of attack (stall) where the relative lift decreases and drag increases.

A spin is caused when the glider's wing exceeds its critical angle of attack (stall) with a sideslip or yaw acting on the glider at, or beyond, the actual stall. During this uncoordinated maneuver, a pilot may not be aware that a critical angle of attack has been exceeded until the glider yaws out of control toward the lowering wing. If stall recovery is not initiated immediately, the glider may enter a spin. If this stall occurs while the glider is in a slipping or skidding turn, this can result in a spin entry and rotation in the direction that the rudder is being applied, regardless of which wingtip is raised.

Many gliders must be forced to spin and require good judgment and technique to get the spin started. These same gliders may be put into a spin accidentally by mishandling the controls in turns, stalls, and flight at minimum controllable airspeeds. This fact is additional evidence of the necessity for the practice of stalls until the ability to recognize and recover from them is developed.

Often a wing drops at the beginning of a stall. When this happens, the nose attempts to move (yaw) in the direction of the low wing. This is when use of the rudder is important during a stall. The correct amount of opposite rudder must be applied to keep the nose from yawing toward the low wing. By maintaining directional control and not allowing the nose to yaw toward the low wing before stall recovery is initiated, a spin is averted. If the nose is allowed to yaw during the stall, the glider begins to skid in the direction of the lowered wing and enters a spin.

A glider must be stalled in order to enter a spin; therefore, continued practice of stall recognition helps the pilot develop a more instinctive and prompt reaction in recognizing an approaching spin. It is essential to learn to apply immediate corrective action any time it is apparent the glider is approaching spin conditions. If it is impossible to avoid a spin, the pilot should immediately execute spin recovery procedures.

The flight instructor should demonstrate spins and spin recovery techniques with emphasis on any special spin procedures or techniques required for a particular glider. Before beginning any spin operations, the following items should be reviewed:

- GFM/POH limitations section, placards, or type certification data sheet, to determine if the glider is approved for spins
- Weight and balance limitations
- Proper recommended entry and recovery procedures
- The requirements for parachutes. It would be appropriate to review current Title 14 of the Code of Federal Regulations (14 CFR) part 91 for the latest parachute requirements.

A thorough glider preflight should be accomplished with special emphasis on excess or loose items that may affect the weight, CG, and controllability of the glider. Slack or loose control cables (particularly rudder and elevator) could prevent full antispin control deflections and delay or preclude recovery in some gliders.

Prior to beginning spin training, the flight area above and below the glider must be clear of other air traffic. Clearing the area may be accomplished while slowing the glider for the spin entry. All spin training should be initiated at an altitude high enough for a completed recovery at or above 1,500 feet AGL within gliding distance of a landing area. There are four phases of a spin: entry, incipient, developed, and recovery.

Entry Phase
In the entry phase, the pilot provides the necessary elements for the spin, either accidentally or intentionally. The entry procedure for demonstrating a spin is similar to a stall. As the glider approaches a stall, smoothly apply full rudder in the direction of the desired spin rotation while applying full back (up) elevator to the limit of travel. Always maintain the ailerons in the neutral position during the spin procedure unless the GFM/POH specifies otherwise.

Incipient Phase
The incipient phase takes place between the time the glider stalls and rotation starts until the spin has fully developed. This change may take up to two turns for most gliders. An incipient spin that is not allowed to develop into a steady-state spin is the most commonly used in the introduction to spin training and recovery techniques. In this phase, the aerodynamic and inertial forces have not achieved a balance. As the incipient spin develops, the indicated airspeed should be near or below stall airspeed. The incipient spin recovery procedure should be commenced prior to the completion of 360° of rotation. The pilot should apply full rudder opposite the direction of rotation.

Developed Phase
The developed phase occurs when the glider's angular rotation rate, airspeed, and vertical speed are stabilized while in a flightpath that is nearly vertical. This is, when glider aerodynamic forces and inertial forces are in balance and the attitude, angles, and self-sustaining motions about the vertical axis are constant or repetitive, the spin is in equilibrium.

Recovery Phase
The recovery phase occurs when the angle of attack of the wings drops below the critical angle of attack and autorotation slows. Then, the nose drops below the spin pitch attitude and rotation stops. This phase may last for a quarter turn to several turns. To recover, control inputs are initiated to disrupt the spin equilibrium by stopping the rotation and stall. To accomplish spin recovery, the manufacturer's recommended procedures should be followed. In the absence of the manufacturer's recommended spin recovery procedures, the following steps for general spin recovery are recommended:

1. Position the ailerons to neutral. Ailerons may have an adverse effect on spin recovery. Aileron control in the direction of the spin may increase the rate of rotation and delay the recovery. Aileron control opposite the direction of the spin may cause the down aileron to move the wing deeper into the stall and aggravate the situation. The best procedure is to ensure that the ailerons are neutral. If the flaps are extended prior to the spin, they should be retracted as soon as possible after spin entry.

2. Apply full opposite rudder against the rotation. Ensure that full (against the stop) opposite rudder has been applied.

3. When rotation stops, apply a positive and brisk, straightforward movement of the elevator control past neutral to break the stall. The forceful movement of the elevator decreases the excessive angle of attack and breaks the stall. The controls should be held firmly in this position.

4. After spin rotation stops, neutralize the rudder. If the rudder is not neutralized at this time, the ensuing increased airspeed acting upon a deflected rudder causes a yawing effect. Slow and overly cautious control movements during spin recovery must be avoided. In certain cases, it has been found that such movements result in the glider continuing to spin indefinitely, even with antispin inputs. A brisk and positive technique, on the other hand, results in a more positive spin recovery.

5. Begin applying back-elevator pressure to raise the nose to level flight. Caution must be used not to apply excessive back-elevator pressure after the rotation stops. Excessive back-elevator pressure can cause a secondary stall and result in another spin. Care should be taken not to exceed the G-load limits and airspeed limitations during recovery.

It is important to remember that the above spin recovery procedures are recommended for use only in the absence of the manufacturer's procedures. Before any pilot attempts to begin spin training, the pilot must be familiar with the procedures provided by the manufacturer for spin recovery.

The most common problems in spin recovery include pilot confusion in determining the direction of spin rotation and whether the maneuver is a spin or a spiral. If the airspeed is increasing, the glider is no longer in a spin but in a spiral. In a spin, the glider is stalled and the airspeed is at or below stalling speed.

Common errors when encountering/practicing spins include:
- Failure to clear area before a spin.

- Failure to establish proper configuration prior to spin entry.
- Failure to correct airspeed for spin entry.
- Failure to recognize conditions leading to a spin.
- Failure to achieve and maintain stall during spin entry.
- Improper use of controls during spin entry, rotation, and/or recovery.
- Disorientation during spin.
- Failure to distinguish a spiral dive from a spin.
- Excessive speed or secondary stall during spin recovery.
- Failure to recover with minimum loss of altitude.
- Failure to recover above minimum altitude with a landing area within gliding distance.

Off-Field Landing Procedures

The possibility of an off-field landing is present on virtually every cross-country soaring flight, even when flying in a self-launching glider. If the engine or power system fails and there is no airport within gliding range, an off-field landing may be inevitable. It should be noted that many glider pilots not flying cross-country have faced the necessity of performing an off-field landing. Causes of off-field landings while soaring in the vicinity of the launching airport, include rapid weather deterioration, a significant change in wind direction, unanticipated amounts of sinking air, disorientation, lack of situational awareness, tow failures, and other emergencies requiring an off-field landing. In these situations, it usually is safer to make a precautionary off-field landing than it is to attempt a low, straight-in approach to the airport. If the glide back to the airport comes up short for any reason, the landing is likely to be poorly executed and may result in damage to the glider or injury to the pilot.

On cross-country soaring flights, off-field landings are not usually considered emergency landings. As a matter of fact, they are expected and are considered while preparing for flight. On the other hand, if equipment failure leads to the necessity of performing an off-field landing, then the landing can be characterized or described as an emergency landing. Whatever the reason for the off-field landing, each glider pilot must be prepared at all times to plan and execute the landing safely.

Unlike airport landings, no off-field landing is entirely routine. An extra measure of care must be undertaken to achieve a safe outcome. The basic ingredients for a successful off-field landing are awareness of wind direction, wind strength at the surface, and approach path obstacles. The glider pilot must be able to identify suitable landing areas, have the discipline to select a suitable landing area while height remains to allow sufficient time to perform a safe approach and landing, and the ability to make consistently accurate landings in the glider type being flown.

These basic ingredients for a successful off-field landing can be summarized as follows:

- Recognizing the possibility of imminent off-field landing.
- Selecting a suitable area, then a suitable landing field within that area.
- Planning the approach with wind, obstacles, and local terrain in mind.
- Executing the approach, land, and then stopping the glider as soon as possible.
- Attempting to contact ground crew and notifying them of off-field landing location.

The most common off-field landing planning failure is denial. The pilot, understandably eager to continue the flight and return to an airport, is often reluctant to initiate planning for an off-field landing because, in the pilot's mind, to do so probably results in such a landing. It would be better, the pilot thinks, to concentrate on continuing the flight and finding a way to climb back up and fly away. The danger of this false optimism is that there is little or no time to plan an off-field landing if the attempt to climb away does not succeed. It is much safer to thoroughly understand the techniques of planning an off-field landing and to be prepared for the occurrence at any time.

Wind awareness, knowing wind direction and intensity, is key when planning an off-field landing. Flying downwind offers a greater geographical area to search than flying upwind. The tailwind during downwind cruise results in a greater range; a headwind during upwind cruise reduces the range. Wind awareness is also essential to planning the orientation and direction of the landing approach. Visualize the wind flowing over and around the intended landing area. Remember that the area downwind of hills, buildings, and other obstructions will probably be turbulent at low altitude. Also, be aware that landing into wind shortens landing rolls.

Decision heights are altitudes at which pilots take critical steps in the off-field landing process. If the terrain below is suitable for landing, select a general area no lower than 2,000 feet above ground level (AGL). Select the intended landing field no lower than 1,500 feet AGL. At 1,000 feet AGL, commit to flying the approach and landing off field. If the terrain below is not acceptable for an off-field landing, the best course of action is to move immediately toward more suitable terrain.

For many pilots, there is a strong temptation during the off-field landing process to select a landing location based primarily on the ease of glider retrieval. The convenience of an easy retrieval is of little consequence if the landing site is unsuitable and results in damage to the glider or injury to the pilot. Select the landing site with safety as the highest priority. During an off-field landing approach, the precise elevation of the landing site is usually unavailable to the pilot. This renders the altimeter more or less useless. Fly the approach and assess the progress by recognizing and maintaining the angle that puts the glider at the intended landing spot safely. If landing into a strong headwind, the approach angle is steep. If headwind is light or nonexistent, the approach angle is shallower unless landing over an obstacle. When landing with a tailwind (due to slope or one-way entry into the selected field due to terrain or obstacles), the angle is shallower. Remember to clear each visible obstacle with safe altitude, clearing any poles and wires by a safe margin. Always keep in mind that from the air, wires are basically invisible until they are right in front of you, whereas towers are visible from a distance. Any time there are two supporting structures (telephone poles) it is safe to assume that there are wires connecting them.

Select a field of adequate length and, if possible, one with no visible slope. Any slope that is visible from the air is likely to be steep. Slope can often be assessed by the color of the land. High spots often are lighter in color than low spots because soil moisture tends to collect in low spots, darkening the color of the soil. If level landing areas are not available and the landing must be made on a slope, it is better to land uphill than downhill. Even a slight downhill grade during landing flare allows the glider to float prior to touchdown, which may result in collision with objects on the far end of the selected field.

Knowledge of local vegetation and crops is also very useful. Tall crops are generally more dangerous to land in than low crops. Know the colors of local seasonal vegetation to help identify crops and other vegetation from the air. Without exception, avoid discontinuities such as lines or crop changes. Discontinuities usually exist because a fence, ditch, irrigation pipe, or some other obstacle to machinery or cultivation is present. Other obstacles may be present in the vicinity of the chosen field. Trees and buildings are easy to spot, but power and telephone lines and poles are more difficult to see from pattern altitude. Take a careful look around to find them. Assume every pole is connected by wire to every other pole. Also assume that every pole is connected by wire to every building, and that every building is connected by wire to every other building. Plan the approach to overfly the wires that may be present, even if you cannot see them. The more visible the landing area is during the approach, the fewer unpleasant surprises there are likely to be.

The recommended approach procedure is to fly the following legs in the pattern:

- Crosswind leg on the downwind side of the field
- Upwind leg
- Crosswind leg on the upwind side of the field
- Downwind leg
- Base leg
- Final approach

This approach procedure provides the opportunity to see the intended landing area from all sides. Use every opportunity while flying this approach to inspect the landing area and look for obstacles or other hazards. *[Figure 8-18]*

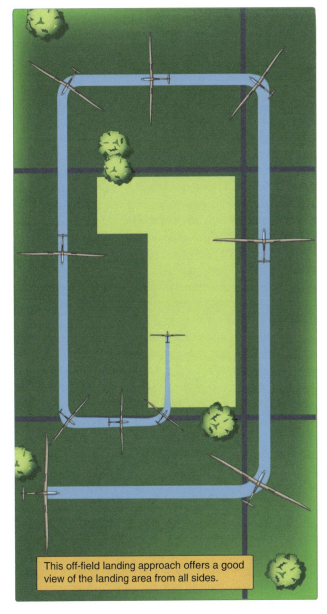

Figure 8-18. *Off field landing approach.*

Landing over an obstacle or a wire requires skill and vigilance. The first goal in landing over an obstacle is to clear the obstacle! Next, consider how the obstacle affects the length of landing area that is actually going to be available for touchdown, roll out, and stopping the glider. If an obstacle is 50 feet high, the first 500 feet or so of the landing area needs to be overflown during the descent to flare and land. If the field selected has obstacles on the final approach path, remember that the field must be long enough to accommodate the descent to flare altitude after clearing the obstacle.

Hold the glider off during the flare and touch down at the lowest safe speed manageable. After touchdown, use the wheel brake immediately and vigorously to stop the glider as soon as possible. Aggressive braking helps prevent collision with small stakes, ditches, rocks, or other obstacles that cannot easily be seen, especially if the vegetation in the field is tall.

Afterlanding Off Field
Off-Field Landing Without Injury

If uninjured, tend to personal needs and then secure the glider. Make contact with the retrieval crew or emergency crew as promptly as possible. If the wait is likely to be long, use the daylight to remove all items necessary for darkness and cold. It is worth remembering that even a normal retrieval can take many hours if the landing was made in difficult terrain or in an area served by relatively few roads. If cellular service is available, use a cell phone to call 911 if you are concerned about personal safety. Glider pilots should always consider alternate means of communication to include satellite telephones and ham radios as cell phone service is not always available. To help identify position, relay the GPS coordinates, if available, to ease the job for the retrieval crew or rescue personnel. It is a good idea to write down the GPS coordinates if the GPS battery is exhausted or if the GPS receiver shuts down for any reason. Use the glider two-way radio to broadcast needs on the international distress frequency 121.5 MHz. Many aircraft, including civil airliners, routinely monitor this frequency. Their great height gives the line-of-sight aviation transceiver tremendous range when transmitting to, or receiving from, these high-altitude aircraft. Calling other glider pilots in the area on the glider-to-glider radio frequency can hasten retrieval or rescue. Another tool for pilots is the personal locator device offered by several companies as a rescue device. These devices use the 406 MHz satellite signal, and global positioning system (GPS) technology to accurately track and relay the pilot's location in the event of an off-field landing requiring assistance.

Once contact has been made with outsiders to arrange for retrieval, attend to minor items, such as collecting any special tools that are needed for glider derigging or installing gust locks on the glider's flight controls.

Off-Field Landing With Injury

If injured, tend to critical injuries first. At the first opportunity, make contact with emergency response personnel, with other aircraft, or any other source of identifiable assistance. Use the glider radio, if operable, to broadcast a Mayday distress call on emergency frequency 121.5 MHz. Also, try any other frequency likely to elicit a response. Some gliders have an Emergency Locator Transmitter (ELT) on board. If the glider is equipped with an ELT and assistance is needed, turn it on. The ELT broadcasts continuous emergency signals on 121.5 MHz. Search aircraft can hone in on this ELT signal using radio equipment designed for search and rescue (SAR). These SAR-equipped aircraft reduce the time spent searching for the pilot's exact location. To transmit a voice message on an operable two-way radio at 121.5 MHz, turn the ELT switch to OFF for the voice message to be heard. The newer ELTs, like the 406 MHz Emergency Position Indicating Radio Beacons (EPIRBs), are becoming more popular because of their substantial benefits. Only ATC ground stations routinely monitor 121.5 MHz anymore and that is line-of-sight reception only. The newer EPIRBs have stronger signals, transmit longer, and are monitored by the satellite network. According to CFR part 91, gliders are not airplanes and therefore old very high frequency (VHF) ELTs are not required, which is why a EPIRB would make a much better choice when flying a glider. If mobile (cell) phone coverage is available, dial 911 to contact emergency personnel. If possible, include a clear description of the location. If the glider is in a precarious position, secure it, if possible, but do not risk further personal injury in doing so. If it is clearly unsafe to stay with the glider, move to a nearby location for shelter but leave clear written instructions in a prominent location in the glider detailing where to find you.

It is best to stay with the glider if at all possible. The glider bulk is likely to be much easier to locate from the air than is an individual person. The pilot might obtain a measure of protection from the elements by crawling into the fuselage or crawling under a wing, or using the parachute canopy to rig a makeshift tent around the glider structure. After attending to medical needs and contacting rescue personnel, attend to clothing, food, and water issues. The pilot should make every attempt to conserve energy.

System and Equipment Malfunctions
Flight Instrument Malfunctions

Instrument failures can result from careless maintenance practices and from internal or external causes. An example of careless maintenance is removal and replacement of the airspeed indicator but failure to connect the instrument correctly to pitot and static lines. A pitot tube clogged by insects or water ingress is an example of an external cause of instrument failure.

Pilots should always be aware of the glider's normal attitudes for all flight regimes. Then, when presented with an instrument failure or erroneous indication, the pilot has a general sense of the glider's normal attitude from outside flying cues to make a safe return and landing. Judging the altitude or airspeed of the glider without the guidance of instruments should not constitute a panic in the cockpit as many pilots can make precision approaches and landings without the use of an altimeter. In fact, many older and vintage gliders do not require an operational altimeter in the cockpit.

Airspeed Indicator Malfunctions

If the airspeed indicator appears to be erratic or inaccurate, fly the glider by pitch attitude. Keep the nose of the glider at the proper pitch attitude for best glide or minimum sink airspeed. Additional cues to airspeed include control "feel" and wind noise. At very low airspeeds, control feel is very mushy and wind noise is generally low. At higher airspeeds, control feel is crisper and wind noise takes on a more insistent hissing quality. The sound of the relative wind can be amplified and made more useful in airspeed control by opening the sliding window installed in the canopy and by opening the air vent control. During the landing approach, maintain adequate airspeed using cues other than the airspeed indicator. Fly the approach with an adequate margin above stall airspeed. If conditions are turbulent or the wind is gusty, additional airspeed is necessary to penetrate the convection and to ensure adequate control authority. If in doubt, it is better to be flying 10 knots faster than optimum airspeed than it is to be 10 knots slower.

Altimeter Malfunctions

Altimeter failure may result from internal instrument failure or from external causes, such as water ingress in the static lines. Regardless of the cause, it is important to maintain sufficient altitude to allow a safe glide to a suitable landing area. During the approach to land without a functioning altimeter, it is necessary to rely on perception of maintaining a safe gliding angle to the target landing area. The primary risk to safety is entering the approach from an altitude that is lower than normal. It is better to enter the approach from a normal height, or even from a higher-than-normal height. During the approach, judge the angle to the target area frequently. If the angle is too steep, apply spoilers/dive brakes to steepen the descent path. If necessary, apply a forward slip or turning slip to lose additional altitude. If the approach angle is beginning to appear shallow, close the spoilers/dive brakes and, if necessary, modify the approach path to shorten the distance necessary to glide to make it to the target landing area.

Static line contamination affects both the altimeter and the airspeed indicator. If it is suspected that either instrument is malfunctioning because of static line contamination, remember that the indications of the other instrument(s) connected to the static line may also be incorrect. Use the external cues described above to provide multiple cross-checks on the indications of all affected instruments. If in doubt about the accuracy of any instrument, it is best to believe the external cues and disregard the instrument indications. After landing and prior to the next flight, have an aviation maintenance professional evaluate the instrument system.

It is essential that a glider pilot be familiar with the procedures for making a safe approach without a functioning airspeed indicator or altimeter. Being accompanied by a glider flight instructor during the flight review provides an excellent opportunity to review these procedures.

Variometer Malfunctions

Variometer failure can make it difficult for the pilot to locate and exploit sources of lift. If an airport is nearby, a precautionary landing should be made so the source of the problem can be uncovered and repaired. If no airport is nearby, search for clues to sources of lift. Some clues may be external, such as a rising smoke column, a cumulus cloud, a dust devil, or a soaring bird. Other sources are internal, such as the altimeter. Use the altimeter to gauge rate of climb or descent in the absence of a functioning variometer. Tapping the altimeter with the forefinger often overcomes internal friction in the altimeter, allowing the hand to move upward or downward. The direction of the movement gives an idea of the rate of climb or descent over the last few seconds. When lift is encountered, stay with it and climb.

Compass Malfunctions

Compass failure is rare, but it does occur. If the compass performs poorly or not at all, cross-check current position with aeronautical charts and with electronic methods of navigation, such as GPS, if available. The position of the sun, combined with knowledge of the time of day, can help with orientation also. Being familiar with section lines and major roads often provides helpful cues to orientation and the direction of flight.

Glider Canopy Malfunctions
Glider Canopy Opens Unexpectedly

Canopy-related emergencies are often the result of pilot error. The most likely cause is failure to lock the canopy in the closed position prior to takeoff. Regardless of the cause, if the canopy opens unexpectedly during any phase of flight, the first duty is to fly the glider. It is important to maintain adequate airspeed while selecting a suitable landing area.

If the canopy opens while on aerotow, it is vital to maintain a normal flying attitude to avoid jeopardizing the safety of the glider occupants and the safety of the towplane pilot. Only when the glider pilot is certain that glider control can be maintained should any attention be devoted to trying to close the canopy. If flying a two-seat glider with a passenger on board, fly the glider while the other person attempts to close and lock the canopy. If the canopy cannot be closed, the glider may still be controllable. Drag is higher than normal; when flying the approach, plan a steeper-than-normal descent path. The best prevention against unexpected opening of the canopy is proper use of the pretakeoff checklist.

Broken Glider Canopy

If the canopy is damaged or breaks during flight, the best response is to land as soon as practicable. Drag increases if the canopy is shattered, so plan a steeper-than-normal descent path during the approach.

Frosted Glider Canopy

Extended flight at high altitude or in low ambient temperatures may result in obstructed vision as moisture condenses as frost on the inside of the canopy. Open the air vents and the side window to ventilate the cabin and to evacuate moist air before the moisture can condense on the canopy. Descend to lower altitudes or warmer air to reduce the frost on the canopy. Flight in direct sunlight helps diminish the frost on the canopy.

Water Ballast Malfunctions

Water ballast systems are relatively simple and major failures are not very common. Nevertheless, ballast system failures can threaten the safety of flight. One example of ballast failure is asymmetrical tank draining (one wing tank drains properly but the other wing tank does not). The result is a wing-heavy glider that may be very difficult to control during slow flight and during the latter portion of the landing rollout. Another example is leakage. Some water ballast systems drain into a central pipe that empties through the landing gear wheel well. If the drain connections from either wing leak significantly, water from the tanks can collect in the fuselage. If the water flows far forward or far aft in the fuselage, pitch control of the glider may be severely degraded. Pitch control can be augmented by flying at mid to high airspeeds, giving the elevator more control authority to correct for the out-of-balance situation, and affording time to determine whether the water can be evacuated from the fuselage. If pitch control is dangerously degraded, abandoning the glider may be the safest choice. The best prevention for water ballast problems is regular maintenance and inspection combined with periodic tests of the system and its components.

Retractable Landing Gear Malfunctions

Landing gear difficulties can arise from several causes. Landing gear failures arising from mechanical malfunction of the gear extension mechanism generally cannot be resolved during flight. Fly the approach at normal airspeed. If the landing gear is not extended, the total drag of the glider is less than it is normally during an approach with the landing gear extended. It may be necessary to use more spoiler/dive brake than normal during the approach. Try to land on the smoothest surface available, preferably an area that has good turf to help reduce the damage to the glider. The landing must be under control and as soft as possible. Slightly above stall speed soft touchdowns are preferable to full stall landings resulting in hard landings. This helps avoid a tailwheel first landing, and a hard touchdown of the glider onto the runway. Avoiding the hard touchdown helps to avoid injury and lessen damage to the glider components.

The glider makes considerable noise as it slides along the runway, and wingtip clearance above the ground is reduced. Keep the wings level for as long as possible. Try to keep the glider going as straight as possible using the rudder to guide the glider. The primary goal is to avoid collision with objects on the ground or along the runway border, including runway lighting and signage. Accept the fact that minor skin damage to the glider is inevitable if the gear cannot be extended and locked. Concentrate on personal safety during the approach and landing. Any damage to the glider can be repaired after an injury-free landing.

Primary Flight Control Systems

Failure of any primary flight control system presents a serious threat to safety. The most frequent cause of control system failure is incomplete assembly of the glider in preparation for flight. To avoid this, use a written checklist to guide each assembly operation and inspect every connection and safety pin thoroughly. Do not allow interruptions during assembly. If interruption is unavoidable, start the checklist again from the very beginning. Perform a positive control check with the help of a knowledgeable assistant. Do not assume that any flight surface and flight control is properly installed and connected during the post-assembly inspection. Instead, assume that every connection is suspect. Inspect and test until certain that every component is ready for flight.

Elevator Malfunctions

The most serious control system malfunction is a failure of the elevator flight control. Causes of elevator flight control failure include the following:

- An improper connection of the elevator control circuit during assembly.

- An elevator control lock that was not removed before flight.

- Separation of the elevator gap seal tape.

- Interference of a foreign object with free and full travel of the control stick or elevator circuit.
- A lap belt or shoulder harness in the back seat that was used to secure the control stick and not removed prior to flight.
- A structural failure of the glider due to overstressing or flutter.

To avoid a failure, ensure that control locks are removed prior to flight, that all flight control connections have been completed properly and inspected, and that all safety pins have been installed and latched properly. Ensure that a positive control check against applied resistance has been performed.

If the elevator irregularity or failure is detected early in the takeoff roll, release the towline (or reduce power to idle), maneuver the glider to avoid obstacles, and use the brakes firmly to stop the glider as soon as possible. If the elevator control irregularity or failure is not noticed until after takeoff, a series of complicated decisions must be made quickly. If the glider is close to the ground and has a flat or slightly nose-low pitch attitude, releasing the towline (or reducing power to zero) is the best choice. If this is an aerotow launch, consider the effect the glider has on the safety of the tow pilot. If there is sufficient elevator control during climb, then it is probably best to stay with the launch and achieve as high an altitude as possible. High altitude gives more time to abandon the glider and deploy a parachute, if worn.

If the decision is to stay with the glider and continue the climb, experiment with the effect of other flight controls on the pitch attitude of the glider. These include the effects of various wing flap settings, spoilers/dive brakes, elevator trim system, and raising or lowering the landing gear. If flying a self-launching glider, experiment with the effect of power settings on pitch attitude.

If aileron control is functioning, bank the glider and use the rudder to moderate the attitude of the nose relative to the horizon. When the desired pitch attitude is approached, adjust the bank angle to maintain the desired pitch attitude. Forward slips may have a predictable effect on pitch attitude and can be used to moderate it. Usually, a combination of these techniques is necessary to regain some control of pitch attitude. While these techniques may be a poor substitute for the glider elevator itself, they are better than nothing. If an altitude sufficient to permit bailing out and using a parachute is achieved, chances of survival are good because parachute failures are exceedingly rare.

Elevator gap seal tape, if in poor condition, can degrade elevator responsiveness. If the adhesive that bonds the gap seal leading edge to the horizontal stabilizer begins to fail, the leading edge of the gap seal may be lifted up by the relative wind. This provides, in effect, a small spoiler that disturbs the airflow over the elevator just aft of the lifted seal. Elevator blanking that occurs across a substantial portion of the span of the elevator seriously degrades pitch attitude control. In extreme cases, elevator authority may be compromised so drastically that the glider elevator is useless.

The pilot may be forced to resort to alternate methods to control pitch attitude as described above. Bailing out may be the safest alternative. Inspection of the gap seal bonds for all flight control surfaces prior to flight is the best prevention.

Aileron Malfunctions

Aileron failures can cause serious control problems. Causes of aileron failure include:

- Improper connection of the aileron control circuit during assembly.
- Aileron control lock that was not removed before flight.
- Separation of the aileron gap seal tape.
- Interference of a foreign object with free and full travel of the control stick or aileron circuit.
- Seat belt or shoulder harness in the back seat that was used to secure the control stick and not removed prior to flight.
- Structural failure and/or aileron flutter.

These failures can sometimes be counteracted successfully, partly because there are two ailerons. If one aileron is disconnected or locked by an external control lock, the degree of motion still available in the other aileron may exert some influence on bank angle control. Use whatever degree of aileron is available to maintain control of the glider. The glider may be less difficult to control at medium to high airspeeds than at low airspeeds.

If the ailerons are not functioning adequately and roll control is compromised, the secondary effect of the rudder can be used to make gentle adjustments in the bank angle so long as a safe margin above stall speed is maintained. The primary effect of the rudder is to yaw the glider. The secondary effect of the rudder is subtler and takes longer to assert itself. In wings-level flight, if left rudder is applied, the nose yaws to the left. If the pressure is held, the wings begin a gentle bank to the left. If right rudder pressure is held and applied, the glider yaws to the right, then begins to bank to the right. This secondary banking effect by the rudder is useful if the pilot must resort to using the rudder to bank the glider wings. The secondary effect of the rudder works best when the wings are level or held in a very shallow bank, and is enhanced at medium to high airspeeds. Try to keep all banks very shallow. If the bank angle becomes excessive, it is difficult or impossible to recover to wings-level flight using the rudder alone. If the bank is becoming too steep, use any aileron influence available, as well as all available rudder to bring the wings back to level. If a parachute is available and the glider becomes uncontrollable at low airspeed, the best chance to escape serious injury may be to bail out of the glider from a safe altitude.

Rudder Malfunctions

Rudder failure is extremely rare because removing and installing the vertical fin/rudder combination is not part of the normal sequence of rigging and de-rigging the glider (as it is for the horizontal stabilizer/elevator and for the wing/aileron combinations). Poor directional control is so obvious to the pilot from the very beginning of the launch that, if rudder malfunction is suspected, the launch can be aborted early.

Rudder malfunctions are most likely to occur after failure to remove the rudder control lock prior to flight or when an unsecured object in the cockpit interferes with the free and full travel of the rudder pedals. Preflight preparation must include removal of all flight control locks and safe stowage of all items on board. The pretakeoff checklist includes checking all primary flight controls for correct, full travel prior to launch.

Although rudder failure is quite rare, the consequences are serious. If a control lock causes the problem, it is possible to control the glider airspeed and bank attitude, but directional control is compromised due to limited rudder movement. In the air, some degree of directional control can be obtained by using the adverse yaw effect of the ailerons to yaw the glider. During rollout from an aborted launch or during landing rollout, directional control can sometimes be obtained by deliberately grounding the wingtip toward the direction of desired yaw. Putting the wingtip on the ground for a fraction of a second causes a slight yaw in that direction; holding the wingtip firmly on the ground usually causes a vigorous yaw or ground loop in the direction of the grounded wingtip.

Careless stowage of cockpit equipment can result in rudder pedal interference at any time during a flight. During flight, if an object is interfering with or jamming the rudder pedals, attempt to remove it. If removal is not possible, attempt to deform, crush, or dislodge the object by applying force on the rudder pedals. It also may be possible to dislodge the object by varying the load factor, but ensure that dislodging the object does not result in its lodging in a worse place where it could jam the elevator or aileron controls. If the object cannot be retrieved and stowed, a precautionary landing may be required.

Commonly misplaced objects that can cause flight control interference include:

- Water bottles,
- Cameras,
- Electronic computers,
- Containers of food and similar items,
- Clothing, and
- Sunglasses.

Control these items by proper planning and good cockpit discipline.

Secondary Flight Controls Systems

Secondary flight control systems include the elevator trim system, wing flaps, and spoilers/dive brakes. Problems with any of these systems can be just as serious as problems with primary controls.

Elevator Trim Malfunctions

Compensating for a malfunctioning elevator trim system is usually as simple as applying pressure on the control stick to maintain the desired pitch attitude, then bringing the flight to safe conclusion. Inspect and repair the trim system prior to the next flight.

Spoiler/Dive Brake Malfunctions

Spoiler/dive brake system failures can arise from rigging errors or omissions, environmental factors, and mechanical failures. Interruptions or distractions during glider assembly can result in failure to properly connect control rods to one or both spoilers/dive brakes. Proper use of a comprehensive checklist reduces the likelihood of assembly errors. If neither of these spoilers/dive brakes is connected, then one or both of the spoilers/dive brakes may deploy at any time and retraction becomes impossible. This is a very hazardous situation for several reasons. One reason is that the spoilers/dive brakes are likely to deploy during the launch or the climb, causing a launch emergency and a possible tow failure incident. Another reason is that the spoilers/dive brakes might deploy asymmetrically: one spoiler/dive brake retracted and the other spoiler/dive brake extended, resulting in yaw and roll tendencies that do not arise when the spoilers/dive brakes deploy symmetrically. A pilot expecting a smooth ,symmetrical deployment would be faced with a control issue that compromises flight safety. Finally, it is not possible to correct the situation by retracting the spoiler/dive brake(s) because the failure to connect the controls properly usually means that pilot control of the spoiler/dive brake has been lost.

If asymmetrical spoiler/dive brake extension occurs and the extended spoiler/dive brake cannot be retracted, several choices must be made. Roll and yaw tendencies due to asymmetry must be overcome or eliminated. One way to solve this problem is to deploy the other spoiler/dive brake to restore the symmetry. The advantages include immediate relief from yaw and roll tendencies and protection against stalling with one spoiler/dive brake extended and the other retracted, which could result in a spin. The disadvantage of deploying the other spoiler/dive brake is that the glide ratio is reduced. If the spoiler/dive brake asymmetry arises during launch or climb, the best choice is to abort the launch, extend the other spoiler/dive brakes to relieve the asymmetry, and make a precautionary or emergency landing.

Environmental factors include low temperature or icing during long, high altitude flights, which may occur during a mountain wave flight. Low temperature causes contraction of all glider components. If the contraction is uneven, the spoilers/dive brakes may bind and be difficult or impossible to deploy. Icing can also interfere with operation of the spoilers/dive brakes. High temperature, on the other hand, causes all glider components to expand. If the expansion is uneven, the spoilers/dive brakes may bind in the closed position. This is most likely to occur while the glider is parked on the ground in direct summer sunlight. The heating can be very intense, particularly for a glider with wings painted a color other than reflective white.

Mechanical failures can cause asymmetrical spoiler/dive brake extension. For example, the spoiler/dive brake extend normally during the prelanding checklist but only one spoiler/dive brake retracts on command. The other spoiler/dive brake remains extended, due perhaps to a broken weld in the spoiler/dive brake actuator mechanism, a defective control connector, or other mechanical failure. The glider yaws and banks toward the wing with the extended spoiler/dive brake. Aileron and rudder are required to counteract these tendencies. To eliminate any possibility of entering a stall/spin, maintain a safe margin above stall airspeed. If the decision to deploy the other spoiler/dive brake is made to relieve the asymmetry, controlling the glider becomes much easier but gliding range is reduced due to the additional drag of the second spoiler/dive brake. This may be a significant concern if the terrain is not ideal for landing the glider. Nevertheless, it is better to make a controlled landing, even in less than ideal terrain, than it is to stall or spin.

Miscellaneous Flight System Malfunctions

Towhook Malfunctions

Towhooks can malfunction as can any other mechanical device. Failure modes include uncommanded towline release and failure to release on command. Pilots must be prepared to abort any towed launch, whether ground or aerotow launch, at any time. Uncommanded towline release must be anticipated prior to every launch. Assess the wind and the airport environment, and then form an emergency plan prior to launch. If the towhook fails to release on command, try to release the towline again after removing tension from the line. Pull the release handle multiple times under varying conditions of towline tension. If the towline still cannot release, alert the towpilot and follow the emergency procedures described in Chapter 7, Flight Maneuvers and Traffic Patterns.

Oxygen System Malfunctions

Oxygen is essential for flight safety at high altitude. If there is a suspected or detected failure in any component of the oxygen system, descend immediately to an altitude at which supplemental oxygen is not essential for continued safe flight. Remember, the first sign of oxygen deprivation is a sensation of apparent well-being. Problem-solving capability is diminished. If the pilot has been deprived of sufficient oxygen, even for a short interval, critical thinking capability has been compromised. Do not be lulled into thinking that the flight can safely continue at high altitude. Descend immediately and breathe normally at these lower altitudes for a time to restore critical oxygen to the bloodstream. Try to avoid hyperventilation, which prolongs the diminished critical thinking capability. Give enough time to recover critical thinking capability before attempting an approach and landing.

Drogue Chute Malfunctions

Some gliders are equipped with a drogue chute to add drag during the approach to land. This drag supplements the drag provided by the spoilers/dive brakes. The drogue chute is packed and stowed in the aft tip (tail cone) of the fuselage or in a special compartment in the base of the rudder. Drogue chutes are very effective when deployed properly and make steep approaches possible. The drogue chute is deployed and jettisoned on pilot command, such as would be necessary if the drag of the glider was so great that the glider would not otherwise have the range to make it to the spot of intended landing. There are several failure modes for drogue chutes. If it deploys accidentally or inadvertently during the launch, the rate of climb seriously degrades and it must be jettisoned. During the approach to land, an improperly packed or damp drogue chute may fail to deploy on command. If this happens, use the rudder to sideslip for a moment, or use the rudder to yaw the tail back and forth. Make certain to attain safe flying speed before attempting the slip or yawing motion. Either technique increases the drag force on the drogue chute compartment that pulls the parachute out of the compartment.

If neither technique deploys the drogue chute, the drogue canopy may deploy at a later time during the approach without further control input from the pilot. This results in a considerable increase in drag. If this happens, be prepared to jettison the drogue chute immediately if sufficient altitude to glide to the intended landing spot has not been reached.

Another possible malfunction is failure of the drogue chute to inflate fully. If this happens, the canopy "streams" like a twisting ribbon of nylon, providing only a fraction of the drag that would occur if the canopy had fully inflated. Full inflation is unlikely after streaming occurs, but if it does occur, drag increases substantially. It is much better to fly with a known drag configuration and adjust for it rather than be faced with a substantially increased drag coefficient at a place and time where a safe landing is no longer possible. If in doubt regarding the degree of deployment of the drogue chute, the safest option may be to jettison the drogue. Regardless of the malfunction type, the pilot should review approach and landing options for the drogue chute conditions.

Self-Launching Gliders

In addition to the standard flight control systems found on all gliders, self-launching gliders have multiple systems to support flight under power. These systems may include but are not limited to the following:

- Fuel tanks, lines, and pumps
- Engine and/or propeller extension and retraction systems
- Electrical system including engine starter system
- Lubricating oil system
- Engine cooling system
- Engine throttle controls
- Propeller blade pitch controls
- Engine monitoring instruments and systems

The complexity of these systems demands thorough familiarity with the GFM/POH for the self-launching glider being flown. Any malfunction of these systems can make it impossible to resume powered flight.

Self-Launching/Sustainer Glider Engine Failure During Takeoff or Climb

Engine failures are the most obvious source of equipment malfunction in self-launching gliders. Engine failures can be subtle (a very slight power loss at full throttle) or catastrophic and sudden (engine crankshaft failing during a full-power takeoff). High on the list of possible causes of power problems are fuel contamination and exhaustion.

To provide adequate power, the engine system must have fuel and ignition, as well as adequate cooling and lubrication. Full power operation is compromised if any of these requirements is not satisfied. Monitor the engine temperature, oil pressure, fuel pressure, and revolutions per minute (rpm) carefully to ensure engine performance is not compromised. Warning signs of impending difficulty include excessively high engine temperatures, abnormal engine oil temperatures, low oil pressure, low rpm despite high throttle settings, low fuel pressure, and erratic engine operation (surging, backfiring, and missing). Abnormal engine performance may be a precursor to complete engine failure. Even if total engine failure does not occur, operation with an engine that cannot produce full power translates into an inability to climb or perhaps an inability to hold altitude despite application of full throttle. The best course of action, if airborne, is to make a precautionary landing first and then discover the source of the trouble.

Regardless of the type of engine failure, the pilot's first responsibility is to maintain flying airspeed and adequate control of the glider. If power failure occurs, lower the nose as necessary to maintain adequate airspeed. Pilots flying self-launching gliders with a pod-mounted external engine above the fuselage need to lower the nose much more aggressively in the event of total power loss than those with an engine mounted in the nose. In the former, the thrust of the engine during full power operations tends to provide a nose-down pitching moment. If power fails, the nose-down pitching moment disappears and is replaced by a nose-up pitching moment due to the substantial parasite drag of the engine pod high above the longitudinal axis of the fuselage. Considerable forward motion on the control stick may be required to maintain flying airspeed. If altitude is low, there is not enough time to stow the engine and reduce the drag that it creates. Land the glider with the engine extended. Glide ratio in this configuration is poor due to the drag of the extended engine and propeller. The authoritative source for information regarding the correct sequence of pilot actions in the event of power failure is contained in the GFM/POH. The pilot must be thoroughly familiar with its contents to operate a self-launching glider safely.

If the power failure occurs during launch or climb, time to maneuver may be limited. Concentrate on flying the glider and selecting a suitable landing area. Remember that the high drag configuration of the glider may limit the distance of the glide without power. Keep turns to a minimum and land the glider as safely as possible. Do not try to restart the engine while at very low altitude because it distracts from the primary task of maintaining flying airspeed and making a safe precautionary landing. Even if power in the engine system were restored, chances are that full power is not available. The problem that caused the power interruption in the first place is not likely to solve itself while trying to maneuver from low altitude and climb out under full power. If the problem recurs, as it is likely to do, the pilot may place the glider low over unlandable terrain with limited gliding range and little or no engine power to continue the flight. Even if the engine continues to provide limited power, flight with partial power may quickly put the glider in a position in which the pilot is unable to clear obstacles, such as wires, poles, hangars, or nearby terrain. If a full power takeoff or climb is interrupted by power loss, it is best to make a precautionary landing. The pilot can sort out the power system problems after returning safely to the ground.

Inability to Restart a Self-Launching/Sustainer Glider Engine While Airborne

Power loss during takeoff roll or climb are serious problems, but they are not the only types of problems that may confront the pilot of a self-launching glider. Other engine failures include an engine that refuses to start in response to airborne start attempts. This is a serious problem if the terrain below is unsuitable for a safe off-field landing.

One of the great advantages of the self-launching glider is having the option to terminate a soaring flight by starting the engine and flying to an airport/gliderport for landing. Nearly all self-launching gliders have a procedure designed to start the engine while airborne. This procedure would be most valuable during a soaring flight with engine off during which the soaring conditions have weakened. The prospect of starting the engine and flying home safely is ideal under such conditions.

As a precaution, an airborne engine start should be attempted at an altitude high enough that, if a malfunction occurs, there is sufficient time to take corrective action. If the engine fails to start promptly, or fails to start at all, there may be little time to plan for a safe landing. If there is no landable area below, then failure to start the engine results in an emergency off-field landing in unsuitable terrain. Glider damage and personal injury may result. To avoid these dangers, self-launching glider pilots should never allow themselves to get into a situation that can only be resolved by starting the engine and flying up and away. It is best to keep a landable field always within easy gliding range.

There are many reasons that a self-launching glider engine may fail to start or fail to provide full power in response to efforts to resume full power operations while airborne. These include lack of fuel or ignition, low engine temperature due to cold soak, low battery output due to low temperatures or battery exhaustion, fuel vapor lock, lack of propeller response to blade pitch controls, and other factors. It is important for the pilot to have an emergency plan in the event that full engine power is not available during any phase of flight.

Self-Launching Glider Propeller Malfunctions

Propeller failures include propeller damage and disintegration, propeller drive belt or drive gear failure, or failure of the variable blade pitch control system. To perform an air-driven engine restart, for example, many self-launching gliders require that the propeller blades be placed in a particular blade pitch position. If the propeller blades cannot be properly adjusted, then the propeller will not deliver enough torque to start the engine. The result is a failure to obtain an air-driven engine start.

Self-Launching Glider Electrical System Malfunctions

An electrical system failure in a self-launching glider may make it impossible to control the propeller pitch if the propeller is electrically controlled. It may also result in the inability to deploy a pod engine successfully for an air restart attempt. Self-launching gliders that require a functioning electric starter for an air restart are unable to resume flight under power. If an airport is within gliding range, an on-airport precautionary landing can be made. If there is no airport within gliding range and the flight can be safely continued without electrical power, the pilot may be able to soar to the vicinity of an airport and land safely. If no airport is within gliding range and flight cannot be sustained without power, an emergency off-airport landing has to be made.

Some self-launching gliders are occasionally used for night flight, cruising under power. All night flights must be conducted in accordance with FAA regulation and the glider must have the appropriate aeronautical lighting required for night time operations (14 CFR part 91, section 91.209). If carrying a passenger(s), the pilot must be qualified to operate the glider at night in accordance with 14 CFR part 61, section 61.57(b).

If an electrical system failure occurs during night operations, pilots of nearby aircraft are not able to see the self-launching glider due to the extinguished position lights. Inside the cockpit, it is difficult or impossible to see the flight instruments or electrical circuit breakers. According to 14 CFR part 135, section 135.159(f), and part 121, section 121.549(b), the FAA requires that commercial and airline pilots have a flashlight "having at least two size D cells or equivalent" for such an emergency. It makes good practical sense for other pilots to follow the same rules.

If smoke or the smell of smoke is present, make no attempt to reset any circuit breakers. In accordance with CE-10-11R, Special Airworthiness Information Bulletin, dated January 14, 2010, and available for download at http://rgl.faa.gov/Regulatory_and_Guidance_Library/rgSAIB.nsf/(LookupSAIBs)/CE-10-11R1?OpenDocument, the best and safest practice is to not reset circuit breakers in the air unless absolutely necessary for safe flight. Resetting a circuit breaker may result in a greater overload and possible fire. *[Figure 8-19]* Head directly for the nearest airport and prepare for a precautionary landing there. Follow nighttime procedures and requirements. The aviation transceiver installed in the instrument panel may not function if electrical failure is total, so it is a good idea to have a portable battery-operated aviation two-way radio onboard for use in such an emergency. It may be necessary to receive landing instruction by air traffic control (ATC) light-signal. Pilot should review 14 CFR part 91, section 125, and the Aeronautical Information Manual (AIM) section 4-2-13, Traffic Control Light Signals, for the proper response.

In-flight Fire

An in-flight fire is the most serious emergency a pilot can encounter. If a fire has ignited, or if there is a smell of smoke or any similar smell, do everything possible to reduce the possibilities that the fire spreads and land as soon as possible. The self-launching glider GFM/POH is the authoritative source for emergency response to suspected in-flight fire. The necessary procedures are:

- Reduce throttle to idle,
- Shut off fuel valves,
- Shut off engine ignition,
- Land immediately and stop as quickly as possible, and
- Evacuate the self-launching glider immediately.

After landing, distance yourself from the glider and try to stay upwind to avoid the harmful fumes. Keep onlookers away from the glider as well. The principal danger after evacuating the glider is fuel ignition and explosion, with the potential to injure personnel at a considerable distance from the glider.

CAUTION: Modern gliders are composed of composite materials and resins that can produce very poisonous fumes. The glider pilot should do whatever is necessary to avoid the fumes to include jettisoning of the canopy, which allows breathable air in and elimination of fumes from the cockpit. This same modern construction also means a fire can spread very quickly. A quick landing or abandoning the glider for a parachute landing may be the only option for the pilot. If the fire is spreading to the wings, bailout at a safe altitude may be the safest choice if the airframe will not last until the landing.

Emergency Equipment and Survival Gear

Emergency equipment and survival gear is essential for safety of flight for all soaring flights.

Survival Gear Checklists

Checklists help the pilot to assemble the necessary equipment in an orderly manner. The essentials for survival include reliable and usable supplies of water, food, and air or oxygen. Maintenance of an acceptable body temperature, which is difficult to manage in extreme cold or extreme heat, is also important. Blankets and appropriate seasonal clothing help to ensure safe body temperatures.

Food and Water

An adequate supply of water and food (especially high-energy foods such as energy bars, granolas, and dried fruits) are of utmost importance during cross-country flight. Water from ballast tanks can be used in an emergency if free of contaminants, such as antifreeze. Water and food should be available and easily accessible during the entire flight.

Clothing

Pilots also need seasonal clothing that is appropriate to the local environment, including hat or cap, shirts, sweaters,

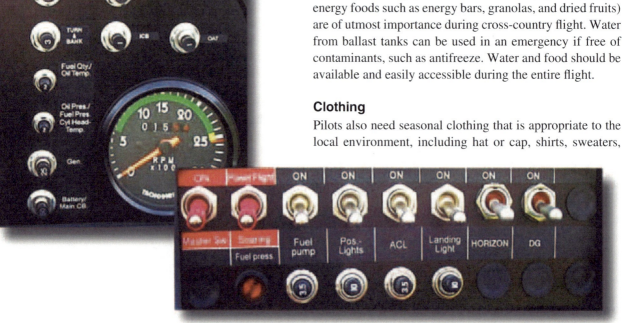

Figure 8-19. *Self-launching glider circuit breakers.*

pants, socks, walking shoes, space blanket, and gloves or mittens. Layered clothing provides flexibility to meet the demands of the environment. Desert areas may be very hot in the day and very cold at night. Prolonged exposure to either condition can be debilitating. Layered clothing traps air between layers, increasing heat retention. The parachute canopy can be used as an effective layered garment when wrapped around the body to conserve body heat or to provide relief from excessive sunlight. Eye protection, such as sunglasses, is more than welcome if conditions during the day are bright, as they often are on good soaring days.

Communication

Communication can be electronic, visual, or audible. Radios, telephones, and cell phones are electronic methods. Signal mirrors, flashlight or light beacons at night, signal fire flames at night, signal smoke during daylight hours, signal flares, and prominent parachute canopy displays are visual methods. Shouting and other noisemaking activities are audible methods but usually have very limited range. A whistle provides a good method for making sound.

Coin, cash, or credit cards are often necessary to operate pay phones. Charged batteries are required to operate cell phones, two-way radios, and emergency locator transmitters. Batteries are also necessary to operate flashlights or position lights on the glider for signal purposes. A list of useful telephone numbers aids rapid communication. The aviation transceiver can be tuned to broadcast and receive on the emergency frequency 121.5 MHz or any other useable frequency that elicits a response. The ELT can be used to provide a continuous signal on 121.5 MHz and/or the newer 406 MHz SAR system. A 406 MHz beacon on a downed aircraft activates either automatically or manually. The ELT transmits a digital identification code to the first satellite that comes into range. The satellites receive the signal and relay it to a ground station. If there is no ground station in view, the satellite records the digital signal in its onboard memory and downloads it to the next ground station. The ground station processor measures the Doppler shift of the signal and calculates its position; this calculation is usually accurate to within 1.5 nautical miles on the first satellite pass and is refined further with each pass. If the beacon has an integrated GPS or is connected into the onboard NAVCOM, the position is imbedded into the initial digital data stream.

After the ground station has completed processing, it transmits the identification and position to the United States Mission Control Center (USMCC). The USMCC attaches the information contained in the 406 MHz beacon registration database for that particular ELT and generates an alert message. If the location lies within the continental U.S., the alert is sent to the Air Force Rescue Coordination Center (AFRCC) at Langley Air Force Base, Virginia. The AFRCC then takes the registration data and attempts to ascertain the aircraft's disposition. By calling the emergency contact numbers, or by calling flight service stations with the N-number, they can quickly determine whether or not the aircraft is safe on the ground.

Since most activations are false alarms, the ability to resolve them over the phone saves the AFRCC (i.e., U.S. taxpayers) millions of dollars. More importantly, it saves SAR assets for actual emergencies. If the AFRCC in unable to verify the aircraft is safe on the ground, they launch a Search and Rescue mission. This normally involves assigning the search to the USAF Auxiliary Civil Air Patrol and may include requesting assistance from the local SAR responders or law enforcement personnel.

The unique digital code of each 406 MHz beacon allows it to be associated with a particular aircraft. The registration contains information, such as tail number, home airport, type and color of aircraft, and several emergency points of contact. This provides rapid access to flight plans and other vital information. This can speed the search effort and can be the difference between life and death.

The parachute canopy and case can be employed to lay out a prominent marker to aid recognition from the air by other aircraft. Matches and a combustible material can provide flame for visibility by night and provide smoke that may be seen during daylight hours.

Navigation Equipment

Aviation charts help to navigate during flight and help pinpoint the location when an off-airport landing is made. Sectional charts have the most useful scale for cross-country soaring flights. Local road maps (with labeled roads) should be carried in the glider during all cross-country flights. Local road maps make it much easier to give directions to the ground crew, allowing them to arrive as promptly as possible. GPS coordinates also help the ground crew if they are equipped with a GPS receiver and appropriate charts and maps. Detailed GPS maps are commercially available and make GPS navigation by land easier for the ground crew.

Medical Equipment

Compact, commercially made medical or first aid kits are widely available. These kits routinely include bandages, medical tape, disinfectants, a tourniquet, matches, a knife or scissors, bug and snake repellent, and other useful items. Ensure that the kit contains medical items suitable to the environment in which the glider is operating. Stow the kit so it is secure from inflight turbulence but would be accessible to injured occupant(s) after an emergency landing, even if injured.

Stowage

Stowing equipment properly means securing all equipment to protect occupants and ensuring integrity of all flight controls and glider system controls. Items carried on board must be secured even in the event that severe inflight turbulence is encountered. Items must also remain secured in the event of a hard or off-field landing. No item carried in the glider should have any chance of becoming loose in flight to interfere with the flight controls. Stowed objects should be adequately secured to prevent movement during a hard landing.

Parachute

The parachute should be clean, dry, and stored in a cool place when not in use. It is imperative to keep the parachute free of contaminants to ensure the integrity the parachutes material. The parachute must have been inspected and repacked within the allowable time frame. The pilot is responsible for ensuring that the parachute meets with the required FAA inspection criteria.

Oxygen System Malfunctions

Oxygen is essential for flight safety at high altitude. If there is a suspected or detected failure in any component of the oxygen system, descend immediately to an altitude where supplemental oxygen is not essential for continued safe flight. Remember, the first sign of oxygen deprivation (hypoxia) is a sensation of apparent well-being. Problem-solving capability is diminished. If the pilot has been deprived of sufficient oxygen, even for a short interval, critical thinking capability has been compromised. Do not be lulled into thinking that the flight can safely continue at high altitude. Descend immediately and breathe normally at these lower altitudes for a time to restore critical oxygen to the bloodstream. Try to avoid hyperventilation, which prolongs diminished critical thinking capability. Give enough time to recover critical thinking capability before attempting an approach and landing.

For high altitude flights, such as a wave flight, the oxygen bailout bottle becomes a necessity. It should be in good condition and be within easy reach if a high altitude escape becomes necessary from the glider. Pilots need to be properly trained for an event requiring abandonment of a glider at a very high altitude, the use of oxygen, and proper use of a parachute at high altitudes.

Accident Prevention

The National Transportation Safety Board (NTSB) generates accident reports anytime a reportable soaring accident occurs. Any interested person can visit the website directly at www.ntsb.gov and look at the NTSB query database page to view summaries of both glider and towplane accidents. It is very important for all pilots to educate themselves on past accidents. In particular, they should look at the cause of the accident and how it could have been prevented. All too often accidents are caused from pilot error or equipment failure that, if trained and educated properly, the pilot could have reacted differently and saved a life, usually their own. The Soaring Safety Foundation is an excellent resource for pilots to educate themselves on glider safety and the website provides pilots with lessons learned information, as well as on-line safety learning. The Soaring Safety Foundation website is www.soaringsafety.org.

Chapter 9
Soaring Weather

Introduction

Glider pilots face a multitude of decisions, starting with the decision to take to the air. Pilots must determine if weather conditions are safe, and if current conditions support a soaring flight. Gliders, being powered by gravity, are always sinking through the air. Therefore, glider pilots must seek air that rises faster than the sink rate of the glider to enable prolonged flight. Glider pilots refer to rising air as lift, not to be confused with the lift created by the wing.

The Atmosphere

The atmosphere is a mixture of gases surrounding the earth. Without it, there would be no weather (wind, clouds, precipitation) or protection from the sun's rays. Though this protective envelope is essential to life, it is extraordinarily thin. When compared to the radius of the earth, 3,438 nautical miles (NM), the vertical limit of the atmosphere represents a very small distance. Although there is no specific upper limit to the atmosphere—it simply thins to a point where it fades away into space—the layers up to approximately 164,000 feet (about 27 NM) contain 99.9 percent of atmospheric mass. At that altitude, the atmospheric density is approximately one-thousandth the density of that at sea level. *[Figure 9-1]*

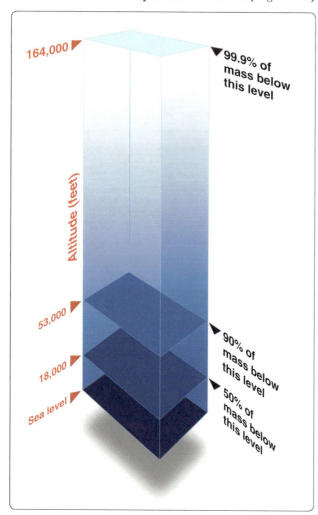

Figure 9-1. *Atmospheric mass by altitude.*

Composition

The earth's atmosphere is composed of a mixture of gases, with small amounts of water, ice, and other particles. Two gases, nitrogen (N_2) and oxygen (O_2), comprise approximately 99 percent of the gaseous content of the atmosphere; the other one percent is composed of various trace gases. Nitrogen and oxygen are both considered permanent gases, meaning their proportions remain the same to approximately 260,000 feet. Water vapor (H_2O), on the other hand, is considered a variable gas. Therefore, the amount of water in the atmosphere depends on the location and the source of the air. For example, the water vapor content over tropical areas and oceans accounts for as much as 4 percent of the gases displacing nitrogen and oxygen. Conversely, the atmosphere over deserts and at high altitudes exhibits less than 1 percent of the water vapor content. *[Figure 9-2]*

Although water vapor exists in the atmosphere in small amounts as compared to nitrogen and oxygen, it has a significant impact on the production of weather. This is because it exists in two other physical states: liquid (water) and solid (ice). These two states of water contribute to the formation of clouds, precipitation, fog, and icing, all of which are important to aviation weather.

Properties

The state of the atmosphere is defined by fundamental variables, namely temperature, density, and pressure. These variables change over time and, combined with vertical and horizontal differences, lead to daily weather conditions.

Temperature

The temperature of a gas is the measure of the average kinetic energy of the molecules of that gas. Fast-moving molecules are indicative of high kinetic energy and warmer temperatures. Conversely, slow-moving molecules reflect lower kinetic energy and lower temperatures. Air temperature is commonly thought of in terms of whether it feels hot or cold. For quantitative measurements, the Celsius (°C) scale is used in aviation, although the Fahrenheit (°F) scale is still used in some applications.

Density

The density of any given gas is the total mass of molecules in a specified volume, expressed in units of mass per volume. Low air density means a smaller number of air molecules in a specified volume while high air density means a greater number of air molecules in the same volume. Air density affects aircraft performance, as noted in Chapter 5, Glider Performance.

Pressure

Molecules in a given volume of air not only possess a certain kinetic energy and density, but they also exert force. The force per unit area defines pressure. At the earth's surface, the pressure exerted by the atmosphere is due to its weight. Therefore, pressure is measured in terms of weight per area. For example, atmospheric pressure is measured in pounds per square inch (lb/in^2). From the outer atmosphere to sea level, a typical value of atmospheric pressure is 14.7 lb/in^2.

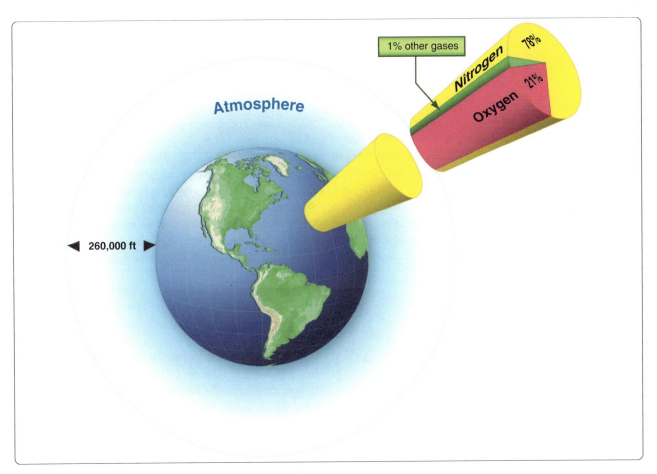

Figure 9-2. *The composition of the atmosphere.*

In aviation weather reports, the units of pressure are inches of mercury ("Hg) and millibars (mb) and 29.92 "Hg equals 1013.2 mb. This force or pressure is created by the moving molecules act equally in all directions when measured at a given point.

In the METAR report, see *Figure 9-3*, the local altimeter setting "A2955", read as 29.55, is the pressure "Hg. In the remarks (RMK) section of this report, sea level pressure expressed as "SLP010", the value expressed in millibars (hPa), is used in weather forecasting.

Dry air behaves almost like an ideal gas, meaning it obeys the gas law given by P/DT = R, where P is pressure, D is density, T is temperature, and R is a constant. This law states that the ratio of pressure to the product of density and temperature must always be the same. For instance, at a given pressure if the temperature is much higher than standard, then the density must be much lower. Air pressure and temperature are usually measured, and using the gas law, density of the air can be calculated and used to determine aircraft performance under those conditions.

Standard Atmosphere

Using a representative vertical distribution of these variables, the standard atmosphere has been defined and is used for pressure altimeter calibrations. Since changes in the static pressure can affect pitot-static instrument operation, it is necessary to understand basic principles of the atmosphere. To provide a common reference for temperature and pressure, a definition for standard atmosphere, also called International Standard Atmosphere (ISA), has been established. In addition to affecting certain flight instruments, these standard conditions are the basis for most aircraft performance data.

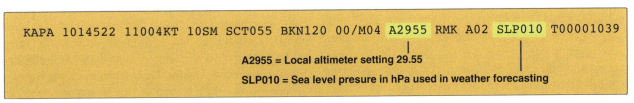

Figure 9-3. *Example of how pressure is used in an aviation weather report.*

At sea level, the standard atmosphere consists of a barometric pressure of 29.92 "Hg, or 1,013.2 mb, and a temperature of 15 °C or 59 °F. Under standard conditions (ISA), a column of air at sea level weighs 14.7 lb/in^2.

Since temperature normally decreases with altitude, a standard lapse rate can be used to calculate temperature at various altitudes. Below 36,000 feet, the standard temperature lapse rate is 2 °C (3.5 °F) per 1,000 feet of altitude change. Pressure does not decrease linearly with altitude, but for the first 10,000 feet, 1 "Hg for each 1,000 feet approximates the rate of pressure change. It is important to note that the standard lapse rates should be used only for flight planning purposes with the understanding that large variations from standard conditions can exist in the atmosphere. *[Figure 9-4]*

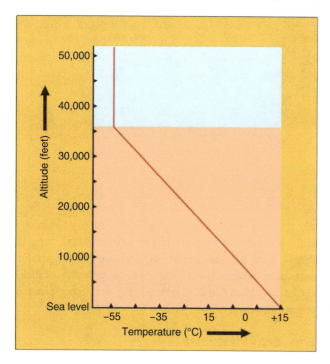

Figure 9-4. *Standard atmosphere.*

Layers of the Atmosphere

The earth's atmosphere is divided into five strata, or layers: troposphere, stratosphere, mesosphere, thermosphere, and exosphere. *[Figure 9-5]* These layers are defined by the temperature change with increasing altitude. The lowest layer, called the troposphere, exhibits an average decrease in temperature from the earth's surface to about 36,000 feet above mean sea level (MSL). The troposphere is deeper in the tropics and shallower in the polar regions. It also varies seasonally, being higher in the summer and lower in the winter months.

Almost all of the earth's weather occurs in the troposphere as most of the water vapor and clouds are found in this layer. The lower part of the troposphere interacts with the land and sea surface, providing thermals, mountain waves, and sea-breeze fronts. Although temperatures decrease as altitude increases in the troposphere, local areas of temperature increase (inversions) are common.

The top of the troposphere is called the tropopause. The pressure at this level is only about ten percent of MSL (0.1 atmosphere) and density is decreased to about 25 percent of its sea level value. Temperature reaches its minimum value at the tropopause, approximately –55 °C (–67 °F). For pilots, this is an important part of the atmosphere because it is associated with a variety of weather phenomena, such as thunderstorm tops, clear air turbulence, and jet streams. The vertical limit altitude of the tropopause varies with season and with latitude. The tropopause is lower in the winter and at the poles; it is higher in the summer and at the equator.

The tropopause separates the troposphere from the stratosphere. In the stratosphere, the temperature tends to first change very slowly with increasing height. However, as altitude increases the temperature increases to approximately 0 °C (32 °F) reaching its maximum value at about 160,000 feet MSL. Unlike the troposphere in which the air moves freely both vertically and horizontally, the air within the stratosphere moves mostly horizontally.

Gliders have reached into the lower stratosphere using mountain waves. At these altitudes, pressurization becomes an issue, as well as the more obvious breathing oxygen requirements. Layers above the stratosphere have some interesting features that are normally not of importance to glider pilots. However, interested pilots might refer to any general text on weather or meteorology.

Scale of Weather Events

When preparing forecasts, meteorologists consider atmospheric circulation on many scales. To aid the forecasting of short- and long-term weather, various weather events have been organized into three broad categories called the scales of circulations. The size and lifespan of the phenomena in each scale are roughly proportional, so that larger size scales coincide with longer lifetimes. The term "microscale" refers to features with spatial dimensions of .10 to 1 NM and lasting for seconds to minutes. An example is an individual thermal. The term "mesoscale" refers to the horizontal dimensions of 1 to 1,000 NM and lasting for many minutes to weeks. Examples include mountain waves, sea breeze fronts, thunderstorms, and fronts. Research scientists break down the mesoscale into further subdivisions to better classify various phenomena. The term "macroscale" refers to the horizontal dimensions greater than 1,000 NM and lasting for weeks to months. These include the long waves in the general global circulation and the jet streams embedded within those waves. *[Figure 9-6]*

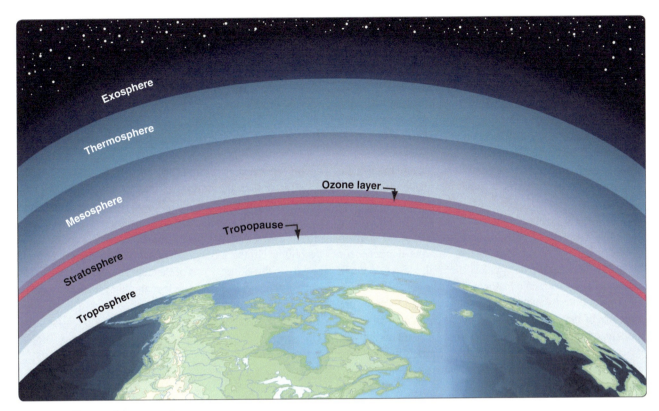

Figure 9-5. *Layers of the atmosphere.*

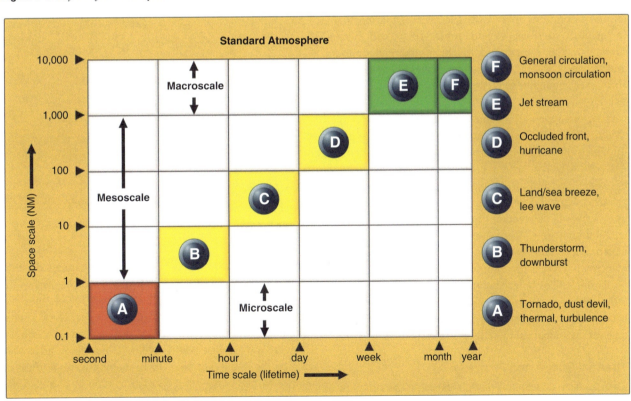

Figure 9-6. *Scale of circulation—horizontal dimensions and life spans of associated weather events.*

Smaller scale features are embedded in larger scale features. For instance, a microscale thermal may be just one of many in a mesoscale convergence line, like a sea breeze front. The sea breeze front may occur only under certain synoptic (i.e., simultaneous) conditions, which is controlled by the macroscale circulations. The scales interact, with feedback from smaller to larger scales and vice versa, in ways that are not yet fully understood by atmospheric scientists. Generally, the behavior and evolution of macroscale features are more predictable, with forecast skill decreasing as scale diminishes. For instance, forecasts of up to a few days for major events, such as a trough with an associated cold front, have become increasingly accurate. However, nobody would attempt to forecast the exact time and location of an individual thermal an hour ahead of time. Since most of the features of interest to soaring pilots lie in the smaller mesoscale and microscale range, prediction of soaring weather is a challenge.

Soaring forecasts should begin with the macroscale, which identifies large-scale patterns that produce good soaring conditions. This varies from site to site and depends, for instance, on whether the goal is thermal, ridge, or wave soaring. Then, mesoscale features should be considered. This may include items such as the cloudiness and temperature structure of the air mass behind a cold front, as well as the amount of rain produced by the front. Understanding lift types, and environments in which they form, is the first step to understanding how to forecast soaring weather.

Thermal Soaring Weather

A thermal is a rising mass of buoyant air. Thermals are the most common updraft used to sustain soaring flight. In the next sections, several topics related to thermal soaring weather are explored, including thermal structure, atmospheric stability, the use of atmospheric soundings, and air masses conducive to thermal soaring.

Convection refers to an energy transfer involving mass motions. Thermals are convective currents and are one means by which the atmosphere transfers heat energy vertically. Advection is the term meteorologists use to describe horizontal transfer; for instance, cold air advection after the passage of a cold front. As a note of caution, meteorologists use the word "convection" to mean deep convection, that is, thunderstorms. Unfortunately, there is often a fine meteorological line between a warm, sunny day with plenty of thermals, and a warm, sunny day that is stable and produces no thermals. To the earthbound general public, it matters little—either is a nice day. Glider pilots, however, need a better understanding of these conditions and must often rely on their own forecasting skills.

Thermal Shape and Structure

Two primary conceptual models exist for the structure of thermals: bubble model and column or plume model. Which model best represents thermals encountered by glider pilots is a topic of ongoing debate among atmospheric scientists. In reality, thermals fitting both conceptual models likely exist. A blend of the models, such as individual strong bubbles rising within one plume, may be what occurs in many situations. These models attempt to simplify a complex and often turbulent phenomenon, so many exceptions and variations are to be expected while actually flying in thermals. Many books, articles, and Internet resources are available for further reading on this subject.

The bubble model describes an individual thermal resembling a vortex ring, with rising air in the middle and descending air on the sides. The air in the middle of the vortex ring rises faster than the entire thermal bubble. The model fits occasional reports from glider pilots. At times, one glider may find no lift, when only 200 feet below another glider climbs away. At other times, one glider may be at the top of the bubble climbing only slowly, while a lower glider climbs rapidly in the stronger part of the bubble below. *[Figure 9-7]* More often, a glider flying below another glider circling in a thermal is able to contact the same thermal and climb, even if the gliders are displaced vertically by 1,000 feet or more. This suggests the column or plume model of thermals is more common. *[Figure 9-8]*

Figure 9-7. *The bubble or vortex ring model of a thermal.*

Which of the two models best describes thermals depends on the source or reservoir of warm air near the surface. If the heated area is rather small, one single bubble may rise and take with it all the warmed surface air. On the other hand, if a large area is heated and one spot acts as the initial trigger, surrounding warm air flows into the relative void left by the initial thermal. The in-rushing warm air follows the same path, creating a thermal column or plume. Since all the warmed air near the surface is not likely to have the exact same temperature, it is easy to envision a column with a few or several imbedded bubbles. Individual bubbles within a thermal plume may merge, while at other times, two adjacent and distinct bubbles seem to exist side by side.

Figure 9-8. *The column or plume model of a thermal.*

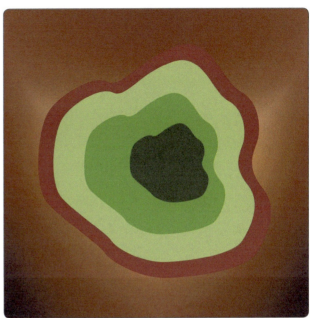

Figure 9-9. *Cross section through a thermal. Darker green is stronger lift; red is sink.*

No two thermals are exactly alike since the thermal sources are not the same.

Whether considered a bubble or column, the air in the middle of the thermal rises faster than the air near the sides of the thermal. A horizontal slice through an idealized thermal provides a bull's-eye pattern. Real thermals usually are not perfectly concentric; techniques for best using thermals are discussed in the next chapter. *[Figure 9-9]*

The diameter of a typical thermal cross-section is on the order of 500–1,000 feet, though the size varies considerably. Typically, due to mixing with the surrounding air, thermals expand as they rise. Thus, the thermal column may actually resemble a cone, with the narrowest part near the ground. Thermal plumes also tilt in a steady wind and can become quite distorted in the presence of vertical shear. If vertical shear is strong enough, thermals can become very turbulent or become completely broken apart. A schematic of a thermal lifecycle in wind shear is shown in *Figure 9-10*.

Atmospheric Stability

Stability in the atmosphere tends to hinder vertical motion, while instability tends to promote vertical motion. A certain amount of instability is desirable for glider pilots; without it, thermals would not develop. If the air is moist enough and the atmospheric instability is deep enough, thunderstorms and associated hazards can form. Thus, an understanding of atmospheric stability and its determination from available weather data is important for soaring flight and safety. As a note, the following discussion is concerned with vertical stability of the atmosphere. Other horizontal atmospheric instabilities, such as the evolution of large-scale cyclones, are not covered here.

Generally, a stable dynamic system is one in which a displaced element returns to its original position. An unstable dynamic system is one in which a displaced element accelerates away from its original position. In a neutrally stable system, the displaced element neither returns to nor accelerates from its original position. In the atmosphere, it is easiest to use a parcel of air as the displaced element. The behavior of a stable or unstable system is analogous to aircraft stability discussed in Chapter 3, Aerodynamics of Flight.

For simplicity, assume first that the air is completely dry. Effects of moisture in atmospheric stability are considered later. A parcel of dry air that is forced to rise expands due to decreasing pressure and cools in the process. By contrast, a parcel of dry air that is forced to descend is compressed due to increasing pressure and warms. If there is no transfer of heat between the surrounding, ambient air and the displaced parcel, the process is called adiabatic. Assuming adiabatic motion, a rising parcel cools at a lapse rate of 3 °C (5.4 °F) per 1,000 feet, known as the dry adiabatic lapse rate (DALR).

Figure 9-10. *Lifecycle of a typical thermal with cumulus cloud.*

The DALR is the rate at which the temperature of unsaturated air changes as a parcel ascends or descends through the atmosphere which is approximately 9.8 °C per 1 kilometer. On a thermodynamic chart, parcels cooling at the DALR are said to follow a dry adiabatic. A parcel warms at the DALR as it descends. In reality, heat transfer often occurs. For instance, as a thermal rises, the circulation in the thermal itself (recall the bubble model) mixes in surrounding air. Nonetheless, the DALR is a good approximation.

The DALR represents the lapse rate of the atmosphere when it is neutrally stable. If the ambient lapse rate in some layer of air is less than the DALR (for instance, 1 °C per 1,000 feet), then that layer is stable. If the lapse rate is greater than the DALR, it is unstable. An unstable lapse rate usually occurs within a few hundred feet of the heated ground. When an unstable layer develops aloft, the air quickly mixes and reduces the lapse rate back to DALR. It is important to note that the DALR is not the same as the standard atmospheric lapse rate of 2 °C per 1,000 feet. The standard atmosphere is a stable one.

Another way to understand stability is to imagine two scenarios, each with a different temperature at 3,000 feet above ground level (AGL), but the same temperature at the surface, nominally 20 °C. In both scenarios, a parcel of air that started at 20 °C at the surface has cooled to 11 °C by the time it has risen to 3,000 feet at the DALR. In the first scenario, the parcel is still warmer than the surrounding air, so it is unstable and the parcel keeps rising—a good thermal day. In the second scenario, the parcel is cooler than the surrounding air, so it is stable and sinks. The parcel in the second scenario would need to be forced to 3,000 feet AGL by a mechanism other than convection, such as being lifted up a mountainside or a front. *[Figure 9-11]*

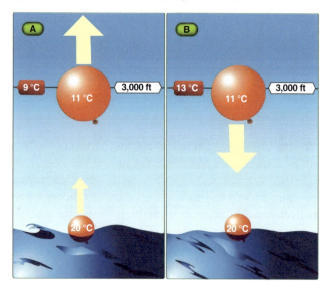

Figure 9-11. *Unstable (A) and stable (B) parcels of air.*

Figure 9-11 also illustrates factors leading to instability. A stable atmosphere can turn unstable in one of two ways. First, if the surface parcel warms by more than 2 °C (to greater than 22 °C), the layer to 3,000 feet then becomes unstable in the second scenario. Thus, if the temperature of the air aloft remains the same, warming the lower layers causes instability and better thermal soaring. Second, if the air at 3,000 feet is cooler, as in the first scenario, the layer becomes unstable. Thus, if the temperature on the ground remains the same, cooling aloft causes instability and better thermal soaring. If the temperatures aloft and at the surface warm or cool by the same amount, then the stability of the layer remains unchanged. Finally, if the air aloft remains the same, but the surface air cools (for instance, due to a very shallow front), then the layer becomes even more stable.

An inversion is a condition in which a layer warms as altitude increases. Inversions can occur at any altitude and vary in strength. In strong inversions, the temperature can rise as much as 10 °C over just a few hundred feet of altitude gain. The most notable effect of an inversion is to cap any unstable layer below. Along with trapping haze or pollution below, it also effectively provides a cap to any thermal activity.

So far, only completely dry air parcels have been considered. However, moisture in the form of water vapor is always present in the atmosphere. As a moist parcel of air rises, it cools at the DALR until it reaches its dewpoint, at which time the air in the parcel begins to condense. During the process of condensation, heat (referred to as latent heat) is released to the surrounding air. Once saturated, the parcel continues to cool, but since heat is now added, it cools at a rate lower than the DALR. The rate at which saturated air cools with height is known as the saturated adiabatic lapse rate (SALR). Unlike the DALR, the SALR varies substantially with altitude. At lower altitudes, it is on the order of 1.2 °C per 1,000 feet, whereas at middle altitudes it increases to 2.2 °C per 1,000 feet. Very high up, above approximately 30,000 feet, little water vapor exists to condense, and the SALR approaches the DALR.

Air Masses Conducive to Thermal Soaring

Generally, the best air masses for thermals are those with cool air aloft, with conditions dry enough to allow the sun's heating at the surface, but not dry enough that cumulus form. Along the West Coast of the continental United States, these conditions are usually found after passage of a pacific cold front. Similar conditions are found in the eastern and midwest United States, except the source air for the cold front is from polar continental regions, such as the interior of Canada. In both cases, high pressure building into the region is favorable, since it is usually associated with an inversion aloft, which keeps cumulus from growing into rainshowers or thundershowers. However, as the high pressure builds after the second or third day, the inversion has often lowered to the point that thermal soaring is poor or no longer possible. This can lead to warm and sunny, but very stable conditions, as the soaring pilot awaits the next cold front to destabilize the atmosphere. Fronts that arrive too close together can also cause poor postfrontal soaring, as high clouds from the next front keep the surface from warming enough. Very shallow cold fronts from the northeast (with cold air only one or two thousand feet deep) often have a stabilizing effect along the plains directly east of the Rocky Mountains. This is due to cool low-level air undercutting warmer air aloft advecting from the west.

In the desert southwest, the Great Basin, and intermountain west, good summertime thermal soaring conditions are often produced by intense heating from below, even in the absence of cooling aloft. This dry air mass with continental origins produces cumulus bases 10,000 feet AGL or higher. At times, this air spreads into eastern New Mexico and western Texas as well. Later in the summer, however, some of these regions come under the influence of the North American Monsoon, which can lead to widespread and daily late morning or early afternoon thundershowers. *[Figure 9-12]*

Cloud Streets

Cumulus clouds are often randomly distributed across the sky, especially over relatively flat terrain. Under the right conditions, however, cumulus can become aligned in long bands, called cloud streets. These are more or less regularly spaced bands of cumulus clouds. Individual streets can extend 50 miles or more while an entire field of cumulus streets can extend hundreds of miles. The spacing between streets is typically three times the height of the clouds. Cloud streets are aligned parallel to the wind direction; thus, they are ideal for a downwind cross-country flight. Glider pilots can often fly many miles with little or no circling, sometimes achieving glide ratios far exceeding the still-air value.

Cloud streets usually occur over land with cold air outbreaks, for instance, following a cold front. Brisk surface winds and a wind direction remaining nearly constant up to cloud base are favorable cloud street conditions. Windspeed should increase by 10 to 20 knots between the surface and cloud base, with a maximum somewhere in the middle of or near the top of the convective layer. Thermals should be capped by a notable inversion or stable layer.

A vertical slice through an idealized cloud street illustrates a distinct circulation, with updrafts under the clouds and downdrafts in between. Due to the circulation, sink between streets may be stronger than typically found away from cumulus. *[Figure 9-13]*

Thermal streets, with a circulation like *Figure 9-13*, may exist without cumulus clouds. Without clouds as markers, use of such streets is more difficult. A glider pilot flying upwind or downwind in consistent sink should alter course crosswind to avoid inadvertently flying along a line of sink between thermal streets.

Thermal Waves

Figure 9-14 shows a wavelike form for the inversion capping the cumulus clouds. If the winds above the inversion are

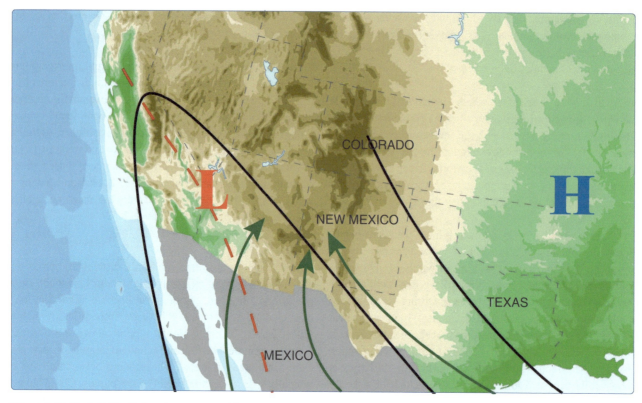

Figure 9-12. *Typical North American monsoon flow.*

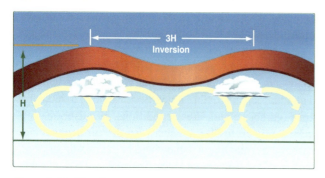

Figure 9-13. *Circulation across a cloud street.*

perpendicular to the cloud streets and increasing at 10 knots per 5,000 feet or more, cloud street waves can form in the stable air above. Though usually relatively weak, thermal waves can produce lift of 100 to 500 fpm and allow smooth flight along streets above the cloud base. *[Figure 9-14]*

So-called cumulus waves also exist. These are similar to cloud street waves, except the cumulus clouds are not organized in streets. Cumulus waves require a capping inversion or stable layer and increasing wind above cumulus clouds. However, directional shear is not necessary. Cumulus waves may also be short lived, and difficult to work for any length of time. An exception is when the cumulus is anchored to some feature, such as a ridge line or short mountain range.

In these cases, the possible influence of the ridge or mountain in creating the wave lift becomes uncertain. Further discussion of atmospheric waves appears later in this chapter. As a final note, thermal waves can also form without clouds present.

Thunderstorms

An unstable atmosphere can provide great conditions for thermal soaring. If the atmosphere is too moist and unstable, however, cumulonimbus (Cb) or thunderclouds can form. Cb clouds are the recognized standard marker of thunderstorms. When Cb builds sufficiently, it changes from rainstorm to thunderstorm status. Well developed Cb clouds are thunderstorms. Not all precipitating, large cumulo-form clouds are accompanied by lightning and thunder, although their presence is usually an indication that conditions are ripe for full-blown thunderstorms. Forecasters sometimes use the term "deep convection" to refer to convection that rises to high levels, which usually means thunderstorms. The tremendous amount of energy associated with Cb stems from the release of latent heat as condensation occurs with the growing cloud.

Thunderstorms can occur any time of year, though they are more common during the spring and summer seasons. They can occur anywhere in the continental United States but are not common along the immediate West Coast, where an average of only about one per year occurs. During the summer months, the desert southwest, extending northeastward into the Rocky Mountains and adjacent Great Plains, experiences an average of 30 to 40 thunderstorms

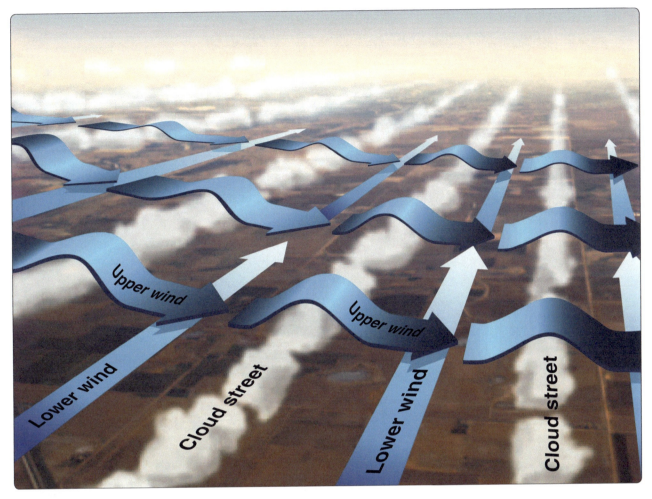

Figure 9-14. *Cloud street wave.*

annually. Additionally, in the southeastern United States, especially Florida, between 30 and 50 thunderstorms occur in an average year. Thunderstorms in the cool seasons usually occur in conjunction with some forcing mechanism, such as a fast moving cold front or a strong upper-level trough. [Figure 9-15]

The lifecycle of an air-mass or ordinary thunderstorm consists of three main stages: cumulus, mature, and dissipating. The term "ordinary" describes the type of thunderstorm consisting of a single Cb, since other types of thunderstorms (described below) can occur in a uniform large scale air mass. The entire lifecycle takes on the order of an hour, though remnant cloud from the dissipated Cb can last substantially longer.

The cumulus stage is characterized by a cumulus growing to a towering cumulus (Tcu), or cumulus congestus. During this stage, most of the air within the cloud is going up. The size of the updraft increases, while the cloud base broadens to a few miles in diameter. Since the cloud has increased in size, the strong updraft in the middle of the cloud is not susceptible to entrainment of dryer air from the outside. Often, other smaller cumulus in the vicinity of the Tcu are suppressed by general downward motion around the cloud. Towards the end of the cumulus stage, downdrafts and precipitation begin to form within the cloud. On some days, small cumulus can be around for hours, before Tcu form, while on other days, the air is so unstable that almost as soon as any cumulus form, they become Tcu. [Figure 9-16]

As the evolution of the thunderstorm continues, it reaches its mature stage. By this time, downdrafts reach the ground and spread out in what are known as downbursts or microbursts. These often lead to strong and sometimes damaging surface winds. Gliders should not be flown or exposed to microbursts and the associated windshears. While increased headwinds can momentarily improve performance, the distance from the landing area may be increased beyond the capabilities of the glider. Attempting to launch with possible windshears can result in fatal consequences.

Note: Launching of a glider either behind a towplane or ground launch is risky. Given the size of windshears, the towplane could be in a tailwind situation while the glider

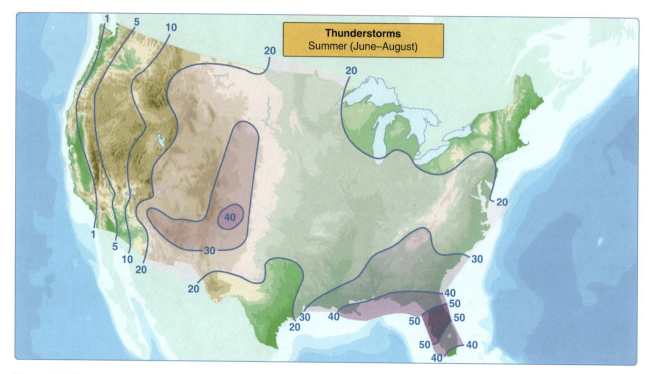

Figure 9-15. *Thunderstorm frequency in the summertime.*

Figure 9-16. *A cumulus growing to a towering cumulus.*

is in a headwind situation. With the likely outcome of that combination of factors, and the hazards of ground handling, operations in such conditions must be severely discouraged.

Pilots need to watch apparently dissipating thunderstorms closely for new dark, firm bases that indicate a new cell forming. In addition, outflow from one Cb may flow several miles before encountering an area where the air is primed for lifting given an extra boost. The relatively cool air in the outflow can provide that boost, leading to new a Cb, which is nearby but not connected to the original Cb.

Lifted Index

The LI is determined by subtracting the temperature of a parcel that has been lifted to 500 mb from the temperature of the ambient air. This index does not give the likelihood of thunderstorm occurrence; rather, it gives an indication of thunderstorm severity if one does occur. In *Figure 9-17*, an LI of −5 indicates moderately severe thunderstorms if they develop.

Lifted Index	Chance of Severe Thunderstorm
0 to −2	Weak
−3 to −5	Moderate
≤ −6	Strong

Figure 9-17. *Lifted index (LI) versus thunderstorm severity.*

K-Index

The KI is used to determine the probability of thunderstorm occurrence and uses information about temperature and moisture at three levels. It is given by the equation KI = (T850 − T500) + Td850 − (T700 − Td700). Here, T stands for temperature, Td is the dewpoint, and 500, 700, or 850 indicates the level in mb. All values are obtained from a morning sounding. Using the following values from a morning sounding KI = (16 − [−9]) + 12 − (6 − 0) = 31. This indicates about a 60 percent probability that thunderstorms will occur. *[Figure 9-18]* As discussed below, charts showing both the LI and KI for all the sounding sites in the continental United States are produced daily.

K Index	Thunderstorm Probability (%)
< 15	near 0
15 to 20	20
21 to 25	20 to 40
26 to 30	40 to 60
31 to 35	60 to 80
36 to 40	80 to 90
> 40	near 100

Figure 9-18. *K-Index (KI) versus probability of thunderstorm occurrence.*

Thunderstorms have several hazards, including turbulence, strong updrafts and downdrafts, strong shifting surface winds, hail, icing, poor visibility and/or low ceilings, lightning, and even tornadoes. Once a cloud has grown to be a Cb, hazards are possible, whether or not there are obvious signs. Since thermal soaring weather can rapidly deteriorate into thunderstorm weather, recognition of each hazard is important. Knowledge of the many hazards may inspire the pilot to land and secure the glider when early signs of thunderstorm activity appear—the safest solution.

Moderate turbulence is common within several miles of a thunderstorm, and it should be expected. Severe or even extreme turbulence (leading to possible structural failure) can occur anywhere within the thunderstorm itself. The inside of a thunderstorm is no place for glider pilots of any experience level. Outside of the storm, severe turbulence is common. One region of expected turbulence is near the surface gust front as cool outflow spreads from the storm. Violent updrafts can be followed a second or two later by violent downdrafts, with occasional side gusts adding to the excitement—not a pleasant proposition while in the landing pattern. At somewhat higher altitudes, but below the base of the Cb, moderate to severe turbulence can also be found along the boundary between the cool outflow and warm air feeding the Cb. Unpredictable smaller scale turbulent gusts can occur anywhere near a thunderstorm, so recognizing and avoiding the gust front does not mean safety from severe turbulence.

Large and strong updrafts and downdrafts accompany thunderstorms in the mature stage. Updrafts under the Cb base feeding into the cloud can easily exceed 1,000 fpm. Near the cloud base, the distance to the edge of the cloud can be deceptive; trying to avoid being inhaled into the cloud by strong updrafts can be difficult. In the later cumulus and early mature stage, updrafts feeding the cloud can cover many square miles. As the storm enters its mature stage, strong downdrafts, called downbursts or microbursts, can be encountered, even without very heavy precipitation present. Downbursts can also cover many square miles with descending air of 2,000 fpm or more. A pilot unlucky enough to fly under a forming downburst, which may not be visible, could encounter sink of 2,000 or 3,000 fpm, possibly greater in extreme cases. If such a downburst is encountered at pattern altitude, it can cut the normal time available to the pilot for planning the approach. For instance, a normal 3-minute pattern from 800 feet AGL to the ground happens in a mere 19 seconds in 2,500 fpm sink!

When a downburst or microburst hits the ground, the downdraft spreads out, leading to the strong surface winds, known as thunderstorm outflow. Typically, the winds strike quickly and give little warning of their approach. While soaring, pilots should keep a sharp lookout between the storm and the intended landing spot for signs of a wind shift. Blowing dust, smoke, or wind streaks on a lake indicating wind from the storm are clues that a gust front is rapidly approaching. Thunderstorm outflow winds are usually at speeds of 20 to 40 knots for a period of 5 to 10 minutes before diminishing. However, winds can easily exceed 60 knots, and in some cases, with a slow-moving thunderstorm, strong winds can last substantially longer. Although damaging outflow winds usually do not extend more than 5 or 10 miles from the Cb, winds of 20 or 30 knots can extend 50 miles or more from large thunderstorms.

Hail is possible with any thunderstorm and can exist as part of the main rain shaft. Hail can also occur many miles from the main rain shaft, especially under the thunderstorm anvil. Pea-sized hail usually does not damage a glider, but the large hail associated with a severe storm can dent metal gliders or damage the gelcoat on composite gliders, whether on the ground or in the air.

Icing is usually a problem only within a cloud, especially at levels where the outside temperature is approximately −10 °C. Under these conditions, supercooled water droplets (water existing in a liquid state 0 °C and below) can rapidly freeze upon contact with wings and other surfaces. At the beginning of the mature stage, early precipitation below cloud base may be difficult to see. At times, precipitation can even be falling through an updraft feeding the cloud. Snow, graupel, or ice pellets falling from the forming storm above can stick to the leading edge of the wing, causing degradation in performance. Rain on the wings can be a problem since some airfoils can be adversely affected by water.

Poor visibility due to precipitation and possible low ceilings as the air below the thunderstorm is cooled is yet another concern. Even light or moderate precipitation can reduce visibility dramatically. Often, under a precipitating Cb, there is no distinction between precipitation and actual cloud.

Lightning in a thunderstorm occurs in cloud, cloud to cloud (in the case of other nearby storms, such as a multicell storm), or cloud to ground. Lightning strikes are completely unpredictable, and cloud-to-ground strikes are not limited to areas below the cloud. Some strikes emanate from the side of the Cb and travel horizontally for miles before turning abruptly towards the ground. Inflight damage to gliders has included burned control cables and blown-off canopies. In some cases, strikes have caused little more than mild shock and cosmetic damage. On the other extreme, a composite training glider in Great Britain suffered a strike that caused complete destruction of one wing; fortunately, both pilots parachuted to safety. In that case, the glider was two or three miles from the thunderstorm. Finally, ground launching, especially with a metal cable, anywhere near a thunderstorm should be avoided.

Severe thunderstorms can sometimes spawn tornadoes, which are rapidly spinning vortices, generally a few hundred to a few thousand feet across. Winds can exceed 200 mph. Tornadoes that do not reach the ground are called funnel clouds. By definition, tornadoes form from severe thunderstorms and should obviously be avoided on the ground or in the air.

Weather for Slope Soaring

Slope or ridge soaring refers to using updrafts produced by the mechanical lifting of air as it encounters the upwind slope of a hill, ridge, or mountain. Slope soaring requires two ingredients: elevated terrain and wind.

Slope lift is the easiest lift source to visualize. When it encounters topography, wind is deflected horizontally, vertically, or in some combination of the two. Not all topography produces good slope lift. Individual or isolated hills do not produce slope lift because the wind tends to deflect around the hill, rather than over it. A somewhat broader hill with a windward face at least a mile or so long, might produce some slope lift, but the lift is confined to a small area. The best ridges for slope soaring are at least a few miles long.

Slope lift can extend to a maximum of two or three times the ridge height. However, the pilot may be able to climb only to ridge height. As a general rule, the higher the ridge above the adjacent valley, the higher the glider pilot can climb. Ridges only 100 or 200 feet high can produce slope lift. The problem with very low ridges is maintaining safe maneuvering altitude, as well as sufficient altitude to land safely in the adjacent valley. Practically speaking, 500 to 1,000 feet above the adjacent valley is a minimum ridge height. *[Figure 9-19]*

In addition to a ridge being long and high enough, the windward slope needs to be steep enough as well. An ideal slope is on the order of 1 to 4. Shallower slopes do not create

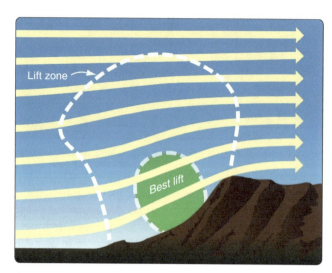

Figure 9-19. *Slope soaring.*

a vertical wind component strong enough to compensate for the glider's sink rate. Very steep, almost vertical slopes, on the other hand, may not be ideal either. Such slopes create slope lift, but can produce turbulent eddies along the lower slope or anywhere close to the ridge itself. In such cases, only the upper part of the slope may produce updrafts, although steeper slopes do allow a quick escape to the adjacent valley. *[Figure 9-20]*

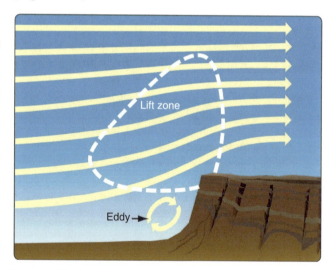

Figure 9-20. *Slope lift and eddy with near-vertical slope.*

A ridge upstream can block the wind flow, so that no low-level flow occurs upwind of an otherwise promising ridge, and no updraft. Additionally, if lee waves are produced by an upstream ridge or mountain, slope lift can be enhanced or destroyed, depending on the wavelength of the lee waves. Locally, the downdraft from a thermal just upwind of the ridge can cancel the slope lift for a short distance. The bottom line: never assume slope lift is present. Always have an alternative.

Just as the flow is deflected upward on the windward side of a ridge, it is deflected downward on the lee side of a ridge. *[Figure 9-21]* This downdraft can be alarmingly strong—up to 2,000 fpm or more near a steep ridge with strong winds (see depiction A). Even in moderate winds, the downdraft near a ridge can be strong enough to make penetration of the upwind side of the ridge impossible. Flat-topped ridges also offer little refuge, since sink and turbulence can combine to make an upwind penetration impossible (see depiction B). Finally, an uneven upwind slope with ledges or "steps" requires extra caution since small-scale eddies, turbulence, and sink can form there (see depiction C).

for heavy sink on the lee side and make sure an alternative is available. *[Figure 9-22]*

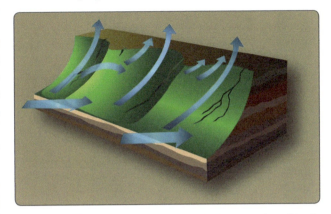

Figure 9-22. *Three-dimensional effects of oblique winds and bowls.*

Depending on the slope, windspeed should be 10–15 knots and blowing nearly perpendicular to the ridge. Wind directions up to 30° or 40° from perpendicular may still produce slope lift. Vertical wind shear is also a consideration. High ridges may have little or no wind along the lower slopes, but the upper parts of the ridge may be in winds strong enough to produce slope lift there.

The area of best lift varies with height. Below the ridge crest, the best slope lift is found within a few hundred feet of the ridge, again depending on the slope and wind strength. As mentioned, very steep ridges require extra speed and caution, since eddies and turbulence can form even on the upwind side. Above the ridge crest, the best lift usually is found further upwind from the ridge the higher one climbs. *[Figure 9-19]*

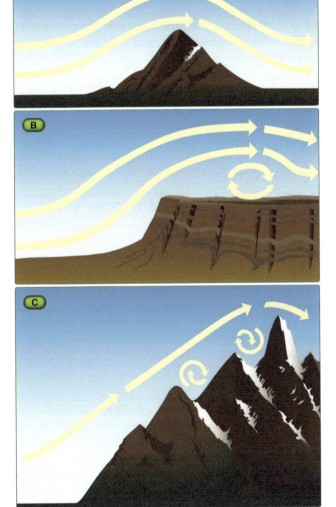

Figure 9-21. *Airflow along different ridges.*

Three-dimensional effects are important as well. For instance, a ridge with cusps or bowls may produce better lift in upwind-facing bowls if the wind is at an angle from the ridge. However, sink may be encountered on the lee side of the bowl. If crossing ridges in windy conditions, always plan

When the air is very stable, and the winds are sufficient but not too strong, slope lift can be very smooth, enabling safe soaring close to the terrain. If the air is not stable, thermals may flow up the slope. Depending on thermal strength and windspeed, the thermal may rise well above the ridge top, or it may drift into the lee downdraft and break apart. Downdrafts on the sides of thermals can easily cancel the slope lift; extra speed and caution are required when the air is unstable, especially below the ridge crest near the terrain. The combination of unstable air and strong winds can make slope soaring unpleasant or even dangerous for the beginning glider pilot.

Moisture must be considered. If air rising in the slope lift is moist and cools sufficiently, a so-called cap cloud may form. The cloud may form above the ridge, and if the air moistens more with time, the cloud slowly lowers onto the ridge and down the upwind slope, limiting the usable height of the slope lift. Since the updraft forms the cloud, it is very easy to climb into the cap cloud *[Figure 9-23]*—a dangerous situation.

Figure 9-23. *Cap cloud.*

Under certain conditions, a morning cap cloud may rise as the day warms, then slowly lower again as the day cools.

Wave Soaring Weather

Where there is wind and stable air, there is the likelihood of waves in the atmosphere. Most of the waves that occur throughout the atmosphere are of no use to the glider pilot. However, mountains or ridges often produce waves downstream, the most powerful of which have lifted gliders to 49,000 feet. Indirect measurements show waves extending to heights around 100,000 feet. If the winds aloft are strong and widespread enough, mountain lee waves can extend the length of the mountain range. Pilots have achieved flights in mountain wave using three turn points of over 2,000 kilometers. Another type of wave useful to soaring pilots is generated by thermals, which were discussed in the previous section.

A common analogy to help visualize waves created by mountains or ridges uses water flowing in a stream or small river. A submerged rock causes ripples (waves) in the water downstream, which slowly dampen out. This analogy is useful, but it is important to realize that the atmosphere is far more complex, with vertical shear of the wind and vertical variations in the stability profile. Wind blowing over a mountain does not always produce downstream waves.

Mountain wave lift is fundamentally different from slope lift. Slope soaring occurs on the upwind side of a ridge or mountain, while mountain wave soaring occurs on the downwind side. (Mountain wave lift sometimes tilts upwind with height. Therefore, at times near the top of the wave, the glider pilot may be almost directly over the mountain or ridge that produced the wave). The entire mountain wave system is also more complex than the comparatively simple slope soaring scenario.

Mechanism for Wave Formation

Waves form in stable air when a parcel is vertically displaced and then oscillates up and down as it tries to return to its original level, illustrated in *Figure 9-24*. In the first frame, the dry parcel is at rest at its equilibrium level. In the second frame, the parcel is displaced upward along the DALR, where it is cooler than the surrounding air. The parcel accelerates downward toward its equilibrium level but it overshoots the level due to momentum and keeps going down. The third frame shows that the parcel is now warmer than the surrounding air, and starts upward again. The process continues with the motion damping out. The number of oscillations depends on the initial parcel displacement and the stability of the air. In the lower part of the figure, wind has been added, illustrating the wave pattern that the parcel makes as it oscillates vertically. If there were no wind, a vertically displaced parcel would just oscillate up and down, while slowly damping, at one spot over the ground, much like a spring. *[Figure 9-24]*

The lower part of *Figure 9-24* also illustrates two important features of any wave. The wavelength is the horizontal distance between two adjacent wave crests. Typical mountain wavelengths vary considerably, between 2 and 20 miles. The amplitude is half the vertical distance between the trough and crest of the wave. Amplitude varies with altitude and is smallest near the surface and at upper levels. As a note, mountain lee waves are sometimes simply referred to as mountain waves, lee waves, and sometimes, standing waves.

In the case of mountain waves, it is the airflow over the mountain that displaces a parcel from its equilibrium level. This leads to a two-dimensional conceptual model, which is derived from the experience of many glider pilots plus postflight analysis of the weather conditions. *Figure 9-25* illustrates a mountain with wind and temperature profiles. Note the increase in windspeed (blowing from left to right) with altitude and a stable layer near mountaintop with less stable air above and below. As the air flows over the mountain, it descends the lee slope (below its equilibrium level if the air is stable) and sets up a series of oscillations downstream. The wave flow itself usually is incredibly smooth. Beneath the smooth wave flow is what is known as a low-level turbulent zone, with an embedded rotor circulation under each crest. Turbulence, especially within the individual rotors, is usually moderate to severe, and can occasionally become extreme. *[Figure 9-25]*

This conceptual model is often quite useful and representative of real mountain waves, but many exceptions exist. For instance, variations to the conceptual model occur when the

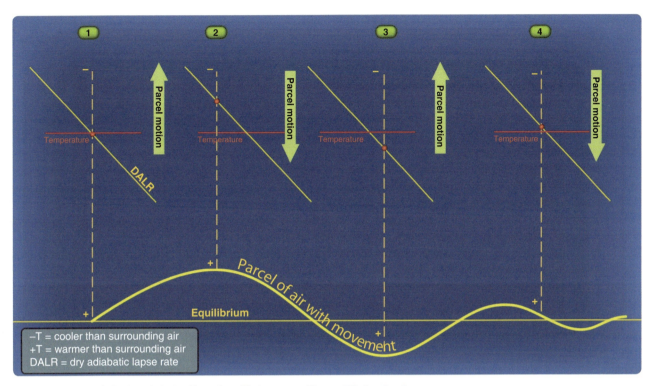

Figure 9-24. *Parcel displaced vertically and oscillating around its equilibrium level.*

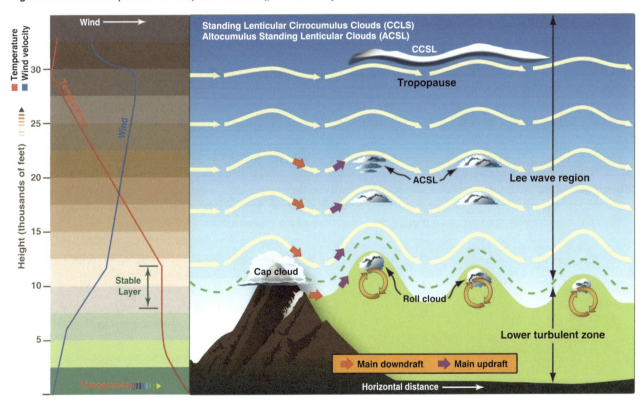

Figure 9-25. *Mountain lee wave system.*

topography has many complex, three-dimensional features, such as individual higher peak, large ridges, or spurs at right angles to the main range. Variations can occur when a north-south range curves to become oriented northeast-southwest. In addition, numerous variations of the wind and stability profiles are possible.

Turbulence associated with lee waves deserves respect. Low-level turbulence can range from unpleasant to dangerous. Glider pilots refer to any turbulence under the smooth wave flow above as "rotor." The nature of rotor turbulence varies from location to location as well as with different weather regimes. At times, rotor turbulence is widespread and fairly uniform; that is, it is equally rough everywhere below the smooth wave flow. At other times, uniformly moderate turbulence is found, with severe turbulence under wave crests. On occasion, no discernable turbulence is noted except for moderate or severe turbulence within a small-scale rotor under the wave crest. Typically, the worst turbulence is found on the leading edge of the primary rotor. Unfortunately, the type and intensity of rotor turbulence are difficult to predict. However, the general rule of thumb is that higher amplitude lee waves tend to have stronger rotor turbulence.

Clouds associated with the mountain wave system are also indicated in *Figure 9-25*. A cap cloud flowing over the mountain tends to dissipate as the air forced down the mountain slope warms and dries. The first (or primary) wave crest features a roll or rotor cloud with one or more lenticulars (or lennies, using glider slang) above. Wave harmonics farther downstream (secondary, tertiary, etc.) may also have lenticulars and/or rotor clouds. If the wave reaches high enough altitudes, lenticulars may form at cirrus levels as well.

It is important to note that the presence of clouds depends on the amount of moisture at various levels. The entire mountain wave system can form in completely dry conditions with no clouds at all. If only lower level moisture exists, only a cap cloud and rotor clouds may be seen with no lenticulars above, as in *Figure 9-26A*. On other days, only mid-level or upper-level lenticulars are seen with no rotor clouds beneath them. When low and mid levels are very moist, a deep rotor cloud may form, with lenticulars right on top of the rotor cloud, with no clear air between the two cloud forms.

Figure 9-26. *Small Foehn Gap under most conditions.*

In wet climates, the somewhat more moist air can advect (meaning to convey horizontally by advection) in, such that the gap between the cap cloud and primary rotor closes completely, stranding the glider on top of the clouds, as in *Figure 9-26B*. Caution is required when soaring above clouds in very moist conditions.

Suitable terrain is required for mountain wave soaring. Even relatively low ridges of 1,000 feet or less vertical relief can produce lee waves. Wave amplitude depends partly on topography, shape, and size. The shape of the lee slope, rather than the upwind slope, is important. Very shallow lee slopes are not conducive to producing waves of sufficient amplitude to support a glider. A resonance exists between the topography width and lee wavelength that is difficult to predict. One particular mountain height, width, and lee slope is not optimum under all weather conditions. Different wind and stability profiles favor different topography profiles. Hence, there is no substitute for experience at a particular soaring site when predicting wave-soaring conditions. Uniform height of the mountaintops along the range is also conducive to better organized waves.

The weather requirements for wave soaring include sufficient wind and a proper stability profile. Windspeed should be at least 15 to 20 knots at mountaintop level with increasing winds above. The wind direction should be within about 30° perpendicular to the ridge or mountain range. The requirement of a stable layer near mountaintop level is more qualitative. A sounding showing a DALR, or nearly so, near the mountaintop would not likely produce lee waves even with adequate winds. A well-defined inversion at or near the mountaintop with less stable air above is best.

Weaker lee waves can form without much increase in windspeed with height, but an actual decrease in windspeed with height usually caps the wave at that level. When winds decrease dramatically with height, for instance, from 30 to 10 knots over two or three thousand feet, turbulence is common at the top of the wave. On some occasions, the flow at mountain level may be sufficient for wave, but then begins to decrease with altitude just above the mountain, leading to a phenomenon called "rotor streaming." In this case, the air downstream of the mountain breaks up and becomes turbulent, similar to rotor, with no lee waves above.

Lee waves experience diurnal effects, especially in the spring, summer, and fall. Height of the topography also influences diurnal effects. For smaller topography, as morning leads to afternoon and the air becomes unstable to heights exceeding the wave-producing topography, lee waves tend to disappear. On occasion, the lee wave still exists but more height is needed to reach the smooth wave lift. Toward evening as thermals again die down and the air stabilizes, lee waves may again form. During the cooler season, when the air remains stable all day, lee waves are often present all day, as long as the winds aloft continue. The daytime dissipation of lee waves is not as notable for large mountains. For instance, during the 1950s Sierra Wave Project (see www.soaringmuseum.org), it was found that the wave amplitude reached a maximum in mid to late afternoon, when convective heating was a maximum. Rotor turbulence also increased dramatically at that time.

Topography upwind of the wave-producing range can also create problems, as illustrated in *Figure 9-27*. In the first case *[Figure 9-27A]*, referred to as destructive interference, the wavelength of the wave from the first range is out of phase with the distance between the ranges. Lee waves do not form downwind of the second range, despite winds and stability aloft being favorable. In the second case *[Figure 9-27B]*, referred to as constructive interference, the ranges are in phase, and the lee wave from the second range has a larger amplitude than it might otherwise.

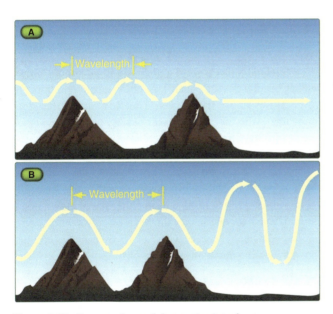

Figure 9-27. *Constructive and destructive interference.*

Wave flight is a unique soaring experience and requires planning, equipment and Federal Aviation Administration (FAA) notification for the flight. The Soaring Society of America (SSA) Awards and Badges offers soaring pilots Lennie Awards for completing and documenting a wave flight. *[Figure 9-28]*

Isolated small hills or conical mountains do not form classic lee waves. In some cases, they do form waves emanating at an angle to the wind flow similar to water waves created by the wake of a ship. A single peak may require only a mile or two in the dimension perpendicular to the wind for high-amplitude lee waves to form, though the wave lift is confined to a relatively small area in these cases.

While working out of the Bishop, California, airport in the late 1940s, mountain pilot and wave pilot pioneer Robert F. Symons created a new and unique system of awards for wave flying, which he called "lennie" pins. Pilots who soared to great heights in the Sierra Wave received a one-lennie pin for attaining an altitude of 25,000 to 35,000 feet, a two-lennie pin for reaching 35,000 to 40,000 feet, and a three-lennie pin for exceeding 40,000 feet.

Very early, Symons recognized the excellent soaring conditions in the Owens Valley and helped organize a soaring group in 1938. As a professional pilot engaged in cloud seeding, he learned first hand of the power generated in the Sierra Wave and became well known for his studies and lectures on mountain wave phenomena. Although his lists are incomplete, it is believed that he issued some 35 one-lennie, 16 two-lennie, and 10 three-lennie pins. The awarding of these pins ceased in 1958, when Symons lost his life in a glider accident.

In 1962 Carl Burson, Jr., saw one of these pins and upon learning of its history, became interested in reestablishing their issuance as a memorial to Bob Symons. In 1963, the program was reestablished under the official auspices of the SSA, with each new pin holder also receiving a handsome wall plaque. The pin itself is 7mm in diameter (the same as the FAI Gold Badge) and has one, two, or three white lenticular clouds against a blue background with a silver rim. Each pin is consecutively numbered.

Figure 9-28. *Lennie Awards are given for completing and documenting a wave flight.*

Lift Due to Convergence

Convergence lift is most easily imagined when easterly and westerly winds meet. When two opposing air masses meet, air is pushed aloft by the two opposing winds. Air does not need to meet head on to go up, however. Wherever air piles up, it leads to convergence and rising air.

One type of convergence line commonly found near coastal areas is the so-called sea-breeze front. Inland areas heat during the day, while the adjacent sea maintains about the same temperature. Inland heating leads to lower pressure, drawing in cooler sea air. As the cooler air moves inland, it behaves like a miniature shallow cold front, and lift forms along a convergence line. Sometimes consistent lift can be found along the sea-breeze front while at other times it acts as a focus for a line of thermals. If the inland air is quite unstable, the sea-breeze front can act as a focus for a line of thunderstorms. Additionally, since the air on the coast side of the sea-breeze front is rather cool, passage of the front can spell the end of thermal soaring for the day.

Sea air often has a higher dewpoint than drier inland air. As shown in *Figure 9-29*, a curtain cloud sometimes forms, marking the area of strongest lift. Due to the mixing of different air along the sea-breeze front, at times the lift can be quite turbulent. At other times, weak and fairly smooth lift is found.

Several factors influence the sea-breeze front character (e.g., turbulence, strength, and speed of inland penetration, including the degree of inland heating and the land/sea temperature difference). For instance, if the land/sea temperature difference at sunrise is small and overcast cirrus clouds prevent much heating, only a weak sea-breeze front, if any, forms. Another factor is the synoptic wind flow. A weak synoptic onshore flow may cause quicker inland penetration of the sea-breeze front, while a strong onshore flow may prevent the sea-breeze front from developing at all. On the other hand, moderate offshore flow generally prevents any inland penetration of the sea-breeze front.

If the sea-breeze front is well defined and marked by a curtain cloud, the pilot can fly straight along the line in fairly steady lift. A weaker convergence line that is not well-defined often produces more lift than sink and the pilot must fly slower in lift and faster in sink. Soaring pilots must be aware that convergence zone lift can be turbulent especially if the colder and warmer air is mixing and be prepared that flying the thermals may be difficult at times.

Convergence can also occur along and around mountains or ridges. In *Figure 9-30A*, flow is deflected around a ridgeline and meets as a convergence line on the lee side of the ridge. The line may be marked by cumulus or a boundary with a sharp visibility contrast. The latter occurs if the air coming around one end of the ridge flows past a polluted urban area, such as in the Lake Elsinore soaring area in southern California. In very complex terrain, with ridges or ranges oriented at different angles to one another, or with passes between high peaks, small-scale convergence zones can be found in adjacent valleys, depending on wind strength and direction. *Figure 9-30B* illustrates a smaller-scale convergence line flowing around a single hill or peak and forming a line of lift stretching downwind from the peak.

Convergence can also form along the top of a ridgeline or mountain range. In *Figure 9-31*, drier synoptic-scale wind flows up the left side of the mountain, while a more moist valley breeze flows up the right side of the slope. The two flows meet at the mountain top and form lift along the entire range. If clouds are present, the air from the moist side condenses first, often forming one cloud with a well-defined step, marking the convergence zone. For this scenario, the better lift conditions will be found on the west side where the air is dryer rather than the east side where clouds are more likely to form.

As a final example, toward evening in mountainous terrain and as heating daytime abates, a cool katabatic, or drainage, wind flows down the slopes. The flow down the slope converges with air in the adjacent valley to form an area of weak lift. Sometimes the convergence is not strong enough for general lifting, but acts as a trigger for the last thermal of the day. In narrow valleys, flow down the slope from both sides of the valley can converge and cause weak lift. *[Figure 9-32]* Many local sites in either flat or mountainous terrain have lines or zones of lift that are likely to be caused or enhanced by convergence. Chapter 10, Soaring Techniques, covers locating and using convergence.

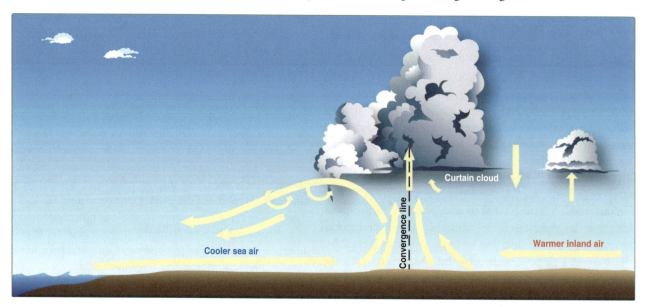

Figure 9-29. *Sea-breeze front.*

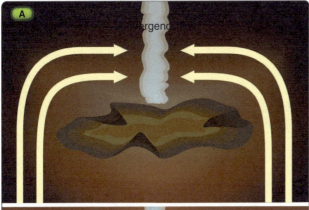

Figure 9-30. *Convergence induced by flow around topography.*

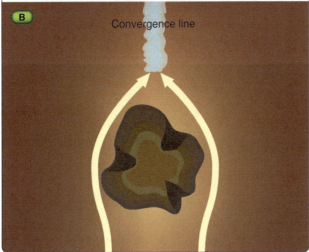

Figure 9-31. *Mountain-top convergence.*

Figure 9-32. *Convergence induced by flow around topography.*

Obtaining Weather Information

One of the most important aspects of flight planning is obtaining reliable weather information. Fortunately, pilots have several outlets to receive reliable weather reports and forecasts to help them determine if a proposed flight can be completed safely. For visual flight rules (VFR) flights, federal regulations require pilots to gather weather reports and forecasts only if they plan to depart the airport vicinity. Nevertheless, it is always a good idea to be familiar with the current and expect weather anytime a flight is planned. Preflight weather information sources include Automated Flight Service Stations (AFSS) and National Weather Service (NWS) telephone briefers, the Direct User Access Terminal System (DUATS), and the Internet. In addition, a multitude of commercial venders provide custom services.

For complete details regarding available weather services and products, refer to the current version of the FAA Advisory Circular (AC) 00-45, Aviation Weather Services, and in the Pilot's Handbook of Aeronautical Knowledge, Chapter 12, Aviation Weather Services.

Preflight Weather Briefing

Often times in order to obtain a preflight weather briefing, certain background information must be given to the weather specialist: type of flight planned, whether flying VFR (Visual Flight Rules) or IFR (Instrument Flight Rules), aircraft registration or pilot's name, aircraft type, departure airport, route of flight, destination, flight altitude(s), estimated time of departure (ETD), and estimated time en route (ETE). Operators of airports, gliderports, or fixed-base operators (FBO) may obtain current reports and forecasts from the AFSS or NWS at various times throughout the day and post them on a bulletin board for easy reference.

Weather briefers do not actually predict the weather; they simply translate and interpret weather reports and forecasts within the vicinity of the airport, route of flight, or the destination airport if the flight is a cross-country. A pilot may request one of four types of briefings: standard, abbreviated, soaring *[Figure 9-33],* or outlook.

Weather-Related Information

Weather-related information can be found on the Internet, including sites directed toward aviation. These sites can be found using a variety of Internet search engines. It is important to verify the timeliness and source of the weather information provided by the Internet sites to ensure the information is up to date and accurate. Pilots should exercise caution when accessing weather information on the Internet, especially if the information cannot be verified. Other sources of accurate weather information are the NWS website located at

9-21

Soaring Forecast
National Weather Service Denver/Boulder, Colorado
645 AM MDT Wednesday August 25, 2010

This forecast is for Wednesday August 25, 2010:

If the trigger temperature of 77.3 F/25.2 C is reached...then
   Thermal Soaring Index....................... Excellent
   Maximum rate of lift....................... 911 ft/min (4.6 m/s)
   Maximum height of thermals.................. 16119 ft MSL (10834 ft AGL)

Forecast maximum temperature................... 89.0 F/32.1 C
Time of trigger temperature.................... 1100 MDT
Time of overdevelopment........................ None
Middle/high clouds during soaring window....... None
Surface winds during soaring window............ 20 mph or less
Height of the -3 thermal index................. 10937 ft MSL (5652 ft AGL)
Thermal soaring outlook for Thursday 08/26..... Excellent

Wave Soaring Index............................. Poor
Wave Soaring Index trend (to 1800 MDT)......... No change
Height of stable layer (12-18K ft MSL)......... None
Weak PVA/NVA (through 1800 MDT)................ Neither
Potential height of wave....................... 14392 ft MSL (9107 ft AGL)
Wave soaring outlook for Thursday 08/26........ Poor

Remarks...

Sunrise/Sunset..................... 06:20:55 / 19:42:44 MDT
Total possible sunshine........... 13 hr 21 min 49 sec (801 min 49 sec)
Altitude of sun at 13:01:25 MDT... 60.82 degrees

Upper air data from rawinsonde observation taken on 08/25/2010 at 0600 MDT

Freezing level.................. 15581 ft MSL (10296 ft AGL)
Additional freezing level....... 54494 ft MSL (49209 ft AGL)
Convective condensation level... 13902 ft MSL (8617 ft AGL)
Lifted condensation level....... 14927 ft MSL (9641 ft AGL)
Lifted index.................... -3.4
K index......................... +9.7

* * * * * * Numerical weather prediction model forecast data valid * * * * * *

   08/25/2010 at 0900 MDT | 08/25/2010 at 1200 MDT

K index... +4.0 | K index... -0.7

This product is issued twice per day, once by approximately 0630 MST/0730 MDT (1330 UTC) and again by approximately 1830 MST/1930 MDT (0130 UTC). It is not continuously monitored nor updated after its initial issuance.

The information contained herein is based on rawinsonde observation and/or numerical weather prediction model data taken near the old Stapleton Airport site in Denver, Colorado at

    North Latitude: 39 deg 46 min 5.016 sec
    West Longitude: 104 deg 52 min 9.984 sec
    Elevation: 5285 feet (1611 meters)

and may not be representative of other areas along the Front Range of the Colorado Rocky Mountains. Note that some elevations in numerical weather prediction models differ from actual station elevations, which can lead to data which appear to be below ground. Erroneous data such as these should not be used.

The content and format of this report as well as the issuance times are subject to change without prior notice. Comments and suggestions are welcome and should be directed to one of the addresses or phone numbers shown at the bottom of this page. To expedite a response to comments, be sure to mention your interest in the soaring forecast.

DEFINITIONS:

Convective Condensation Level - The height to which an air parcel possessing the average saturation mixing ratio in the lowest 4000 feet of the airmass, if heated sufficiently from below, will rise dry adiabatically until it just becomes saturated. It estimates the base of cumulus clouds that are produced by surface heating only.

Convection Temperature (ConvectionT) - The surface temperature required to make the airmass dry adiabatic up to the given level. It can be considered a "trigger temperature" for that level.

Freezing Level - The height where the temperature is zero degrees Celsius.

Height of Stable Layer - The height (between 12,000 and 18,000 feet above mean sea level) where the smallest lapse rate exists. The location and existence of this feature is important in the generation of mountain waves.

K Index - A measure of stability which combines the temperature difference between approximately 5,000 and 18,000 feet above the surface, the amount of moisture at approximately 5,000 feet above the surface, and a measure of the dryness at approximately 10,000 feet above the surface. Larger positive numbers indicate more instability and a greater likelihood of thunderstorm development. One interpretation of K index values regarding soaring in the western United States is given in WMO Technical Note 158 and is reproduced in the following table:

   below -10   no or weak thermals
   -10 to 5   dry thermals or 1/8 cumulus with moderate thermals
   5 to 15   good soaring conditions
   15 to 20   good soaring conditions with occasional showers
   20 to 30   excellent soaring conditions, but increasing probability of showers and thunderstorms
   above 30   more than 60 percent probability of thunderstorms

Lapse Rate - The change with height of the temperature. Negative values indicate inversions.

Lifted Condensation Level - The height to which an air parcel possessing the average dewpoint in the lowest 4000 feet of the airmass and the forecast maximum temperature must be lifted dry adiabatically to attain saturation.

Lifted Index - The difference between the environmental temperature at a level approximately 18,000 feet above the surface and the temperature of an air parcel lifted dry adiabatically from the surface to its lifted condensation level and then pseudoadiabatically thereafter to this same level. The parcel's initial temperature is the forecast maximum temperature and its dewpoint is the average dewpoint in the lowest 4000 feet of the airmass. Negative values are indicative of instability with positive values showing stable conditions.

Lift Rate - An experimental estimate of the strength of thermals. It is computed the same way as the maximum rate of lift but uses the actual level rather than the maximum height of thermals in the calculation. Also, none of the empirical adjustments based on cloudiness and K-index are applied to these calculations.

Maximum Height of Thermals - The height where the dry adiabat through the forecast maximum temperature intersects the environmental temperature.

Figure 9-33. *Soaring forecast.*

Maximum Rate of Lift - An estimate of the maximum strength of thermals. It is computed from an empirical formula which combines the expected maximum height of thermals with the difference in the environmental temperatures between the maximum height of thermals and the temperature 4,000 feet above the ground. After this computation, further empirical adjustments are made based on the value of the K-index and the amount and opacity of middle and high level cloudiness expected between the time of trigger temperature and the time of overdevelopment.

Middle/High Clouds - The amount and opacity of middle (altostratus, altocumulus) or high (cirrus, cirrostatus, cirrocumulus) clouds. Broken means that between 60% and 90% of the sky is covered by the cloud, with overcast conditions occurring when more than 90% of the sky is covered by the cloud. Thin implies that the clouds are predominantly transparent, meaning that some sunlight is reaching the ground, in contrast to opaque which suggests that little sunlight is reaching the ground.

Potential Height of Wave - The minimum of the following two heights:
1. Level above the height of stable layer (or 14,000 feet if none exists) where the wind direction changes by 30 degrees or more
2. Level above the height of stable layer (or 14,000 feet if none exists) where the wind speed no longer increases with height

PVA/NVA - Positive vorticity advection (PVA)/negative vorticity advection (NVA) on the 500 millibar isobaric surface (approximately 18,000 feet above mean sea level). Weak PVA has been shown to assist in mountain wave soaring.

Soaring Window - The time between the time the trigger temperature is reached and the time of overdevelopment.

Thermal Index - The difference between the environmental temperature and the temperature at a particular level determined by following the dry adiabat through the forecast maximum temperature up to that level. Negative values are indicative of thermal lift.

Thermal Soaring Index - An adjective rating (for sailplanes) based on the computed maximum rate of lift, and the wind speed and middle and high cloud cover expected during the soaring window (the time of the trigger temperature and the time of overdevelopment) according to the following:

Maximum rate of lift	Adjective Rating
≥ 800 fpm	Excellent
≥ 400 and < 800 fpm	Good
≥ 200 and < 400 fpm	Fair
< 200 fpm	Poor

Time of Overdevelopment - The time one or more of the following phenomena, which essentially shut off thermal lift, is expected to occur:
1. formation of broken to overcast convective cloud cover
2. formation of scattered to numerous downbursts
3. initiation of widespread precipitation

Time of Trigger Temperature - The time the surface temperature is expected to reach the trigger temperature.

Trigger Temperature - The surface temperature required to make the first 4000 feet of the atmosphere dry adiabatic.

Wave Soaring Index - An empirical, adjective rating (for sailplanes) which attempts to combine a variety of phenomena important in mountain wave soaring into a single index number. Objective points are assigned to these phenomena: wind speed and direction at 14,000 ft MSL, the static stability in the 12,000-18,000 ft MSL layer, the wind speed gradient above the stable layer, jet stream location and frontal and upper trough movements.

Figure 9-33. *Soaring forecast (continued).*

www.nws.noaa.gov, the NOAA site at http://aviationweather.gov/adds/metars/ and Dr. Jack's regional forecasts at http://www.drjack.info/BLIP/RUC.

Interpreting Weather Charts, Reports, and Forecasts

Knowing how and where to gather weather information is important but the ability to interpret and understand the information requires additional knowledge and practice. Weather charts and reports are merely records of observed atmospheric conditions at certain locations at specific times. Trained observers using electronic instruments, computers, and personal observations produce the weather products necessary for pilots to determine if a flight can be conducted safely. This same information can be used by soaring pilots to determine where they can find lift and how long the lift is usable for soaring flight.

Graphic Weather Charts

Reports of observed weather are graphically depicted in a number of weather products. Among them are the surface analysis chart, radar summary chart, weather depiction chart, winds and temperature aloft chart, and the composite moisture stability chart. For detailed information about the surface analysis chart, weather depiction charts, and radar summary chart, refer to the Pilot's Handbook of Aeronautical Knowledge and Advisory Circular 00-45G, "Aviation Weather Services."

Winds and Temperatures Aloft Forecast

The winds and temperatures aloft forecast (FB) is a 12-hour product that is issued at 0000Z and 1200Z daily. *[Figure 9-34]* It is used primarily to determine expected wind direction and velocity, and temperatures for the altitude of a planned cross-country flight. The forecast contains nine columns that correspond to forecast levels 3,000; 6,000; 9,000; 12,000; 18,000; 24,000; 30,000; 34,000; and 39,000 feet MSL. Soaring pilots planning to attempt proficiency for altitude should be aware that the levels below 18,000 feet are based on local altimeter settings. Above 18,000 feet, flight levels are based on standard altimeter setting of 29.92 "Hg. For example 19,000 feet is FL190. Wind direction is from true north. No winds are forecast within 1,500 feet of station elevation. Also, no temperatures are forecast for the 3,000 foot level or for any level within 2,500 feet of station elevation. Temperature is in whole degrees Celsius and assumed to be negative above 24,000 feet. *Figure 9-34* shows an example winds aloft message as well as how to decode it.

Sample winds aloft
DATA BASED ON 010000Z
VALID 010600Z FOR USE 0500-0900Z. TEMPS NEG ABV 24000
FT 3000 6000 9000 12000 18000 24000 30000 34000 39000
MKC 2426 2726-09 2826-14 2930-21 2744-32 2751-41 275550 276050 276547

Sample message decoded:
DATA BASED ON 010000Z

Forecast data is based on computer forecasts generated the first day of the month at 0000 UTC.
VALID 010600Z FOR USE 0500-0900Z. TEMPS NEG ABV 24000

The valid time of the forecast is the first day of the month at 0600 UTC. The forecast winds and temperature are to be used between 0500 and 0900 UTC. Temperatures are negative above 24,000 feet.
FT 3000 6000 9000 12000 18000 24000 30000 34000 39000

FT indicates the forecast location, the numbers indicate the forecast levels.
MKC 2426 2726-09 2826-14 2930-21 2744-32 2751-41 275550 276050 276547

This example shows data for MKC (Kansas City, MO). The 3,000 foot wind is forecast to be 240 degrees at 26 knots. The 6,000 foot wind is forecast to be 270 degrees at 26 knots and the air temperature is forecast to be -9 degrees Celsius. The 30,000 foot wind is forecast to be 270 degrees at 55 knots with the air temperature forecast to be -50 degrees Celsius.

If a coded direction is more than "36," then the wind speed is 100 knots or more. Therefore, if the direction number is between 51 and 86, the wind speed will be over 100 knots. For example, a forecast at 39,000 feet of "731960" shows a wind direction from 230 degrees (73-50=23) and the speed is 119 knots (100+19=119). The temperature is minus 60 degrees Celcius.

If the wind speed is forecast to be 200 knots or greater, the wind group is coded as 199 knots. For example, "7799" is decoded as 270 degrees at 199 knots or greater.
Wind direction is coded to the nearest 10 degrees. When the forecast speed is less than 5 knots, the coded group is "9900" and read, "LIGHT AND VARIABLE."

Figure 9-34. *Types of briefings.*

NOTE: The winds aloft forecasts were formally known as FD.

Composite Moisture Stability Chart

The composite moisture stability chart is a four-panel chart, which depicts stability, precipitable water, freezing level, and average relative humidity. It is a computer-generated chart derived from upper-air observation data and is available twice daily with a valid time of 0000Z and 1200Z. This chart is useful for determining the characteristics of a particular weather system with regard to atmospheric stability, moisture content, and possible aviation hazards, such as thunderstorms and icing. *[Figure 9-35]*

For the purpose of soaring flight, the stability panel located in the upper left corner of the chart *[Figure 9-35 Panel A]* can be useful when obtaining weather as it outlines areas of stable and unstable air. The numbers on this panel resemble fractions; the top number is the lifted index (LI) and the lower number is the K index (KI). *[Figure 9-36]* The LI is

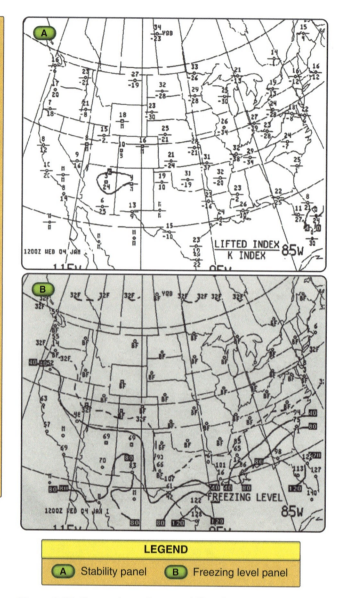

Figure 9-35. *Composite moisture stability chart.*

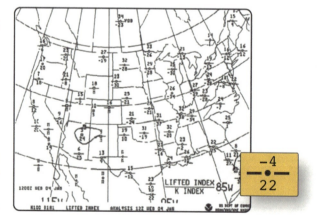

Figure 9-36. *Stability panel.*

9-24

the difference between the temperature of a parcel of air being lifted from the surface to the 500 mb level (approximately 18,000 feet MSL) and the actual temperature at the 500 mb level. If the number is positive, the air is considered stable. For example, a lifted index of +8 is very stable, and the likelihood of severe thunderstorms is weak. Conversely, an index of –6 or less is considered very unstable, and severe thunderstorms are likely to occur; however, the instability may give rise to favorable soaring conditions. A zero index is neutrally stable. *[Figure 9-37]*

THUNDERSTORM POTENTIAL	
Lifted index (LI)	Severe Potential
0 to –2	Weak
–3 to –5	Moderate
≤ –6	Strong

Figure 9-37. *Airmass stability.*

The chart in *Figure 9-37* shows relative instability in two ways. First, the station circle is darkened when the lift index is zero or less. Second, solid lines are used to delineate areas that have an index of +4 or less at intervals of 4 (+4, 0, –4, –8). The stability panel is an important preflight planning tool because the relative stability of an airmass is indicative of the type of clouds that can be found in a given area. For example, if the airmass is stable, a pilot can expect smooth air and, given sufficient moisture, steady precipitation. On the other hand, if the airmass is unstable, convective turbulence and showery precipitation can be expected.

The K index indicates whether the conditions are favorable for airmass thunderstorms. The K index is based on temperature, low-level moisture, and saturation. A K index of 15 or less would be forecast as a 0 percent probability for airmass thunderstorms, and an index of 40 or more would be forecast as 100 percent probability. *[Figure 9-38]*

THUNDERSTORM POTENTIAL	
K index	Airmass Thunderstorm Probability
<15	near 0%
15–19	20%
20–25	21–40%
26–30	41–60%
31–35	61–80%
36–40	81–90%

Figure 9-38. *Thunderstorm potential.*

Caution should be exercised if the K index is high, indicating moisture is sufficient for storm development. Although the lifting index may be very negative and good for soaring, too much moisture can make good soaring conditions very dangerous once the storms develop. A very negative LI with high KI may mean a better day to soar close to the gliderport, whereas very negative LI and low KI values make for clear soaring conditions in general.

Chapter 10
Soaring Techniques

Introduction

Soaring flight, maintaining or gaining altitude rather than slowly gliding downward, is the reason most glider pilots take to the sky. After learning to stay aloft for two or more hours at a time, the urge to set off cross-country often overcomes the soaring pilot. The goal is the same whether on a cross-country or a local flight—to use available updrafts as efficiently as possible. This involves finding and staying within the strongest part of the updraft. This chapter covers the basic soaring techniques.

In the early 1920s, soaring pilots discovered the ability to remain aloft using updrafts caused by wind deflected by the very hillside from which they had launched. This allowed time aloft to explore the air. Soon afterward, they discovered thermals in the valleys adjacent to the hills. In the 1930s, mountain waves, which were not yet well understood by meteorologists, were discovered, leading pilots to make the first high altitude flights. Thermals are the most commonly used type of lift for soaring flight, since they can occur over flat terrain and in hilly country.

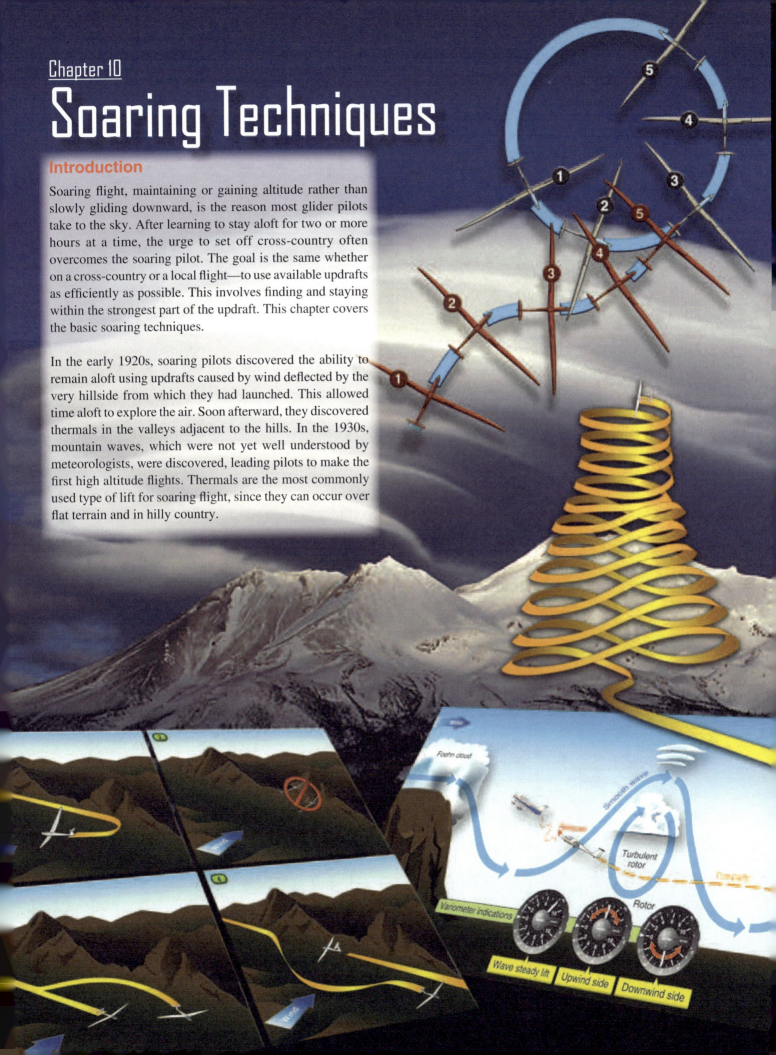

There are two favored theories of thermal characteristics. One is that thermals are continuous updrafts like a plume of smoke from a campfire rising up and sometimes twisting depending on the wind currents. This theory requires the glider pilot to locate the rising thermal current and estimate the amount of slant caused by the winds shifting the rising updraft downwind from the heat source. Just like a campfire, the winds may tend to twist and oscillate around the hotter origin.

The other theory is that thermals can be more like a hot water bubble rising in a pan on a stove. If you can stay in the bubble, you can climb. If you spill out of the bubble, there is no lift even just under where you were climbing because the lift is not a continuous vertical stream. The glider pilot must search for the next rising bubble to obtain lift.

In the practical world, the nature of thermals is probably a blend of these theories. The sun produces heat, and often that heating is unequal on the surface of the earth, so winds occur as natural forces that work to equalize the atmosphere. Some of these winds are vertical currents. We call them updrafts and downdrafts. Updrafts provide lift and downdrafts provide sink. Since the atmosphere always seeks equality, if there is an updraft, there must be a downdraft or drafts close to replace the upward flowing air. The goal of soaring pilots is to maximize time in lifting currents and minimize their time in sinking currents.

The contemporary models and experience seem to support the theory of a central updraft surrounded by compensating downdrafts. The skill involves staying in the lift as long as possible and exiting or passing through the sink as quickly as possible.

As a note, glider pilots refer to rising air as lift. This is not the lift generated by the wings as discussed in Chapter 3, Aerodynamics of Flight. The use of this term may confuse new pilots, but when used in the context of updrafts, the energy in a rising column of air is translated as lift. This chapter refers to lift as the rising air within an updraft and sink as the descending air in downdrafts.

Thermal Soaring

Locating Thermals

When locating and utilizing thermals for soaring flight, called thermaling, glider pilots must constantly be aware of any nearby lift indicators. Successful thermaling requires several steps: locating the thermal, entering the thermal, centering the thermal, and, finally, leaving the thermal. Keep in mind that every thermal is unique in terms of size, shape, and strength.

Cumulus Clouds

According to the last chapter, if the air is moist enough and thermals rise high enough, cumulus clouds, or Cu (pronounced like the word "cue") form. Glider pilots seek Cu in the developing stage, while the cloud is still being built by a thermal underneath it. The base of the Cu should be sharp and well defined. Clouds that have a fuzzy appearance are likely to be well past their prime and probably have little lift left or even sink as the cloud dissipates. *[Figure 10-1]*

Judging which clouds have the best chance for a good thermal takes practice. On any given day, the lifetime of an individual Cu can differ from previous days, so it becomes important to observe Cu lifecycle on a particular day. A good looking Cu may already be dissipating by the time it is reached. Soaring pilots refer to such Cu as rapid or quick cycling, which means the Cu forms, matures, and dissipates in a short time. The lifetime of Cu often varies during a given day as well; quick cycling Cu early in the day often become well formed and longer lived as the day develops.

Sometimes Cu cover enough of the sky that seeing the cloud tops becomes difficult. Hence, glider pilots should learn to read the bases of Cu. Generally, a dark area under the

Figure 10-1. *Photographs of (A) mature cumulus probably producing good lift, and (B) dissipating cumulus.*

cloud base indicates a deeper cloud and, therefore, a higher likelihood of a thermal underneath. Also, several thermals can feed one cloud, and it is often well worth the deviation to those darker areas under the cloud. At times, an otherwise flat cloud base under an individual Cu has wisps or tendrils of cloud hanging down from it, producing a particularly active area. Cloud hanging below the general base of a Cu indicates that the air is more moist, and hence more buoyant. Note the importance of distinguishing features under Cu that indicate potential lift from virga. Virga is precipitation in the form of rain, snow, or ice crystals, descending from the cloud base that is evaporating before it strikes the ground. Virga often signals that the friendly Cu has grown to cumulus congestus or thunderstorms. *[Figure 10-2]*

Another indicator that one area of Cu may provide better lift is a concave region under an otherwise flat cloud base. This indicates air that is especially warm, and hence more buoyant, which means stronger lift. This can cause problems for the unwary pilot, since the lift near cloud base often dramatically increases, for instance from 400 to 1,000 feet per minute (fpm). When trying to leave the strong lift in the concave area under the cloud, pilots can find themselves climbing rapidly with cloud all around—another good reason to abide by required cloud clearances. See Title 14 of the Code of Federal Regulations (14 CFR) part 91, section 91.155, Basic VFR Weather Minimums.

After a thermal rises from the surface and reaches the convective condensation level (CCL), a cloud begins to form. At first, only a few wisps form. Then, the cloud grows to a cauliflower shape. The initial wisps of Cu in an otherwise blue (cloudless) sky indicate where an active thermal is beginning to build a cloud. When crossing a blue hole (a region anywhere from a few miles to several dozen miles of cloud-free sky in an otherwise Cu-filled sky), diverting to an initial wisp of Cu is often worthwhile. On some days, when only a few thermals are reaching the CCL, the initial wisps may be the only cloud markers around. The trick is to get to the wisp when it first forms, to catch the thermal underneath.

Lack of Cu does not necessarily mean lack of thermals. If the air aloft is cool enough and the surface temperature warms sufficiently, thermals form whether or not enough moisture exists for cumulus formation. These dry, or blue thermals as they are called, can be just as strong as their Cu-topped counterparts. Glider pilots can find blue thermals, without Cu markers, by gliding along until stumbling upon a thermal. With any luck, other blue thermal indicators exist, making the search less random.

Other Indicators of Thermals

One indicator of a thermal is another circling glider. Often the glint of the sun on wings is all that can be seen, so finding other gliders thermaling requires keeping a good lookout, which glider pilots should be doing anyway. Circling birds are also good indicators of thermal activity. Thermals tend to transport various aerosols, such as dust, upward with them. When a thermal rises to an inversion, it disturbs the stable air above it and spreads out horizontally, thus depositing some of the aerosols at that level. Depending on the sun angle and the pilot's sunglasses, haze domes can indicate dry thermals. If the air contains enough moisture, haze domes often form just before the first wisp of Cu.

On blue, cloudless days, gliders and other airborne indicators are not around to mark thermals. In such cases, pay attention to clues on the ground. First, think about previous flight experiences. It is worth noting where thermals have been found previously since certain areas tend to be consistent thermal sources. Remember that weather is fickle, so there is never a guarantee that a thermal currently exists where one existed before. In addition, if a thermal has recently formed, it takes time for the sun to reheat the area before the next thermal is triggered. Glider pilots new to a soaring location should ask the local pilots about favored spots—doing so might save the cost of a tow. Glider pilots talk about house thermals, which are simply thermals that seem to form over and over in the same spot or in the same area.

Stay alert for other indicators, as well. In drier climates, dust devils mark thermals triggering from the ground. In hilly or

Figure 10-2. *Photographs of (A) cumulus congestus, (B) cumulonimbus (Cb), and (C) virga.*

mountainous terrain, look for sun-facing slopes. Unless the sun is directly overhead, the heating of a sun-facing slope is more intense than that over adjacent flat terrain because the sun's radiation strikes the slope at more nearly right angles. *[Figure 10-3]* Also, cooler air usually pools in low-lying areas overnight; taking longer to warm during the morning. Darker ground or surface features heat quicker than grass covered fields. Huge black asphalt parking lots can produce strong thermals. A large tilled black soil field can be a good source of lift if the pilot can find the sometimes very narrow plume of rising air. Finally, slopes often tend to be drier than surrounding lowlands, and tend to heat better. Given the choice, it usually pays to look first to the hills for thermals.

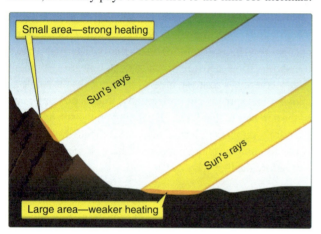

Figure 10-3. *Sun's rays are concentrated in a smaller area on a hillside than on adjacent flat ground.*

Whether soaring over flat or hilly terrain, some experts suggest taking a mental stroll through the landscape to look for thermals. Imagine strolling along the ground where warmer areas would be found. For instance, walk from shade into an open field where the air suddenly warms. A town surrounded by green fields is likely to heat more than the surrounding farmland. Likewise, a yellowish harvested field feels warmer than an adjacent wet field with lush green vegetation. Wet areas tend to use the sun's radiation to evaporate the moisture rather than heat the ground. Thus, a field with a rocky outcrop might produce better thermals. Rocky outcrops along a snowy slope heat much more efficiently than surrounding snowfields. Although this technique works better when at lower altitudes, it can also be of use at higher altitudes in the sense of avoiding cool-looking areas, such as a valley with many lakes.

Wind

Wind has important influences not only on thermal structure, but on thermal location as well. Strong winds at the surface and aloft often break up thermals, making them turbulent and difficult or impossible to work at all. Strong shear can break thermals apart and effectively cap their height even though the local sounding indicates that thermals should extend to higher levels. On the other hand, as discussed in Chapter 9, Soaring Weather, moderately strong winds without too much wind shear sometimes organize thermals into long streets, a joyous sight when they lie along a cross-country course line. *[Figure 10-4]*

Figure 10-4. *Photograph of cloud streets.*

In lighter wind conditions, consideration of thermal drift is still important, and search patterns should become "slanted." For instance, in Cu-filled skies, glider pilots need to search upwind of the cloud to find a thermal. How far upwind depends on the strength of the wind, typical thermal strength on that day, and distance below cloud base (the lower the glider, the further upwind the gliders needs to be). The task can be challenging when you add to this the fact that windspeed does not always increase at a constant rate with height, and/or the possibility that wind direction also can change dramatically with height.

Wind direction and speed at cloud base can be estimated by watching the cloud shadows on the ground. The numerous variables sometimes make it difficult to estimate exactly where a thermal should be. Pay attention to where thermals appear to be located in relation to clouds on a given day, and use this as the search criterion for other clouds on that day. If approaching Cu from the downwind side, expect heavy sink near the cloud. Head for the darkest, best defined part of the cloud base, then continue directly into the wind. Depending on the distance below cloud base, just about the time of passing upwind of the cloud, fly directly into the lift forming the cloud. If approaching the cloud from a crosswind direction (for instance, heading north with westerly winds), try to estimate the thermal location from others encountered that day. If only reduced sink is found, there may be lift nearby, a short leg upwind or downwind may locate the thermal.

Thermals drift with the wind on blue days as well, and similar techniques are required to locate thermals using airborne or ground-based markers. For instance, if heading toward a circling glider but at a thousand feet lower, estimate how much the thermal is tilted in the wind and head for the most likely spot upwind of the circling glider. *[Figure 10-5]* When in need of a thermal, pilots might consider searching on a line upwind or downwind once abeam the circling glider. This may or may not work; if the thermal is a bubble rather than a column, the pilot may be below the bubble. It is easy to waste height while searching in sink near one spot, rather than leaving and searching for a new thermal. Remember that a house thermal will probably be downwind of its typical spot on a windy day. Only practice and experience enable glider pilots to consistently find good thermals.

Cool, stable air can also drift with the wind. Avoid areas downwind of known stable air, such as large lakes or large irrigated regions. On a day with Cu, stable areas can be indicated by a big blue hole in an otherwise Cu-filled sky. If the area is broad enough, a detour upwind of the stabilizing feature might be in order. *[Figure 10-6]*

The Big Picture

When the sky is full of Cu, occasional gliders are marking thermals, and dust devils move across the landscape, the sky becomes glider pilot heaven. If gliding in the upper part of the height band, it is best to focus on the Cu, and make choices based on the best clouds. Sometimes lower altitudes cause glider pilots to go out of synch with the cloud. In that circumstance, use the Cu to find areas that appear generally active, but then start focusing more on ground-based indicators, like dust devils, a hillside with sunshine on it,

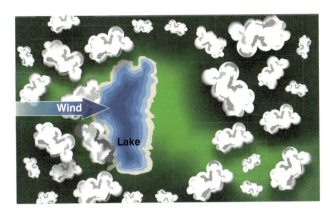

Figure 10-6. *Blue hole in a field of cumulus downwind of a lake.*

or a circling bird. When down low, accept weaker climbs. Often the thermal cycles again, and hard work is rewarded.

When searching for lift, use the best speed to fly, that is, best L/D speed plus corrections for sink and any wind. This technique allows glider pilots to cover the most ground with the available altitude. See Chapter 3, Aerodynamics of Flight, to review shifting of the polar for winds and sink.

Entering a Thermal

Once a thermal has been located, enter it so you do not lose it right away. The first indicator of a nearby thermal is often, oddly enough, increased sink. Next, a positive G-force is felt, which may be subtle or obvious, depending on the thermal strength. The "seat-of-the-pants" indication of lift is the quickest, and is far faster than any variometer, which has a small lag. Speed should have been increased in the sink adjacent to the thermal; as the positive G-force increases, reduce speed to between L/D and minimum sink. Note the trend of the variometer needle (should be an upswing) or the

Figure 10-5. *Thermal tilt in shear that (A) does not change with height, and that (B) increases with height.*

audio variometer going from the drone to excited beeping. At the right time in the anticipated lift, begin the turn. If everything has gone perfectly, the glider will roll into a coordinated turn, at just the right bank angle, at just the right speed, and be centered perfectly. In reality, it rarely works that well.

Before going further, what vital step was left out of the above scenario? CLEAR BEFORE TURNING! The variometer is hypnotic upon entering lift, especially at somewhat low altitudes. This is exactly where pilots forget that basic primary step before any turn—looking around first. An audio variometer helps avoid this.

To help decide which way to turn, determine which wing tends to be lifted. For instance, when entering the thermal and the glider is gently banking to the right, CLEAR LEFT, then turn left. A glider on its own tends to fly away from thermals. *[Figure 10-7]* As the glider flies into the first thermal, but slightly off center, the stronger lift in the center of the thermal banks the glider right, away from the thermal. It then encounters the next thermal with the right wing toward the center and is banked away from lift to the left, and so on. Avoid letting thermals bank the glider even slightly. Sometimes the thermal-induced bank is subtle, so be light on the controls and sensitive to the air activity. At other times, there is no indication on one wing or another. In this case, take a guess, CLEAR, then turn. As a note, new soaring pilots often get in the habit of turning in a favorite direction, to the extreme of not being able to fly reasonable circles in the other direction. If this happens, make an effort to thermal in the other direction half the time—being proficient in either direction is important, especially when thermaling with traffic.

As a glider encounters lift on one side, some gliders tend to slip laterally as indicated by the yaw string. The glider pilot must bring the climbing wing down, not just to level the wings but further to begin the turn into the lifting columns of air. In these instances, the soaring pilot should turn towards the tip of the yaw string to seek the lift.

Inside a Thermal
Bank Angle

Optimum climb is achieved when proper bank angle and speed are used after entering a thermal. The shallowest possible bank angle at minimum sink speed is ideal. Thermal size and associated turbulence usually do not allow this. Large-size, smooth, and well-behaved thermals can be the exception in some parts of the country. Consider first the bank angle. The glider's sink rate increases as the bank angle increases. However, the sink rate begins to increase more rapidly beyond about a 45° bank angle. Thus, a 40° compared to a 30° bank angle may increase the sink rate less than the gain achieved from circling in the stronger lift near the center of the thermal. As with everything else, this takes practice, and the exact bank angle used depends on the typical thermal, or even a specific thermal, on a given day. Normally, bank angles in excess of 50° are not needed, but exceptions always exist. It may be necessary, for instance, to use banks of 60° or so to stay in the best lift. Thermals tend to be smaller at lower levels and expand in size as they rise higher. Therefore, a steeper bank angle is required at lower altitudes, and shallower bank angles can often be used while climbing higher. Remain flexible with techniques throughout the flight.

Speed

If turbulence is light and the thermal is well formed, use the minimum sink speed for the given bank angle. This should optimize the climb because the glider's sink rate is at its lowest, and the turn radius is smaller. As an example, for a 30° bank angle, letting the speed increase from 45 to 50 knots increases the diameter of the circle by about 100 feet. In some instances, this can make the difference between climbing or not. Some gliders can be safely flown several knots below minimum sink speed. Even though the turn radius is smaller, the increased sink rate may offset any gain achieved by being closer to strong lift near the thermal center.

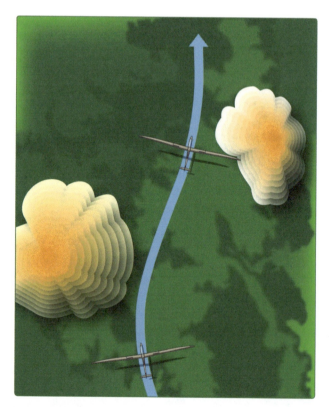

Figure 10-7. *Effect of glider being allowed to bank on its own when encountering thermals.*

There are two other reasons to avoid thermaling speeds that are too slow: the risk of a stall and lack of controllability.

Distractions while thermaling can increase the risk of an inadvertent stall and include, but are not limited to: studying the cloud above or the ground below (for wind drift), quickly changing bank angles without remaining coordinated while centering, thermal turbulence, or other gliders in the thermal. Stall recovery should be second nature, so that if the signs of an imminent stall appear while thermaling, recovery is instinctive. Depending on the stall characteristics of the particular glider or in turbulent thermals, a spin entry is always possible. Glider pilots should carefully monitor speed and nose attitude at lower altitudes. Regardless of altitude, when in a thermal with other gliders below, maintain increased awareness of speed control and avoid any stall/spin scenario. Controllability is a second, though related, reason for using a thermaling speed greater than minimum sink. The bank angle may justify a low speed, but turbulence in the thermal may make it difficult or impossible to maintain the desired quick responsiveness, especially in aileron control, in order to properly remain in the best lift. Using sufficient speed ensures that the pilot, and not the thermal turbulence, is controlling the glider.

Soaring pilots' opinions differ regarding how long to wait after encountering lift and before rolling into the thermal. Some pilots advocate flying straight until the lift has peaked. Then, they start turning, hopefully back into stronger lift. It is imperative not to wait too long after the first indication that the thermal is decreasing for this maneuver. Other pilots favor rolling into the thermal before lift peaks, thus avoiding the possibility of losing the thermal by waiting too long. Turning into the lift too quickly causes the glider to fly back out into sink. There is no one right way; the choice depends on personal preference and the conditions on a given day. Timing is everything, and practice is key to developing good timing.

Centering

Usually upon entering a thermal, the glider is in lift for part of the circle and sink for the other part. It is rare to roll into a thermal and immediately be perfectly centered. The goal of centering the thermal is to determine where the best lift is and move the glider into it for the most consistent climb. One centering technique is known as the 270° correction. *[Figure 10-8]* In this case, the pilot rolls into a thermal and almost immediately encounters sink, an indication of turning the wrong way. Complete a 270° turn, straighten out for a few seconds, and if lift is encountered again, turn back into it in the same direction. Avoid reversing the direction of turn. The distance flown while reversing turns is more than seems possible and can lead away from the lift completely. *[Figure 10-9]*

Often, stronger lift exists on one side of the thermal than on the other, or perhaps the thermal is small enough that lift exists on one side and sink on the other, thereby preventing

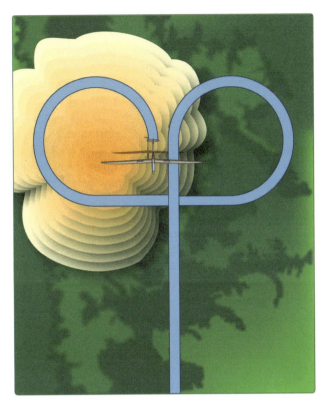

Figure 10-8. *The 270° centering correction.*

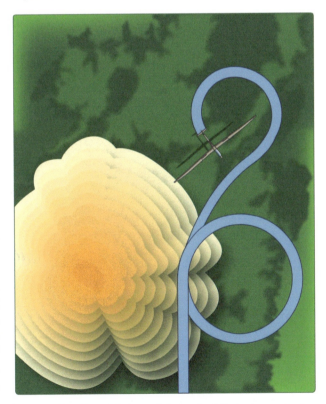

Figure 10-9. *Possible loss of thermal while trying to reverse directions of circle.*

a climb. There are several techniques and variations to centering. One method involves paying close attention to where the thermal is strongest; for instance, toward the northeast or toward some feature on the ground. To help judge this, note what is under the high wing when in the best lift. On the next turn, adjust the circle by either straightening or shallowing the turn toward the stronger lift. Anticipate things and begin rolling out about 30° before actually heading toward the strongest part. This allows rolling back toward the strongest part of the thermal rather than flying through the strongest lift and again turning away from the thermal center. Gusts within the thermal can cause airspeed indicator variations; therefore, avoid "chasing the airspeed indicator." Paying attention to the nose attitude helps pilots keep their focus outside the cockpit. How long a glider remains shallow or straight depends on the size of the thermal. *[Figure 10-10]* Other variations include the following: *[Figure 10-11]*

1. Shallow the turn slightly (consider 5° or 10°) when encountering the weaker lift, then as stronger lift is encountered again (feel the positive G, variometer swings up, audio variometer starts to beep) resume the original bank angle. If shallowing the turn too much, it is possible to fly completely away from the lift.

2. Straighten or shallow the turn for a few seconds 60° after encountering the weakest lifts or worst sink indicated by the variometer. This allows for the lag in the variometer since the actual worst sink occurred a couple of seconds earlier than indicated. Resume the original bank angle.

3. Straighten or shallow the turn for a few seconds when the stronger seat-of-the-pants surge is felt. Then, resume the original bank. Verify with the variometer trend (needle or audio).

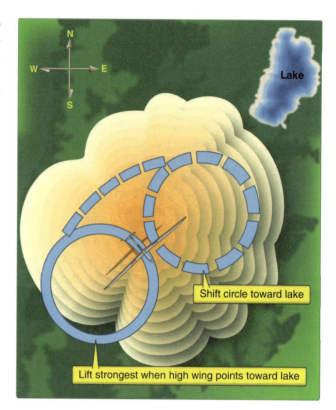

Figure 10-10. *Centering by shifting the circle turn toward stronger lift.*

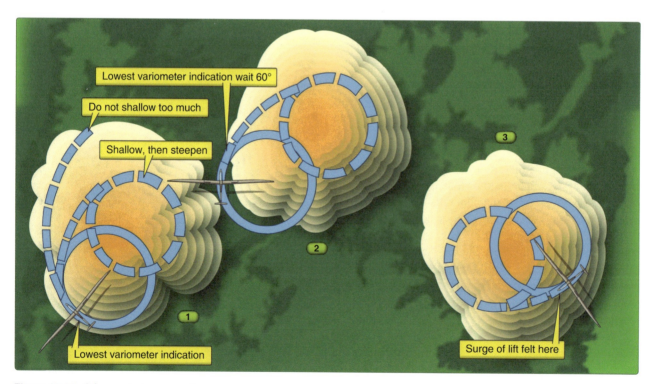

Figure 10-11. *Other centering corrections.*

For the new glider pilots, it is best to become proficient using one of the above methods first, and then experiment with other methods. As an additional note, thermals often deviate markedly from the conceptual model of concentric gradients of lift increasing evenly toward the center. For instance, it sometimes feels as if two (or more) nearby thermal centers exist, making centering difficult. Glider pilots must be willing to constantly adjust, and recenter the thermal to maintain the best climb.

In addition to helping pilots locate lift, other gliders can help pilots center a thermal as well. If a nearby glider seems to be climbing better, adjust the turn to fly within the same circle. Similarly, if a bird is soaring close by, it is usually worth turning toward the soaring bird. Along with the thrill of soaring with a hawk or eagle, it usually leads to a better climb.

Collision Avoidance

Collision avoidance is of primary importance when thermaling with other gliders. The first rule calls for all gliders in a particular thermal to circle in the same direction. The first glider in a thermal establishes the direction of turn and all other gliders joining the thermal should turn in the same direction. Ideally, two gliders in a thermal at the same height or nearly so should position themselves across from each other so they can maintain best visual contact. *[Figure 10-12]* When entering a thermal, strive to do so in a way that does not interfere with gliders already in the thermal, and above all, in a manner that does not cause a hazard to other gliders. An example of a dangerous entry is pulling up to bleed off excess speed in the middle of a crowded thermal. A far safer technique is to bleed off speed before reaching the thermal and joining the thermal at a "normal" thermaling speed. Collision avoidance, not optimum aerodynamic efficiency, is the priority when thermaling with other gliders. Announcing to the other glider(s) on the radio that you are entering the thermal enhances collision avoidance. *[Figure 10-12]*

Different types of gliders in the same thermal may have different minimum sink speeds, and it may be difficult to remain directly across from another glider in a thermal. Avoid a situation where the other glider cannot be seen or the other glider cannot see you. Radio communication is helpful. Too much talking clogs the frequency, and may make it impossible for a pilot to broadcast an important message. Do not fly directly above or below another glider in a thermal since differences in performance, or even minor changes in speed can lead to larger than expected altitude changes. If sight of another glider is lost in a thermal and position cannot be established via a radio call, leave the thermal. After 10 or 20 seconds, come back around to rejoin the thermal, hopefully with better traffic positioning. It cannot be stressed enough that collision avoidance when thermaling is a priority! Mid-

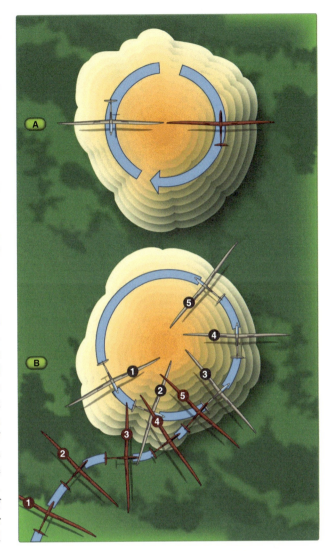

Figure 10-12. *Proper positioning with two gliders at the same altitude. Numbers represent each glider's position at that time.*

air collisions can sometimes be survived, but only with a great deal of luck. Unsafe thermaling practices endanger everyone. *[Figure 10-13]*

Exiting a Thermal

Leaving a thermal properly can also save some altitude. While circling, scan the full 360° of sky with each thermaling turn. This first allows the pilot to continually check for other traffic in the vicinity. Second, it helps the pilot analyze the sky in all directions to decide where to go for the next climb. It is better to decide where to go next while still in lift rather than losing altitude in sink after leaving a thermal. Exactly when to leave depends on the goals for the climb—whether the desire is to maximize altitude for a long glide or leave when lift weakens in order to maximize time on a cross-country flight. In either case, be ready to increase speed to penetrate the sink often found on the edge of the thermal, and leave the thermal in a manner that does not hinder or endanger other gliders.

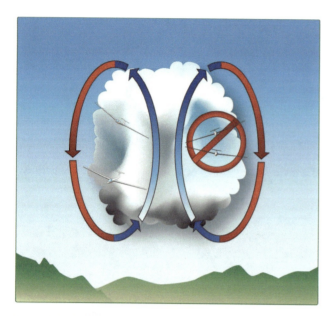

Figure 10-13. *When thermaling, avoid flying in another glider's blind spot, or directly above or below another glider.*

Atypical Thermals

Exceptions to normal or typical thermals are numerous. For instance, instead of stronger sink at the edge of a thermal, weak lift sometimes continues for a distance after leaving a thermal. Glider pilots should be quick to adapt to whatever the air has to offer at the time. The mechanics of simply flying the glider become second nature with practice, as do thermaling techniques. Expect to land early because anticipated lift was not there on occasion—it is part of the learning curve.

If thermal waves are suspected, climb in the thermal near cloud base, then head toward the upwind side of the Cu. Often, only very weak lift, barely enough to climb at all, is found in smooth air upwind of the cloud. Once above cloud base and upwind of the Cu, climb rates of a few hundred fpm can be found. Climbs can be made by flying back and forth upwind of an individual Cu, or by flying along cloud streets if they exist. If no clouds are present, but waves are suspected, climb to the top of the thermal and penetrate upwind in search of smooth, weak lift. Without visual clues, thermal waves are more difficult to work. Thermal waves are most often stumbled upon as a pleasant surprise.

Ridge/Slope Soaring

Efficient slope soaring (also called ridge soaring or ridge running) is fairly easy; simply fly in the updraft along the upwind side of the ridge. Although the appearance may seem simple, it is very complicated and can be very hazardous for the untrained glider pilot. Ridge soaring can also be very demanding on the glider and the pilot. Even though it is easy to fly, there are many situations in which a glider pilot can be exposed to hazards if proper training has not been received. A thorough preflight and route planning needs to be accomplished. This planning also includes ridge selection based on the current winds. The horizontal distance from the ridge varies with height above the ridge, since the best lift zone, or optimum lift zones (OLZ) tilts upwind with height above the ridge. These zones, or OLZ, vary but usually are slightly off the top of the ridge, with a slight angle into the prevailing wind. The bottom of the OLZ may be slightly down from the top line under normal conditions. These OLZ vary with the size and terrain makeup of the ridge. *[Figure 10-14]*

Figure 10-14. *Optimum lift zone of a ridge.*

Surface winds of 15–20 knots that are perpendicular to the ridge are ideal. Wind flow within 45° of the perpendicular line also provides adequate lift. Winds less than 10 knots have also produced adequate ridge soaring dependent on the terrain, but with 10 knots of wind or less, pilots should avoid flying low over any ridge due to the possibility of encountering sink. Local ridge pilots know about of these conditions and the need for good preflight planning and training is required. *[Figure 10-15]*

- Airflow mirrors a hill or ridge shape. Imagine a flow of water around the ridge instead of air. However, air is thinner and can be compressed as in a "venturi effect" and can be "squeezed" and accelerated, especially along the ridge. *[Figure 10-16]*

- Ridges that have an irregular profile are hazardous. The more complicated the ridge is, the more erratic the airflow may become. *[Figure 10-17]*

Traps

Even though the idea is simple, traps exist for both new and expert glider pilots. Obtain instruction when first learning to ridge soar/slope soar. Avoid approaching from the upwind side perpendicularly to the ridge. Instead, approach the ridge

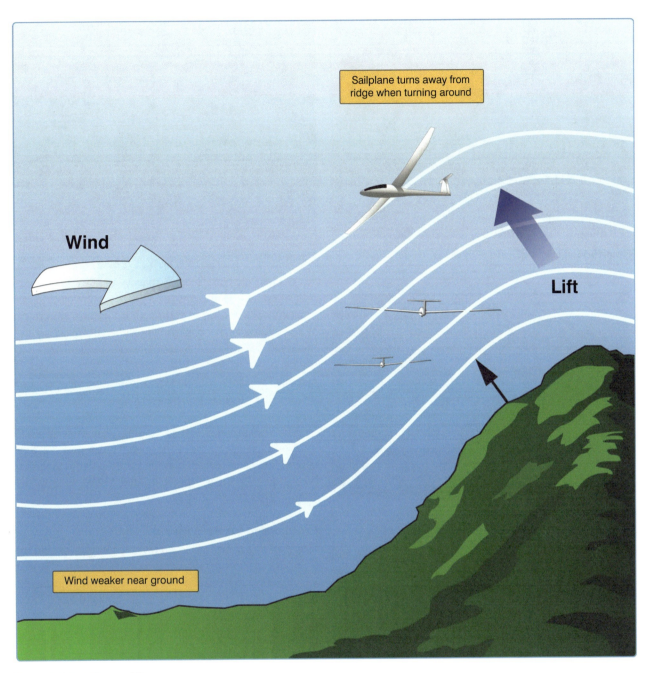

Figure 10-15. *Ridge wind flow.*

at a 45° angle, so that a quick egress away from the ridge is possible should lift not be contacted.

NOTE: When approaching the ridge from downwind, approach the ridge at a diagonal. If excess sink is encountered, this method allows a quick turn away from the ridge. *[Figure 10-18]*

While flying along the ridge, a crab angle is necessary to avoid drifting too close to the ridge or, if gliding above the ridge, to avoid drifting over the top into the leeside downdraft.

Thermal sink can turn the glider upside down, a phenomenon known as upset. A thermal may appear anywhere. When it appears from the opposite side of the ridge, it has strong energy. When flying in strong conditions (winds and thermals), fly with extra speed for positive control of the glider. DO NOT fly on the ridge crest or below the ridge on the downwind side. *[Figure 10-19]*

For the new glider pilot, crabbing along the ridge may be a strange sensation, and it is easy to become uncoordinated while trying to point the nose along the ridge. This is both

Figure 10-16. *Airflow reflects a hill's shape.*

Figure 10-19. *Thermal sink can roll the craft toward the mountain.*

Figure 10-17. *Irregular profiles are hazardous.*

Figure 10-18. *From downwind, approach ridges diagonally.*

inefficient and dangerous, since it leads to a skid toward the ridge. *[Figure 10-20]*

In theory, to obtain the best climb, it is best to slope soar at minimum sink speed. However, flying that slowly may be unwise for two reasons. First, minimum sink speed is relatively close to stall speed, and flying close to stall speed near terrain has obvious dangers. Second, maneuverability at minimum sink speed may be inadequate for proper control near terrain, especially if the wind is gusty and/or thermals are present. When gliding at or below ridge top height, fly faster than minimum sink speed—how much faster depends on the glider, terrain, and turbulence. When the glider is at least several hundred feet above the ridge and shifting upwind away from it in the best lift zone, reduce speed. If in doubt, fly faster.

NOTE: When flying close to the ridge, use extra speed for safety—extra speed gives the glider more positive flight control input and also enables the glider to fly through areas of sink quickly. Ensure that seat and lap belts are tightened. *[Figure 10-21]*

Procedures for Safe Flying

Slope soaring comes with several procedures to enable safe flying and to allow many gliders on the same ridge. The rules are explained in the following paragraphs and illustrated in *Figure 10-22*.

Make all turns away from the ridge. *[Figure 10-22A]* A turn toward the ridge is dangerous, even if gliding seemingly well away from the ridge. The groundspeed on the downwind portion of the turn is difficult to judge properly, and striking the ridge is a serious threat. Even if above the ridge, it is easy to finish the turn downwind which may take the glider over the ridge crest; this puts the glider into heavy sink.

Do not fly directly above or below another glider. *[Figure 10-22B]* Gliders spaced closely together in the vertical are in each other's blind spots. A slight change in climb rate between the gliders can lead to a collision.

Pass another glider on the ridge side, anticipating that the other pilot will make a turn away from the ridge. *[Figure 10-22C]* Sometimes the glider to be passed is so close to the ridge that there is inadequate space to pass between

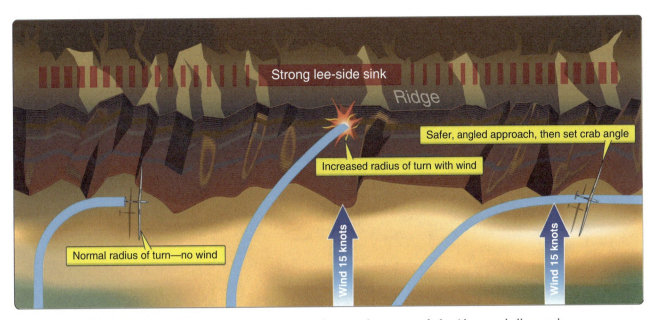

Figure 10-20. *Flying with a wind increases the turn radius over the ground, so approach the ridge at a shallow angle.*

Figure 10-21. *When flying close to a ridge, use extra speed for more control and to pass quickly through sink.*

the glider and the ridge. In that case, either turn back in the other direction (away from the ridge) if traffic permits or fly upwind away from the ridge and rejoin the slope lift as traffic allows. If using a radio, try to contact the glider by the completion number and then coordinate the passing. When soaring outside of the United States, be aware that this rule may differ.

The glider with its right side to the ridge has the right of way. *[Figure 10-22D]* Title 14 of the Code of Federal Regulations (14 CFR) requires both aircraft approaching head-on to give way to the right. A glider with the ridge to the right may not have room to move in that direction. The glider with its left side to the ridge should give way. Additionally, when overtaking a slower glider along the ridge, always pass on the ridge side. If the overtaking glider encounters sink, turbulence, etc., it must maneuver away from the ridge. This is acceptable. When piloting the glider with its right side to the ridge, ensure the approaching glider sees you and is yielding in plenty of time. In general, gliders approaching head-on are difficult to see; therefore, extra vigilance is needed to avoid collisions while slope soaring. The use of a radio during ridge soaring is recommended. Pilots must be familiar with 14 CFR part 91, section 91.113, Right-of-way rules: Except water operations, and section 91.111, Operating near other aircraft.

Bowls and Spurs

If the wind is at an angle to the ridge, bowls or spurs (i.e., recessed or protruding rock formations) extending from the main ridge can create better lift on the upwind side and sink on the downwind side. If at or near the height of the ridge, it may be necessary to detour around the spur to avoid the sink, then drift back into the bowl to take advantage of the better lift. After passing such a spur, do not make abrupt turns toward the ridge. Always consider what the general flow of traffic is doing. If soaring hundreds of feet above a spur, it may be possible to fly over it and increase speed in any sink. This requires caution since a thermal in the upwind bowl, or even an imperceptible increase in the wind, can cause greater than anticipated sink on the downwind side. Always have an escape route or, if in any doubt, detour around. *[Figure 10-23]*

Slope Lift

It is not uncommon for thermals to exist with slope lift. Indeed, slope soaring can often be used as a "save" when thermals have temporarily shut down. Working thermals from slope lift requires special techniques. When a thermal is encountered along the ridge, a series of S-turns can be made into the wind. Drift back to the thermal after each turn if needed and, of course, never continue the turn to the point that

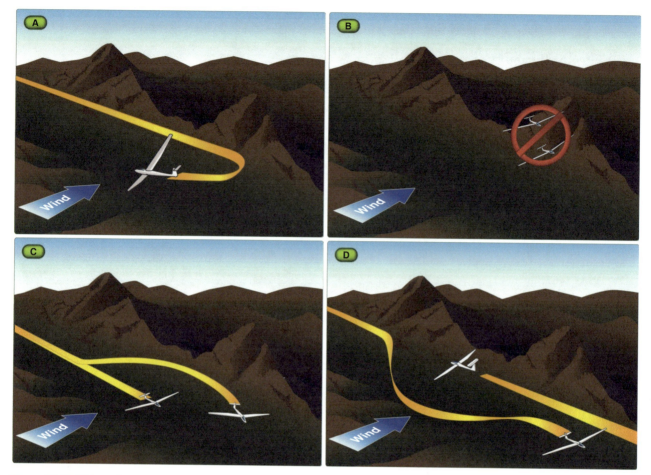

Figure 10-22. *Ridge rules.*

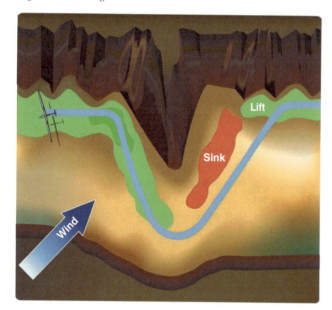

Figure 10-23. *Avoid sink on the downwind side of spurs by detouring around them.*

the glider is turning toward the ridge. Speed is also important, since it is easy to encounter strong sink on the sides of the thermal. It is very likely that staying in thermal lift through the entire S-turn is not possible. The maneuver takes practice, but when done properly, a rapid climb in the thermal can be made well above the ridge crest, where thermaling turns can begin. Even when well above the ridge, caution is needed to ensure the climb is not too slow as to drift into the lee-side sink. Before trying an S-turn, make sure it would not interfere with other traffic along the ridge. *[Figure 10-24]*

A second technique for catching thermals when slope soaring is to head upwind away from the ridge. This works best when Cu mark potential thermals, and aids timing. If no thermal is found, the pilot should cut the search short while still high enough to dash back downwind to the safety of the slope lift. *[Figure 10-25]*

Obstructions

As a final note, caution is also needed to avoid obstructions when slope soaring. Obstructions include wires, cables, and power lines, all of which are very difficult to see. When flying at extremely low altitudes along the ridge (tree top level), the glider and pilot may be placed at a high risk of collision with wires. Ensure an adequate reconnaissance has been completed when flying at these altitudes. Aeronautical charts show high-tension towers that have many wires between them. Soaring pilots familiar with the area should

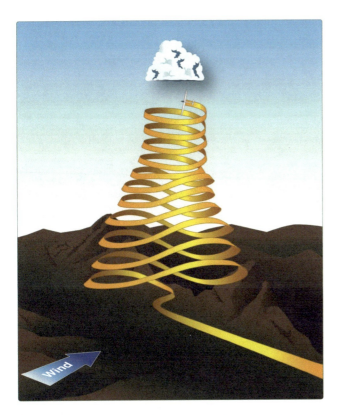

Figure 10-24. *One technique for catching a thermal from ridge lift.*

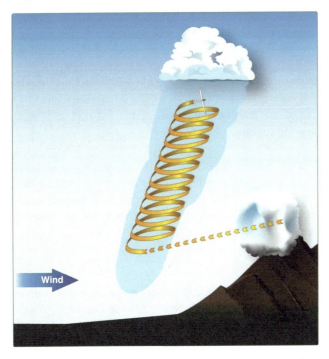

Figure 10-25. *Catching a thermal by flying upwind away from the slope lift.*

be able to provide useful information on any problems with the local ridge.

Tips and Techniques

Observe the ridges slope for collectors or dividers of the wind flow. Plan to determine which of the slopes is gathering wind flow. *[Figure 10-26]* Due to the changes in wind directions and or sun angles, any portion on the ridge can change in only a few minutes.

- Collectors are mountain/ridge bowls and canyon ends that can offer extreme areas of lift when the wind is blowing into them. Remember to have a way out.

- Dividers are ridges parallel with the wind and tend to have airflow separation. A collector that may be downwind from a divider may receive more airflow, making better lift possible.

Figure 10-26. *Analyze sloping ground for collectors and dividers of wind.*

The downwind side of any ridge or hill produces turbulence and sink. The larger or higher the ridge and the greater the wind velocity, the wider the turbulence may be. During these conditions, remember to ensure that seat and shoulder harnesses are tight. Sink calls for speed. Turbulence and speed are very hard on the glider airframe and pilot comfort. Pilots must obey glider limitations set forth in the GFM/POH. Also, do not exceed the design speed for maximum gust intensity (V_b). *[Figure 10-27]*

The ridge crest is where all airflow starts down. Steep ridges with narrow ridge tops can collect thermal action from both sides of the crest. The best lift could be directly above the crest. However, this terrain can be very hazardous as a pilot cannot see it or may not have visual cues. If wind is the only source of lift, the crest can be very dangerous. Always stay upwind of the crest. *[Figure 10-28]*

Areas along the ridge that are in deep shade is where the air goes down and sink can be found. If there is strong lift on the sunny side of the ridge, then chances are that strong sink

Figure 10-27. *Expect turbulence and sink in the downwind of any hill.*

Figure 10-28. *The crest is where rising air starts back down.*

can be found on the shady or dark side of the ridge. This is true when the sun angle is low or late in the afternoon. *[Figure 10-29]*

Figure 10-29. *Deep shade is where colder air goes down.*

Thermal source can be found where drainages area along the ridge meet. Where the ridge or peaks are numerous and slope down into a valley, thermal sources may be found. Canyons or large bowls hold areas of warm air.

Ridges may form cloud streets above the ridge. A glider pilot should try to climb in a thermal to reach these streets. Fast cruising speeds can be found under these streets. The glider pilot must stay upwind to stay in this type of lift near the ridge.

Since gliders tend to seek the same conditions for lift, thermals and areas of ridge lift are areas for special diligence for avoiding other aircraft. To some extent, for the same reasons that gliders seek rising air, other low flying airplanes and helicopters will plan to use that area for flights, so be aware for all aircraft. A portable VHF radio and sharing a common channel for traffic calls is an enhancement for safety, but nothing replaces a good visual scan at all times looking for other aircraft.

Density altitude is increasing as the glider climbs. At 10,000 feet mean sea level (MSL), a pilot is required to have approximately 40 to 45 percent more room to maneuver a glider. The air is less dense by 2 percent per one thousand feet of altitude gained. *[Figure 10-30]*

Wave Soaring

Almost all high-altitude flights are made using mountain lee waves. As covered in Chapter 9, Soaring Weather, lee wave systems can contain tremendous turbulence in the rotor, while the wave flow itself is usually unbelievably smooth. In more recent years, the use of lee waves for cross-country soaring has led to flights exceeding 1,500 miles, with average speeds of over 100 mph. *[Figure 10-31]*

Figure 10-30. *At 10,000' MSL, 44 percent more room is needed to complete a turn due to density altitude.*

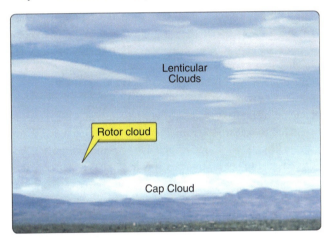

Figure 10-31. *Rotor and cap clouds with lenticulars above.*

Preflight Preparation

The amount of preflight preparation depends on the height potential of the wave itself. Assume that the pilot is planning a flight above 18,000 feet MSL during the winter. (Pilots planning wave flights to much lower altitudes can reduce the list of preparation items accordingly.)

At all times during flights above 14,000 feet MSL, and for flights of more than 30 minutes above 12,500 feet MSL up to and including 14,000 feet MSL, 14 CFR states that required crewmembers must use supplemental oxygen. Pilots must be aware of their own physiology; however, it may be wise to use oxygen at altitudes well below 14,000 feet MSL. In addition, pilots should recognize signs of hypoxia.

When flying at higher altitudes, the inside of the glider can get cold. The portions of your body exposed to the sun through the canopy might feel comfortable but your feet will probably feel the temperature drop and could get cold. It is important to prepare for this and pack thermal underwear, wear warm socks and shoes and have gloves easily accessible during the flight.

Within the continental United States, Class A airspace lies between 18,000 and 60,000 feet MSL (flight level (FL) 180 to FL 600). Generally, flights in Class A airspace must be conducted under instrument flight rules (IFR). However, several clubs and glider operations have established so-called wave windows. These are special areas, arranged in agreement with air traffic control (ATC), in which gliders are allowed to operate above 18,000 feet MSL under visual flight rules (VFR) operations. Wave windows have very specific boundaries. Thus, to maintain this privilege, it is imperative to stay within the designated window. On any given day, the wave window may be opened to a specific altitude during times specified by ATC. Each wave window has its own set of procedures agreed upon with ATC. All glider pilots should become familiar with the procedures and required radio frequencies.

True airspeed (TAS) becomes a consideration at higher altitudes. To avoid the possibility of flutter, some gliders require a reduced indicated never-exceed speed (V_{NE}) as a function of altitude. For instance, the Pilot's Operating Handbook (POH) for one common two-seat glider, list a V_{NE} at sea level of 135 knots. However, at 19,000 feet MSL, it is only 109 knots. Study the glider's POH carefully for any limitations on indicated airspeeds.

There is always the possibility of not contacting the wave. Sink on the downside of a lee wave can be high—2,000 fpm or more. In addition, missing the wave often means a trip back through the turbulent rotor. The workload and stress level in either case can be high. To reduce the workload, it is a good idea to have minimum return altitudes from several locations calculated ahead of time. In addition, plan for some worse case scenarios. For instance, consider what off-field landing options are available if the planned minimum return altitude proves inadequate.

A normal preflight of the glider should be performed. In addition, check the lubricant that has been used on control fittings. Some lubricants can become very stiff when cold. Also, check for water from melting snow or a recent rain in the spoilers or dive brakes. Freezing water in the spoilers or drive brakes at altitude can make them difficult to open. Checking the spoilers or dive brakes occasionally during a high climb helps avoid this problem. A freshly charged battery is recommended, since cold temperatures can reduce battery effectiveness.

Check the radio and accessory equipment, such as a microphone in the oxygen mask even if it is not generally used. As mentioned, the oxygen system is vital. Other specific items to check depend on the system being used.

A briefing with the tow pilot is even more important before a wave tow. Routes, minimum altitudes, rotor avoidance (if possible), anticipated tow altitude, and eventualities should be discussed on the ground prior to flight.

After all preparations are complete, it is time to get in the glider. Some pilots may be using a parachute for the first time on wave flights, so become familiar with its proper fitting and use. The parachute fits on top of clothing that is much bulkier than for normal soaring, so the cockpit can suddenly seem quite cramped. It takes several minutes to get settled and organized. Make sure radio and oxygen are easily accessible. If possible, the oxygen mask should be in place, since the climb in the wave can be very rapid. At the very least, the mask should be set up so that it is ready for use in a few seconds. All other gear (mittens, microphone, maps, barograph, etc.) should be securely stowed in anticipation of the rotor. Check for full, free rudder movement since footwear is probably larger than normal. In addition, given the bulky cold-weather clothing, check to make sure the canopy clearance is adequate. The pilot's head can break a canopy in rotor turbulence, so seat and shoulder belts should be tightly secured. This may be difficult to achieve with the extra clothing and accessories, but take the time to ensure everything is secure. There will not be time to attend to such matters once the rotor is encountered.

Getting Into the Wave

There are two ways to get into the wave: soaring into it or being towed directly into it. Three main wave entries while soaring are thermaling into the wave, climbing the rotor, and transitioning into the wave from slope soaring.

At times, an unstable layer lower than the mountaintop is capped by a strong, stable layer. If other conditions are favorable, the overlying stable layer may support lee waves. On these days, it is sometimes possible to avoid the rotor and thermal into the wave. Whether lee waves are suspected or not, the air near the thermal top may become turbulent. At this point, attempt a penetration upwind into smooth wave lift. A line of cumulus downwind of and aligned parallel to the ridge or mountain range is a clue that waves may be present. *[Figure 10-32]*

Another possibility is to tow into the upside of the rotor, then climb the rotor into the wave. This can be rough, difficult, and prone to failure. The technique is to find a part of the rotor that is going up and try to stay in it. The rotor lift is usually stationary over the ground. Either perform a figure 8 in the rotor lift to avoid drifting downwind, fly several circles with an occasional straight leg, or fly straight into the wind for several seconds until lift diminishes. Then, circle to reposition in the lift. The choice that works depends on the size of the lift and the wind strength. Since rotors have rapidly changing regions of very turbulent lift and sink, simple airspeed and bank angle control can become difficult. This wave-entry technique is not for new pilots.

Depending on the topography near the soaring site, it may be possible to transition from slope lift into a lee wave that is created by upwind topography as shown in *Figure 9-27*. In this case, climb as high as possible in slope lift, then penetrate upwind into the lee wave. When the lee waves are in phase with the topography, it is often possible to climb from slope to wave lift without the rotor. At times, the glider pilot may not realize wave has been encountered until finding lift steadily increasing as the glider climbs from the ridge. Climbing in slope lift and then turning downwind to encounter possible lee waves produced downwind of the ridge is generally not recommended. Even with a tailwind, the lee-side sink can put the glider on the ground before the wave is contacted.

Figure 10-32. *Thermaling into wave.*

Towing into the wave can be accomplished by either towing ahead of the rotor or through the rotor. Complete avoidance of the rotor generally increases the tow pilot's willingness to perform future wave tows. If possible, tow around the rotor and then directly into the wave lift. This may be feasible if the soaring site is located near one end of the wave-producing ridge or mountain range. A detour around the rotor may require more time on tow, but it is well worth the diversion. *[Figure 10-33]*

Often, a detour around the rotor is not possible and a tow directly through the rotor is the only route to the wave. The rotor turbulence is, on rare occasion, only light. However, moderate to severe turbulence is usually encountered. The nature of rotor turbulence differs from turbulent thermal days, with sharp, chaotic horizontal and vertical gusts along with rapid accelerations and decelerations. At times, the rotor can become so rough that even experienced pilots may elect to remain on the ground. Any pilot inexperienced in flying through rotors should obtain instruction before attempting a tow through rotor.

When towing through a rotor, being out of position is normal. Glider pilots must maintain position horizontally and vertically as best they can. Pilots should also be aware that an immediate release may be necessary at any time if turbulence becomes too violent. Slack-producing situations are common, due to a rapid deceleration of the towplane. The glider pilot must react quickly to slack if it occurs and recognize that slack is about to occur and correct accordingly. The vertical position should be the normal high tow. Any tow position that is lower than normal runs the risk of the slack line coming back over the glider. On the other hand, care should be taken to tow absolutely no higher than normal to avoid a forced release should the towplane suddenly drop. Gusts may also cause an excessive bank of the glider, and it may take a moment to roll back to level. Full aileron and rudder deflection, held for a few seconds, is sometimes needed.

Progress through the rotor is often indicated by noting the trend of the variometer. General downswings are replaced by general upswings, usually along with increasing turbulence. The penetration into the smooth wave lift can be quick—in a matter of few seconds—while at other times it can be more gradual. Note any lenticulars above; a position upwind of the clouds helps confirm contact with the wave. If in doubt, tow a few moments longer to be sure. Once confident about having contacted the wave lift, make the release. If heading into more or less crosswind, the glider should release and fly straight or with a crab angle. If flying directly into the wind, the glider should turn a few degrees to establish a crosswind crab angle. The goal is to avoid drifting downwind and immediately losing the wave. After release, the towplane should descend and/or turn away to separate from the glider. Possible nonstandard procedures need to be briefed with the tow pilot before takeoff. *[Figures 10-34 and 10-35]*

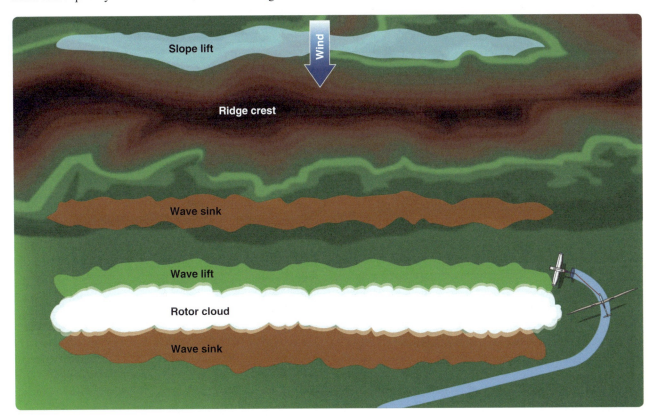

Figure 10-33. *If possible, tow around the rotor directly into the wave.*

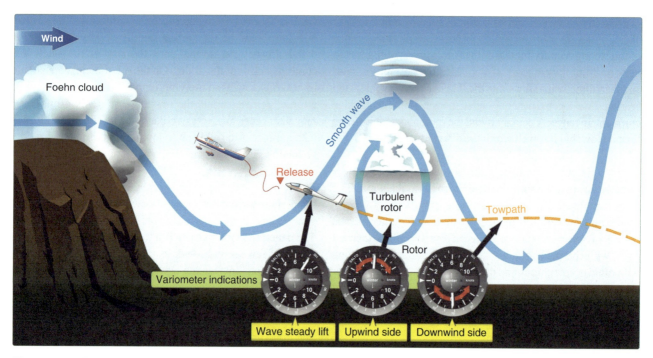

Figure 10-34. *Variometer indications during the penetration into the wave.*

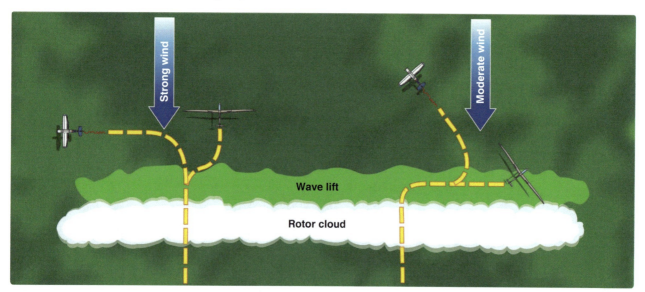

Figure 10-35. *Possible release and separation on a wave tow.*

Flying in the Wave

Once the wave has been contacted, the best techniques for utilizing the lift depend on the extent of the lift (especially in the direction along the ridge or mountain range producing the wave) and the strength of the wind. The lift may initially be weak. In such circumstances, be patient and stay with the initial slow climb. Patience is usually rewarded with better lift as the climb continues. At other times, the variometer may be pegged at 1,000 fpm directly after release from tow.

If the wind is strong enough (40 knots or more), find the strongest portion of the wave and point into the wind, and adjust speed so that the glider remains in the strong lift. The best lift is found along the upwind side of the rotor cloud or just upwind of any lenticulars. In the best-case scenario, the required speed is close to the glider's minimum sink speed. In quite strong winds, it may be necessary to fly faster than minimum sink to maintain position in the best lift. Under those conditions, flying slower allows the glider to drift downwind (fly backward over the ground) and into the down side of the wave. This can be a costly mistake since it is difficult to penetrate back into the strong headwind. When the lift is strong, it is easy to drift downwind while climbing into stronger winds aloft, so it pays to be attentive to the position relative to rotor clouds or lenticulars. If no clouds exist, special attention is needed to judge wind drift by finding nearby ground references. It may be necessary to increase speed with altitude to maintain position in the best lift. Often the wind is strong, but not quite strong enough for the glider to remain stationary over the ground so that the glider slowly moves upwind out of the best lift. If this occurs, turn slightly from a direct upwind heading, drift slowly downwind into better lift, and turn back into the wind before drifting too far. *[Figure 10-36]*

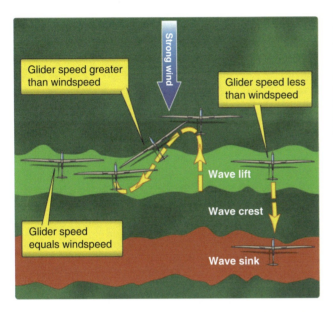

Figure 10-36. *Catching a thermal by flying upwind away from the slope lift.*

Often, the wave lift is not perfectly stationary over the ground since small changes in windspeed and/or stability can alter the wavelength of the lee wave within minutes. If lift begins to decrease while climbing in the wave, one of these things has occurred: the glider is nearing the top of the wave, the glider has moved out of the best lift, or the wavelength of the lee wave has changed. In any case, it is time to explore the area for better lift, and it is best to search upwind first. Searching upwind first allows the pilot to drift downwind back into the up part of the wave if he or she is wrong. Searching downwind first can make it difficult or impossible to contact the lift again if sink on the downside of the wave is encountered. In addition, caution is needed to avoid exceeding the glider's maneuvering speed or rough-air redline, since a penetration from the down side of the wave may put the glider back in the rotor. *[Figure 10-37]*

If the winds are moderate (20 to 40 knots), and the wave extends along the ridge or mountain range for a few miles, it is best to fly back and forth along the wave lift while crabbing into the wind. This technique is similar to slope soaring, using the rotor cloud or lenticular as a reference. All turns

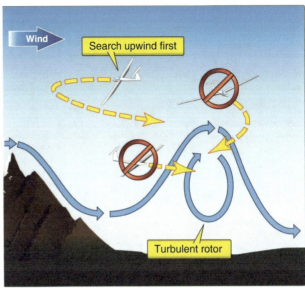

Figure 10-37. *Search upwind first to avoid sink behind the wave crest or the rotor.*

should be into the wind to avoid being on the down side of the wave or back into the rotor. Once again, it is easy to drift downwind into sink while climbing higher, and searching for better lift should be done upwind first. When making an upwind turn to change course 180°, remember that the heading change will be less, depending on the strength of the wind. Note the crab angle needed to stay in lift on the first leg, and assume that same crab angle after completing the upwind turn. This prevents the glider from drifting too far downwind upon completing the upwind turn. With no cloud, ground references are used to maintain the proper crab angle, and avoid drifting downwind out of the lift. While climbing higher into stronger winds, it may become possible to transition from crabbing back and forth to a stationary upwind heading. *[Figure 10-38]*

Weaker winds (15 to 20 knots) sometimes require different techniques. Lee waves from smaller ridges can form in relatively weak winds of approximately 15 knots. Wave lift from larger mountains rapidly decreases when climbing to a height where winds aloft diminish. As long as the lift area is big enough, use a technique similar to that used in moderate winds. Near the wave top, there sometimes remains only a small area that still provides lift. In order to attain the maximum height, fly shorter figure 8 patterns within the remaining lift. If the area of lift is so small that consistent climb is not possible, fly a series of circles with an occasional leg into the wind to avoid drifting too far downwind. Another possibility is an oval-shaped pattern—fly straight into the wind in lift and, as it diminishes, fly a quick 360° turn to reposition. These last two techniques do not work as well in moderate winds, and not at all in strong winds since it is too easy to be downwind of the lift and into heavy sink. *[Figure 10-39]*

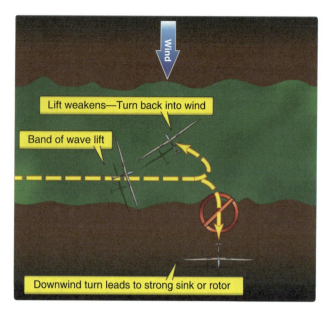

Figure 10-38. *Proper crabbing to stay in lift and effects of upwind turn (correct) or downwind turn (incorrect).*

In the discussion thus far, a climb in the primary wave has been assumed. It is also possible to climb in the secondary or tertiary lee wave (if existing on a given day) and then penetrate into the next wave upwind. The success of this depends on wind strength, clouds, the intensity of sink downwind of wave crests, and the performance of the glider. Depending on the height attained in the secondary or tertiary lee wave, a trip through the rotor of the next wave upwind is a distinct possibility. Caution is needed if penetrating upwind at high speed. The transition into the downwind side of the rotor can be as abrupt as on the upwind side, so speed should be reduced at the first hint of turbulence. In any case, expect to lose a surprising amount of altitude while penetrating upwind through the sinking side of the next upwind wave. *[Figure 10-40]*

If a quick descent is needed or desired, the sink downwind of the wave crest can be used. Sink can easily be twice as strong as lift encountered upwind of the crest. Eventual descent into downwind rotor is also likely. Sometimes the space between a rotor cloud and overlying lenticulars is inadequate and a transition downwind cannot be accomplished safely. In this case, a crosswind detour may be possible if the wave is produced by a relatively short ridge or mountain range. If clouds negate a downwind or crosswind departure from the wave, a descent on the upwind side of the wave crest is needed. Spoilers or dive brakes may be used to descend through the updraft, followed by a transition under the rotor cloud and through the rotor. A descent can be achieved by moving upwind of a very strong wave lift if spoilers or dive brakes alone do not allow an adequately fast descent. A trip back through the rotor is at best unpleasant. At worst, it can be dangerous if the transition back into the rotor is done with too much speed. In addition, strong wave lift and lift on the upwind side of the rotor may make it difficult to stay out of the rotor cloud. This wave descent requires a good deal of caution and emphasizes the importance of an exit strategy before climbing too high in the wave, keeping in mind that conditions and clouds can rapidly evolve during the climb.

Some of the dangers and precautions associated with wave soaring have already been mentioned. Those and others are summarized below.

- If any signs of hypoxia appear, check the oxygen system and immediately begin a descent to lower altitudes below which oxygen is not needed. Do not delay!

- Eventually, a pilot becomes cold at altitude regardless of how warmly the pilot is dressed. Descend well before it becomes uncomfortably cold.

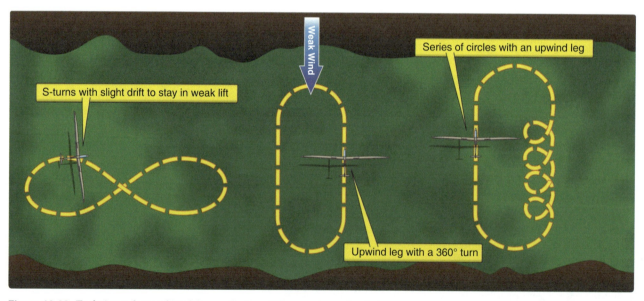

Figure 10-39. *Techniques for working lift near the top of the wave in weak winds.*

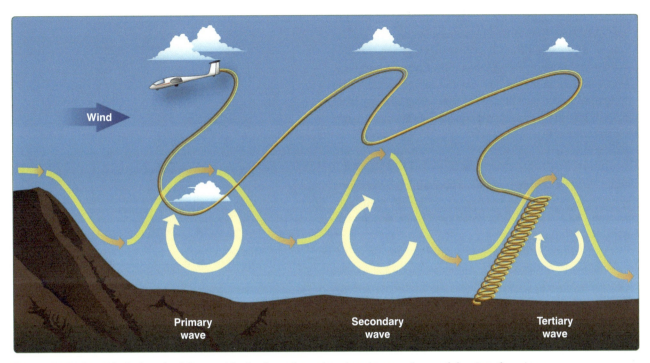

Figure 10-40. *Possible flightpath while transitioning from the tertiary into the secondary and then into the primary.*

- Rotor turbulence can be severe or extreme. Caution is needed on tow and when transitioning from smooth wave flow (lift or sink) to rotor. Rotors near the landing area can cause strong shifting surface winds of 20 or 30 knots. Wind shifts up to 180° sometimes occur in less than a minute at the surface under rotors.

- Warm, moist exhaled air can cause frost on the canopy, restricting vision. Opening air vents may alleviate the problem or delay frost formation. Clear vision panels may also be installed. If frost cannot be controlled, descend before frost becomes a hazard.

- In wet waves, those associated with a great deal of cloud, beware of the gaps closing beneath the glider. If trapped above cloud, a benign spiral mode is an option, but only if this mode has been previously explored and found stable for the glider.

- Know the time of actual sunset. At legal sunset, bright sunshine is still found at 25,000 feet while the ground below is already quite dark. Even at an average 1,000 fpm descent, it takes 20 minutes to lose 20,000 feet.

Caution: Flights under a rotor cloud can encounter high sink rates and should be approached with extreme caution.

Soaring Convergence Zones

Convergence zones are most easily spotted when cumulus clouds are present. They appear as a single, straight, or curved cloud street, sometimes well defined and sometimes not. The edge of a field of cumulus can mark convergence between a mesoscale air mass that is relatively moist and/or unstable from one that is much drier and/or more stable. Often, the cumulus along convergence lines have a base lower on one side than the other, similar to that in *Figure 9-31*.

With no cloud present, a convergence zone is sometimes marked by a difference in visibility across it, which may be subtle or distinct. When there are no clues in the sky itself, there may be some clues on the ground. If lakes are nearby, look for wind differences on lakes a few miles apart. A lake showing a wind direction different from the ambient flow for the day may be a clue. Wind direction shown by smoke can also be an important indicator. A few dust devils, or—even better—a short line of them, may indicate the presence of ordinary thermals versus those triggered by convergence. Spotting subtle clues takes practice and good observational skills, and is often the reason a few pilots are still soaring while others are already on the ground.

The best soaring technique for this type of lift depends on the nature of the convergence zone itself. For instance, a sea-breeze front may be well defined and marked by curtain clouds; the pilot can fly straight along the line in fairly steady lift. A weaker convergence line often produces more lift than sink; the pilot must fly slower in lift and faster in sink. An even weaker convergence line may simply serve as focus for more frequent thermals; normal thermal techniques are used along the convergence line. Some combination of straight legs along the line with an occasional stop to thermal is often used.

Convergence zone lift can at times be somewhat turbulent, especially if air from different sources is mixing, such as along a sea-breeze front. The general roughness may be the only clue of being along some sort of convergence line. There can also be narrow and rough (but strong) thermals within the convergence line. Work these areas like any other difficult thermals, using steeper bank angles and more speed for maneuverability.

Combined Sources of Updrafts

Finally, lift sources have been categorized into four types: thermal, slope, wave, and convergence. Often, more than one type of lift exists at the same time, such as thermals with slope lift, thermaling into a wave, convergence zones enhancing thermals, thermal waves, and wave and slope lift. In mountainous terrain, it is possible for all four lift types to exist on a single day. The glider pilot needs to remain mentally nimble to take advantage of various types and locations of rising air during the flight.

Nature does not know that it must only produce rising air based on these four lift categories. Sources of lift that do not fit one of the four lift types discussed probably exist. For instance, there have been a few reports of pilots soaring in travelling waves, the source of which was not known. At some soaring sites, it is sometimes difficult to classify the type of lift. This should not be a problem. Simply work the mystery lift as needed, then ponder its nature after the flight.

Chapter 11
Cross-Country Soaring

Introduction

A cross-country flight is defined as one in which the glider has flown beyond gliding distance from the local soaring site. Cross-country soaring seems simple enough in theory; in reality, it requires a great deal more preparation and decision-making than local soaring flights. Items that must be considered during cross-country flights are how good the thermals ahead are, and if they will remain active, what the landing possibilities are, which airport along the course has a runway that is favorable for the prevailing wind conditions. What effect will the headwind have on the glide? What is the best speed to fly in sink between thermals?

Flying cross-country using thermals is the basis of this chapter. A detailed description of cross-country soaring using ridge or wave lift is beyond the scope of this chapter.

Flight Preparation and Planning

Adequate soaring skills form the basis of the pilot's preparation for cross-country soaring. Until the pilot has flown several flights in excess of 2 hours and can locate and utilize thermals consistently, the pilot should focus on improving those skills before attempting cross-country flights.

Any cross-country flight may end in an off-field landing, so short-field landing skills are essential. These landings should be practiced on local flights by setting up a simulated off-field landing area. Care is needed to avoid interfering with the normal flow of traffic during simulated off-field landings. The first few simulated landings should be done with an instructor, and several should be done without the use of the altimeter.

The landing area can be selected from the ground, but the best training is selecting one from the air. A self-launching glider or other powered aircraft for landing area selection training and simulated approaches to these areas is a good investment, if one is available.

Once soaring skills have been honed, the pilot needs to be able to determine position along a route of flight. A Sectional Aeronautical Chart, or sectional, is a map soaring pilots use during cross-country flights. They are updated every 6 months and contain general information, such as topography, cities, major and minor roads and highways, lakes, and other features that may stand out from the air, such as a ranch in an otherwise featureless prairie. In addition, sectionals show the location of private and public airports, airways, restricted and warning areas, and boundaries and vertical limits of different classes of airspace. Information on airports includes field elevation, orientation and length of all paved runways, runway lighting, and radio frequencies in use. Each sectional features a comprehensive legend. A detailed description of the sectional chart is found in FAA-H-8083-25, the Pilot's Handbook of Aeronautical Knowledge. *Figure 11-1* shows a sample sectional chart.

The best place to become familiar with sectional charts is on the ground. It is instructive to fly some "virtual" cross-country flights in various directions from the local soaring site. In addition to studying the terrain (hills, mountains, large lakes) that may affect the soaring along the route, study the various lines and symbols. What airports are available on course? Do any have a control tower? Can all the numbers and symbols for each airport be identified? If not, find them on the legend. Is there Class B, C, or D airspace en route? Are there any restricted areas? Are there airways along the flightpath? Once comfortable with the sectional from ground study, it can be used on some local flights to practice locating features within a few miles of the soaring site.

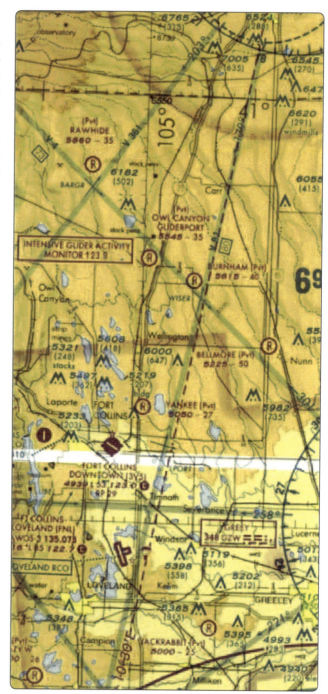

Figure 11-1. *Excerpt from a Sectional Aeronautical Chart.*

Any cross-country flight may end with a landing away from the home soaring site, so pilots and crews should be prepared for the occurrence prior to flight. Sometimes an aerotow retrieve can be made if the flight terminates at an airport; however, trailer retrieval is more typical. Both the trailer and tow vehicle need a preflight before departing on the flight. The trailer should be roadworthy and set up for the specific glider. Stowing and towing a glider in an inappropriate trailer can lead to damage. The driver should be familiar with procedures for towing and backing a long trailer. The tow vehicle should be strong and stable enough for towing. Both radio and telephone communication options should be discussed with the retrieval crew.

Before any flight, obtain a standard briefing and a soaring forecast from the Automated Flight Service Station (AFSS). As discussed in Chapter 9, Soaring Weather, the briefer supplies general weather information for the planned route, as well as any NOTAMs, AIRMETs, or SIGMETs, winds aloft, an approaching front, or areas of likely thunderstorm activity. Depending on the weather outlook, beginners may find it useful to discuss options with more experienced cross-country pilots at their soaring site.

Many pilots have specific goals in mind for their next cross-country flight. Several options should be planned ahead based on the area and different weather scenarios. For instance, if the goal is a closed-course 300 nautical mile (NM) flight, several likely out-and-return or triangle courses should be laid out ahead of time, so that on the specific day, the best task can be selected based on the weather outlook. There are numerous final details that need attention on the morning of the flight, so special items should be organized and readied the day before the flight.

Lack of preparation can lead to delays, which may mean not enough of the soaring day is left to accomplish the planned flight. Even worse, poor planning leads to hasty last-minute preparation and a rush to launch, making it easy to miss critical safety items.

Inexperienced and experienced pilots alike should use checklists for various phases of the cross-country preparation in order to organize details. When properly used, checklists can help avoid oversights, such as sectionals left at home, barograph not turned on before takeoff, etc. Checklists also aid in making certain that safety of flight items, such as all assembly items, are checked or accomplished, oxygen turned on, drinking water is in the glider, etc. Examples of checklists include the following:

- Items to take to the gliderport (food, water, battery, charts, barograph).
- Assembly must follow the Glider Flight Manual/Pilot's Operating Handbook (GFM/POH) and add items as needed.
- Positive control check.
- Prelaunch (water, food, charts, glide calculator, oxygen on, sunscreen, cell phone).
- Pretakeoff checklist itself.
- Briefing checklist for tow pilot, ground crew, and retrieval crew.

Being better organized before the flight leads to less stress during the flight, enhancing flight safety.

Personal and Special Equipment

Many items not required for local soaring are needed for cross-country flights. Pilot comfort and physiology is even more important on cross-country flights since these flights often last longer than local flights. An adequate supply of drinking water is essential to avoid dehydration. Many pilots use the backpack drinking system with readily accessible hose and bite valve that is often used by bicyclists. This system is easily stowed beside the pilot, allowing frequent sips of water. A relief system also may be needed on longer flights. Cross-country flights can last up to 8 hours or more, so food of some kind is also a good idea.

Several items should be carried in case there is an off-field landing. (For more details, see Chapter 8, Abnormal and Emergency Procedures.) First, a system for securing the glider is necessary, as is a land-out kit for the pilot. The kit varies depending on the population density and climate of the soaring area. For instance, in the Great Basin in the United States, a safe landing site may be many miles from the nearest road or ranch house. Since weather is often hot and dry during the soaring season, extra water and food should be added items. Taking good walking shoes is a good idea as well. A cell phone may prove useful for landouts in areas with some telephone coverage. Some pilots elect to carry an Emergency Position Indicating Radio Beacon (EPIRB) in remote areas in case of mishap during an off-field landing.

Cross-country soaring requires some means of measuring distances to calculate glides to the next source of lift or the next suitable landing area. Distances can be measured using a sectional chart and navigational plotter with the appropriate scale, or by use of Global Positioning System (GPS). If GPS is used, a sectional and plotter should be carried as a backup. A plotter may be made of clear plastic with a straight edge on the bottom marked with nautical or statute miles for a sectional scale on one side and World Aeronautical Chart (WAC) scale on the other. On the top of the plotter is a protractor or semicircle with degrees marked for measuring course angles. A small reference index hole is located in the center of the semicircle. *[Figure 11-2]* Prior to taking off, it may be handy to prepare a plotter for the specific glider's performance by applying some transparent tape over the plotter marked with altitudes versus range rings in still air. After a little use, the glider pilot should gain a perception of the glide angle most often evident in the conditions of the day.

Glide calculations must take into account any headwind or tailwind, as well as speeds to fly through varying sink rates as discussed in chapter 5. Tools range widely in their level

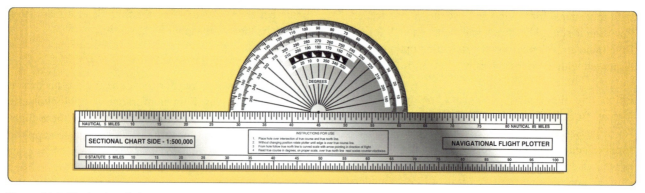

Figure 11-2. *Navigational plotter.*

of sophistication, but all are based on the performance polar for the particular glider. Most high-performance gliders usually have glide/navigation computers that automatically computer the glide ratio (L/D). The simplest glide aid is a table showing altitudes required for distance versus wind, which can be derived from the polar. To avoid a table with too many numbers, which could be confusing, some interpolation is often needed. Another option is a circular glide calculator as shown in *Figure 11-3*. This tool allows the pilot to read the altitude needed for any distance and can be set for various estimated headwinds and tailwinds. Circular glide calculators also make it easy to determine whether a pilot is actually achieving the desired glide, since heavy sink or a stronger-than-estimated headwind can cause a loss of more height with distance than was indicated by the calculator. For instance, the settings in *Figure 11-3* indicate that for the estimated 10 knot headwind, 3,600 feet is required to glide 18 miles. After gliding 5 miles, there is still 2,600 feet. Note that this only gives the altitude required to make the glide.

The pilot can also use simple formulas to mentally compute an estimated L/D. One hundred feet per minute (fpm) is approximately 1 knot. To compute your glide ratio, take groundspeed divided by vertical speed as indicated on a vertical speed indicator (VSI) or variometer, then divide by 100 (just drop the zeros). If groundspeed is not available, use indicated airspeed, which will not yield as accurate a result as groundspeed. In this case, groundspeed or indicated airspeed is 60 knots. VSI shows 300 fpm down. Calculate the glide ratio.

$$\frac{VSI}{100} = \text{vertical speed in knots}$$

$$\frac{300 \text{ fpm}}{100} = 3 \text{ knots}$$

$$\frac{\text{Groundspeed}}{\text{Vertical speed}} = \text{Glide ratio}$$

$$\frac{60 \text{ knots}}{3 \text{ knots}} = 20, \text{ a glide ratio of } 20:1$$

This is a good approximation of the current L/D.

Another method is to basically recompute a new L/D by utilizing this standard formula. Glide ratio, with respect to the air (GRA) or L/D, remains constant at a given airspeed. For example, your glider's glide ratio, lift over drag (L/D) is 30 to 1 expressed as 30:1 at a speed of 50 knots. At 50 knots with an L/D of 30:1, a 10-knot tailwind results in an effective L/D of 36:1. *[Figure 11-4]*

Figure 11-3. *Circular glider calculator.*

In addition to a glide calculator, a MacCready ring on the variometer allows the pilot to easily read the speed to fly for different sink rates. MacCready rings are specific to the type of glider and are based on the glider performance polar. (See Chapter 4, Flight Instruments, for a description of the MacCready ring.) Accurately flying the correct speed in sinking air can extend the achieved glide considerably.

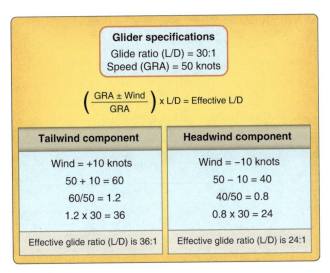

Figure 11-4. *Glide calculation example.*

Many models of electronic glide calculators now exist. Often coupled with an electronic variometer, they display the altitude necessary for distance and wind as input by the pilot. In addition, many electronic glide calculators feature speed-to-fly functions that indicate whether the pilot should fly faster or slower. Most electronic speed-to-fly directors include audio indications, so the pilot can remain visually focused outside the cockpit. The pilot should have manual backups for electronic glide calculators and speed-to-fly directors in case of a low battery or other electronic system failure.

Other equipment may be needed to verify soaring performance to receive a Federation Aeronautique Internationale (FAI) badge or record flights. These include turn-point cameras, barographs, and GPS flight recorders. For complete descriptions of these items, as well as badge or record rules, check the Soaring Society of America website (www.ssa.org) for details.

Finally, a notepad or small leg-attached clipboard on which to make notes before and during the flight is often handy. Notes prior to flight could include weather information such as winds aloft forecasts or distance between turn points. In flight, noting takeoff and start time, as well as time around any turn points, is useful to gauge average speed around the course.

Navigation

Airplane pilots navigate by pilotage (flying by reference to ground landmarks) or dead reckoning (computing a heading from true airspeed and wind, and then estimating time needed to fly to a destination). Glider pilots use pilotage since they generally cannot remain on a course line over a long distance and do not fly one speed for any length of time. Nonetheless, it is important to be familiar with the concepts of dead reckoning since a combination of the two methods is sometimes needed.

Using the Plotter

Measuring distance with the plotter is accomplished by using the straight edge. Use the Albuquerque sectional chart and measure the distance between Portales Airport (Q34) and Benger Airport (Q54), by setting the plotter with the zero mark on Portales. Read the distance of 47 nautical miles (NM) to Benger. Make sure to set the plotter with the sectional scale if using a sectional chart (as opposed to the WAC scale), otherwise the measurement will be off by a factor of two. *[Figure 11-5]*

The true heading between Portales and Benger can be determined by setting the top of the straightedge along the course line, then slide it along until the index hole is on a line of longitude intersecting the course line. Read the true heading on the outer scale, in this case, 48°. The outer scale should be used for headings with an easterly component. If the course were reversed, flying from Benger to Portales, use the inner scale, for a westerly component, to find 228°. *[Figure 11-6]*

A common error when first using the plotter is to read the course heading 180° in error. This error is easy to make by reading the scale marked W 270° instead of the scale marked E 09°. For example, the course from Portales to Benger is towards the northeast, so the heading should be somewhere between 30° and 60°, therefore the true heading of 48° is reasonable.

A Sample Cross-Country Flight

For training purposes, plan a triangle course starting at Portales Airport (PRZ), with turn points at Benger Airport (X54), and the town of Circle Back. As part of the preflight preparation, draw the course lines for the three legs. Using the plotter, determine the true heading for each leg, then correct for variation and make a written note of the magnetic heading on each leg. Use 9° east (E) variation as indicated on the sectional chart (subtract easterly variations, and add westerly variations). The first leg distance is 47 NM with a heading of 48° (48° − 9° E = 39° magnetic); the second leg is 38 NM at 178° true (178° − 9° E = 169° magnetic); the third leg is 38 NM at 282° true (282° − 9° E = 273° magnetic). *[Figure 11-7]*

Assume the base of the cumulus is forecast to be 11,000 MSL, and the winds aloft indicate 320° at 10 knots at 9,000 MSL and 330° at 20 knots at 12,000 MSL. Make a written note of the winds aloft for reference during the flight. For instance, the first leg has almost a direct crosswind from the left; on the second leg, a weaker crosswind component from the right; while the final leg is almost directly into the wind. Knowing courses and approximate headings aids the navigation and helps avoid getting lost, even though deviations to stay with the best lift are needed. During the flight, if the sky ahead

11-5

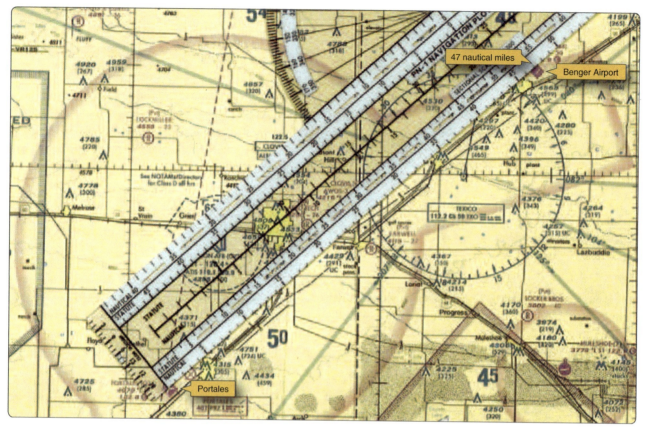

Figure 11-5. *Measuring distance using the navigation plotter.*

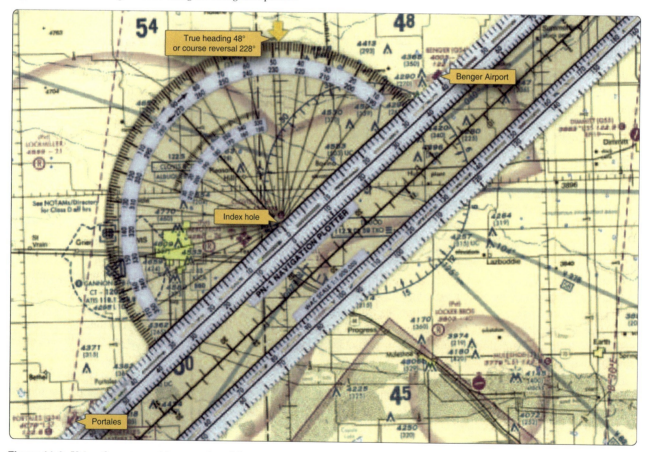

Figure 11-6. *Using the outer and inner scales of the navigation plotter.*

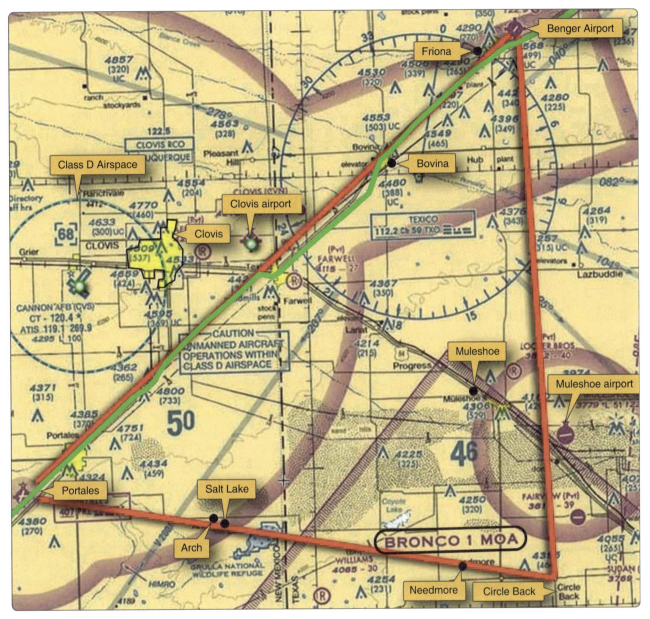

Figure 11-7. *Cross-country triangle.*

shows several equally promising cumulus clouds, choosing the one closest to the course line makes the most sense.

During preflight preparation, study the course line along each leg for expected landmarks. For instance, the first leg follows highway and parallel railroad tracks for several miles before the highway turns north. The town of Clovis should become obvious on the left. Note the Class D airspace around Cannon Air Force Base (CVS) just west of Clovis—this could be an issue if there is better soaring north of course track because of military traffic operating into Cannon. With the northwesterly wind, it is possible to be crossing the path of aircraft on a long final approach to the northwest-southeast runway at the air base.

Next is the Clovis airport (CVN) with traffic to check operating in and out of the airport. Following Clovis are Bovina and Friona; these towns can serve as landmarks for the flight. The proximity of the Texico (TXO) VOR, a VHF Omnidirectional Range station near Bovina, indicates the need for alertness for power traffic in the vicinity. The VOR serves as an approach aid to the Clovis airport.

The first turn point is easy to locate because of good landmarks, including Benger Airport (X54). *[Figure 11-8]* The second leg has fewer landmarks. After about 25 miles, the town of Muleshoe and the Muleshoe airport (2T1) should appear. The town should be on the right and the airport on the left of the intended course. Next, the course enters the Bronco 1 Military Operations Area (MOA). The dimensions of the

Figure 11-8. *Benger Airport (X54).*

MOA can be found on the sectional chart, and the automated flight service station (AFSS) should be consulted concerning the active times of this airspace. Approaching the second turn point, it is easy to confuse the towns of Circle Back and Needmore. *[Figure 11-9]* The clues are the position of Circle Back relative to an obstruction 466 feet above ground level (AGL) and a road that heads north out of Needmore. Landmarks on the third leg include power transmission lines, Salt Lake (possibly dry), the small town of Arch, and a major road coming south out of Portales. About eight miles from Portales a VOR V-280 airway is crossed.

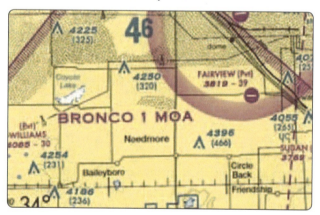

Figure 11-9. *Circle Back and Needmore.*

After a thorough preflight of the glider and all the appropriate equipment is stowed or in position for use in flight, it is time to go fly. Once in the air and on course, try to verify the winds aloft. Use pilotage to remain as close to the course line as soaring conditions permit. If course deviations become necessary, stay aware of the location of the course line to the next turn point. For instance, the Cu directly ahead indicates lift, but the one 30° off course indicates possibly even more lift,

it may be better not to deviate. If the Cu left of course indicates a possible area of lift compared to the clouds ahead and only requires a 10° off course deviation, proceed towards the lift. Knowing the present location of the glider and where the course line is located is important for keeping situational awareness.

Sometimes it is necessary to determine an approximate course once already in the air. Assume a few miles before reaching the town of Muleshoe, on the second leg, the weather ahead is not as forecast and has deteriorated—there is now a shower at the third turn point (Circle Back). Rather than continuing on to a certain landing in the rain, the decision is made to cut the triangle short and try to return directly to Portales. Measure and find that Portales is about 37 miles away, and the estimated heading is about 240°. Correct for variation (9°) for a compass heading of about 231° (240° − 9° = 231°). The northwesterly wind is almost 90° to the new course and requires a 10° or 20° crab to the right, so a heading between 250° and 270° should work, allowing for some drift in thermal climbs. With practice, the entire thought process should take little time.

The sky towards Portales indicates favorable lift conditions. However, the area along the new course includes sand hills, an area that may not have good choices for off-field landings. It may be a good idea to fly more conservatively until beyond this area and then back to where there are suitable fields for landing. Navigation, evaluation of conditions ahead, and decision-making are required until arrival back at Portales or until a safe off-field landing is completed.

Navigation Using GPS

The GPS navigation systems are available as small hand-held units. (See Chapter 4, Flight Instruments, for information on GPS and electronic flight computers.) Some pilots prefer to use existing flight computers for final glide and speed-to-fly information and add a hand-held GPS for navigation. A GPS system makes navigation easier. A GPS unit displays distance and heading to a specified point, usually found by scrolling through an internal database of waypoints. Many GPS units also continuously calculate and display ground speed. If TAS is also known, the headwind component can be calculated from the GPS by subtracting ground speed from TAS. Many GPS units also feature a moving map display that shows past and present positions in relation to various prominent landmarks like airports. These displays can often zoom in and out to various map scales. Other GPS units allow marking a spot for future reference. This feature can be used to mark the location of a thermal before going into a turn point, with the hopes that the area will still be active after rounding the turn point.

One drawback to GPS units is their attractiveness—it is easy to be distracted by the unit at the expense of flying the glider and finding lift. This can lead to a dangerous habit of focusing too much time inside the cockpit rather than scanning outside for traffic. Like any electronic instrument, GPS units can fail, so it is important to have a backup for navigation, such as a sectional and plotter.

Cross-Country Techniques

The number one rule of safe cross-country soaring is always stay within glide range of a suitable landing area. The alternate landing area may be an airport or a farmer's field. If thermaling is required just to make it to a suitable landing area, safe cross-country procedures are not being practiced. Sailplane pilots should always plan for high sink rates between thermals as there are always areas of sink around a lifting thermal to fill in the void vacated by the lifting air.

Before venturing beyond gliding distance from the home airport, thermaling and cross-country techniques can be practiced using small triangles or other short courses. Three examples are shown in *Figure 11-10*. The length of each leg depends on the performance of the glider, but they are typically small, around 5 or 10 miles each. Soaring conditions do not need to be excellent for these practice tasks but should not be so weak that it is difficult just to stay aloft. On a good day, the triangle may be flown more than once. If other airports are nearby, practice finding and switching to their communication frequency and listening to traffic in the traffic pattern. As progress is made along each leg of the triangle, frequently cross check the altitude needed to return to the home airport and abandon the course if needed. Setting a minimum altitude of 1,500 feet or 2,000 feet AGL to arrive back at the home site adds a margin of safety. Every landing after a soaring flight should be an accuracy landing.

Determining winds aloft while en route can be difficult. Often an estimate is the best that can be achieved. A first estimate is obtained from winds aloft forecasts provided by the AFSS. Once aloft, estimate windspeed and direction from the track of cumulus shadows over the ground, keeping in mind that the winds at cloud level are often different than those at lower levels. On cloudless days, obtain an estimate of wind by noting drift while thermaling. If the estimate was for a headwind of 10 knots but more height is lost on glides than the glide calculator indicates, the headwind estimate may be too low and will need to be adjusted. When flying with GPS, determine windspeed from TAS by simple subtraction. Some flight computers automatically calculate the winds aloft while other GPS systems estimate winds by calculating the drift after several thermal turns.

It is important to develop skill in quickly determining altitude needed for a measured distance using one of the glide calculator tools. For instance, while on a cross-country flight and over a good landing spot with the next good landing site a distance of 12 miles into a 10-knot headwind. [*Figure 11-11*] The glide calculator shows that 3,200 feet is needed to accomplish the glide. Add 1,500 feet above ground to allow time to set up for an off-field landing if necessary, to make the total needed 4,700 feet. The present height is only 3,800 feet, not high enough to accomplish the 12-mile glide, but still high enough to start along course. Head out adjusting the speed based on the MacCready ring or other speed director. After two miles with no lift, altitude is almost 3,300 feet, still not high enough to glide the remaining 10 miles, but high enough to turn back to the last landing site. After almost 4 miles, a 4-knot thermal is encountered at about 2,700 feet and provides for a climb to 4,300 feet.

When using the glide calculator tool, keep in mind that these calculations account for only the glider's calm air rate of descent. Any sink can drastically affect these calculations and make them worthless. In times of good lift, there will also be areas of strong sink. A sailplane pilot must learn to read the sky to find the lift and avoid or pass through the sink as quickly as possible. Time in lift is good and time in sink is bad. A good sailplane pilot will be thoroughly aware of that particular sailplane's polar curves and the effects from different conditions of lift, sink, and winds.

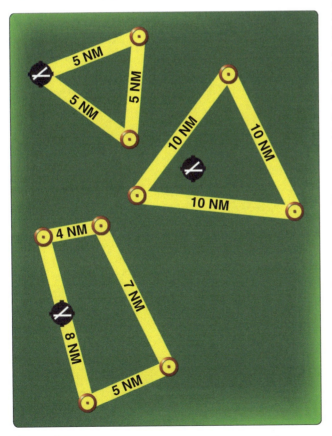

Figure 11-10. *Examples of practice cross country courses.*

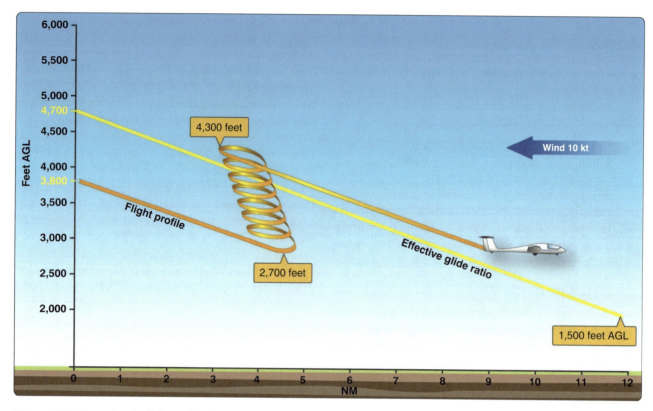

Figure 11-11. *Example of a flight profile during a cross-country course.*

During the climb, the downwind drift of the thermal moves the glider back on course approximately a half mile. Now, there is almost 9 miles to glide to the next landing spot, and a check of the glide calculator indicates 2,400 feet are needed for the glide into the 10-knot headwind, plus 1,500 feet at the destination, for a total of 3,900 feet. Now, there is 400 feet above the minimum glide with a margin to plan the landing. In the previous example, had the thermal topped at 3,600 feet (instead of 4,300 feet) there would not be enough altitude to glide the 9 miles into the 10-knot headwind. However, there would be enough height to continue further on course in hopes of finding more lift before needing to turn downwind back to the previous landing spot. Any cross-country soaring flight involves dozens of decisions and calculations such as this. In addition, safety margins may need to be more conservative if there is reason to believe the glide may not work as planned, for example, other pilots reporting heavy sink along the intended course.

On any soaring flight, there is an altitude when a decision must be made to cease attempts to work thermals and commit to a landing. This is especially true of cross-country flights in which landings are often in unfamiliar places and feature additional pressures like those discussed in Chapter 8, Abnormal and Emergency Procedures. It is even more difficult on cross-country flights to switch the mental process from soaring to committing to a landing. For beginners, an altitude of 1,000 feet AGL is a recommended minimum to commit to landing. A better choice is to pick a landing site by 1,500 feet AGL, which still allows time to be ready for a thermal while further inspecting the intended landing area. The exact altitude where the thought processes should shift from soaring to landing preparation depends on the terrain. In areas of the Midwest in the United States, landable fields may be present every few miles, allowing a delay in field selection to a lower altitude. In areas of the desert southwest or the Great Basin, landing sites may be 30 or more miles apart, so focusing on a landing spot must begin at much higher altitudes above the ground.

Once committed in the pattern, do not try to thermal away again. Accidents occur due to stalls or spins from thermaling attempts in the pattern. Damage to the glider's airframe can and has occurred after a pilot drifted away from a safe landing spot while trying to thermal from low altitudes. When the thermal dissipates, the pilot is too far beyond the site to return for a safe landing and is left with a less suitable landing choice. It is easy to fall into this trap. In the excitement of preparing for an off-field landing, do not forget a prelanding checklist.

A common first cross-country flight is a 50-kilometer (32 statute miles) straight distance flight with a landing at another field. The distance is short enough that it can be flown at a leisurely pace on an average soaring day and also qualifies for part of the FAI Silver Badge. Prepare the course well and find out about all available landing areas along the way. Get to the soaring site early so there is no rush in the preflight preparations. Once airborne, take time to get a feel for the day's thermals. If the day looks good enough and height is adequate to set off on course, commit to the task! Landing away from the home field for the first time requires skill, planning, and knowledge but is a confidence builder whether the task was accomplished or not.

Soaring Faster and Farther

Early cross-country flights, including small practice triangles within gliding range of the home field, are excellent preparation and training for longer cross-country flights. The FAI Gold Badge requires a 300-kilometer (187 statute miles) cross-country flight, which can be straight out distance or a declared triangle or out-and-return flight. An average cross-country speed of 20 or 30 miles per hour (mph) may have been adequate for a 32-mile flight, but that average speed is too low on most days for longer flights. Flying at higher average cross-country speeds also allows for farther soaring flights.

Improvement of cross-country skills comes primarily from practice, but reviewing theory as experience is gained is also important. A theory or technique that initially made little sense to the beginner has real meaning and significance after several cross-country flights. Postflight self-critique is a useful tool to improve skills.

In the context of cross-country soaring, flying faster means achieving a faster average groundspeed. The secret to faster cross-country flight lies in spending less time climbing and more time gliding. This is achieved by using only the better thermals and spending more time in lifting air and less time in sinking air. Optimum speeds between thermals are given by MacCready ring theory and/or speed-to-fly theory, and can be determined through proper use of the MacCready speed ring or equivalent electronic speed director.

Height Bands

On most soaring days there is an altitude range, called a height band, in which the thermal strength is at a maximum. Height bands can be defined as the optimum altitude range in which to climb and glide on a given day. For instance, a thermal in the 3,000 feet AGL range may have 200 to 300 fpm thermals, increasing to 500 fpm at 5,000 feet AGL range then weaken before topping out at 6,000 feet AGL. In this case, the height band would be 2,000 feet deep between 3,000 feet and 5,000 feet AGL. Staying within the height band gives the best (fastest) climbs. Avoid stopping for weaker thermals while within the height band unless there is a good reason.

On another day, thermals may be strong from 1,000 feet to 6,000 feet AGL before weakening, which would suggest a height band 5,000 feet deep. In this case, however, depending on thermal spacing, terrain, pilot experience level, and other factors, the height band would be 2,000 feet or 3,000 feet up to 6,000 feet AGL. Avoid continuing to the lower bounds of strong thermals (1,000 feet AGL) since failure to find a thermal there gives no extra time before committing to a landing. *[Figure 11-12]*

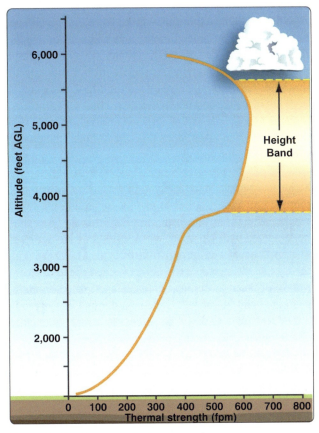

Figure 11-12. *Example of the height band.*

NOTE: Automated Flight Service Stations (AFSS) report cloud levels as AGL in METARS, and PIREPS are reported as MSL. Area forecasts gives clouds as MSL if above 1,000' AGL. Pilots must be careful to determine which value is being presented. This is very important when glider pilots travel to higher elevation airports and must subtract field elevation from MSL reports to ensure cloud clearances.

Determining the top of the height band is a matter of personal preference and experience, but a rule of thumb puts the top at an altitude where thermals drop off to 75 percent of the best achieved climb. If maximum thermal strength in the height band is 400 fpm, leave when thermals decrease to 300 fpm for more than a turn or two. The thermal strength used to determine the height band should be an average achieved climb. Many electronic variometers have an average function that displays average climb over specific time intervals.

Another technique involves simply timing the altitude gained over 30 seconds or 1 minute.

Theoretically, the optimum average speed is attained if the MacCready ring is set for the achieved rate of climb within the height band. To do this, rotate the ring so that the index mark is at the achieved rate of climb (for instance, 400 fpm) rather than at zero (the setting used for maximum distance). A series of climbs and glides gives the optimum balance between spending time climbing and gliding. The logic is that, on stronger days, the extra altitude lost by flying faster between thermals is more than made up in the strong lift during climbs. Flying slower than the MacCready setting does not make the best use of available climbs. Flying faster than the MacCready setting uses too much altitude between thermals; it then takes more than the optimum amount of time to regain the altitude.

Strict use of the MacCready ring assumes that the next thermal is at least as strong as that set on the ring and can be reached with the available altitude. Efforts to fly faster must be tempered with judgment when conditions are not ideal. Factors that may require departure from the MacCready ring theory include terrain (extra height needed ahead to clear a ridge), distance to the next landable spot, or deteriorating soaring conditions ahead. If the next thermal appears to be out of reach before dropping below the height band, either climb higher, glide more slowly, or both.

To illustrate the use of speed-to-fly theory, assume there are four gliders at the same height. Ahead are three weak cumulus clouds, each produced by 200-fpm thermals, then a larger cumulus with 600 fpm thermals under it, as in *Figure 11-13*.

- Pilot 1 sets the ring to 6 knots for the anticipated strong climb under the large cumulus, but the aggressive approach has the glider on the ground before reaching the cloud.

- Pilot 2 sets the ring for 2 knots and climbs under each cloud until resetting the ring to 6 knots after climbing under the third weak cumulus, in accordance with strict speed-to-fly theory.

- Pilot 3 is conservative and sets the ring to zero for the maximum glide.

- Pilot 4 calculates the altitude needed to glide to the large cumulus using an intermediate setting of 3 knots, and finds the glider can glide to the cloud and still be within the height band.

By the time pilot 4 has climbed under the large cumulus, the pilot is well ahead of the other two pilots and is relaying retrieve instructions for pilot 1. This example illustrates the science and art of faster cross-country soaring. The science is provided by speed-to-fly theory, while the art involves interpreting and modifying the theory for the actual conditions. Knowledge of speed-to-fly theory is important as a foundation. How to apply the art of cross-country soaring stems from practice and experience.

Tips and Techniques

The height band changes during the day. On a typical soaring day, thermal height and strength often increases rapidly

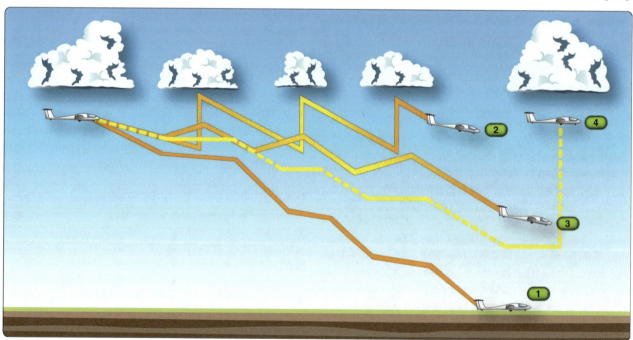

Figure 11-13. *Example of glides achieved for different MacCready ring settings.*

during late morning, and then both remain somewhat steady for several hours during the afternoon. The height band rises and broadens with thermal height. Sometimes the top of the height band is limited by the base of cumulus clouds. Cloud base may slowly increase by thousands of feet over several hours, during which the height band also increases. Thermals often "shut off" rapidly late in the day, so a good rule of thumb is to stay higher late in the day. *[Figure 11-14]*

It is a good idea to stop and thermal when at or near the bottom of the height band. Pushing too hard can lead to an early off-field landing. Pushing too hard leads to loss of time at lower altitudes because the pilot is trying to climb in weak lift conditions.

Another way to increase cross-country speed is to avoid turning at all. A technique known as dolphin flight can be used to cover surprising distances on thermal days with little or no circling. The idea is to speed up in sink and slow down in lift while only stopping to circle in the best thermals. The speed to fly between lift areas is based on the appropriate MacCready setting. This technique is effective when thermals are spaced relatively close together, as occurs along a cloud street.

As an example, assume two gliders are starting at the same point and flying under a cloud street with frequent thermals and only weak sink between thermals. Glider 1 uses the conditions more efficiently by flying faster in the sink and slower in lift. In a short time, glider 1 has gained distance on glider 2. Glider 2 conserves altitude and stays close to cloud base by flying best L/D through weak sink. To stay under the clouds, he is forced to fly faster in areas of lift, exactly opposite of flying fast in sink, slow in lift. At the end of the cloud street, one good climb quickly puts glider 1 near cloud base and well ahead of glider 2. *[Figure 11-15]* The best speed to fly decreases time in sink and therefore

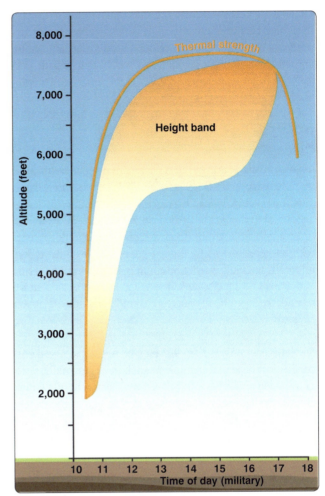

Figure 11-14. *Thermal height and height band versus time of day.*

decreases the overall amount of descent but produces the best forward progress. Being slower in sink increases time descending and slows forward progress, while being fast in lift decreases time in lift and altitude gained.

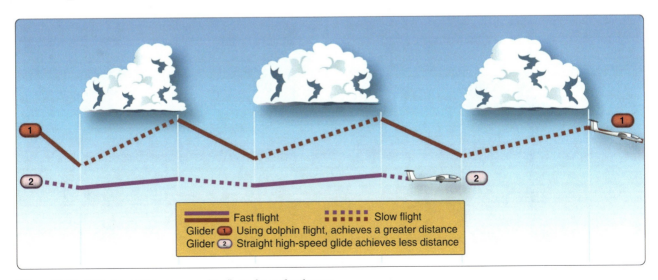

Figure 11-15. *Advantage of proper speed to fly under a cloud street.*

On an actual cross-country flight, a combination of dolphin flight and classic climb and glide is frequently needed. In a previous example, the two pilots who decided not to stop and circle in the weaker thermals would still benefit from dolphin flight techniques in the lift and sink until stopping to climb in the strong lift.

Special Situations

Course Deviations

Diversion on a soaring cross-country flight is the norm rather than the exception. Some soaring days supply fair weather cumulus evenly spaced across all quadrants, and it is still beneficial to deviate toward stronger lift. Deviations of 10° or less add little to the total distance and should be used without hesitation to fly toward better lift. Even deviations up to 30° are well worthwhile if they lead toward better lift and/or avoid suspected sink ahead. The sooner the deviation is started, the less total distance is covered during the deviation. *[Figure 11-16]*

Deviations of 45° or even 90° may be needed to avoid poor conditions ahead. An example might be a large cloudless area or a shaded area where cumulus have spread out into stratus clouds. Sometimes deviations in excess of 90° are needed to return to active thermals after venturing into potentially stable air.

Deviations due to poor weather ahead should be undertaken before the flight becomes unsafe. For instance, if cloud bases are lowering and showers developing, always have the option for a safe, clear landing area before conditions deteriorate too much. Generally, glider pilots will encounter stable air or sinking air which will put them on the ground before VFR conditions disappear. If the sky becomes cloudy, thermaling will cease. Ridge lift might remain but will be in the clouds so either way the glider pilot must get on the ground. It is better to land on your terms rather than be forced down by total lack of lift. Thunderstorms along the course are a special hazard, since storm outflow can affect surface winds for many miles surrounding the storm. Do not count on landing at a site within 10 miles of a strong thunderstorm—sites farther removed are safer. Thunderstorms ahead often warrant large course deviations of up to 180° (i.e., retreat to safety).

NOTE: Cloud development can and does shade the earth, decreasing the heating, and hence decreasing lift. Be aware of cloud shadowing.

Lost Procedures

Navigation has become far easier with the advent of GPS. Since GPS systems are not 100 percent free from failure, pilots must still be able use the sectional chart and compass for navigation. It is important to have an alternate plan in the event of becoming lost. As discussed earlier, preflight

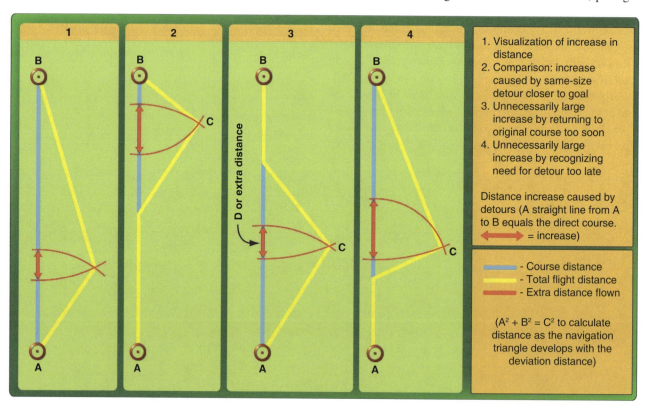

Figure 11-16. *Effects of starting course deviations at different times. Red arrows show extra course distance and indicate the benefit of early course deviations.*

preparation can help avoid becoming lost. Spend some time studying the sectional chart for airports or other notable landmarks along the route.

If you are still lost after some initial searching, try to remain calm. The first priority is to make sure there is a suitable landing area within gliding distance. Then, if possible, try to find lift, even if it is weak, and climb. This buys time and gives a wider view of the area. Next, try to estimate the last known position, the course flown, and any possible differences in wind at altitude. For instance, maybe the headwind is stronger than anticipated and not as far along the course as expected. Try to pinpoint the present position from an estimate of the distance traveled for a given period of time and confirm it with visible landmarks by reference to the sectional chart. For instance, if at point X, averaging about 50 knots, heading north for about 30 minutes should put the glider at point Y. Look again at the sectional chart for landmarks that should be nearby point Y, then search the ground for these landmarks. Thermaling while searching has the added advantage of allowing a wider area of scan while circling.

Once a landmark is located on the sectional and on the ground, confirm the location by finding a few other nearby landmarks. For instance, if that is a town below, then the highway should curve like the one shown on the chart. Does it? If you are lost and near a suitable landing area, stay in the area until certain of location. Airports and airport runways provide valuable clues, like runway orientation and markings or the location of town or a city relative to the airport.

If all efforts fail, attempt a radio call to other soaring pilots in the area. A description of what is below and nearby may bring help from a fellow pilot more familiar with the area.

Cross-Country Flight in a Self-Launching Glider

A self-launching glider can give the pilot much more freedom in exchange for a more complex and expensive aircraft. First, a self-launching glider allows the pilot to fly from airports without a towplane or tow pilot. Second, the engine can be used to avoid off-field landings and extend the flight. In theory, when low in a self-launching glider, simply start the engine and climb to the next source of lift. This second advantage has pitfalls and dangers of its own and has led to many accidents due to engine failure and/or improper starting procedures. Engines on self-launching gliders generally are less reliable than those on airplanes and are susceptible to special problems. For instance, in the western United States, summer thermals often extend to altitudes where the air is cold. The self-launching engine can become cold soaked after several hours of flight, and may take more time to start or may fail to start.

Overreliance on the engine may result in a false sense of security. This can lead pilots to glide over unlandable terrain, something they might not normally do. If the engine then fails when needed most, the pilot has no safe place to land. Some accidents have occurred in which the engine starting system was actually fully functional, but in the rush to start the engine to avoid landing, the pilot did not perform a critical task, such as switching the ignition on. Other accidents have occurred in which the engine did not start immediately, and while trying to solve the starting problem, the pilot flew too far from a suitable landing area. For a self-launching glider with an engine that stows in the fuselage behind the cockpit, the added drag of an extended engine can reduce the glide ratio by 50 to 75 percent. *[Figure 11-17]*

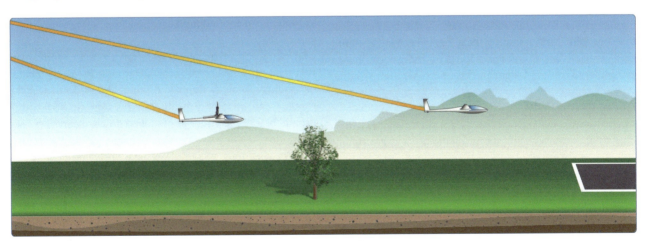

Figure 11-17. *Effects on the glide ratio of the engine being extended but not running.*

The critical decision height to commit to an engine start on a self-launching glider is typically higher than the critical decision height for a nonpowered glider. This is due to a combination of the time needed to start the engine and extra drag during the starting process. It may take anywhere from 200 feet to 500 feet of altitude to extend and then start the engine. Whereas a pure glider may commit to landing at 1,000 feet AGL, the pilot of a self-launching glider probably opts for 1,500 feet AGL, depending on the glider and landing options should the engine fail. In this sense, the self-launching glider becomes more restrictive.

Cross-country flight can also be done under power with a self-launching glider, or a combination of powered and soaring flight. For some self-launching gliders, the most efficient distance per gallon of fuel is achieved by a maximum climb under power followed by a power-off glide. Check the GFM/POH for recommendations.

Another type of glider features a sustainer engine. These engines are not powerful enough to self-launch but are able to keep the glider airborne if lift fails. Sustainers can only produce enough power to overcome the glider's sink rate, and the higher sink rates can easily overwhelm the climb rate capability of many sustainer powerplants. The sustainer engine is typically less complex to operate than their self-launching counterparts, and can eliminate the need for a time-consuming retrieval. Pilots flying with a sustainer are susceptible to the same pitfalls as their self-launching counterparts.

High-Performance Glider Operations and Considerations

Extended cross-country flights have been made in relatively low-performance gliders. However, on any given soaring day, a glider with a 40:1 glide ratio is able to fly farther and faster than one with 20:1, assuming the pilots in both have similar skill levels. Often, a glider pilot looks for more performance in a glider to achieve longer and faster cross-country flights.

Glider Complexity

Most high-performance gliders have a single seat. If a two-seat, high-performance glider is available, the pilot should obtain some instruction from an authorized flight instructor before attempting to fly a single seat high-performance glider for the first time. Before flying any single-seat glider, pilots should thoroughly familiarize themselves with the GFM/POH, including important speeds, weight and balance issues, and all operating systems in the glider GFM/POH, such as landing gear, flaps, and wheel brake location.

High-performance gliders are usually more complex and somewhat more difficult to fly, but they vary considerably.

Current Standard Class gliders (15 meter wingspan and no flaps) are easy to assemble, and newer types are comparatively easier to fly. On the other end of the spectrum, Open Class gliders (unlimited wingspan with flaps) can feature wingspans of 24 meters or more with wings in four sections. The experience required to fly a high-performance glider cannot be quantified simply in terms of a pilot's total glider hours. Types of gliders flown (low and high performance) must be considered.

Almost all high-performance gliders have retractable landing gear, so pilots must make certain that "landing gear down" is on their prelanding checklist. Most landing gear handles are on the right side of the cockpit, but a few are on the left side, so caution is required when reaching for a handle to make sure it is not flaps or airbrakes. A common error is to neglect to retract the landing gear and then mistakenly retract it as part of the prelanding checklist. A gear-up landing in a glider usually causes only embarrassment and minor damage. The distance between the pilot and the runway with the landing gear up is minimal, providing no real "cushioning" protection for the pilot during a hard landing.

Many high-performance gliders have flaps. A few degrees of positive flap can be used when thermaling, and some gliders have 30° or more positive flap settings for lower landing speeds. Flaps can be set to 0° for relatively low-speed glides, while negative flap settings are available for glides at higher speeds. The GFM/POH and glider polar provide recommended flap settings for different speeds, as well as maximum speeds allowed for different flap settings. A few high-performance gliders have no air brakes and use only large positive flap settings for landing. This system allows steep approaches but can be uncomfortable for a pilot who has only used spoilers or dive brakes for landing. A thorough ground briefing is required.

Many high-performance gliders have greater wingspans that require special care to avoid ground loops on takeoff or landing. Runway lights and other obstructions near the runway can become a problem. If a wingtip strikes the ground before the glider has touched down, a cartwheel is a possibility, leading to extensive damage and serious injury. Gliders with long wings often have speed restrictions for dive brake use to avoid severe bending loads at the wingtips.

The feel of the controls on high-performance gliders is light, and pilot-induced oscillations (PIOs) occur easily with the sensitive elevator. Elevator movements using the wrist only, while the forearm rests on the thigh, can aid in avoiding PIOs.

Some high-performance gliders have only one center of gravity (CG) towhook either ahead of the landing gear or in the landing gear well. If the CG hook is within the landing gear well, retracting the gear on tow interferes with the towline. Even if the glider has a nose hook, retracting the gear on tow is not recommended, since the handle is usually on the right cockpit side and switching hands to raise the gear can lead to loss of control on tow. A CG hook, as compared to a nose hook, makes a crosswind takeoff more difficult since the glider can weathervane into the wind more easily. In addition, a CG hook makes the glider more susceptible to "kiting" on takeoff, especially if the flying CG is near the aft limit. This can present a serious danger to the tow pilot.

Water Ballast

To maximize average cross-country speed on a day with strong thermals, water ballast can be used. The gain in speed between thermals outweighs the lost time due to slightly slower climbs with water ballast. If thermals are weak, ballast should not be used. If strong thermals become weak, the water ballast can be dumped. In any case, water ballast should be dumped before landing because heavy wings are more difficult to keep level on the ground roll, and a hard landing is more likely to lead to damage with a heavier glider. Water dumping times vary but are typically between 2 and 5 minutes.

Water ballast is carried in the wings in built-in tanks or water bags. The latter works well but has been known to have problems with leaks. Filling and dumping systems vary from glider to glider, and it is vital to be familiar with the ballast system as described in the GFM/POH. Filling without proper venting can lead to structural damage. Care must be taken to ensure that both wings are filled with the same amount of water. If one wing has a few extra gallons, it can be lead to ground loops and loss of control on takeoff, especially in the presence of a crosswind.

Water expands when going from the liquid state to the solid state. The force of the water ballast freezing can be enough to split composite wing skins. If anticipating flying at levels where the temperature might be below 0 °C, follow the GFM/POH recommended additive to avoid freezing.

Some gliders have a small ballast tank in the tail, as well as ballast in the wings. Tail ballast is an effective means to adjust for a CG that is too far forward. It should be used with caution, however, since the position of the tail ballast tank gives it a long arm aft of the empty CG. A careless calculation can lead to too much water in the tail tank and a flying CG that is aft of the limit.

Cross-Country Flight Using Other Lift Sources

Many world distance and speed records have been broken using ridge or wave lift. Under the right conditions, these lift sources can extend for hundreds of miles from sunrise to sunset. Ridge or wave lift is often more consistent than thermals, allowing long, straight stretches at high speed.

Cross-country flight on ridge lift poses some special problems and considerations. Often, the best lift is very close to the ridge crest where the air can be quite turbulent. Great pilot concentration is needed over several hours close to terrain in rough conditions for longer flights. On relatively low ridges, (e.g., in the eastern United States) ridge lift may not extend very high, so the pilot is never too far from a potential off-field landing. These are not conditions for the beginning cross-country pilot. In milder conditions, gaps in the ridge may require thermaling to gain enough height to cross the gap. Ridge lift can provide a place to temporarily wait for thermals to generate. For instance, if cumulus have spread out to form a stratus layer shading the ground and eliminating thermals, a wind facing slope can be used to maintain soaring flight until the sun returns to regenerate thermals.

Wave lift can also provide opportunities for long and/or fast cross-country flights. Most record flights have been along mountain ranges; flights in excess of 2,000 kilometers having been flown in New Zealand and along the Andes. In the United States, speed records have been set using the wave in the lee of the Sierra Nevada Mountains. In theory, long-distance flights could also be made by climbing high in wave, then gliding with a strong tailwind to the next range downwind for another climb. Special consideration for pilot physiology (cold, oxygen, etc.) and airspace restrictions are needed when considering a cross-country flight using wave lift.

Convergence zones can also be used to enhance cross-country speed. Even if the convergence is not a consistent line but merely acts as a focus for thermals, dolphin flight is often possible, making glides over long distances possible without thermaling. When flying low, awareness of local, small-scale convergence can help the pilot find thermal triggers, enabling climb back to a comfortable cruising height.

It is possible to find ridge, thermal, wave, and even convergence lift during one cross-country flight. Optimum use of the various lift sources requires mental agility but makes for an exciting and rewarding flight.

Chapter 12
Towing

Introduction

Tow planes are the most common way that a glider obtains altitude. *[Figure 12-1]* Winch or automobile tows are being used less and less as they require more crew, are more difficult to set up, and the altitude gain for the glider is just a fraction of what a tow plane can offer. Pilots of gliders and powered aircraft must abide by all federal air regulations listed in the appropriate Code of Federal Regulations (CFR) governing flight. The CFRs that are applicable to pilot certification for towing gliders is covered by Title 14 of the Code of Federal Regulations (14 CFR) part 61, Certification: Pilots, Flight Instructors, and Ground Instructors," and 14 CFR Part 91, General Operating and Flight Rules. The following sections are also applicable:

- 14 CFR Part 61, section 61.23—Medical Certificates: Requirements and Duration
- 14 CFR Part 61, section 61.56—Flight Review
- 14 CFR Part 61, section 61.69—Gliders and Unpowered Ultralight Vehicle Towing: Experience and Training Requirements. *[Figure 12-2]*
- 14 CFR Part 91, section 91.15—Dropping Objects
- 14 CFR Part 91, section 91.309—Towing: Gliders and Unpowered Ultralight Vehicles *[Figure 12-3]*

Guidance and towing procedures can also be found in the Aeronautical Information Manual (AIM) and pertain to flight in the National Airspace (NAS).

How does a private pilot obtain towing privileges? CFR, part 61, section 61.69, outlines the requirements for towing privileges.

You must

1. Hold at least a private pilot certificate with the appropriate category rating;
2. Have logged a minimum of 100 hours as pilot in command in the same category aircraft us
3. Have a logbook endorsement from an authorized instructor certifying you have received gro unpowered ultralight vehicles, and is proficient in the areas listed in part 61.69(a)(3)(i)(ii)(iii) a
4. Have a logbook endorsement from a pilot that already meets the requirements of part 61.69 (the pilot on three flights which has certified them to have accomplished at least three flights in or unpowered ultralight vehicle, or while simulating towing flight procedures; and In the precedin ee actual or simulated tows accompanied by a qualified pilot or has been towed for three fligh ight vehicle. In accordance with part 61.52, pilots towing under an ultralight exemption may c ht vehicles for their towing experience and endorsements.

To meet the rule below, the tow plane safety link strength requirement must be greater than 1,000 lbs. and not more than 1,250 lbs.

The 1,400 lbs. strength requirement is not a player since 1,250 lbs. is the maximum.

1000 lbs. x 25% = 250 lbs.
1000 lbs. + 250 lbs. = 1250 lbs.
700 lbs. x 2 = 1400 lbs.

Glider safety link breaking strength 1,000 lbs.

700 lbs. MGW

RULE: Greater, but not more than 25 percent greater than that of the safety link at the glider end, and not greater than twice the glider MGW.

Maximum Aero Tow Speed	MPH	Knots
Blanik L-23	93 mph	81 knots
Blanik L-13	87 mph	76 knots
SGS 2-33	98 mph	85 knots
SGS 1-26	95 mph	83 knots
ASK 21	108 mph	94 knots

Figure 12-1. *Gliders use tow planes to launch and obtain altitude.*

Equipment Inspections and Operational Checks

Tow Hook

There are typically two types of tow hooks used in the United States: Tost or Schweizer. The tow hook must be inspected for proper operation daily and prior to any tow activity. *[Figure 12-4]*

Schweizer Tow Hook

Prior to use, the tow hook and release arm should be inspected for damage, cracks, deformation, and freedom of movement on the pivot bolt. Visually check the tow hook and ensure that the hook properly engages the release arm. Inspect the rubber spacer for general condition and check the condition of the release cable. Inside the cockpit, check to see that the manual release lever is not rubbing against the aircraft seat or any other obstructions, and check the security of the release handle assembly and the cable attachment.

The following operation checks should be performed to the tow hook:

- Attach the tow line to the tow hook and apply tension on the line in the direction of tow.
- With tension on the tow line, have another person pull the release control in the tow plane cockpit and check for proper release of the tow line.
- If the tow line does not properly release, restrict the tow plane from towing duties until repairs can be made.
- Reattach the tow line and apply a moderate tug in the direction of tow.
- Inspect the release assembly to ensure it has remained completely closed.
- If the release assembly has opened, even partially, restrict the tow plane from towing duties and repair the tow assembly.

Tost Tow Hook

Before use, ensure that the release hook opens completely when the cockpit release is pulled to its fullest extent. The release hooks should touch the tow hook ring. If the release mechanism is not working correctly, it should not be repaired by anyone other than the Tost Factory. Inside the cockpit, check to see that the manual release lever is not rubbing against the aircraft seat or any other obstructions, and check the security of the release handle assembly and the cable attachment. When the cockpit manual release lever is released, the tow hook should return to the fully closed position. Before each use, check the tow hook and ensure that

---

How does a private pilot obtain towing privileges?
CFR, part 61, section 61.69, outlines the requirements for towing privileges.

You must

1. Hold at least a private pilot certificate with the appropriate category rating;
2. Have logged a minimum of 100 hours as pilot in command in the same category aircraft used for towing;
3. Have a logbook endorsement from an authorized instructor certifying you have received ground and flight training in gliders or unpowered ultralight vehicles, and is proficient in the areas listed in part 61.69(a)(3)(i)(ii)(iii) and (iv);
4. Have a logbook endorsement from a pilot that already meets the requirements of part 61.69 (c) and (d), who has accompanied the pilot on three flights which has certified them to have accomplished at least three flights in an aircraft while towing a glider or unpowered ultralight vehicle, or while simulating towing flight procedures; and In the preceding 12 months has performed three actual or simulated tows accompanied by a qualified pilot or has been towed for three flights in a glider or unpowered ultralight vehicle. In accordance with part 61.52, pilots towing under an ultralight exemption may credit experience obtained in ultralight vehicles for their towing experience and endorsements.

You must

1. Hold at least a private pilot certificate with the appropriate category rating;
2. Have logged a minimum of 100 hours as pilot in command in the same category aircraft used for towing;
3. A logbook endorsement from an authorized instructor who has reviewed their logged ultralight towing experience and who has verified their aero tug pilot endorsement card received from USHPA, verifying they have received the authorized training to become a tow pilot of gliders and/or unpowered ultralight vehicles; and In the preceding 12 months has performed three actual or simulated tows accompanied by a qualified pilot, or has been towed for three flights in a glider or unpowered ultralight vehicle.

Figure 12-2. *Excerpt from the Code of Federal Regulations, part 61, section 61.69.*

> **Title 14: Aeronautics and Space**
> **PART 91—GENERAL OPERATING AND FLIGHT RULES**
> **Subpart D—Special Flight Operations**
> **§ 91.309 Towing: Gliders and unpowered ultralight vehicles**
>
> (a) No person may operate a civil aircraft towing a glider or unpowered ultralight vehicle unless—
>   (1) The pilot in command of the towing aircraft is qualified under §61.69 of this chapter;
>   (2) The towing aircraft is equipped with a tow-hitch of a kind, and installed in a manner, that is approved by the Administrator;
>   (3) The towline used has breaking strength not less than 80 percent of the maximum certificated operating weight of the glider or unpowered ultralight vehicle and not more than twice this operating weight. However, the towline used may have a breaking strength more than twice the maximum certificated operating weight of the glider or unpowered ultralight vehicle if—
>   (i) A safety link is installed at the point of attachment of the towline to the glider or unpowered ultralight vehicle with a breaking strength not less than 80 percent of the maximum certificated operating weight of the glider or unpowered ultralight vehicle and not greater than twice this operating weight;
>   (ii) A safety link is installed at the point of attachment of the towline to the towing aircraft with a breaking strength greater, but not more than 25 percent greater, than that of the safety link at the towed glider or unpowered ultralight vehicle end of the towline and not greater than twice the maximum certificated operating weight of the glider or unpowered ultralight vehicle;
>   (4) Before conducting any towing operation within the lateral boundaries of the surface areas of Class B, Class C, Class D, or Class E airspace designated for an airport, or before making each towing flight within such controlled airspace if required by ATC, the pilot in command notifies the control tower. If a control tower does not exist or is not in operation, the pilot in command must notify the FAA flight service station serving that controlled airspace before conducting any towing operations in that airspace; and
>   (5) The pilots of the towing aircraft and the glider or unpowered ultralight vehicle have agreed upon a general course of action, including takeoff and release signals, airspeeds, and emergency procedures for each pilot.
>
> (b) No pilot of a civil aircraft may intentionally release a towline, after release of a glider or unpowered ultralight vehicle, in a manner that endangers the life or property of another.

Figure 12-3. *Excerpt from the Code of Federal Regulations, part 91, section 91.309.*

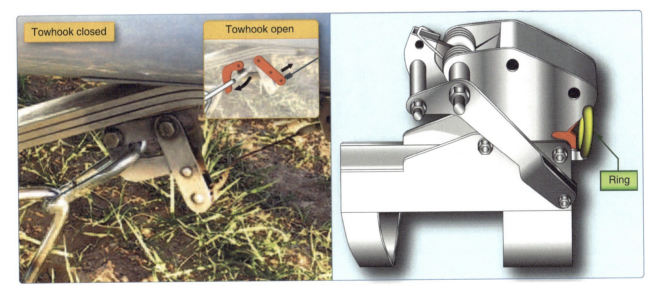

Figure 12-4. *Schweizer tow hook (left) and a Tost tow hook (right).*

it is free of dirt and/or corrosion. It is important to confirm that the tow plane end of the tow rope is fitted with a Tost tow ring.

The following operation checks should be performed to the tow hook:

- Attach the tow line to the tow hook and apply tension on the line in the direction of tow.

- With tension on the tow line, have another person pull the release control in the tow plane cockpit and check for proper release of the tow line.

- If the tow line does not properly release, restrict the tow plane from towing duties until repairs can be made.

- Reattach the tow line and apply a moderate tug in the direction of tow.

- Inspect the release assembly to ensure it has remained completely closed.
- If the release assembly has opened, even partially, restrict the tow plane from towing duties and repair the tow assembly.

Tow Ring Inspection

Tow ring inspection should begin with checking for wear and tear. The rings should not be used if they have deep scratches or dents. Like the tow hitch assembly, there are two types of tow rings: Schweizer and Tost. *[Figure 12-5]* The Schweizer tow ring is two inches in diameter and made of high grade, one-quarter inch steel that has been magnafluxed with good weld. The Tost tow ring is also made of high grade steel and available through most glider supply companies.

Figure 12-6. *It is both the tow pilot and glider pilots responsibility to check the condition of the tow rope before flight.*

- Check the entire length of the tow line for abrasions, security of splices, and general condition.
- The tow line should be free from excess wear; all strands should be intact, and the line should be free from knots (knots in the tow line reduces its strength by up to 50 percent and causes a high spot in the rope that is more susceptible to wear).
- Pay particular attention to the ring area to which the glider attaches because this is also a high-wear area.
- Consideration should be given in replacing the tow rope after a period of time due to usage and ultraviolet (UV) exposure from being in the sun and exposed to the elements.
- Ensure tow line strength is appropriate for the glider being towed.

Figure 12-5. *Schweizer tow ring and a Tost tow ring.*

Always ensure that the tow line is configured for the proper type of hitch being used. For example, a Schweizer tow ring will not fit into a Tost tow hitch, but a Tost tow ring can be placed on a Schweizer type tow hitch (with the great possiblility that the Tost tow ring will become stuck in the hitch mechanism making tow rope release impossible).

Tow Rope Inspection

Although the pilot of the glider is primarily responsible for the selection and inspection of the proper tow line, it is also the duty of the tow pilot to confirm that the tow line selected meets the requirements of the Federal Aviation Administration (FAA) Regulations and is acceptable for use. *[Figure 12-6]* The tow line should be inspected as follows:

Tow Rope Strength Requirements

Stated in the 14 CFR part 91, section 91.309, the minimum tow rope strength is eighty percent of the gliders maximum certificated operating weight. The maximum strength is twice the maximum certificated operating weight. The maximum certificated operating weight can be found in the specific pilot's operating handbook (POH) for the glider and may be the maximum certificated gross weight at takeoff. *Figure 12-7* shows the strength of some ropes that are typically used. If the tow rope has a breaking strength more than twice the maximum certificated operating weight of the glider being towed, a safety link (weak link) has to be installed at the point of attachment of the glider and the tow plane with the following breaking strength requirements:

Diameter	Nylon	Dacron	Polyethylene Hollow braid	Polypropylene Monofilament	Polypropylene Multifilament
3/16"	960	720	700	800	870
1/4"	1,500	1,150	1,200	1,300	1,200
5/16"	2,400	1,750	1,750	1,900	2,050

Figure 12-7. *Rope strengths.*

- Safety link (weak link) at the glider end:
  - Minimum strength = eighty percent of the glider maximum certificated operating weight.
  - Maximum strength = twice the maximum certificated operating weight. *[Figure 12-8]*
- Safety link (weak link) at the tow plane end:
  - Strength requirements = greater, but not more than twenty five percent greater than that of the safety link on the glider end, and not more than twice the maximum certificated operating weight of the glider.

Tow ropes and cables are made of many different reliable materials, such as nylon, step-index fiber from Red Polyester, Hollow Braid POLYPRO, Dacron, steel, and Polyethylene. *[Figure 12-9]*

Take Off Planning

After all inspections are complete, compute the takeoff performance for the tow plane using the approved POH. As a rule of thumb, the tow plane is normally airborne in about twice the computed distance. If your tow plane does not have takeoff performance charts, make a normal takeoff without the glider in tow and note the lift-off point. Use this physical point in lieu of computed takeoff data. Pay particular attention to your altitude over the departure end of the runway and the clearance of any barriers.

Figure 12-9. *Tow ropes and cables are made of many different reliable materials such as nylon, step-index fiber from Red Polyester, Hollow Braid POLYPRO, Dacron, steel, and Polyethylene.*

Using the computed takeoff data or actual takeoff point, choose a physical abort point on the runway. *[Figure 12-10]* Thoroughly brief the glider pilot on the abort point and abort procedures. If the tow plane is not off the ground by the chosen abort point, the glider should release, or be released, allowing the tow plane to accomplish a normal takeoff.

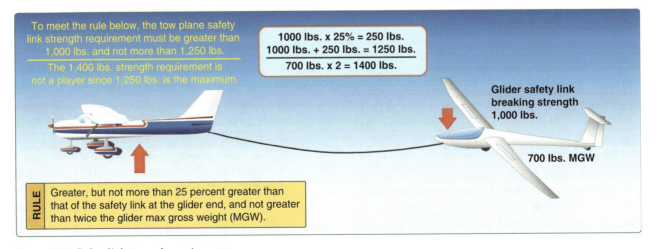

Figure 12-8. *Safety link strength requirements.*

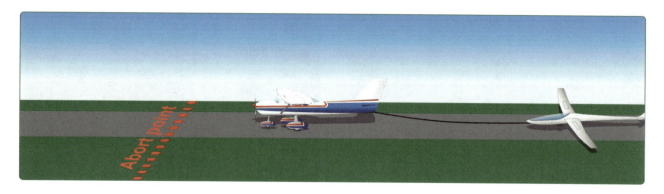

Figure 12-10. *A physical abort point on the runway should be determined and briefed to the glider pilot before starting the towing procedures.*

Since density altitude is perhaps the single most important factor affecting airplane performance, a review of the effects of density altitude is in order. An increase in air temperature and/or humidity significantly decreases power output and propeller efficiency.

The engine produces power in proportion to the weight or density of the air. Therefore, as air density decreases (high density altitude), the power output of the engine decreases. Also, the propeller produces thrust in proportion to the mass of air being accelerated through the rotating blades. If the air is less dense, propeller efficiency is decreased.

The problem of high density altitude operation is compounded by the fact that when the air is less dense, more engine power and increased propeller efficiency are needed to overcome the decreased lift efficiency of the tow plane's wing. This additional power and propeller efficiency are not available under high density altitude conditions; consequently, tow plane performance decreases considerably.

The winds aloft should be continuously evaluated to help determine the glider release area and always attempt to release the glider upwind of the airport. Code of Federal Regulations (CFR), part 91, section 91.309 (a)(5) states, "The pilot of the towing aircraft and the glider have agreed upon a general course of action, including takeoff and release signals, airspeeds, and emergency procedures for each pilot." If there is any doubt that this rule has not been complied with through briefings or published and agreed upon standard operating procedures, ensure both you as the tow pilot and the glider pilot are absolutely clear on all aspects of the upcoming tow.

On the Airport

The tow pilot must develop an awareness of the direction of the tow plane's prop blast. Blasting launch personnel and glider canopies with all sorts of debris is undesirable and potentially dangerous. Whenever possible, turn away from any ground operations. Prior to taking the active runway for tow line hook-up and takeoff, if available, monitor and announce your intentions on the Common Traffic Advisory Frequency (CTAF).

Ground Signals

In most cases, the Standard American Soaring Signals are used to communicate between the launch crew and tow plane. In some cases, however, specific local procedures may be in effect. The tow pilot should be thoroughly briefed on any specific local procedures. The tow pilot may be required to observe these signals through the mirror or through an additional signal relay person positioned safely on the side of the runway adjacent to the tow plane. The ground signals are listed below and are also presented as illustrations in Chapters 7 and 8 of this handbook.

- Take up slack—the take up slack signal is given by the ground crewmember moving his or her lowered arm from side to side. When you receive this signal, slowly taxi the tow plane forward to take up the slack in the tow line. When all the slack has been taken from the tow line, expect to receive the "hold" signal from the ground crew.

- Hold—this signal is given by holding the arms out straight.

- Pilot ready, wings level—when the glider pilot is ready for takeoff, a thumbs up signal is given and the wing runner will level the wing to the takeoff position.

- Begin takeoff—the glider pilot waggles the rudder with the wings level and the wing runner signals with a circular motion of the arm. When ready for takeoff, the tow pilot should broadcast on the CTAF that a glider launch is about to be initiated. For example, "Tallahasee traffic, N12345 taking off Runway 33, glider in tow, Tallahasee." Remember, 14 CFR part 91, section 91.309, requires that before conducting towing operations within Class B, C, D, or E airspace designated for an airport, or before making each towing flight within such controlled airspace if required by ATC, the pilot in charge (PIC) must notify the control tower. If a control tower does not exist or is not in operation, the PIC must notify the FAA flight service station (FSS) serving that controlled airspace before conducting any towing operations.

- Stop engine/release tow line—this signal is given by moving a hand back and forth across the throat.

- Tow plane ready—prior to takeoff, carefully look at the glider to ensure the glider dive brakes are closed and no one is standing in front of the wings or so close to the launch path to create a hazard. It is important to note, however, that some high-performance gliders may make their initial takeoff roll with spoilers open. Know your gliders and if in doubt, do not be ashamed to question the glider pilot. Better to be a bit embarrassed than to end up in the trees at the end of the runway. Additionally, the tow pilot should ensure that the traffic pattern is clear of aircraft. Once assured that the glider is ready and the briefed departure path is clear, the ready for takeoff signal may be given with a waggle of the tow plane rudder.

- Stop operation or emergency—this signal is given by a waving motion of the arms above the head.

Takeoff and Climb

The takeoff is done by advancing the throttle smoothly and quickly in one motion. *[Figure 12-11]* If the tow plane is allowed to accelerate and then slow down, the glider may overrun the tow line. This may result in the tow line becoming tangled in the landing gear of the glider. The glider may then be unable to release. Accelerate to liftoff speed keeping in mind that during the takeoff phase of flight, ground effect produces some important relationships. The tow plane leaving ground effect will:

Figure 12-11. *The takeoff is done by smoothly and quickly advancing the throttle in one motion so that the glider does not overrun the tow line.*

- Require an increase in the angle of attack (AOA) to maintain the same lift coefficient;

- Experience an increase in induced drag and thrust required;

- Experience a decrease in stability and a nose-up change in moment; and

- Produce a reduction in static source pressure and increase in indicated airspeed.

These general effects should point out the possible danger in attempting takeoff prior to achieving the recommended lift-off speed. Due to the reduced drag in ground effect, the tow plane may seem capable of takeoff well below the recommended speed; however, lifting out of ground effect with a lower than normal lift off speed may result in very marginal initial climb performance.

The glider will normally liftoff first. The pilot of the glider should correct for crosswind until the tow plane becomes airborne.

At this point, the tow pilot must remain extra alert. The tail of the tow plane may be lifted if the glider climbs too high. Should this happen, the application of full-up elevator on the tow plane may not be sufficient to prevent an accident from happening. The tow pilot must be ready to pull the release handle, releasing the glider and regaining control. As a rule of thumb, the use of a 200 foot tow line would require the glider to climb to over 20 feet above the altitude of the tow plane to present a danger of upset.

After liftoff, a constant airspeed climb should be established. The pilot of the glider should establish a position directly behind the tow plane. The pilot of the tow plane should maintain a constant ground track on the initial climb. Upon reaching a safe altitude, a turn may be established to maintain the desired departure path. Bank angle should be limited to a maximum of 15–20°.

Climb at full throttle unless otherwise required by the POH. The fuel/air mixture should be leaned only in accordance with the POH for maximum power. Each specific model of glider has a published maximum aerotow speed, and the tow pilot must be familiar with this speed, which may be very close to the minimum safe speed of the tow plane. *[Figure 12-12]*

The tow pilot should understand that these are maximum airspeeds. Plan to fly at a speed slower than the maximum while maintaining safe tow plane flying speed. When towing a different model of glider for the first time, obtain a briefing from the glider pilot to ensure compliance with maximum

Maximum Aero Tow Speed	MPH	Knots
Blanik L-23	93 mph	81 knots
Blanik L-13	87 mph	76 knots
SGS 2-33	98 mph	85 knots
SGS 1-26	95 mph	83 knots
ASK 21	108 mph	94 knots

Figure 12-12. *Maximum aerotow speeds.*

operating speeds. Also note fiberglass gliders, like the ASK-21, are towed faster than other popular training gliders.

Recommended towing speed is determined by considering stall speed and maximum aerotow speed of the glider, minimum speed for proper engine cooling of the tow plane, and stall speed of the tow plane. Generally speaking, aerotow should be conducted at the slowest speed possible considering these factors and safety. Speed should be at least thirty percent above stall speed of the glider and twenty percent above the stall speed of the tow plane.

Because of the potential for low altitude emergencies, the initial climb must remain upwind and within gliding distance of the airport. If circumstances do not permit an upwind departure, plan the climb to remain in a position that allows the glider to return to the traffic pattern with the existing headwind component.

When towing, expect the glider to practice maneuvers such as "Boxing the Wake," which is explained and illustrated in Chapter 7 of this handbook. A thoughtful glider pilot communicates the intention to maneuver behind the tow plane. However, the tow pilot should remain alert for unannounced maneuvering. Glider pilot's normally begin the "Box the Wake" maneuver by descending vertically from high tow position to low tow position. Once a similar maneuver is detected, maintain a constant heading and a wings level attitude. After the "Box the Wake" maneuver is completed and the glider is stabilized in the hig-tow position, turns can be resumed.

During tow, the glider instructor may demonstrate and practice slack rope recovery procedures. This maneuver normally involves a climb to one side or the other followed by a small dive to create the slack in the tow line. The instructor will then have the student take the slack out of the tow line without breaking the rope. Be alert for these maneuvers and do not mistake the climb and dive maneuver as a release. This maneuver is discussed in further detail in Chapter 8 of this handbook.

Tow Positions, Turns, and Release
Glider Tow Positions
The high tow is normally used for glider tow operations. However, a low-tow position may be used in some instances, a cross-country tow for example. The main goal of both positions is to place the glider in a position that avoids the wake of the tow plane. *[Figure 12-13]*

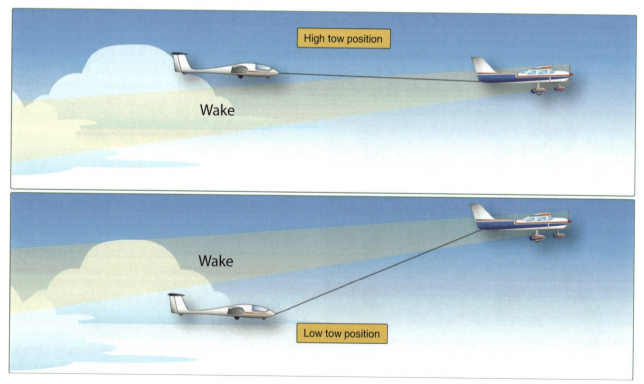

Figure 12-13. *Aerotow climb-out.*

Turns on Tow

All turns should be performed in a gentle and gradual manner. The pilot of the glider will attempt to fly the exact flightpath of the tow plane. To do this, the pilot points the nose of the glider at the outside wing tip of the tow plane during a turn.

Turns may be initiated upon reaching a safe altitude. Consideration should be given to obstruction clearance, terrain, and wind gradient. Turbulence and differential wing speed of the glider during turns are potential sources of problems.

Due to the length of the wingspan, the roll rate of a glider is typically slower than that of the tow plane. Consequently, the tow pilot should plan all turns with the understanding that the angle of bank determines the turn radius. Since the bank angles of the tow plane and glider must match to fly the same path, normally a maximum of 15–20° of bank is used.

Approaching a Thermal

When approaching a thermal, be vigilant of other gliders. Since the first glider in the thermal establishes the direction of turn, any glider joining the thermal is required to circle in the same direction as the first glider. This requires the tow pilot to position the flight in a manner that allows the glider proper and safe entry to the thermal. Be super alert when approaching thermals with circling gliders. Expect other gliders to be inbound to the thermal from all directions. Give the thermal traffic a wide berth. If the thermal appears to be especially crowded, steer clear of the activity.

Release

Standard glider release procedures are as follows *[Figure 12-14]*:

1. The pilot of the glider should ensure the tow line is relatively tight, with no excessive slack, prior to release. This allows the tow pilot to feel the release of the glider. If the tow rope is visible in the mirror, look for the wrinkle in the tow rope after the glider has released.

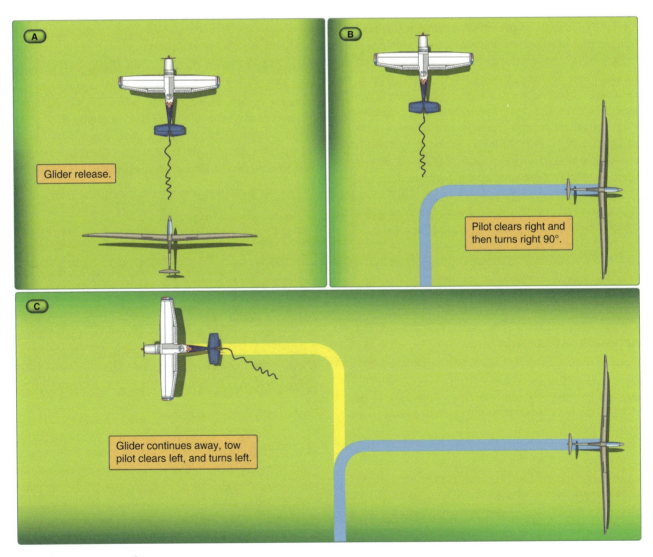

Figure 12-14. *Aerotow release.*

2. Once it has been confirmed that the glider has released and is clear, the tow pilot should clear the airspace to the left and start a medium bank, descending left turn.

3. The glider should turn right after release but may proceed straight ahead a few moments before turning right. Always be alert for non-standard maneuvering by the glider.

When the tow pilot has positively observed and confirmed the release of the tow line (assumption of release is not acceptable), the pilot of the tow plane may begin a left turn and initiate the descent. In some instances, the glider will release with slack in the tow line. This soft release may not be detectable by the tow pilot. If there is any doubt of the release status in the mind of the tow pilot, the tow pilot should continue the tow and confirm the release via radio or visually.

Descent, Approach and Landing
Descent
During the descent, proper engine management is essential. Good engine conservation practices require a gradual power reduction and conservative descent airspeeds. In fact, studies indicate that airspeed may be more critical than power reduction. Therefore, every attempt should be made to avoid airspeed acceleration and power reduction for 3 minutes after glider release. Full flaps or slipping turns can be used to obtain a suitable rate of descent. Closing cowl flaps, if available, further reduces the rate of engine cooling. Realize oil temperature is not as reliable as cylinder head temperature for managing temperature change. Each airplane requires slightly different techniques; however, the goal is to keep the engine as warm as possible while descending at a reasonable rate.

Collision avoidance is always a high priority, since descending flight attitudes increase the potential of a mid-air collision. Consider developing and using specific descent corridors that are void of glider and power traffic.

Approach and Landing
A 200-foot tow line hangs down behind the tow plane at a 30 to 40 degree angle. The altitude of the tow plane must be adjusted to ensure the tow line does not become entangled in obstructions at close proximity to the ground.

Ensure you are thoroughly briefed and familiar with the obstructions around the airport, especially obstructions on the approach end of the runway to be used. Briefings should include a minimum above ground level (AGL) obstruction crossing height and any factors that may influence altitude judgment, such as visual illusions or other airport distractions.

Landing with the tow line attached is not prohibited by regulation; however, the following points should be considered:

1. Obstructions are cleared by more than the tow line length (altimeter lag considered).

2. The field is well turfed. It is simply inviting early tow line failure from abrasion to land with the tow line on hard ground or paved runways. Landing with the tow line should never be attempted unless the field has clear approaches and is at least 2,500 feet in length.

Other situations require the tow line to be dropped, normally in the glider launch area, during short approach to the runway. If the tow line is to be dropped, the tow pilot must be constantly aware of the launch area situation. The tow line drop area must be defined and ground personnel must be briefed and aware of the drop area. Ground personnel must stay clear of the drop area, and the presence of an individual in the drop area requires an immediate go-around by the pilot of the tow plane without dropping the tow line.

Cross-Country Aerotow
Planning is the key for a successful and safe cross-county tow. *[Figure 12-15]* Fuel consumption during any tow operation is high. Plan conservatively, using the maximum fuel consumption for your particular tow plane and also plan for the possibility of a diversion along your route of flight. Study your route of flight on current sectional charts paying particular attention to airspace, both controlled and special use.

Figure 12-15. *Cross-country tow.*

Since a tow line break is a constant possibility, always plan your route of flight over landable terrain and, while in flight, strive to keep the glider over landable terrain. Tow and glider pilot fatigue is a real hazard. Make sure you are properly rested and in good medical condition prior to the flight. If the flight is particularly long, plan rest stops along the way, if feasible. Think about water requirements to keep hydrated and the inevitable physiological requirement. Use aircraft trim to ensure the maximum tow speed of the glider is not exceeded and to help reduce pilot fatigue.

Two-way communication between the glider and the tow plane is essential during cross-country tows. Ensure portable radios and glider batteries are fully charged prior to the flight and conduct a radio check as part of your pre-flight activities. *[Figure 12-16]*

Figure 12-16. *On a cross-country tow, the tow pilot and glider pilot should have two way communication using portable radios.*

Emergencies

Takeoff Emergencies

The key to ensuring successful emergency management is the development of an emergency plan. Prior to takeoff, an emergency release point should be selected somewhere along the takeoff runway. This release point should leave sufficient room to land straight ahead, using normal stopping techniques, in the event conditions are such that a safe takeoff with the glider in tow cannot be completed.

During the initial climb out, the pilot of the glider will be noting certain altitudes that correspond to actions he or she will take in the event of a low-altitude emergency.

Tow Plane Power Failure on the Runway During Takeoff Roll

The following actions should be taken in the event the tow plane has a power failure on the runway during the takeoff roll:

- The glider should release or be released by the tow plane and, if possible, maneuver right of the runway.

- The tow plane should maneuver to the left of the runway if space is available. (Realize each individual airfield layout and obstacles may dictate an alternate procedure, so take the time to plan your actions prior to takeoff.)

- Survey the abort area carefully and know where you can exit the runway (grass or taxi-way) without causing a hazard. Always have a plan.

- Realize the glider will probably be airborne, therefore try and give the glider as much space as possible to land on the remaining runway and brake to a stop.

- Know the stopping characteristics of the glider you are towing. Some models have very effective brakes, others do not.

Glider Releases During Takeoff With Tow Plane Operation Normal

The pilot of the tow plane should continue the takeoff eliminating a collision hazard with the glider.

Tow Plane Power Failure or Tow Rope Break After Takeoff but Below 200 Feet Above Ground Level

The pilot of the glider will normally release and descend straight ahead or maneuver using slight turns to make a specific forced landing. Because of airport obstructions in close proximity to the airport, the options available for a tow plane or glider land out may be limited. Discuss these options during the pilot briefing or safety meetings. Again, a plan will go a long way in ensuring a successful land out as a result of a takeoff emergency.

Tow Plane Power Failure or Tow Rope Break After Takeoff Above 200 Feet

The glider can more than likely return to the field in the event of engine failure or rope break. Since the tow plane requires considerably more altitude to return to the field in the event of a power failure, the pilot should have a specific plan in mind that includes pre-selected landing areas for each runway.

Glider Climbs Excessively High During Takeoff

The tail of the tow plane may be lifted if the glider climbs excessively high during takeoff. Should this happen, the application of full-up elevator on the tow plane may not be sufficient to prevent an accident. The tow pilot must be ready to pull the release handle in order to regain control of the tow plane. As a rule of thumb, use of a 200-foot tow line would require the glider to climb to over 20 feet above the altitude of the tow plane to present a danger of upset.

If at any time the nose of the tow plane is pulled uncontrollably by the glider to a dangerously high or low pitch attitude—PULL THE RELEASE.

If a Schweizer tow hitch is being used, it may be possible for the release mechanism to become jammed due to the excessively high position of the glider.

Airborne Emergencies
Glider Release Failure

If the pilot of the glider is unable to release, the tow pilot should be informed by means of the aircraft radio or by the following airborne signal. The glider will move out to the left side of the towplane and rock its wings. *[Figure 12-17]* Be sure not to mistake the wing rock as the beginning of a normal release. Wait a few seconds to ensure the glider's wings are rocking. Once the tow pilot has determined the glider cannot release the tow plane should return to the airfield and release the glider at a safe altitude over the field.

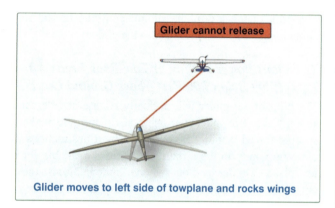

Figure 12-17. *Glider release failure.*

Neither the Tow Plane or Glider Can Release

This is an extremely rare event. Although as improbable as this situation may be, you must be prepared. The pilot of the tow plane should inform the pilot of the glider by aircraft radio or airborne signal. The signal is accomplished by yawing the tail of the tow plane.

The glider should move to the low tow position. Then the tow plane should begin a slow descent toward an airfield of suitable length. Fly a wide pattern ending up on an extended final approach. Set up a very stabilized and gradual (200–300 foot per minute (fpm)) descent. Plan on landing long and allowing sufficient altitude while on short final for the glider to avoid approach obstacles.

Since the glider is lower than the tow plane, it lands first. The glider should not apply brakes until the tow plane has touched down. After touchdown, apply brakes gently or not at all, slowly coming to a stop. Remember, most glider brakes are not that effective, so allow the glider plenty of runway to stop.

While not well defined in soaring literature, some glider pilots are taught to attempt to break the tow rope rather than land behind the tow plane. If the glider does attempt to break the rope, maintain the tow plane in a straight and level attitude in an attempt to reduce the total gravity forces of the glider's maneuver.

Glider Problem

You may notice the glider has a problem that is obviously not being detected by the glider pilot. The most common is the failure of the glider pilot to close and lock the glider's spoilers/airbrakes prior to takeoff, resulting in an inadvertent undetected deployment of spoilers as the glider accelerates during takeoff. If you notice a problem with the glider, inform the glider pilot via radio and visual signal. The visual signal for "Glider Problem" is waggling the rudder while airborne.

Immediate Release

This situation requires immediate action by the pilot of the glider. Should the tow pilot rock the wings of the tow plane, the pilot of the glider must release immediately. Obviously, this would be appropriate during a time critical tow plane emergency, such as engine-failure or fire. *[Figure 12-18]*

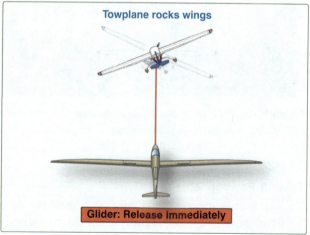

Figure 12-18. *The towplane is telling the glider to release immediately.*

Chapter 13
Human Factors

Introduction

The term human factors is often associated with ergonomics and is documented as the only discipline that focuses on the interaction of humans and technology. *[Figure 13-1]* When referring to human factors, we immediately think of the 3 Ds: development, design, and deployment of systems and devices that improve system-human interface. While there is much more to human factors than the 3 Ds, behavior intervention and modification is a necessary component to ensuring a safer aviation environment. As there have been great strides over recent decades to decrease the number of aviation accidents, human error remains the biggest hurdle for safety professionals. Research has shown nearly 80 percent of aviation accidents are attributed to human error. As a result of this finding, the aviation environment must rely heavily on minimizing human error to ensure a safer air space. This chapter focuses specifically on key elements associated with human error and systems related to glider flying operations as well as some of the physiological issues involved in soaring.

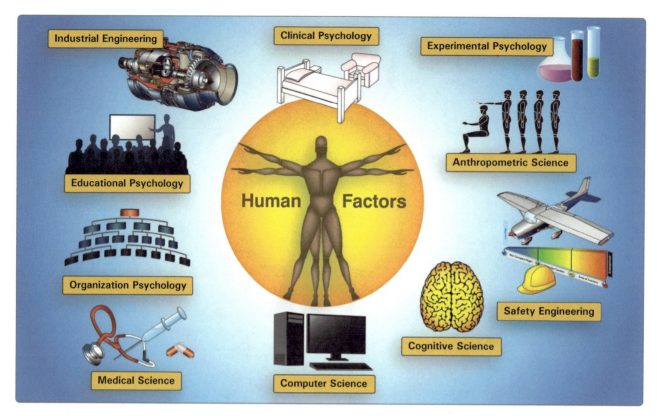

Figure 13-1. *1 Human factor disciplines.*

Learning from Past Mistakes

The National Transportation Safety Board (NTSB) generates accident reports any time a reportable glider accident occurs. This information is open to the public and can be found at www.ntsb.gov/ntsb. Once on the accident query page, enter the term "glider," which retrieves all reports pertaining to gliders to include tow plane accidents. It is important for pilots to review NTSB accident reports and learn what the common errors and hazards are that apply to glider operations. Learning from others mistakes helps reduce future accident rates.

An NTSB query from November 1, 2010, through October 31, 2011, shows 27 glider accidents. Shown in *Figure 13-2* are some of the accidents reported during that time to include the type of aircraft, injuries, and the probable cause of the accident (if given).

Recognizing Hazardous Attitudes

It is important that pilots ensure their flight is safe by following procedures and checklists rather than hope for a safe flight and doing things they know are not right. As technological advances have contributed to fewer mechanical failures, which in turn has created a much safer air space, human error remains a constant factor in aviation accidents. There is a wealth of information available that focuses on unsafe behaviors and attitudes. For the purpose of this chapter, three common behaviors are addressed: complacency, indiscipline, and overconfidence. While complacency, indiscipline, and overconfidence share a common theme (each stem from experience), it is necessary to further delineate on the contributions of attitude-behavior linkage. To do so, we must further explore each term respectively.

Complacency

Often glider operations can seem less stressful than other modes of flight for no other reason than the "meditative silence" that accompanies gliding through the air. This is why complacency can easily materialize. Complacency is when a person has a sense of security about one's surrounding yet fails to recognize or lacks awareness of possible danger. As pilots accrue flight time, their experience increases and, while one might view this as positive, their experience complacency may emerge. All too often, with experience comes boredom, a desire to cut corners, distractibility, feelings of content, minimal performance, and intentionally overlooking basic safety precautions (i.e., "I've done this a million times, it is not necessary to follow a checklist.").

A few countermeasures include:

- Never assume all facets related to the flight will go smoothly.
- Always prepare and expect the unexpected.

Aircraft Type	Injuries	Probable Cause
Burkhart GROB G-103A Twin II ACRO	2 uninjured	The certified flight instructor's inadequate compensation for the crosswind and delayed remedial action during landing, which resulted in a ground loop.
Schweizer SGS 1-23D	1 minor	The pilot's loss of control during an intentional aerobatic maneuver (spin) resulting in a collision with trees.
Mcholland C L Solitare	2 uninjured	The glider pilot's misjudgment while approaching to land, which resulted in an off-airport landing.
AMS-Flight D.O.O. DG-500 Elan Orion	2 uninjured	The in flight loss of lift while landing, resulting in a collision with a fence.
Glasflugel Standard Libelle	1 fatal	Probable cause not yet released.
Rolladen-Schneider GMBH LS-3	1 serious	The glider pilot's delayed response to changing weather conditions, which resulted in an off-airport landing into trees.
Burkhart GROB Flugzeugbau G102 Club Astir IIIB	1 fatal	Probable cause not yet released.
LET L 33 Solo	1 fatal	Probable cause not yet released.
Doktor Fiberglass H101 Salto	1 uninjured	The glider's encounter with turbulence and loss of lift, which resulted in a ditching in a lake.
Schleicher ASW-27	1 minor	Glider struck two transmission lines.
Schweizer SGS 2-33A	2 uninjured	Each pilot thought that the other had control of the aircraft.
Eiriavion OY PIK 20B	1 uninjured	Probable cause has not been determined.
Schleicher ASW-20	1 fatal	Probable cause has not been determined.
Schweizer SGS 2-32	1 fatal, 1 serious	Probable cause has not been determined.
Schweizer SGS 2-32	1 serious, 2 uninjured	The pilot's inadequate altitude to clear a ridgeline while maneuvering over a mountainous area.

Figure 13-2. *Some accidents reported by the National Transportation Safety Board (NTSB) from November 1, 2011 through October 31, 2012.*

- Play the "what if" game and offer solutions to the scenarios you create.

The key to preventing complacency is keeping your mind sharp at all times by "being proactive rather than reactive."

Indiscipline
Much like complacency, as pilots gain experience the failure to comply with certain standards seem to be evident in many aviation accidents. Either they feel their experience has taught them an easier or faster way to do certain tasks, or their attitude is not in alignment with the guidelines set forth by more experienced aviators. Nevertheless, indiscipline can be a very dangerous attitude that can easily lead to unsafe behaviors.

Overconfidence
Similarly to complacency, familiar circumstances or repetition can lead to a state of overconfidence. Developing and maintaining a sense of confidence toward your abilities is acceptable unless it leads to cutting corners and ignoring proper procedure.

Human Error
Human error is defined as a human action with unintended consequences. There is nothing inherently wrong or troublesome with error itself, but when you couple error with aviation and the negative consequences that it produces it becomes extremely troublesome. Training, flight examinations (written or oral), and operational checks should not be restricted to attempt to avoid errors but rather to make them visible and identify them before they produce damaging and regrettable consequences. Simply put, human error is not avoidable but it is manageable. *[Figure 13-3]*

Types of Errors
Unintentional

An unintentional error is an unintentional wandering or deviation from accuracy. This can include an error in your action (a slip), opinion, or judgment caused by poor reasoning, carelessness or insufficient knowledge (a mistake). For example, a pilot reads the glider performance numbers from

Figure 13-3. *Safety awareness will help foresee and mitigate the risk of human error.*

the Pilot's Operating Handbook (POH) and unintentionally transposed the number 62 to 26. He or she did not mean to make that error but unknowingly and unintentionally did.

Intentional

In aviation, an intentional error should really be considered a flight violation. If someone knowingly or intentionally chooses to do something wrong, it is a violation, which means that one has deviated from safe practices, procedures, standards, or regulations.

Human and Physiological Factors that Affect Flight

Fatigue

Fatigue is a major human factor that has contributed to many maintenance errors resulting in accidents. Fatigue can be mental or physical in nature. Emotional fatigue also exists and effects mental and physical performance. A person is said to be fatigued when a reduction or impairment in any of the following occurs: cognitive ability, decision-making, reaction time, coordination, speed, strength, and balance. Fatigue reduces alertness and often reduces a person's ability to focus and hold attention on the task being performed. [*Figure 13-4*]

Symptoms of fatigue may also include short-term memory problems, channeled concentration on unimportant issues while neglecting other factors that may be more important, and failure to maintain a situational overview. A fatigued person may be easily distracted or may be nearly impossible to distract. He or she may experience abnormal mood swings. Fatigue results in an increase in mistakes, poor judgment, and poor decisions or perhaps no decisions at all. A fatigued person may also lower his or her standards.

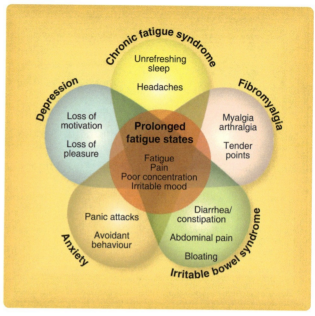

Figure 13-4. *Fatigue can be mental or physical and effects both mental and physical performance.*

Tiredness is a symptom of fatigue. However, sometimes a fatigued person may feel wide awake and engaged in a task. The primary cause of fatigue is a lack of sleep. Good restful sleep free from drugs or alcohol is a human necessity to prevent fatigue. Fatigue can also be caused by stress and by overworking. A person's mental and physical state also naturally cycles through various levels of performance each day. Variables such as body temperature, blood pressure, heart rate, blood chemistry, alertness, and attention rise and fall in a pattern daily. This is known as one's circadian rhythm. [*Figure 13-5*] A person's ability to work (and rest) rises and falls during this cycle. Performance counter to circadian rhythm can be difficult. Until it becomes extreme, a person may be unaware that he or she is fatigued. It is easier recognized by another person or in the results of tasks being performed. Flying alone when fatigued is particularly dangerous.

The best remedy for fatigue is to get enough sleep on a regular basis. Pilots must be aware of the amount and quality of sleep obtained. Countermeasures to fatigue are often used. Effectiveness can be short lived and many countermeasures may make fatigue worse. Caffeine is a common fatigue countermeasure. Pseudoephedrine found in sinus medicine and amphetamines are also used. While effective for short periods, a fatigued person remains fatigued and may have trouble getting the rest needed once they try to sleep.

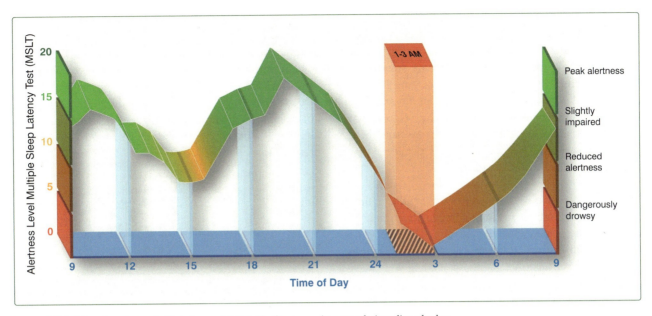

Figure 13-5. *Many human variables rise and fall daily due to one's natural circadian rhythm.*

If you find yourself suffering from acute fatigue, stay on the ground. Glider pilots often become fatigued while flying due to soaring in close proximity to other gliders in areas of lift or because of the constant requirement to see and avoid other traffic. Getting adequate rest is the only way to prevent fatigue from occurring. You should avoid flying when you have not had a full night's rest, when you have been working excessive hours, or have had an especially exhausting or stressful day. If you suspect you are suffering from chronic fatigue, consult your doctor.

Hyperventilation

Hyperventilation occurs when you are experiencing emotional stress, fright, or pain, and your breathing rate and depth increase, although the carbon dioxide is already at a reduced level in the blood. This can happen to both the experienced and novice pilot. Hyperventilation causes an excessive loss of carbon dioxide from your body, which can lead to unconsciousness due to the respiratory system's overriding mechanism to regain control of breathing.

Glider pilots who encounter extreme or unexpected turbulence or strong areas of sink over rough terrain or water may unconsciously increase their breathing rate. When flying at higher altitudes, either with or without oxygen, a tendency to breathe more rapidly than normal may occur, which can lead to hyperventilation.

It is important to know the symptoms of hyperventilation and correctly treat for it. *[Figure 13-6]* Treatment for hyperventilation involves restoring the proper carbon dioxide level back in the body. Breathing normally is both the best

Common Symptoms of Hyperventilation
Headache
Decreased reaction time
Impaired judgment
Euphoria
Visual impairment
Drowsiness
Lightheaded or dizzy sensation
Tingling in fingers and toes
Numbness
Pale, clammy appearance
Muscle spasms

Figure 13-6. *Common symptoms of hyperventilation.*

prevention and the best cure for hyperventilation. In addition to slowing the breathing rate, you also can breathe into a paper bag or talk aloud to over-come hyperventilation. Recovery is usually rapid once the breathing rate is returned to normal.

Inner Ear Discomfort

Gliders are not pressurized, therefore, pressure changes can affect glider pilots that are flying at high altitudes. Inner ear pain and a temporary reduction in ability to hear are caused by the ascents and descents of the glider. The physiological explanation for this discomfort is a difference between the pressure of the air outside the body and the air inside the middle ear. The middle ear cavity is small and located in the bone of the skull. While the external ear canal is always at the same pressure as the outside air, the pressure in the middle ear often changes more slowly. Even a slight difference between external pressure and middle ear pressure can cause discomfort.

When a glider ascends, middle ear air pressure may exceed the pressure of the air in the external ear canal, causing the eardrum to bulge outward. This pressure change becomes apparent when you experience alternate sensations of "fullness" and "clearing." During a descent, the reverse happens. While the pressure of the air in the external ear canal increases, the middle ear cavity, which equalized with the lower pressure at altitude, is at lower pressure than the external ear canal. The result is higher outside pressure, causing the eardrum to bulge inward.

This condition can be more difficult to relieve due to the fact that air must be introduced into the middle ear through the eustachian tube to equalize the pressure. The inner ear is a partial vacuum and tends to constrict the walls of the eustachian tube. To correct this often painful condition, which causes temporary reduction in hearing sensitivity, pinch your nostrils, close your mouth and lips, and blow slowly and gently in the mouth and nose. This procedure, called the valsalva maneuver, forces air up the eustachian tube into the middle ear.

Spatial Disorientation

For glider pilots, prevention is the best remedy for spatial disorientation. If the glider you are flying is not equipped for instrument flight, and you do not have many hours of training in controlling the glider by reference to instruments, it is best to avoid flight in reduced visibility or at night when the horizon is not visible. Susceptibility to disorienting illusions can be reduced through training, awareness, and learning to rely totally on your flight instruments. *[Figure 13-7]*

Figure 13-7. *Learning to rely totally on flight instruments to fly will reduce the likelihood of experiencing a disorienting illusion while in flight.*

Dehydration

Dehydration is the term given to a critical loss of water from the body. The first noticeable effect of dehydration is fatigue, which in turn makes top physical and mental performance difficult, if not impossible. Glider pilots often fly for a long period of time in hot summer temperatures or at high altitudes. This makes dehydration very likely for two reasons: the gliders clear canopy offers no protection from the sun and, at high altitudes, there are fewer air pollutants to diffuse the sun's rays. The result is continual exposure to heat that the body attempts to regulate by perspiration. If this fluid is not replaced, fatigue progresses to dizziness, weakness, nausea, tingling of hands and feet, abdominal cramps, and extreme thirst. *[Figure 13-8]*

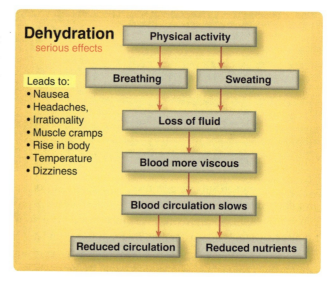

Figure 13-8. *Symptoms of dehydration.*

Water should be taken on every flight to prevent dehydration. The effects of dehydration on a pilot's performance are subtle, but can be dangerous and are especially a factor in warmer climates. Some glider pilots wear a hat to block the sun from distracting their ability to fly and see the instruments. Pilots should ensure that the brim of the hat is not too large, which can interfere with the ability to scan for other gliders and air traffic.

Heatstroke

Heatstroke is a condition caused by any inability of the body to control its temperature. Onset of this condition may be recognized by the symptoms of dehydration, but also has been known to be recognized only by complete collapse. To prevent these symptoms, it is recommended that you carry an ample supply of water and use it at frequent intervals on any long flight, whether you are thirsty or not. Wearing light colored, porous clothing and a hat provides protection from the sun. It is also helpful to keep the cockpit well ventilated, which aids in dispelling excess heat.

Cold Weather

When flying at higher altitudes, the inside of the glider can get cold. Proper clothing is a must since temperatures of −30° to −60 °C may be encountered at altitude. Proper preparation for the cold is especially difficult since temperatures on the ground are often pleasant on wave soaring days. Sunshine through the canopy keeps the upper body amazingly warm for a time, but shaded legs and feet quickly become cold. Frostbite is a very real threat. After an hour or two at such temperatures, even the upper body can become quite cold. Layered, loose-fitting clothing helps insulate body heat. Either wool gloves or light, fitted gloves with mittens over them work best for the hands. Mittens make tasks such as turning radio knobs difficult. For the feet, two or three pairs of socks (inner, silk; outer, wool) with an insulated boot are recommended.

In addition, the low temperatures can cause two other symptoms: it frosts your exhaled breath on the inside of the canopy and it causes the kidneys to excrete liquid at an accelerated rate.

A clean piece of cloth (that will not damage the canopy) can be used to wipe the condensation or frost from the canopy, if needed, but the best way to clear the canopy is a little fresh air through the side or front vent to help delay the buildup of frost. Unfortunately, this also quickly lowers the inside temperature, so it is best to wear clothing in layers so that you can easily take off or put on what is needed. There is little that can be done for the kidneys excreting liquid at an accelerated rate. The best course of action is to plan for it in advance by making a bathroom stop before you take off. Remember that the body is dehydrating more rapidly because of the cold and always be looking for signs of dehydration.

Cockpit Management

Prior to launch, passengers should be briefed on the use of safety belts, shoulder harnesses, and emergency procedures. If ballast is used, it must be properly secured. Organize the cockpit so items needed in flight are accessible. All other items must be securely stowed. The necessary charts and cross-country aids should be stowed within easy reach of the pilot.

Personal Equipment

If a parachute of the approved type is to be available for emergencies, Title 14 of the Code of Federal Regulations (14 CFR) part 91 requires that a certificated and appropriately-rated parachute rigger repack it within the preceding 180 days if it is made of nylon. The packing date information is usually found on a card contained in a small pocket on the body of the parachute.

Oxygen System

14 CFR part 91 also requires that the pilot in command (PIC) use supplemental oxygen for flights more than 30 minutes in duration above 12,500 feet and at all times during a flight above 14,000 feet. If supplemental oxygen is used, the system should be checked for flow, availability, and the PRICE checklist should be used:

- P = Pressure
- R = Regulator
- I = Indicator
- C = Connections
- E = Emergency bail-out bottle

The importance of understanding the need for oxygen equipment in gliders has been heightened in recent years by a considerable increase in the number of high-altitude soaring flights. The exploration of mountain waves has led to numerous flights at altitudes in excess of 30,000 feet with several record flights in excess of 40,000 feet. In some parts of the country, it is frequently possible to soar to a 16,000- to 18,000-foot cloud base in thermals. In almost all parts of the United States such altitudes are attainable in cumulonimbus clouds.

At 18,000 feet, air density is only one-half that at sea level. The purpose of breathing is to supply oxygen to the blood and remove carbon dioxide. In each breath at 18,000 feet, the pilot breathes in only half as much oxygen as at sea level. This is not enough to deliver an adequate supply of oxygen to the blood, and the situation worsens as altitude increases. The automatic reaction is to breathe twice as fast. This hyperventilation, or overbreathing, is almost worse than going up without oxygen in the first place because it results in eliminating too much carbon dioxide from the blood. The immediate effects of hyperventilation are:

- Spots before the eyes
- Dizzy feeling
- Numbing of fingers and toes, followed by possible unconsciousness

The dangers of oxygen deprivation should not be taken lightly. At around 20,000 feet MSL, pilots might have only 10 minutes of "useful consciousness." By 30,000 feet MSL, the time frame for "useful consciousness" decreases to 1 minute or less. For planned flights above 25,000 feet MSL, an emergency oxygen backup or bailout bottle should be carried.

The U.S. Air Force in cooperation with the Federal Aviation Administration (FAA) provides a 1-day, high-altitude orientation and chamber ride for civilian pilots. The experience is invaluable for any pilot contemplating high-altitude soaring and is even required by many clubs and operations as a prerequisite.

Aviation Oxygen Systems

Aviation oxygen systems are designed for airborne aviation applications. Unlike a medical-type oxygen system, an aviation system is generally much lighter, compact, and calibrated to deliver oxygen based on extensive research in human flight physiology. Prior to purchasing any type of oxygen system, pilots should research the different options and choose an oxygen system that is appropriate for the type of flying that they do because there are many manufacturers and types of system available. Two common types of systems used today are the Continuous-Flow System and the Electronic Pulse Demand Oxygen System (EDS).

Continuous-Flow System

The continuous-flow system uses a high-pressure storage tank and a pressure-reducing regulating valve that reduces the pressure in the cylinder to approximately atmospheric pressure at the mask. *[Figure 13-9]* The oxygen flow is continuous as long as the system is turned on. In some installations, it is possible to adjust the amount of oxygen flow manually for low, intermediate, and high altitudes; automatic regulators adjust the oxygen flow by means of a bellows, which varies the flow according to altitude. When using the continuous-flow oxygen system, the pilot can use either an oxygen mask or a nasal cannula. *[Figures 13-10 and 13-11]*

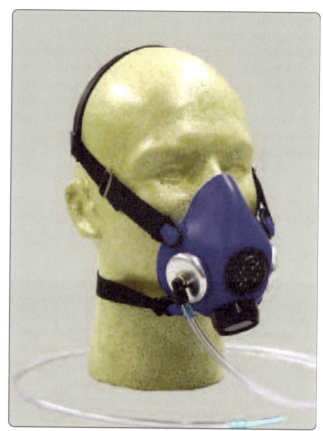

Figure 13-10. *Oxygen mask.*

Figure 13-9. *Continuous-flow oxygen system.*

Electronic Pulse Demand Oxygen System (EDS)

The EDS is the lightest, smallest, and most capable on-demand oxygen system available that delivers altitude-compensated pulses of oxygen only as you inhale, using as little as ⅛, typically ⅙ the amount of oxygen at ¼ the weight and volume over conventional constant-flow systems that deliver one liter per minute per 10,000 feet. *[Figure 13-12]* The EDS has a precision micro-electronic pressure altitude barometer that automatically determines the volume for each oxygen pulse up to pressure altitudes of 32,000 feet and higher altitudes are compensated with pulses of greater volume. The EDS automatically goes to a 100 percent pulse-demand mode at pressure altitudes above 32,000 feet.

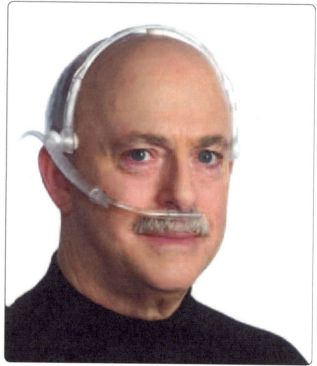

Figure 13-11. *Nasal cannula.*

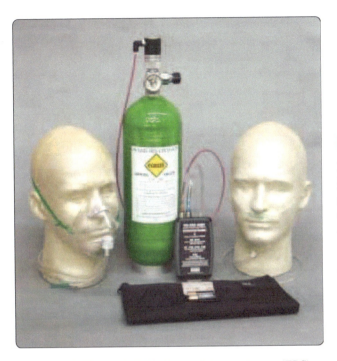

Figure 13-12. *Electronic Pulse Demand Oxygen System (EDS).*

The EDS can be set to one of three D (day or delayed) modes and delays, responding with oxygen until it senses pressure altitudes of approximately 5,000 or 10,000 feet, conserving oxygen when it is not needed. It can also be set to N (night or now) mode for night flying where it responds from sea-level and up. Both modes provide the same amount of oxygen, automatically tracking pressure altitude changes. The EDS limits its response to a maximum respiration rate of about 20 breaths per minute, virtually eliminating hyperventilation usually encountered in stressful situations. There are no scales to observe or knobs to turn as you climb or descend. Adjusting (zeroing) for new barometric pressures is not needed because the EDS responds directly to pressure altitude, as do the physiological properties of your body.

Transponder Code

The Federal Aviation Administration (FAA) has assigned transponder code 1202 for use by gliders not in contact with an air traffic control (ATC) facility with an effective date of March 7, 2012. The notice was published in JO 7110.577, a copy of which is available on the FAA website at www.faa.gov. Gliders operating in areas where there is an agreement with local ATC to use a different code should contact the agreement sponsor for guidance on which code to use.

Definitions

- SQUAWK: The 4-digit code set in the transponder, such as 1202.
- IDENT or SQUAWK IDENT: A controller may ask you to "ident" or "squawk ident" to verify your location on the radar screen. Do NOT push the ident button unless they ask you to. When asked, push the button on the transponder marked IDENT. This causes the target on the controllers radar screen to change, identifying your transponder location.
- Tow planes are to Squawk 1200, as normal.

Risk Management

Risk management, a formalized way of dealing with hazards, is the logical process of weighing the potential costs of risks against the possible benefits of allowing those risks to stand uncontrolled. In order to better understand risk management, the terms "hazard" and "risk" needs to be understood.

Hazard identification is a process used to identify all possible situations where people may be exposed to injury, illness, or disease. Typical hazards are weather, mountains, obstacles, and operational and equipment failure.

Risk is the chance of a hazard actually causing damage and/or injury. Risk is measured in terms of consequences and likelihood. Risk management is the overall process of risk identification, risk analysis, control of risks, and risk evaluation. Risk control is part of risk management that involves the implementation of policies, standards, procedures, and physical changes to eliminate or minimize adverse risks. For example, the pilot understands the risk of a tow line break during launch. An acceptable risk that he or she can mitigate by understanding the risk and having a plan of actions to follow after a tow line breaks.

Safety Management System (SMS)

The Safety Management System (SMS) is a formal, top-down business approach to managing safety risk, which includes a systemic approach to managing safety, including the necessary organizational structures, accountabilities, policies and procedures. SMS is becoming a worldwide standard throughout the aviation industry integrating risk management, occupational safety, health, security, environment, and other concepts for the management of a complete safety program. SMS is a comprehensive program designed for a formal organization. The individual pilot can learn from the process and apply the concept for his or her own personal safety considerations, such as:

- Risk management decision-making.
- Management capabilities before a system failure
- Risk controls through safety assurance
- Knowledge sharing between regulations and the pilot
- Promoting a safety framework by having a sound safety culture or attitude

Aeronautical Decision-Making (ADM)

Aeronautical decision-making (ADM) is a mental process used by pilots (systematically) to determine a course of action in response to a given set of circumstances.

- Circumstance: My oxygen system has a slow leak. Soaring conditions are prefect and I do not need oxygen for today.

- Circumstance: High winds are forecast later today, but I should return before the wind changes.

- Circumstance: My batteries are low, but I am only planning a short flight.

Learning effective ADM skills cannot be overemphasized. As advancement in training methods, airplane equipment and systems, and services continue for pilots, incidents and accidents still occur. Despite all the changes in technology to improve flight safety, the human factor is the same. The human factor is still involved in a high percent of all aviation accidents.

Circumstances as mundane as a "slow oxygen leak," a "high wind forecast," or "low batteries" are parts of a decision chain leading to an incident or accident. The term "pilot error" has been used to describe the causes of these accidents meaning that an action or decision made by the pilot was the cause or a contributing factor that led to the accident. In the previous circumstances, the chain is broken if the pilot—has the "slow oxygen leak" repaired—respects the "high wind forecast" and delays the flight—charges the "low batteries" before the next flight. The pilot error definition also includes the pilot's failure to make a decision or take action. Human factor-related accidents are accidents that did not involve a single decision but a chain of decision and factors leading to the accident. A "poor judgment chain," referred to as the error chain, describe the concept of contributing factors in a human factors-related accident. Breaking one link in the chain normally is all that is necessary to change the outcome of the sequence of events.

Advisory Circular (AC) 60-22, "Aeronautical Decision Making," provides introductory material, background information, and reference material on ADM. The material in this AC provides a systematic approach to risk assessment and stress management in aviation, illustrates how personal attitudes can influence decision-making, and how those attitudes can be modified to enhance safety in the cockpit. This AC also provides instructors with methods for teaching ADM techniques and skills in conjunction with conventional flight instruction.

Appendix A
Soaring Safety Foundation (SSF): Safety Advisory 00-1, Glider Critical Assembly Procedures

Introduction

The Soaring Society of America (SSA) and the Soaring Safety Foundation (SSF) issued Safety Advisory 00-1 concerning glider assembly procedures to aid the pilot by providing some critical information to consider when assembling a glider. Due to a number of recent accidents involving improper assembly of the glider as a causal factor, the SSF is issuing this Safety Advisory to address the critical components of glider assembly. Improper glider assembly has been identified as having caused injuries to pilots and destruction of aircraft.

This safety advisory presents suggested procedures for ensuring proper assembly without specific detail that is available in Pilot Operating Handbooks (POHs) and other checklists developed by the manufacturer. Other knowledgeable individuals have also presented methods to confirm proper assembly, as well as emergency procedures for flying the aircraft should any control function improperly due to improper assembly. The latter may or may not be approved by the manufacturer of the glider or sailplane, and will not be discussed herein.

History

Prior to 1960, most gliders required significant effort to assemble. Many had containers of bicycle chains, bolts, nuts, washers, retaining pins, and other pieces that had to be assembled in sequence. An improperly assembled glider would not pass a simple control check. For example, the horizontal tail assembly (including elevator) may not have been detached during disassembly; the control cables for the rudder and elevator were never disconnected nor did they require assembly later.

Later, manufacturers developed quicker and easier methods for assembling gliders and sailplanes. This made it possible to install both wings by simply inserting the wing root into the fuselage and using a pin to secure the attachment. Horizontal stabilizers and elevators were removed during disassembly and reassembled with as little as one simple attach bolt or pin. The SSA and the SSF encouraged all manufacturers to go to the next level and provide "automatic hook-ups" for ailerons, flaps, glidepath control devices, and elevators, anticipating a reduction in the potential to attempt flight without the controls properly attached. Many of the gliders and sailplanes today have these automatic attachments.

Although the annual numbers of reported incidents and accidents resulting from failure to attach controls have decreased, disturbing numbers of recent incidents and accidents indicate a need for further investigation of the causes. Subsequent structural improvements and/or revisions of assembly and/or disassembly procedures could help prevent many future incidents and accidents.

The SSF recognized four factors that frequently appeared when investigation of such accidents were made:

1. Distractions from other people while assembling the glider,
2. Failure to follow manufacturer-recommended assembly procedures,
3. Failure to do a positive control check, and
4. Rushing the procedure to get into the air.

Ensuring Airworthiness

The pilot in command (PIC) is directly responsible and the final authority for operation of the aircraft in accordance with Title 14 of the Code of Federal Regulations (14 CFR) part 91, section 91.3. It is also the responsibility of the PIC to determine if the aircraft is in condition for safe flight (14 CFR part 91, section 91.7). During assembly of the glider or sailplane, the PIC assumes that responsibility.

During the assembly procedure, no outside interference should be allowed. It is difficult to keep observers from attempting to converse or ask questions, but such action has frequently been the cause of incomplete and/or inaccurate assembly. The crew person or assistant can be of great assistance by immediately deflecting this unintentional interference.

To ensure the glider is properly assembled, the manufacturer's checklist should be followed and positive control check performed. The assembly should proceed in a relaxed and thorough manner and never be hurried. Rushing to squeeze in between landings or to be number one on the grid has resulted in improperly assembled sailplanes and subsequent accidents. To enhance the checking of the assembly process, it is suggested that the PIC ask another person to assist by examining critical items to ensure proper installation. This person does not necessarily need to be familiar with a specific aircraft or manufacturer, but should have a basic understanding of how to assemble a glider or sailplane. If such a person is not available, the PIC may benefit from explaining to an assistant how each part is installed and attached; in effect, checking the pilot's own work.

Critical Items

The following list, although not totally inclusive, offers items that should be checked prior to flight. Failure to have these items correctly assembled may result in difficult or impossible flight characteristics. With the help of an assistant, and usually performed by simply walking around the aircraft, starting and ending at the cockpit area, check each of the following items as appropriate to the aircraft being flown for proper installation and security. After a thorough check of the following items is complete, a positive control check should be conducted.

- Main wing pin(s)
- Drag spar pin(s)
- Control rods attached
- Ailerons, drag devices, flaps
- Hotellier connectors
- Spring-loaded connectors
- Locking collars
- Safety pins installed
- Safety collars installed
- Outer wing panels installed
- Control rods attached and properly secured
- Horizontal tail properly installed
- Elevator control rod attached
- Safety pin installed
- Rudder cables attached

The SSA and the SSF agree that adherence to this safety advisory will prevent accidents that occur as a result of improper assembly of gliders. The SSF strongly encourages each PIC to develop a list of critical items for each glider being flown to assist in ensuring that critical items are properly installed and secured during the assembly process.

After the assembly is completed, the pilot should conduct a preflight as recommended by the manufacturer. This preflight ensures that all assembly has been conducted properly, and the pilot can determine if the glider is airworthy for flight. During the preflight, it is essential that the pilot completes a positive control check. This check ensures that the glider has been assembled correctly and that all controls are connected and secured as per the manufacturer recommendations.

Glossary

A

Advection. The transport of an atmospheric variable due to mass motion by the wind. Usually the term as used in meteorology refers only to horizontal transport.

Ailerons. The hinged portion of the trailing edge of the outer wing used to bank or roll around the longitudinal axis.

Air density. The mass of air per unit volume.

Airfoil. The surfaces on a glider that produce lift.

Air mass. A widespread mass of air having similar characteristics (e.g., temperature), that usually helps to identify the source region of the air. Fronts are distinct boundaries between air masses.

Amplitude. In wave motion, one half the distance between the wave crest and the wave trough.

Angle of attack. The angle formed between the relative wind and the chord line of the wing.

Angle of incidence. The angle between the chord line of the wing and the longitudinal axis of the glider. The angle of incidence is built into the glider by the manufacturer and cannot be adjusted by the pilot's movements of the controls.

Aspect ration. The ratio between the wing span and the mean chord of the wing.

Asymmetrical airfoil. One in which the upper camber differs from the lower camber.

Atmospheric sounding. A measure of atmospheric variables aloft, usually pressure, temperature, humidity, and wind.

Atmospheric stability. Describes a state in which an air parcel resists vertical displacement or, once displaced (for instance by flow over a hill), tends to return to its original level.

B

Bailout bottle. Small oxygen cylinder connected to the oxygen mask supplying several minutes of oxygen. It can be used in case of primary oxygen system failure or if an emergency bailout at high altitude became necessary.

Ballast. Term used to describe any system that adds weight to the glider. Performance ballast employed in some gliders increases wing loading using releasable water in the wings (via integral tanks or water bags). This allows faster average cross-country speeds. Trim ballast is used to adjust the flying CG, often necessary for light-weight pilots. Some gliders also have a small water ballast tank in the tail for optimizing flying CG.

Barograph. Instrument for recording pressure as a function of time. Used by glider pilots to verify flight performance for badge or record flights.

Best glide speed (best L/D speed). The airspeed that results in the least amount of altitude loss over a given distance. This speed is determined from the performance polar. The manufacturer publishes the best glide (L/D) airspeed for specified weights and the resulting glide ratio. For example, a glide ratio of 36:1 means that the glider will lose 1 foot of altitude for every 36 feet of forward movement in still air at this airspeed.

C

Camber. The curvature of a wing when looking at a cross section. A wing has upper camber on its top surface and lower camber on its bottom surface.

Cap cloud. Also called a foehn cloud. These are clouds forming on mountain or ridge tops by cooling of moist air rising on the upwind side followed by warming and drying by downdrafts on the lee side.

Centering. Adjusting circles while thermalling to provide the greatest average climb.

Center of pressure. The point along the wing chord line where lift is considered to be concentrated.

Centrifugal force. The apparent force occurring in curvilinear motion acting to deflect objects outward from the axis of rotation. For instance, when pulling out of a dive, it is the force pushing you down in your seat.

Centripetal force. The force in curvilinear motion acting toward the axis of rotation. For instance, when pulling out of a dive, it is the force that the seat exerts on the pilot to offset the centrifugal force.

Chord line. An imaginary straight line drawn from the leading edge of an airfoil to the trailing edge.

Cloud streets. Parallel rows of cumulus clouds. Each row can be as short as 10 miles or as long as a 100 miles or more.

Cold soaked. Condition of a self-launch or sustainer engine making it difficult or impossible to start in flight due to long-time exposure to cold temperatures. Usually occurs after a long soaring flight at altitudes with cold temperatures (e.g., a wave flight).

Convection. Transport and mixing of an atmospheric variable due to vertical mass motions (e.g., updrafts).

Convective condensation level (CCL). The level at which cumulus forms from surface-based convection. Under this level, the air is dry adiabatic and the mixing ratio is constant.

Conventional tail. A glider design with the horizontal stabilizer mounted at the bottom of the vertical stabilizer.

Convergence. A net increase in the mass of air over a specified area due to horizontal wind speed and/or direction changes. When convergence occurs in lower levels, it is usually associated with upward air motions.

Convergence zone. An area of convergence, sometimes several miles wide, at other times very narrow. These zones often provide organized lift for many miles (e.g., a sea-breeze front).

Critical angle of attack. Angle of attack, typically around 18°, beyond which a stall occurs. The critical angle of attack can be exceeded at any airspeed and at any nose attitude.

Cross-country. In soaring, any flight out of gliding range of the takeoff airfield. Note that this is different from the definitions in the 14 CFR for meeting the experience requirements for various pilot certificates and/or ratings.

Cumulus congestus. A cumulus cloud of significant vertical extent and usually displaying sharp edges. In warm climates, these sometimes produce precipitation. Also called towering cumulus, these clouds indicate that thunderstorm activity may soon occur.

Cumulonimbus (CB). Also called thunderclouds, these are deep convective clouds with a cirrus anvil and may contain any of the characteristics of a thunderstorm: thunder, lightning, heavy rain, hail, strong winds, turbulence, and even tornadoes.

D

Dead reckoning. Navigation by computing a heading from true airspeed and wind, then estimating time needed to fly to a destination.

Density altitude. Pressure altitude corrected for nonstandard temperature variations. Performance charts for many older gliders are based on this value.

Dewpoint (or dewpoint temperature). The temperature to which a sample of air must be cooled, while the amount of water vapor and barometric pressure remain constant, in order to attain saturation with respect to water.

Dihedral. The angle at which the wings are slanted upward from the root to the tip.

Diurnal effects. A variation (may be in temperature, moisture, wind, cloud cover, etc.) that recurs every 24 hours.

Downburst. A strong, concentrated downdraft, often associated with a thunderstorm. When these reach the ground, they spread out, leading to strong and even damaging surface winds.

Drag. The force that resists the movement of the glider through the air.

Dry adiabat. A line on a thermodynamic chart representing a rate of temperature change at the dry adiabatic lapse rate.

Dry adiabatic lapse rate (DALR). The rate of decrease of temperature with height of unsaturated air lifted adiabatically (not heat exchange). Numerically the value is 3 °C or 5.4 °F per 1,000 feet.

Dust devil. A small vigorous circulation that can pick up dust or other debris near the surface to form a column hundreds or even thousands of feet deep. At the ground, winds can be strong enough to flip an unattended glider over on its back. Dust devils mark the location where a thermal is leaving the ground.

Dynamic stability. A glider's motion and time required for a response to static stability.

E

Elevator. Attached to the back of the horizontal stabilizer, if controls movement around the lateral axis.

Empennage. The tail group of the aircraft usually supporting the vertical stabilizer and rudder, as well as the horizontal stabilizer and elevator, or on some aircraft, the V-Tail.

F

Flaps. Hinged portion of the trailing edge between the ailerons and fuselage. In some gliders, ailerons and flaps are interconnected to produce full-span flaperons. In either case, flap change the lift and drag on the wing.

Flutter. Resonant condition leading to rapid, unstable oscillations of part of the glider structure (e.g., the wing) or a control surface (e.g., elevator or aileron). Flutter usually occurs at high speeds and can quickly lead to structural failure.

Forward slip. A slide used to dissipate altitude without increasing the glider's speed, particularly in gliders without flaps or with inoperative spoilers.

G

Glider. A heavier-than-air aircraft that is supported in flight by the dynamic reaction of the air against its lifting surfaces, and whose free flight does not depend on an engine.

Graupel. Also called soft hail or snow pellets, these are white, round or conical ice particles $\frac{1}{8}$ to $\frac{1}{4}$ inch in diameter. They often form as a thunderstorm matures and indicate the likelihood of lightning.

Ground effect. A reduction in induced drag for the same amount of lift produced. Within one wingspan above the ground, the decrease in induced drag enables the glider to fly at a lower airspeed. In ground effect, a lower angle of attack is required to produce the same amount of lift.

H

Height band. The altitude range in which the thermals are strongest on any given day. Remaining with the height band on a cross-country flight should allow the fastest average speed.

House thermal. A thermal that forms frequently in the same or similar location.

Human factors. The study of how people interact with their environments. In the case of general aviation, it is the study of how pilot performance is influenced by such issues as the design of cockpits, the function of the organs of the body, the effects of emotions, and the interaction and communication with the other participants of the aviation community, such as other crewmembers and air traffic control personnel.

I

Induced drag. Drag that is the consequence of developing lift with a finite-span wing. It can be represented by a vector that results from the difference between total and vertical lift.

Inertia. The tendency of a mass at rest to remain at rest or, if in motion, to remain in motion unless acted upon by some external force.

Instrument meteorological conditions (IMC). Meteorological conditions expressed in terms of visibility, distance from cloud, and ceiling less than the minimum specified for visual meteorological conditions (VMC). Gliders rarely fly in IMC due to instrumentation and air traffic control requirements.

Inversion. Usually refers to an increase in temperature with height, but may also be used for other atmospheric variables.

Isohumes. Lines of equal relative humidity.

Isopleth. A line connecting points of constant or equal value.

Isotherm. A contour line of equal temperature.

K

Katabatic. Used to describe any wind blowing down slope.

Kinetic energy. Energy due to motion, defined as one half mass times velocity squared.

L

Lapse rate. The decrease with height of an atmospheric variable, usually referring to temperature, but can also apply to pressure or density.

Lateral axis. An imaginary straight line drawn perpendicularly (laterally) across the fuselage and through the center of gravity. Pitch movement occurs around the lateral axis, and is controlled by the elevator.

Lenticular cloud. Smooth, lens-shaped clouds marking mountain-wave crests. They may extend the entire length of the mountain range producing the wave and are also called wave clouds or lennies by glider pilots.

Lift. Produced by the dynamic effects of the airstream acting on the wing, lift opposes the downward force of weight.

Limit load. The maximum load, expressed as multiples of positive and negative G (force of gravity), that an aircraft can sustain before structural damage becomes possible. The load limit varies from aircraft to aircraft.

Load factor. The ratio of the load supported by the glider's wings to the actual weight of the aircraft and its contents.

Longitudinal axis. An imaginary straight line running through the fuselage from nose to tail. Roll movement occurs around the longitudinal axis, and is controlled by the ailerons.

M

Mesoscale convection system (MCS). A large cluster of thunderstorms with horizontal dimensions on the order of 100 miles. MCSs are sometimes organized in a long line of thunderstorms (e.g., a squall line) or as a random grouping of thunderstorms. Individual thunderstorms within the MCS may be severe.

Microburst. A small-sized downburst of 2.2 nautical mile or less horizontal dimension.

Minimum sink airspeed. Airspeed, as determined by the performance polar, at which the glider achieves the lowest sink rate. That is, the glider loses the least amount of altitude per unit of time at minimum sink airspeed.

Mixing ration. The ratio of the mass of water vapor to the mass of dry air.

Multicell thunderstorm. A group or cluster of individual thunderstorm cells with varying stages of development. These storms are often self propagating and may last for several hours.

O

Olphin flight. Straight flight following speed-to-fly theory. Glides can often be extended and average cross-country speeds increased by flying faster in sink and slower in lift without stopping to circle.

P

Parasite drag. Drag caused by any aircraft surface that deflects or interferes with the smooth airflow around the airplane.

Pilotage. Navigational technique based on flight by reference to ground landmarks.

Pilot-induced oscillation (PIO). Rapid oscillations caused by the pilot's overcontrolled motions. PIOs usually occur on takeoff or landings with pitch-sensitive gliders and in severe cases can lead to loss of control or damage.

Pitch attitude. The angle of the longitudinal axis relative to the horizon. Pitch attitude serves as a visual reference for the pilot to maintain or change airspeed.

Pitot-static system. System that powers the airspeed altimeter and variometer by relying on air pressure differences to measure glider speed, altitude, and climb or sink rate.

Placards. Small statements or pictorial signs permanently fixed in the cockpit and visible to the pilot. Placards are used for operating limitations (e.g., weight or speeds) or to indicate the position of an operating lever (e.g., landing gear retracted or down and locked).

Precipitable water. The amount of liquid precipitation that would result if all water vapor were condensed.

Pressure altitude. The height above the standard pressure level of 29.92 "Hg. It is obtained by setting 29.92 in the barometric pressure window and reading the altimeter.

R

Radiant energy. Energy due to any form of electromagnetic radiation (e.g., from the sun).

Radius of turn. The horizontal distance an aircraft uses to complete a turn.

Rate of turn. The amount of time it takes for a glider to turn a specified number of degrees.

Relative wind. The airflow caused by the motion of the aircraft through the air. Relative wind, also called relative airflow, is opposite and parallel to the direction of flight.

Rotor. A turbulent circulation under mountain-wave crests, to the lee side and parallel to the mountains creating the wave. Glider pilots use the term rotor to describe any low-level turbulent flow associated with mountain waves.

Rotor streaming. A phenomenon that occurs when the air flow at mountain levels may be sufficient for wave formation, but begins to decrease with altitude above the mountain. In this case, the air downstream of the mountain breaks up and becomes turbulent, similar to rotor, with no lee waves above.

Rudder. Attached to the back of the vertical stabilizer, the rudder controls movement about the vertical axis.

S

Sailplane. A glider used for traveling long distances and remaining aloft for extended periods of time.

Saturated Adiabatic Lapse Rate (SALR). The rate of temperature decrease with height of saturated air. Unlike the dry adiabatic lapse rate (DALR), the SALR is not a constant numerical value but varies with temperature.

Self-launching glider. A glider equipped with an engine, allowing it to be launched under its own power. When the engine is shut down, a self-launching glider displays the same characteristics as a non-powered glider.

Side slip. A slip in which the glider's longitudinal axis remains parallel to the original flightpath but in which the flightpath changes direction according to the steepness of the bank.

Slip. A descent with one wing lowered and the glider's longitudinal axis at an angle to the flightpath. A slip is used to steepen the approach path without increasing the airspeed, or to make the glider move sideways through the air, counteracting the drift resulting from a crosswind.

Speed to fly. Optimum speed through the (sinking or rising) air mass to achieve either the furthest glide or fastest average cross-country speed depending on the objectives during a flight.

Spin. An aggravated stall that results in the glider descending in a helical, or corkscrew, path.

Spoilers. Devices on the tops of wings to disturb (spoil) part of the airflow over the wing. The resulting decrease in lift creates a higher sink rate and allows for a steeper approach.

Squall line. A line of thunderstorms often located along or ahead of a vigorous cold front. Squall lines may contain severe thunderstorms. The term is also used to describe a line of heavy precipitation with an abrupt wind shift but no thunderstorms, as sometimes occurs in association with fronts.

Stabilator. A one-piece horizontal stabilizer used in lieu of an elevator.

Stability. The glider's ability to maintain a uniform flight condition and return to that condition after being disturbed.

Stall. Condition that occurs when the critical angle of attack is reached and exceeded. Airflow begins to separate from the top of the wing, leading to a loss of lift. A stall can occur at any pitch attitude or airspeed.

Standard atmosphere. A theoretical vertical distribution of pressure, temperature and density agreed upon by international convention. It is the standard used, for instance, for aircraft performance calculations. At sea level, the standard atmosphere consists of a barometric pressure of 29.92 inches of mercury ("Hg) or 1013.2 millibars, and a temperature of 15 °C (59 °F). Pressure and temperature normally decrease as altitude increases. The standard lapse rate in the lower atmosphere for each 1,000 feet of altitude is approximately 1 "Hg. and 2 °C (3.5 °F). For example, the standard pressure and temperature at 3,000 feet mean sea level (MSL) is 26.92 "Hg. (29.92 – 3) and 9 °C (15 °C – 6 °C).

Static stability. The initial tendency to return to a state of equilibrium when disturbed from that state.

Supercell thunderstorm. A large, powerful type of thunderstorm that forms in very unstable environments with vertical and horizontal wind shear. These are almost always associated with severe weather, strong surface winds, large hail, and/or tornadoes.

T

T-tail. A type of glider with the horizontal stabilizer mounted on the top of the vertical stabilizer forming a T.

Thermal. A buoyant plume or bubble of rising air.

Thermal index (TI). For any given level is the temperature of the air parcel having risen at the dry adiabatic lapse rate (DALR) subtracted from the ambient temperature. Experience has shown that a TI should be –2 for thermals to form and be sufficiently strong for soaring flight.

Thermal wave. Waves, often but not always marked by cloud streets, that are excited by convection disturbing an overlying stable layer. Also called convection waves.

Thermodynamic diagram. A chart presenting isopleths of pressure, temperature, water vapor content, as well as dry and saturated adiabats. Various forms exist, the most commonly used in the United States being the Skew-T/Log-P.

Thrust. The forward force that propels a powered glider through the air.

Total drag. The sum of parasite and induced drag.

Towhook. A mechanism allowing the attachment and release of a towrope on the glider or towplane. On gliders, it is located near the nose or directly ahead of the main wheel. Two types of towhooks commonly used in gliders are manufactured by Tost and Schweizer.

Trim devices. Any device designed to reduce or eliminate pressure on the control stick. When properly trimmed, the glider should fly at the desired airspeed with no control pressure from the pilot (i.e., hands off). Trim mechanisms are either external tabs on the elevator (or stabilator) or a simple spring-tension system connected to the control stick.

True altitude. The actual height of an object above mean sea level.

V

V-tail. A type of glider with two tail surfaces mounted to form a V. V-tails combine elevator and rudder movements.

Variometer. Sensitive rate of climb or descent indicator that measures static pressure between the static ports and an external capacity. Variometers can be mechanical or electrical and can be compensated to eliminate unrealistic indications of lift and sink due to rapid speed changes.

Vertical axis. An imaginary straight line drawn through the center of gravity and perpendicular to the lateral and longitudinal axes. Yaw movement occurs around the vertical axis and is controlled by the rudder.

Visual meteorological conditions (VMC). Meteorological conditions expressed in terms of visibility, distance from cloud, and ceiling equal to or better than a specified minimum. VMC represents minimum conditions for safe flight using visual reference for navigation and traffic separation. Ceilings and visibility below VMC constitutes instrument meteorological conditions (IMC).

W

Washout. Slight twist built in towards the wingtips, designed to improve the stall characteristics of the wing.

Water vapor. Water present in the air while in its vapor form. It is one of the most important of atmospheric constituents.

Wave length. The distance between two wave crests or wave troughs.

Wave window. Special areas arranged by Letter of Agreement (LOA) with the controlling ATC wherein gliders may be allowed to fly under VFR in Class A Airspace at certain times and to certain specified altitudes.

Weight. Acting vertically through the glider's center of gravity, weight opposes lift.

Wind triangle. Navigational calculation allowing determination of true heading with a correction for crosswinds on course.

Index

A

Abnormal procedures..8-8, 8-14
Absolute altitude..4-11
Accelerated stalls..7-34
Accident prevention..8-30
A cross-country flight..11-1
Aeronautical Decision-Making (ADM)................................13-10
Aerotow abnormal and emergency procedures.....................8-8
Aerotow climb-out...7-6
Aerotow release..7-8
After landing and securing..7-27
Afterlanding off field...8-20
Aileron malfunctions...8-23
Airborne emergencies...12-12
    Glider problem...12-12
    Glider release failure..12-12
    Immediate release..12-12
    Neither the tow plane or glider can release..................12-12
Air masses conducive to thermal soaring..............................9-9
Airspeed indicator...4-2
Airspeed indicator malfunctions...8-21
Airspeed indicator markings...4-5
Airspeed limitations..4-6
    Best glide speed..4-6
    Landing gear operating speed..4-6
    Maneuvering speed...4-6
    Maximum aerotow or ground launch speed....................4-6
    Minimum sink speed...4-6
Altimeter..4-6
Altimeter malfunctions..8-21
Altitude..5-3
Angle of bank...7-29
Approach...12-10
Approaching a thermal...12-9
A sample cross-country flight...11-5
Assembly and storage techniques...6-2
Atmosphere..9-2
Atmospheric pressure...5-2
Atmospheric pressure and altitude..4-6
Atmospheric stability..9-7
Attitude..1-6
Atypical thermals..10-10
Automobile launch..7-14

B

Ballast...5-14
    Performance ballast..5-14
    Water ballast...5-14
Boundary layer...3-3
    Laminar boundary layer..3-3
    Turbulent boundary layer..3-4
Bowls and spurs...10-13
Boxing the wake..7-10
Broken glider canopy...8-22
Bubble model...9-6

C

Cable..1-6
Centrifugal force..3-13
CG hooks...7-11
Classes of gliders eligible for European and World Championships..2-3
    15 Meter class..2-3
    18 Meter class..2-3
    Club class...2-3
    Open class..2-3
    Standard class...2-3
    Two-seat class...2-3
    World class...2-4
Classes of turns...7-28
Climb..12-7
Climb-out and release procedures......................................7-16
Climb-out and shutdown procedures..................................7-19
Clothing..8-28
Cloud streets..9-9
Cockpit management..13-7
Collision avoidance...10-9
Combined sources of updrafts..10-24
Communication...8-29
Compass malfunctions...8-21
Complacency...13-2

Composition 9-2
Convection 9-6
Convergence lift..9-19
Convergence zones 10-23
Converting meters to feet..1-6
Course deviations...11-14
Cross-country aerotow 12-10
Cross-country flight in a self-launching glider 11-15
Cross-country flight using other lift sources.............11-17
Cross-country techniques..11-9
Crossed-control stalls..7-35
Crosswind landing 7-25
Crosswinds...5-3
Crosswind takeoff 7-5, 7-19
    Assisted 7-5
    Unassisted..7-6
Crosswind takeoff and climb 7-14
Cumulus clouds...10-2

D

Density 9-2
Density altitude 4-11
Descent..12-10
Dive brakes 2-5
Downwind landing 7-27
Drogue chute malfunctions 8-25
Dry adiabatic lapse rate..9-7

E

Effect of nonstandard pressure and temperature............4-7
Efficient slope soaring...10-10
Electronic flight computers 4-15
Elevator 1-6, 2-6
Elevator malfunctions..8-22
Elevator trim malfunctions 8-24
Emergencies..12-11
Emergency equipment and survival gear....................8-28
Emergency procedures............................. 7-17, 8-14, 8-15
Empennage..2-6
Entering a thermal..10-5
Entripetal force..3-13
Equipment inspections and operational checks 12-2
European aviation safety agency 2-3
Exiting a thermal..10-9

F

Factors influencing PIOs...8-2
Fatigue..13-4
Federation Aeronautique Internationale 2-3
Flaps..2-5

Flight instrument malfunctions 8-20
Flight instruments 4-1
Flight manuals..5-8
Flight preparation and planning 11-2
Flying in the wave..10-20
Food and water...8-28
Forecasts 9-23
Forces of flight..3-2
Forward slip 3-16, 7-26
Frosted glider canopy...8-22
Fuselage 2-4
    Wings and components 2-4

G

Getting into the wave...10-18
Glider 1-3
Glide ratio 3-8
    Aspect ratio..3-9
Glider canopy malfunctions.......................................8-21
Glider canopy opens unexpectedly 8-21
Glider care...6-7
Glider certificate eligibility requirements 1-5
Glider complexity 11-16
Glider design..2-2
Glider-induced oscillations 8-6
Glider mechanical failure...8-8
Glider pilot schools 1-4
    14 CFR part 61 school..1-5
    14 CFR part 141 school..1-5
Glider polars...5-8
Glider preflight inspection 6-6
Gliders—the early years 1-2
Glider tow positions 12-8
G-loads..4-17
G-meter 4-17
    Negative G..4-17
    Positive G..4-17
GPS navigation systems...11-8
Graphic weather charts 9-23
    Composite moisture stability chart.......................9-24
    Winds and temperatures aloft chart......................9-23
Ground effect..3-19
Ground handling 6-4
Ground launch abnormal and emergency
procedures..8-14
Ground launch takeoff procedures..............................7-11
Ground signals 12-6

Begin takeoff 12-6
Hold 12-6
Pilot ready, wings level 12-6
Stop engine/release tow line 12-7
Stop operation or emergency 12-7
Take up slack 12-6
Tow plane ready 12-7
Gust-induced oscillations 8-5
Gyroscopic instruments 4-17

H

Hazardous attitudes 13-2
Headwind 5-3
Heatstroke 13-6
Height bands 11-11
High density altitude 5-2
High-performance glider operations and
considerations 11-16
Human and physiological factors that affect flight 13-4
Human error 13-3
Intentional 13-4
Unintentional 13-3
Hyperventilation 13-5

I

Impact air pressure lines 4-2
Improper elevator trim setting 8-3
Improper wing flaps setting 8-3
Inability to restart a self-launching/sustainer glider
engine while airborne 8-27
Inclinometer 4-16
Indicated altitude 4-10
Indiscipline 13-3
Induced drag 3-5
Total drag 3-6
Inflight fire 8-28
Inflight signals 7-3, 7-12
Initial point 7-22
Inner ear discomfort 13-5
Inside a thermal 10-6
Bank angle 10-6
Centering 10-7
Speed 10-6
Interpreting weather charts 9-23
Inversion 9-9

K

K-index 9-12
Knots 1-6

L

Landing 7-21, 12-10
Landing checklist 7-22
Landing gear 2-8
Launch equipment inspection 6-5
Layers of the atmosphere 9-4
Exosphere 9-4
Mesosphere 9-4
Stratosphere 9-4
Thermosphere 9-4
Troposphere 9-4
Lift 1-6, 3-2
Lift/drag devices 2-5
Lifted index 9-12
Limitations 5-10
Load factor 3-13
Locating thermals 10-2
Lost procedures 11-14
Low density altitude 5-2

M

Magnetic compass 4-16
Malfunctions, airspeed indicator 8-21
Maneuvering at minimum controllable airspeed 7-31
Mechanism for wave formation 9-16
Medical equipment 8-29
Minimum sink rate 5-8
Miscellaneous flight system malfunctions 8-25

N

National Transportation Safety Board (NTSB) 8-30
Navigation equipment 8-29
Negative flap 2-5
Netto 4-14
Normal approach and landing 7-22
Normal assisted takeoff 7-4
Normal into-the-wind launch 7-15
Normal takeoff 7-19
Nosewheel glider oscillations during launches
and landings 8-7

O

Obstructions 10-14
Obtaining weather information 9-21
Off-field landing procedures 8-18
Off-field landing with injury 8-20
Off-field landing without injury 8-20
On the airport 12-6
Operating airspeeds 7-36

Best glide airspeed..7-37
    Minimum sink airspeed 7-36
    Speed to fly...7-37
Outside air temperature gauge 4-18
Overconfidence 13-3
Oxygen system..8-30
Oxygen system malfunctions 8-25, 8-30

P

Parachute..8-30
Parasite drag...3-3
    Form drag 3-3
    Interference drag..3-5
    Skin friction drag...3-3
Performance information 5-8
Performance maneuvers..7-27
Personal equipment...13-7
    Oxygen system 13-7
        Aviation oxygen systems..........................13-7
        Continuous-flow system 13-8
        Electronic Pulse Demand Oxygen
        System (EDS) 13-8
Pilotage..11-5
Pilot-induced oscillations..8-2
    Pitch oscillations during landing 8-6
    Pitch oscillations during launch 8-2
    Roll oscillations during launch............................8-3
    Yaw oscillations during launch 8-4
Pitch 1-6
Pitch influence of the glider towhook position 8-6
Pitot-static instruments...4-2
Placards 5-8
Plume 9-6
Porpoising 8-2
Practical test standards 1-5
Preflight preparation..10-16
Preflight weather briefing...9-21
Prelaunch checklist 6-7
Preparation and engine start...7-17
Pressure 9-2
Pressure altitude 4-11
Pretakeoff check...7-18
Preventive maintenance 6-8
Primary flight control systems....................................8-22
Principles of operation 4-6
Problems associated with CG 5-12
    Aft of aft limit...5-13
    Forward of forward limit...................................5-12
Procedures for safe flying 10-12
Properties 9-2

R

Radius of the turn 3-14, 7-29
Rate of climb..5-7
Rate of turn 3-14
Release 12-9
Reports 9-23
Retractable landing gear malfunctions........................8-22
Ridge/slope soaring..10-10
Risk management...13-9
Roll...1-6
Roll-in 7-29
Roll-out 7-30
Rudder..2-6
Rudder malfunctions..8-24

S

Safety Management System (SMS)..............................13-9
Sailplane...1-3
Sample weight and balance problems.........................5-13
Scale of weather events..9-4
Secondary flight controls systems...............................8-24
Secondary stall...7-34
Securing 6-4
Self-launching gliders 2-7, 8-26
    Electrical system malfunctions.........................8-27
    Engine failure during takeoff or climb.............8-26
    Oscillations during powered flight 8-7
    Propeller malfunctions 8-27
    Takeoff emergency procedures 8-15
Self-launch takeoff procedures 7-17
Setting the altimeter 4-8
Sideslip...7-26
Signals.. 7-2, 7-11
    Prelaunch signals 7-2, 7-11
Sink 1-6
Skidding turn..7-30
Slack line... 7-9, 8-13
Slipping turn...7-30
Slips..7-25
    Forward slip...3-15
    Sideslip 3-17
Slope lift... 9-14, 10-13
Soaring faster and farther...11-11
Soaring Safety Foundation (SSF).................................8-30
Soaring Society of America (SSA)................................1-1
Spatial disorientation 13-6
Spins...3-17, 3-18, 8-15, 8-16
    Developed phase...8-17
    Entry phase...8-17
    Incipient phase..8-17

Recovery phase..8-17
Spiral dives...8-15
Spoiler/dive brake malfunctions 8-24
Spoilers 2-5
Stabilator 2-6
Stability 3-10
Dihedral 3-12
Dynamic stability 3-10
Flutter 3-11
Lateral stability 3-12
Static stability 3-10
Stall recognition and recovery 7-32
Stalls..3-17
Stall speed 5-6
Standard atmosphere 9-3
Static pressure lines...4-2
Stowage 8-30
Straight glides 7-27
Strop 1-6
Survival gear checklists 8-28
Sustainer engines 2-8
Swept-forward wing...3-7
System and equipment malfunctions 8-20

T

Tailwheel/tailskid equipped glider oscillations
during launches and landings...................................8-8
Tailwind 5-3
Takeoff 12-7
Takeoff emergencies 12-11
Glider climbs excessively high during takeoff......12-11
Glider releases during takeoff with tow plane
operation normal...12-11
Tow plane power failure on the runway during
takeoff roll 12-11
Tow plane power failure or tow rope break after
takeoff above 200 feet 12-11
Tow plane power failure or tow rope break after
takeoff but below 200 feet above ground level 12-11
Take off planning 12-5
Takeoff procedures and techniques 7-3
Taxiing 7-18
Temperature 5-3, 9-2
Thermal 9-6
Thermal characteristics theories 10-2
Thermal indicators 10-3
Thermal shape and structure 9-6
Thermal soaring weather..9-6
Thermal waves 9-9
Thrust 3-9

Thunderstorms 9-10
Cumulus stage 9-11
Dissipating stage 9-12
Mature stage 9-11
Tiedown 6-4
Tips and techniques..10-15
Total energy system 4-14
Tow failure 7-9, 8-10
Above 800' AGL 8-12
Above return to runway alititude.....................8-11
Above traffic pattern altitude...........................8-13
Without runway to land below returning altitude 8-11
With runway to land and stop...........................8-11
Tow hook 12-2
Schweizer tow hook 12-2
Tost tow hook 12-2
Towhook devices 2-7
Towhook malfunctions 8-25
Towhook system failures 8-8
Tow ring inspection 12-4
Tow rope inspection 12-4
Tow rope strength requirements.......................12-4
Tow speeds..7-12
Trailering..6-3
Transponder code 13-9
Traps 10-10
Trim ballast 5-14
Trim devices...2-6
True airspeed 10-17
True altitude 4-10
Turn coordination..3-15
Turns 7-28
Medium turns 7-28
Shallow turns 7-28
Steep turns 7-31
Turns on tow..12-9
Types of airspeed 4-3
Calibrated airspeed 4-3
Indicated airspeed 4-3
True airspeed 4-4
Types of altitude 4-10
Types of drag 3-3

U

Unassisted takeoff...7-5
Using the plotter...11-5

V

Variometer 4-11
Audio variometers 4-13
Electric variometers..4-11

Variometer malfunctions 8-21
Vertical gusts during high-speed cruise 8-5

W

Water ballast 11-17
    Malfunctions 8-22
Wave soaring 10-16
Wave soaring weather 9-16
Weak link 1-6
Weather for slope soaring 9-14
Weather reiated information 9-21
Weight 3-9, 5-5
Weight and balance 5-12
Wheel brakes 2-8
Wind 10-4
Wing planform 3-6
    Elliptical 3-6
    Rectangular 3-7
    Tapered 3-7
    Washout 3-7

Y

Yaw 1-6, 3-10
Yaw string 4-16, 7-30